C000184392

Cols and Passes
of
the British Isles

Graham Robb is an acclaimed historian and biographer,
a Fellow of the Royal Society of Literature and a Chevalier
dans l'Ordre des Arts et des Lettres. He has won the
Whitbread Biography Prize and the Heinemann Award
for *Victor Hugo*, as well as the Ondaatje Prize and Duff
Cooper Prize for *The Discovery of France*. He lives on the
English-Scottish border, and within a day's ride of one
hundred and seventy cols.

Also by the author

*Balzac*
*Victor Hugo*
*Rimbaud*
*Unlocking Mallarmé*
*Strangers: Homosexual Love in the Nineteenth Century*
*The Discovery of France*
*Parisians: An Adventure History of Paris*
*The Ancient Paths: Discovering the Lost Map of Celtic Europe*

# COLS AND PASSES
## of the British Isles

GRAHAM ROBB

PARTICULAR
BOOKS

PARTICULAR BOOKS

UK | USA | Canada | Ireland | Australia
India | New Zealand | South Africa

Particular Books is part of the Penguin Random House group of companies
whose addresses can be found at global.penguinrandomhouse.com.

First published 2016

001

Maps and illustrations by Neil Gower
Book design by Richard Marston
Set in Quadraat and Quadraat Sans
Printed in Germany by GGP

A CIP catalogue record for this book is available from the British Library

ISBN: 978–1–846–14873–6

MIX
Paper from
responsible sources
FSC® C018179

# Contents

Dedicated to the first person to cross all 2002 cols of the British Isles (without the aid of a car).

# Prologue

This book was already well down the road, composing itself at a leisurely pace, when it occurred to me that it ought to be heading somewhere in particular. The writing mind caught up with it, pushed a little harder and, after thousands of miles and two years in the workshop, a brand-new reference work was ready to be wheeled out: the first complete guide to the cols and passes of the British Isles.*

Only then was I struck by the strangeness of the project: it seemed incredible that a whole aspect of the cultural and geographical heritage of the British Isles had remained undiscovered or, at least, undescribed. Even now, the coordinates of the catalogue seem to refer to an imaginary realm of trials and adventures in which every fold of the landscape contains an untold tale.

This sense of magical revelation reflects the nature of cols themselves. A col is a gap or depression in a ridge or a range of hills which serves as a gateway to the lands on either side. A person or an animal who wishes to cross the hills with the least effort will naturally head for the col, which provides the lowest crossing.

*Fig. 1* Lairig Noe (Lorn, Scotland)

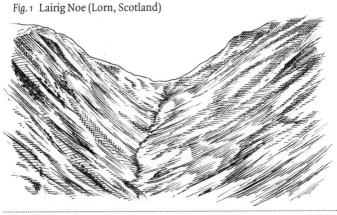

---

* For definitions of 'col' and 'pass', see pp. 14–18.

Cols are among the most distinctive of geographical features, but, like any natural feature, they can take many different forms. Some, like Lairig Noe (fig. 1), are broad 'saddles' between two high mountains. Others, like Castle Nick and Sycamore Gap on Hadrian's Wall (fig. 2), are narrow clefts or gullies.

Modern transport effectively erased these crucial passageways from the national consciousness. Their names disappeared even from the most detailed maps. Now, cols are once again becoming noticeable features of the landscape. For walkers and climbers, the cradle of a col is a place to rest before tackling a summit or continuing on the lowest route over the ridge. There are usually views in more than one direction and a reassuring sense of being able to comprehend the whole landscape. For cyclists, the word 'col' tends to conjure up the gigantic Alpine and Pyrenean passes of the Tour de France, referred to in sporting hyperbole as *mythique* – which, in fact, some of them are: the Tour's publicity machine bestows the prestigious word 'col' on steep climbs that no animal or shepherd would ever have attempted. Cols were used and named not because someone wanted to conquer them but because they provided the most efficient route from one valley to the next. Cols are portals rather than obstacles, which is why walkers and cyclists who travel for pleasure rather than punishment soon learn to appreciate their magical qualities.

During cycling expeditions through France, one of these convenient gateways would occasionally appear – often at the

top of a climb but sometimes on a descent. The spot would be marked by a small rectangular sign with white letters on a black background: 'Col de l'Homme Mort', 'Pas du Voltigeur', etc. The sign (always just the right height for a commemorative photograph) was an invitation to stop and dismount. In the silence of the pass, when the road was no longer spinning out its tale, fragments of another story would come into focus: a ruined hut or the pedestal of a cross, a meeting of tracks, the first glimpse of a new horizon, a change in the wind which brought the smells of a different *pays*. Named cols are among the oldest traces of a human presence in the landscape. Many of them occur along the ancient trails of shepherds and thieves, migrants and merchants, armies and refugees, and since these sites of otherwise unrecorded history also make useful markers in regions where few other waypoints exist, I acquired the habit of including them in outlines of each future journey.

After returning to Britain in the fume-filled hold of a ferry, we (which is to say, I, my wife Margaret and our bicycles) set off every Sunday before dawn and ranged over the Cotswolds and the Chilterns, wondering whether or not we were crossing any cols. Michelin and IGN maps indicate even minor cols, but they are almost entirely absent from British maps, and col signs are nowhere to be seen. At some of the most impressive summits of the British road system, the traveller is greeted with nothing but instructions and advice: 'Keep Your Dog on a Leash', 'Lock Your Car', 'Take Your Litter Home'. Could it be that cols were a French

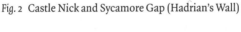

Fig. 2  Castle Nick and Sycamore Gap (Hadrian's Wall)

speciality and that the geological forces which shaped the planet had operated differently on the other side of the Channel?

Given the national penchant for challenges and quests, one might have expected British ramblers and cyclists to 'collect' cols as hill walkers 'bag' Munros, but the only lists were of vicious hill roads celebrated for their steepness. Most of these 'killer climbs' are not cols at all. They appeal to a particular breed of cyclist who, not requiring the bicycle for daily use, is free to hammer both vehicle and rider into a state of collapse whilst viewing the landscape through a veil of pain and perspiration and then through the windows of a 'support vehicle'. In France, a different form of hill cycling has evolved in which the curse of gravity is treated as a heavenly gift. Groups of wives drive their elderly husbands to the top of an Alp or a Pyrenee, deposit them there with their lithe and youthful machines, and then wait for them confidently in a restaurant in the valley below. In Britain, this would be considered cheating, but it takes a great deal of skill, experience and stamina to spiral down a mountain on a skittish *vélo de course* at sixty kilometres an hour.

A few years ago, the French Club des Cent Cols ('Hundred Cols Club') put *les Anglais* to shame by producing a list of 'the 533 cols of the British Isles'. (There are, as I discovered, nearly four times that number, and several cols in their list are not actually cols.) By comparison, the catalogue of French cols lists 10,892. This appeared to confirm the superiority of France in matters of the *terroir* – the untranslatable term for the soil of the *patrie*, considered as a source of gastronomic delights. 'England is on the whole a rather flat country,' the introduction to the club's list of British cols loftily avers.

It turns out that, by geological chance, the Cotswolds and the Chilterns are sadly lacking in cols. We continued to cycle over the nameless passes of our home region, baptising them, as British cyclists often do, with faux-French names such as le Col de Watlington or le Pas du Cheval Blanc. Meanwhile, each spring and autumn, our tally of French cols grew larger, and I forgot about the problem of the missing British cols until we moved to the English–Scottish border.

It was while plotting walking and cycling routes through northern Cumbria and the Borders that I began to come across some certifiable cols on the largest-scale Ordnance Survey maps, on old charts and surveys of the turnpike system, in ballads, tales and travellers' guides. Sometimes, the only clue to a col's existence lay in the record of a cattle raid or a smugglers' route. These Border cols had exotic names such as 'hass', 'hause' and 'swire'. A few days to the west and the north, in the patchwork of Gaelic, Norse and Anglo-Saxon, there were 'nicks' and 'snecks', 'slaps' and 'slochs', 'bealachs' and 'lairigs'. Nearly all these cols were missing from the list of the Club des Cent Cols, and most of them seemed to be unknown to walkers and cyclists, yet these out-of-the-way places were nerve centres of British history: the eleven cols of the Whin Sill crags which were incorporated into Hadrian's Wall; Windy Swire, through which the young Mary, Queen of Scots, rode into Liddesdale in 1566; Whitrope Hass on the cloudy watershed above the disused tunnel of the old North British Railway.

To see these cols for the first time is to feel the thrill of a Victorian explorer: the place itself may be known, but the discoverer of cols arrives simultaneously in the present and the past. At Carter Bar, the highest crossing of the English–Scottish border, a piper in a kilt and the radio of a burger van offered up their music like a Tibetan prayer to the winds that sweep over the magnificent desolation. 'You Are Here', says the information panel, an arrow pointing at 'Carter Bar'. But Carter Bar refers to the eighteenth-century toll-gate. Long before there was a road, this was Redeswire, the 'swire', or col, of the river Rede, where Scots and English fought their last major skirmish in 1575.

For three years, I stored up the coordinates of these magical places, along with the names of lost cols which were mentioned in documents but had vanished from the map. The final impetus for the book came from two chance encounters in the border-lands in the spring of 2014.

We were climbing up into the forested moors between Eskdale and Annandale towards the forgotten col of Fenton Yet. I heard the click and whisper of a well-tuned gear and a cyclist materi-alized at my side. He had the unmistakeable calf muscles of a racer and an ice-blue bike with a Scottish thistle painted on its down tube. Courteously matching my slow pace, he welcomed me to 'the rainiest part of Scotland', and asked where we were headed. I told him Glasgow and the Trossachs, two days' ride to the north. As an organizer of bike races, he was able to give me a bend-by-bend description of the Duke's Pass near Aberfoyle, which features in the Tour des Trossachs time trial. The hill arched its back and steepened. 'We've dropped your companion,' he noted. I glanced back and, before I had a chance to tell him of the col we were about to cross, he disappeared like a moorland bird, leaving us to the hailstorm that swept down over the pass.

A week later, I was walking across an upland bog in search of the route by which Mary, Queen of Scots, had reached the lonely fortress called the Hermitage. The Queen's Mire, as part of the moor is known, sometimes reveals traces of the long-abandoned road, but the surest guide is the double dip on the ridge ahead – Moss Patrick Swire on the right, Windy Swire on the left – beyond which a track slopes down into Teviotdale. For miles around, there was not a soul to be seen. Then a figure appeared in the gap of Windy Swire, dressed in pink Lycra and striding south at a surprising speed. Intent on the act of self-propulsion, she passed with the briefest of greetings and vanished in the direction of the Hermitage.

It struck me then that a catalogue of British cols might be something more than a compendium of geographical data. It would have enabled the man with the thistle on his bike to include some authentic *cols mythiques* in his race routes. The aerodynamic walker, had she known that she was crossing a col, might have paused to drink in the view. Each would have had a reference point around which the day's memories might have gathered in the evening. I saw the machinery of coordinates precisely adjusted to the evocative names and reflected that, quite apart from its navigational use, a catalogue of cols and passes would also be the perfect prelude to ten hours of restorative sleep.

## Cols

Cols were formed either gradually or violently, by glaciation, seismic activity or tectonic movement. In every case, the process was completed – for the time being – by erosion and occasionally by mechanical diggers. The raw material of a col is a rocky ridge. Sometimes, the ridge was carved into a graceful parabola by glaciers sliding down from the crest or by meltwater widening and deepening a fault or fissure in the rock as it forced its way out of the valley containing the glacier. Other cols, known as 'wind gaps', were created when ancient rivers were 'captured' by other rivers or diverted by landslides.

Fig. 3 The distribution of cols in the British Isles

The uneven distribution of the 2,002 cols of the British Isles reflects the geological history of the islands. Some cols are isolated, but most occur in groups. They are usually found in upland areas, but some lie only a few metres above sea level. In some regions, they are entirely absent. The snaky chalk and limestone ridges of the Chilterns and the Cotswolds are almost col-less, whereas the ragged granite fells of Cumbria account for nearly half the cols in England.

The word 'col' ('neck'), in the sense of a narrow passage between hills, was first recorded in French in 1635. In English, it came into use as a geological term in the mid-nineteenth century. Since then, it has acquired two subsidiary meanings, one highly specialized, the other resulting from a misconception.

To mountaineers, a col is the lowest point between two summits. It may or may not have the geological characteristics of a col. The point is simply to determine the height of a given climb and the relative prominence of a summit.

In the world of cycling, 'col' is often taken to be a synonym of 'climb', especially a long, steep climb which causes pain and exhaustion and evokes heroic images of the Tour de France. A French and British cyclists' club, the Ordre des Cols Durs ('Hard Cols Club'), applies the word to any road which goes up and then, if followed in the same direction, down into another valley, the idea being to accumulate as many metres of ascent as possible. In this sense, the list of 'cols' would be practically endless. The misconception comes from the hasty idiom of professional bike racing, in which 'the Col d'Aubisque', for example, is shorthand for 'the climb to the Col d'Aubisque'.

The definition used in this book is the geological definition. Every col identified in the catalogue is a true col in the scientific sense. The only difference is that, while geologists work in four dimensions, this catalogue is rooted in the present. A geologist who views the landscape as the result of processes stretching over millennia might identify a col in a region which now appears flat and featureless. These ancient cols are generally referred to as 'Gaps' with a capital 'G'. The Watford Gap, for instance, through which the River Thames flowed in the Pleistocene epoch, no longer has the clear characteristics of a col and is therefore not included in the catalogue.

## Passes

The words 'col' and 'pass' are not interchangeable. Mennock Hass is the col which looks down on Wanlockhead in Dumfriesshire; Mennock Pass is the long defile to which the road descends on the other side. Confusingly, many cols have the word 'pass' in their name (Buttertubs Pass, Pass of Glenogle, etc.), but 'pass' is a slippery term which can also be applied to roads with no noticeable summit or gradient. 'Col' is scientific; 'pass' is a vague umbrella term applied not only to cols but also to a great variety of passages and crossings. The catalogue contains 105 passes which are not cols and which are therefore listed separately. The criterion of inclusion is that the route or its summit must be commonly referred to as a pass or recorded as such on a map.

Typically, a pass is a road which runs through a steep-sided valley of menacing demeanour, a defile darkened by crags or looming forests which the traveller will be relieved or thrilled to have negotiated. Some passes cling to hillsides above crashing burns; others creep through tunnels of vegetation before rising on to treeless moors. Few passes were named as such on maps until the late nineteenth century, when the word came into use for the convenience of speakers of standard English. Newlands Pass in the Lake District is still often referred to (at least in print) as Newlands Hause, but no one now uses the older names – 'scarth', 'hals' and 'yeat' – of the passes known as Hardknott, Wrynose and Kirkstone. There is no trace at all of the older name of the Hampshire col which was first identified implicitly in 1910, when the Ordnance Survey recorded the 'Khyber Pass Plantation'.

In Wales, 'pass' was imported as a more pronounceable sub-stitute for *bwlch*. As in Scotland, it usually came with a metalled road, and the name of the *bwlch* was sometimes removed at the same time. Bwlch Oernant, or Coldstream Col, became the Horseshoe Pass (from the great curve of the road), and Bwlch y Gorddinan, or Pass of the Impulsive River, became the unWelsh Crimea Pass (from the name of an inn). These relatively recent passes, in Wales and in Scotland, are associated with the arrival of tourism. The word 'pass' dates from Norman times, but its modern application to spectacular or merely picturesque roads such as the five passes of the Trossachs was supposed to conjure up the prestigious passes of the Alps and the classical world. The Pass of Llanberis was the Saint Bernard of Snowdonia, and the Pass of Glencoe the Thermopylae of the Highlands.

In Ireland, a 'pass' is sometimes just a flat road in low country which cuts through otherwise impenetrable bog or forest. In England, 'pass' tends to refer to a difficult, inter-regional high road which is sometimes impassable and at most other times clogged with traffic because, for geographical reasons, no other route exists.

## How the catalogue was compiled

The first step was to find all the words that were ever used to refer to a col in the languages of the British Isles. The initial list contained about sixty words. Many more, not previously recognized as words for 'col', came to light in the course of research. The glossary, which was originally conceived as a brief checklist, ended up as a mini-dictionary.

The main sources were the eighty-nine volumes of the Survey of English Place-names, the archives coordinated by the 'ScotlandsPlaces' project, the Placenames Database of Ireland, the 'name books' of the Ordnance Survey's surveyors and the larger toponymic guides and gazetteers. Works which draw on title deeds and estate maps proved especially valuable, since to find and decipher all such documents would be the work of several lifetimes. These works in turn provided clues to ballads, novels, surveys and travellers' accounts in which otherwise unknown cols are mentioned.

I then read all the maps I could find, beginning with Christopher Saxton's maps of Welsh and English counties (1574–79) and Timothy Pont's handwritten maps of Scotland (c. 1583–96). Most pre-Ordnance Survey maps can be read in less than a day, but the key reference is the Ordnance Survey 'six-inch' map in its various incarnations. Joined together, each series would cover an area of almost six hundred square metres.* As the landscape of cols changed in the light of increasing information, these maps had to be reread more than once. It soon became apparent that

---

* Except in built-up areas, the original '25-inch' series contains the same information as the '6-inch' series. Though the Ordnance Survey made no secret of the fact, it is not widely known that the scale of the '25-inch' map is metric: 1:2500, or 25.344 inches to the mile.

*Fig. 4* Lairig Noe (Lorn, Scotland). Contour lines at ten-metre intervals. The col itself is shown in fig. 1.

some cols and passes are shown only on smaller-scale maps which seem at first unlikely to yield any fresh data. One British pass is named only on a French Michelin map.

Since not every col name was recorded and hundreds of cols were incorrectly placed, the maps must also be read for relief. Contour lines, first used in the early eighteenth century, must be one of the most satisfyingly efficient inventions in the history of cartography. With a little practice, the eye can spot the characteristic swirl and eddy of lines as quickly as an angler spots the ripples made by a fish, though not every col produces the classic 'hour-glass' shape (fig. 4).

Several paper and digital maps now show relative height in various forms: these provided a useful means of testing the original survey. A col can be any height and so the survey was extended to every part of the British Isles, including East Anglia, which, not surprisingly (but not predictably), turned out to be devoid of cols.

The result was a working catalogue of British and Irish cols and passes with their past and present names, a note of the terrain, and approximate latitude and longitude coordinates. At this stage, the catalogue included every *bealach*, *bwlch*, gap, gate, hass, etc., and any other feature whose name might have indicated a col. I then winnowed out all those that are clearly not cols. For those that remained, I established precise coordinates, noted cases where reality disagrees with the map, and organized them all by county.

In the meantime, I was visiting as many cols as time and weather permitted. Even at a rate of one col or pass every day of the year, it would take six years to cross them all, and so these expeditions were organized with two principal aims. One was to cross every col described in the later section of this book. The other was to become acquainted with their types and peculiarities.

Finally, the catalogue entry for each col was completed with National Grid coordinates, its height above sea level, the geographical location and any significant physical or historical details. This information might have been added at an earlier stage, but the fewer concurrent tasks the better, and in this way, each entry was rechecked several times.

## Finding cols on the map

The first clue to a col on an Ordnance Survey map is the pattern of contour lines (fig. 4); the second is the name. Some of these names – *bealach* in Scotland or *bwlch* in Wales – are extremely common, but a *bealach* or a *bwlch* is not necessarily a col. Apart from the scientific term itself, no single word means 'col' and nothing else. A *bealach* may be an opening or a gap of any kind – a road, path, valley, gorge, inlet or gate. However, when applied to a col, most of the 138 terms listed in the glossary precisely describe the nature of the col in question. A *lairig* is a broad mountain pass, a *dìollaid* ('saddle') is a col on a ridge, a *uinneag* ('window') is a high col with plunging views. At a *feadan*, the wind whistles through a narrow gap, a *slack* is always wet, and at an *aisir* or an *eag*, one step in the wrong direction could lead to sudden death.

The richest source of col names is the first series of Ordnance Survey maps.* Even this monumental masterpiece is not exhaustive. Every map reflects the age in which it was produced. The original surveyors used local informants – clergymen and teachers, lords of the manor, post-masters and -mistresses, estate agents, rate collectors and antiquarians. The 'best authorities' were held to be 'respectable inhabitants' rather than 'small farmers and cottagers [who] are not to be depended on, even

---

* Ireland, 1827–46; Scotland, 1843–82; England and Wales, 1842–93, with revisions.

for the names of the places they occupy'. Many names that were familiar to these lesser mortals were never recorded, and not all the 'authorities' knew the meaning of the Welsh, Gaelic or dialectal terms. The advantage for the Ordnance Survey was that educated people could be counted on to have a settled opinion and to make sense of what an early surveyor in County Kerry called 'the barbarous pronunciation in this wild barony'.

Later map-makers relied heavily – and still do – on these original surveys. Sometimes, errors were corrected, but many more were introduced. Cols and passes which had once been major landmarks and stages on local or long-distance routes were omitted as unimportant. Once it became possible to obliterate a hill with the touch of an accelerator pedal, cols began to disappear from the map. A *bealach* spelt *baelach* and a *bwlch* spelt *bwich* on modern Ordnance Survey maps show that these names are no longer the everyday words they once were.

Many cols have suffered from what might be called caption creep: between one edition and the next, names that were no longer recognized were misattributed – attached to the tail instead of the head of a caption – and eventually found themselves a long way from their original home. The old Ordnance Survey maps are not just keys to a vanished world. In many parts of the British Isles, that world still exists, and rediscovering it on paper is an adventure in itself.

## Finding cols on the ground

One of the best ways in which to become acquainted with a landscape is to set off in search of a col, because, even with maps and a well-planned route, it very often *is* a search. Some cols reveal themselves only at the end of a long, circuitous journey; others appear distinctly on the horizon and then vanish when approached. A bicycle will sometimes stop at exactly the right spot, as it feels the road level out and the wind drop or stiffen. At other times, topography seems to defy the map: gradients and contours play tricks on the eye, and then the site has to be examined like a crime scene.

The first clue might be a puddle on the road on a rainless day, a field of reeds and reluctant streams or a subterranean gurgling: these are often signs of a watershed, which might also be indicated by a covered reservoir or some other hydrological installation.

One of the very few signs in England on which the name of a col is inscribed stands at the top of a quiet lane in Derbyshire, near the perimeter of the Chadwick Nick sewage-treatment plant.

Where the waters divide, there may be a meeting of the ways – a busy road junction or a disused path detectable only in a gap in the hedge or the flattened grass of a deer track. There may be a sudden view and, if the col is enshrouded in fog, its strategic value may still be apparent in a hill fort, a machine-gun emplacement or the memorial to a battle. Some cols which are barely noticeable to a vigorous walker or a wind-propelled cyclist were quite obvious to heavily laden soldiers and their artillery officers.

Many (perhaps all) cols stand on ancient or modern boundaries. These can take the form of a fence, a drystone wall, a ditch or the straight edge of a wood. The col summit may be occupied by a cattle-grid dividing one animal tribe from another, and there may be different breeds of sheep in the adjacent fields. A bicycle often registers the crossing of a boundary in the tremor of its tubing and the hum of its tyres where a change in the road surface marks the point at which one council's road-mending crew took over (or didn't) from another. At county and national borders there may be a 'Welcome' sign, or, if souvenir hunters have struck, the mangled remnant of its support.

A few cols (far fewer than in France) are marked by a cross, to guide or to protect travellers. Crosses were often erected between one parish and the next, on the spiritual watershed from which blessings would flow in all directions. Sometimes, as well as a cross, there was a gibbet on which the tarred corpse of a criminal swayed in the breeze. Today, there may be a monument of rubbish left by fly-tippers and signs threatening official prosecution. Some of these consecrated cols were places of local pilgrimage; many are still used as meeting points by walkers' clubs, which unconsciously reenact the pilgrimage.

In the absence of a col sign, mysterious abbreviations and symbols may be painted on the road. In the code of race organizers, these indicate the summit of a climb or a 'feed station' – a poignant sight for a hungry traveller passing several months after the event. Increasingly often in the last ten or fifteen years, an actual cyclist will appear, whether or not the col is known to be a col. Failing that, spreadeagled on the verge or hanging from a hedge, there may be the almost infallible indicator of a cyclists' route: a banana skin. Discarded plastic tubes of energy gel, which litter the approaches to some of the famous French cols, are still a relatively rare sight in the British Isles.

Finally, the col's name is an invaluable clue. The generic name will show what sort of col to expect. The particular name can pinpoint the location, which is especially useful when the name is in the wrong place on the map. At the Bwlch y Clawdd (Dyke Pass), there is an earthen embankment; at Bwlch-castell, a hill fort marks the col, which lies five hundred metres from the farm which took the col's name. At the Rest and Be Thankful in Argyll, often erroneously identified with the Bealach an Easain Duibh, there is no 'dark waterfall', but there is one further up the road at the true Bealach an Easain Duibh. With the passing of time, some names have become as unreliable as ghosts. No cow is ever seen at Milking Gap on Hadrian's Wall, and there is nothing in the denuded moorland of northern Mull to reveal the location of the col named Bealach nan Craobh ('Pass of the Trees').

## Anonymous, lost and wandering cols

In the British Isles, where true wilderness is rare, practically every col was named, whether or not it was on a recognized route. Even cols which are impassable can serve as navigational aids: a gap between two hills usually gives a more precise bearing than the summits, which are seldom as conveniently pointy as they are in paintings.

Many cols which appear to be nameless lent their names to other sites and features – usually a hill, a stream or a farm. The only verbal remnant of the Cumbrian col once known as Moss Hause is Mosshause Gill, which has its source at the col. This also explains the otherwise perplexing name of the mountain above Caernarfon Bay, Bwlch Mawr, which means 'Great Pass'. In Wales and Ireland, col names tended to slide downhill and become attached to the nearest inhabited place, or even to an entire administrative area. In England, some cols seemed to vanish from the map when their old names, unused and unmodernized, became incomprehensible. To speakers of Anglo-Saxon, the *corfes* of Dorset and the *yates* of the Malvern Hills were self-evidently 'cuttings' and 'gateways'.

It is surprising how often the trace of a name survives. At a moorland col below Pendle Hill in Lancashire, Ordnance Survey maps show nothing but 'Annel [or Hannell] Cross (Site of)'.

Almost within living memory, there was an annual gathering
on the first Sunday in May at which bonfires were lit and a feast
consumed. The gathering – or *thing* in Anglo-Saxon times – was
known as the Nick o' Thungs. 'Nick' is a common term for 'col' in
this part of Britain, and since the site is indeed a col, the Nick o'
Thungs can now be restored to the map.

Only a handful of cols whose names are recorded in documents must be given up as lost. A crossing of the English–
Scottish border called Whithaugh Swire is listed in a document
of 1597 and vaguely located as 'Whytehoope Suyre' on a map
of 1654. If it was a col, it was a remarkably discreet feature. A
Hardhaugh, or Hindhaugh, Swire appears in two Border ballads,
but even Walter Scott and other local authorities were unable to
identify it correctly. Perhaps both swires *are* known, but under
different names. Hethouswyre, on the other hand, which was
last heard of in the Middle Ages and never shown on a map, can
be identified with a col in the Cheviot Hills simply by following
the boundary lines described in the document.

As rural populations dwindled, many names were forgotten
and lost for ever. But in the English Lake District, which has by
far the largest concentration of anonymous cols, the process is
reversed. Until the late eighteenth century, the scowling fells
were considered a natural horror to be avoided at all costs.
Before the advent of Romantic poets and mountaineers, some
remote cols were probably used only by wild animals. Now, the
descendants of those creatures are witnessing a mutation of
the bipedal species. New col names are appearing all the time,
as though the region were still being colonized – which, in a
sense, it is, by a race of hardy, booted aliens heading for the
upper atmosphere. More than a quarter of Lake District cols
are still nameless, but the maps are becoming more crowded
by the year. Several 'innominate' passes were named by Alfred
Wainwright in the 1950s. More recently, the imported word 'col'
made its first appearance on an English Ordnance Survey map
at Lingmell Col below Scafell Pike, and the great buttress of
England's highest mountain at last acquired a name.

# Glossary

This is a glossary of all the words used in the British Isles since the tenth century to denote a col or a pass. Each entry shows the word as it appears in documents or on maps, the language(s) to which it belongs, its dictionary definitions, and the area(s) in which it occurs. The geographical definitions have been derived from the physical attributes of all the cols which bear the name in question.

*Languages*

| | | | |
|---|---|---|---|
| C | Cornish | OE | Old English |
| E | English | ON | Old Norse |
| F | French | S | Scots |
| HE | Hiberno-English | SG | Scottish Gaelic |
| IG | Irish Gaelic | SKG | St Kildan Gaelic |
| M | Manx | W | Welsh |
| N | Norn (Shetland) | | |

*Areas*

| | | | |
|---|---|---|---|
| E | England | ME | Midlands (England) |
| ES | Eastern Scotland | NE | Northern England |
| HS | Highland Scotland | NI | Northern Ireland |
| I | Republic of Ireland | S | Scotland |
| IOM | Isle of Man | SE | Southern England |
| LS | Lowland Scotland | W | Wales |

**adwy** W: gap, breach, gate, inlet; a relatively indistinct saddle; W

**aisir, aisre, aisridh** SG: path, pass, defile; col on a narrow ridge; HS

**baarney** M: gap; IOM

**ballagh** HE: mutation of 'bearna'; I

**balloch** S: pass (mutation of 'bealach'); common place name, only rarely with the sense of 'col' and often from 'baile an loch' ('town', 'village' or 'farm' 'of the loch'); LS

**barna** HE: mutation of 'bearna'; I

**béal** IG: mouth; usually a broad col with a steep drop; I

**bealach** SG: any kind of col or pass (including trackless); also other kinds of opening: a road or path, valley or gorge, a gap, gate, inlet, etc.; fewer than two-thirds of sites named 'bealach' are cols; HS, I, NI

**beàrn** SG: gap, breach; more frequent in anglicized forms, 'barn(s)'; HS

**bearna** IG: gap; any kind of col or pass (as 'bealach'); more frequently applied to a path or track than to a col; I, NI

**bearradh** SG: dictionaries define as 'mountain top', 'cliff' or 'pinnacle'; applied to two cols on Arran with the sense of 'cutting' (usually of hair); HS

**beul** SG: mouth; rough and rocky col; HS

**beum** SG: wound, gash, stream; gap; ES

**blaid** SKG: mouth; col on a ridge; St Kilda

**bolgh, volgh** C: presumed Cornish equivalent of 'bwlch'; unattested, probably because Cornwall lacks cols

**braaid** M: gullet, gorge; applied to two cols, neither very gorge-like; IOM

**bráid** IG; neck, throat; defile; I

**bràid** SG: horse-collar; broad-shouldered col; HS

**bràigh, braighe** SG: uplands, mountain top; neck, throat; a high saddle; HS, especially Outer Hebrides

**breabag** SG: kick; rocky col or cleft; HS

**bridge** E: applied to an asymmetrical saddle; NE

**briseadh, bristeadh, briste** SG: breach, rocky col; HS

**brisleach** IG: breach, asymmetrical saddle; I

**bwlch** W: gap, notch, battlement; topographic senses include all kinds of pass and col; also applied to gaps, nooks, hollows, roads and paths (as 'bealach'); ME, W

**bylchau** W: plural of 'bwlch'; W

**cab** SG: head, mouth or gap; col at the head of a corrie; HS

**cadha** SG: porch; pass, ravine; typically a col on a narrow ridge; HS

**caol** IG, SG: throat; firth; a strait or narrow; HS, I

**caolas** IG, SG: firth; a strait or narrow; Jura, I

**carcair** IG: prison (or narrow place); pen (for animals); hill slope, large rock; applied to a flattish pass; I

**céim** IG: step; pass or ravine; usually a mountain col with fairly gentle drops; I

**chair** E: a broad pass; Orkney

**chuingeal** SG: defile; anglicized as 'fungle'; ES

**clais** SG: furrow, trench, gutter, groove; ES, HS

**clash** S: anglicized 'clais'; Angus

**cock** E: prefix occasionally associated with a col in SE; perhaps from ON *kok* ('gullet', 'throat')

**coimín** IG: little hollow, glen; I

**coiscéim** IG: footstep; a high saddle; *see* also **céim** above; I

**col** F (but perhaps SG, with the sense of 'plateau'): on OS maps, applied to a low col near Glen Turret and to Lingmell Col in the Lake District; HS, NE

**com, cúm** IG: hollow, coomb; either a low col in rolling hills or a high saddle; I

**comar** IG: ravine, rut; a precipitous col; I

**conair** IG: path(way), narrow passage; col on a high, narrow ridge; I

**coom, coum** HE: *see* **com**

**corfe** (from OE *ceorfan*): cutting; col in a cutting or hollow way; ME, SE

**corse** S: cross or crossing; LS

**còs** SG: hollow, crevice, recess; HS

**crasg, cròsg** SG (locally, 'charsk'): cross, crossing; a col sufficiently broad to be a meeting of four ways; ES, HS

**cró** IG: hollow, hole; applied to a broad saddle; I

**crò** SG: a strait or narrow; HS

**cròsg** SG *see* **crasg**

**cross** E: cross or crossing; anglicized 'corse', not always indicating a cruciform monument; LS NE, SE

**cúil** IG: corner, nook; applied to a broad col; I

**cùil** SG: corner, nook; HS

**cùl** SG: back, behind; applied to four rocky cols; but perhaps originally 'cùil' (*see* **cúil** and Bealach Cùil (now 'Cùl') a' Choire); HS

**cúm** IG *see* **com**

**cumhang**, **cumhann** SG: a strait or narrow; HS

**cunglach** SG: cleft, defile, strait; HS

**cut** E: *see* **gearradh**

**cutting** E: applied to the col of Baldyate (*see* **yate**), now the Wyche Cutting; ME

**cwm** W: coomb, glen, hollow (especially with 'bwlch'); generally, a high, rocky col; W

**dìollaid** SG: saddle; HS

**door** E, S: various types of col; often plural; sometimes 'dore'; LS, NE

**drochaid** SG: bridge; typically applied to a col on a broad, flattish ridge; HS

**drws** W: door, entrance; pass, deep saddle, col on a narrow ridge; W

**eag** IG, **eang** SG: nick, notch; usually a col marked by a rocky cleft or a steep descent; HS, I

**eisc**, **easca** IG: channel, fissure, hollow; I

**feadan** SG: pipe, spout, whistle, flute, bagpipe chanter or gun barrel; col through which the wind whistles; HS

**ford** S: broad col at a watershed; LS

**fungle** *see* **chuingeal**

**gabhal**, **gabhlán** IG: fork, junction, inlet; applied to various cols by analogy with an inlet rather than in reference to the bifurcation of a road, or perhaps by association with 'gabháil' in the sense of 'yoke'; I; perhaps also HS (SG *gobhal*)

**gàg**, **gàig** SG: cleft, notch; applied to two passes and one col; also Gaick Pass; HS

**gap** E, S: gap, pass; in Scotland, a distinct col between two hills of similar size; in England and Ireland, applied to several kinds of col or pass but more often to a road or a cleft; in Ireland, a common translation of 'bearna'; E, HS, LS, I, NI. Also a geological term (e.g. 'wind gap', the Watford Gap) denoting cols which may be perceptible only in geological time.

**gate** E, S: col or pass; occasionally with this sense but more often meaning gate, road or way; in Ireland, common translation of 'bearna'; in England, applied to most kinds of col or pass, or to the roads that cross them; sometimes plural; E, HS, I, LS, W

**gearradh** IG: cutting; anglicized as 'cut'; I

**gil** SG: mountain stream; rift, gully; Caithness

**gill**, **geall** SG: notch; Hebrides

**glac**, **glack** S: hollow, ravine, valley; col at the head of a small valley; mostly ES, some HS

**goul**, **gowl(e)**, **goyle**, **gyle** OE, S: throat, deep hollow; a defile or cutting (not always a col); LS, NE, SE

**gowlane** HE: anglicized 'gabhal' (*see* **gabhal**), but perhaps 'little gowl' (*see* **goul**); I

**hals** ON (*see* **hass**); in historical forms, but survives in Hallshot and Halsway; NE, SE

**hass** S (from OE and ON *hals*): neck, throat, gullet; inlet, isthmus; various types of lowland col, often a subtle depression in a ridge; LS, NE

**hause**, **hawse** E, S: *see* **hass**; sometimes 'halse' or, erroneously, 'horse', 'house' or 'hows'; ridge; col; LS, NE (all in Cumbria)

**head** E: often applied to a col at the headwaters of a river or stream and combined with 'dore', 'hause' and 'nick' NE, SE

**imir**, **iomaire** SG: ridge, furrow; Jura

**ladder** S: (col on a) steep path; anglicized SG 'fàradh'; LS

**ladhar** IG: fork, crotch; mountain saddle; I

**lag** SG: hollow between hills, dell; HS

**lagan** SG: diminutive of 'lag'; HS

**làirig** SG: broad mountain pass; a typical *làirig* has very long approaches; HS

**léim** IG: leap; chasm, headland; I

**loup** S: leap (usually applied to a waterfall which fish ascend, or to the site of a legendary leap by a saint or a soldier); applied to saddle cols in Aberdeenshire and Ayrshire; perhaps also in Hart Leap or Hartleap (Windy House) and the Devil's Leap in Yorkshire; LS

**malaidh** IG: brow (of eye or hill); a broad col; I

**mám** IG: a high col; usually an obvious saddle in high mountains; a *mám* is also a yoke; I

**mam**, **màm** SG: gap, pass or col; often with a steep drop on one or both sides; also a round, breast-shaped hill; HS

**maam**, **maum** HE: *see* **mám**

**mouth** E, S: col; LS, ME, NE

**neive** S: col on a ridge? ('neive' = 'fist', but the local sense is obscure); Galloway

**nick** E, S: a col (not necessarily narrow and sometimes indistinct); occasionally 'neuk'; 'nick' can also refer to a road, path or watercourse; LS, ME, NE

**nook** E: applied to a ridge col in the Peak District, perhaps also to a col in the Lake District; NE

**pant** W: valley; hollow, depression, dent; W

**pass** E: for definitions, *see* p. 17; a pass is not necessarily a col; 'pass' can refer to the summit or to the road or path which crosses it; E, I, NI, S, W

**path** E, S: occasionally used for 'pass' in LS

**pole** E: as 'pivot', in Burwarton Pole? The resemblance to a col name may be fortuitous, though Pegwn-y-bwlch ('pegwn' = 'pole' or 'axis') has a similar star-pattern of paths; ME

**poll** IG: hole, pit, pool, burrow; applied to three cols, perhaps coincidentally; I

**saddle** E: col on a ridge; HS, I, LS, NE, SE

**scailp** IG: gap, cleft, chasm; a col in a deep glen; I

**scar** S: cliff, ridge; gullet, throat; LS

**score** S: notch, cut, rift; LS

**scarth** E (from ON *skarð*): notch, cleft; usually a distinct col on a high mountain ridge; modernized as 'gap', 'nick' or 'pass'; NE

**scord** N, S: col; same origin as 'scarth'; the name of all cols on Shetland; almost two-thirds of scords are coves, inlets, gullies, hill slopes or upland tracks (as 'bealach')

**sheard** OE: gap, cleft; I, NE, SE

**shelve** E (from OE *scylf*): probably in the sense of a sloping plateau; SE

**slack**, **slake** S: dell, shallow gully; col, generally indistinct and watery; LS, NE

**slap**, **slop** S: a low col; a gap or breach; LS

**sloc**, **slochd** M, SG: dell, gully, hollow way, defile; ES, HS, IOM

**slogg** S: bog – but in 'Slogg of Buchromb' probably confused with 'sloc(hd)'; ES

**sloggan**, **slugan** SG: neck of a bottle, gullet, narrow pass; ES, HS

**slop** S *see* **slap**; LS

**slot** S: hollow, dip, gully; LS

**slug** S (from SG *sloc*): gorge, narrow pass; ES

**slugan** SG *see* **sloggan**

**sneck** S: a saddle col, often at a gully on a long ridge; ES

**sreang** SG: a col and / or the path or road which crosses it; anglicized as 'string'; HS

**stairs** E: nick, notch; NE (Hadrian's Wall)

**stairsneach** SG: threshold; open, flattish pass; HS

**step** E: col or pass; in Ireland, anglicized 'coiscéim'; in the Lake District, possible translation of French *pas*; I, NE

**stile** HE: col or pass; English rendering of *céim*; I

**straits**, **straights** E: col on a narrow ridge; NE

**string** E, S *see* **sreang**

**suidhe** SG: seat; as a geographical term, usually a hill or flat area on a hillside; applied to the flattish summit of Learg Mheuran (Argyll / Perth & Kinross); HS

**sware**, **swire**, **swyre** (more rarely **swair**, **square**) E, S: a 'neck' of land or the end of a ridge; a dip or flat area on a ridge, often indistinct; LS, NE, SE

**torc** SG: notch, cleft, indentation (the usual meaning is 'boar'); HS

**trough** E: hollow; channel of river or stream; col; NE

**uinneag** SG: high col with plunging views; anglicized as 'window'; HS

**wick**, **wyke** S: notch, cleft (from ON *vík*) in Orkney; col on a high, narrow ridge in NE

**window** E, S *see* **uinneag**

**yate**, **yatt** E: gate; pass or col; may also refer to the road or path; E

**yet**, **yett** S: gate; pass or defile; LS

# Regions

## London

An enormous, overstuffed walrus – a creature unknown to
the Victorian taxidermist, who assumed it to have had a taut,
unwrinkled hide – is one of many unique objects of the natural
world displayed in the Horniman Museum in south London.
The museum's rarest treasure, however, lies on its very doorstep,
unnamed and unrecognized – until now.

London has many hills but only one col. It cuts through the
Norwood Ridge, one mile to the north of the Crystal Palace
Transmitter. For a long time, the gap in the Norwood Ridge was
not particularly useful. London grew up around a crossing of
the Thames and expanded along its tributaries. The city's main
arteries followed valleys and unbroken ridges. But eventually,
the burgeoning suburbs developed their own arterial system
and it became possible to orbit the city without passing through
its centre. The road which crosses the col now forms part of
the South Circular. It was already a busy route in 1868, when
Frederick Horniman, a tea merchant and collector, bought a
house and gardens with distant views of central London and
began to organise his collection of curiosities, which he left to
the people of London in 1901.

Natural features can be hard to find in a city. In that part of
south London, there are signs to everything except the col,

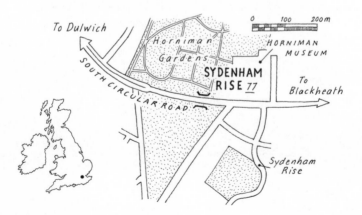

which reveals its classic shape – two elegantly intersecting encolures – only at the very top. Streams which flowed from the watershed have been sent underground, and the place has to be imagined without its buildings and roads (a soothing mental exercise for anyone who has reached the col after shooting the rapids of the worst cycling black spots in London). It can be seen as it was in quieter days on the right of Camille Pissarro's *Lordship Lane Station*, where it appears as a grassy cleft dotted with suburban villas. This is the only British col to be painted by a French Impressionist, and the first to be crossed on a bicycle by a major French novelist. During the Dreyfus Affair, Émile Zola lived in a hotel on the Norwood Ridge, velocipeding all over the place with his camera and admiring the lacy bloomers of English lady cyclists.

Though it stands in one of the most densely populated parts of Britain, this is perhaps the loneliest of British cols. Its nearest col-neighbour lies more than twenty miles to the south-west, and no col lies further to the east. It makes up for loneliness with sociability. No other col has a pedestrian crossing at its summit, no col is served by more bus-lines and none has more cycle traffic. On a chilly February afternoon, I counted half a dozen cyclists in as many minutes. Photographing them as they crossed the col entubed in dark clothing, I wondered whether Émile Zola would have bothered to record the scene.

By far the commonest humanpowered vehicle making use of the col has four wheels and is piloted almost exclusively by women. At certain times of day, London's only col is congested with pushchairs. The bloated walrus, the disembodied dogs' heads, the aquarium, the park and the infant-friendly staff are a powerful attraction for the under-fives of Sydenham and Dulwich, who regularly have themselves wheeled up to the col. If col-baggers are allowed to count the same col more than once, some of those juvenile museum-goers already have more col-crossings to their credit than the most experienced fell-walker or cyclist.

I have attached the name 'Sydenham Rise' to the anonymous col because this is one of the streets which form the sides of the col-cradle. It might have been given a different name, in keeping with all the passes of 'the cattle', 'the sheep', 'the deer', and so on. The unwrinkled behemoth, originally from Canada, was purchased by Mr Horniman and brought up to the col from

Kensington in 1901. Two years ago, it descended on the other side when it was moved to Margate for an exhibition and thus, unbeknownst to everyone, became, probably, the first walrus to cross a col.

## Wessex

Nowhere is the strategic value of cols more obvious than at Corfe Castle in Dorset. Three miles from the Channel coast, on the chalk ridge of the Purbeck Hills, the gaunt and jagged ruins of this eleventh-century fortress loom over the village to which it gave its name. On either side of a stubborn rock, two streams cut through the ridge, creating a double gateway. The cutting was known in the tenth century as Corfes Geat, which makes it one of the earliest attested cols in Britain. The name comes from the Old English *ceorfan*, 'to cut'. In the novels of Thomas Hardy, who named the region Wessex, after the Anglo-Saxon kingdom, it is called Corvsgate. In modern English, its name would be Col Castle.

Col Castle, where King Edward the Martyr was murdered, might be thought of as the prime English col. The western side of Corfes Geat is the lowest col in England, fifteen metres

above sea level. More significantly, it stands just west of the meridian which was chosen by the Ordnance Survey as its line of mid-longitude (two degrees west of Greenwich). This is the line marked 'oo' on Ordnance Survey maps, and it is the only line on the map which runs due north all the way through England. Since no law states that a cyclist must ride from Land's End to John o'Groats in order to claim to have ridden the length of Britain, this would make an ideal start to an End to End. It makes an especially good beginning for a col-bagging End to End because, simply by circumcycling Corfe Castle (using the shortcut provided by the Purbeck Way), the end-to-ender will be able to tick off two cols within the first half-mile.

Double cols appear to be a Dorset speciality. Another of these rare features – also called Corfe Gate – lies twenty miles to the west, just outside Dorchester, on a limestone ridge. It is mentioned in a land grant by King Cnut in 1024: *on corf getes westran cotan*. The two 'corfes' forming the double col are less than half a mile apart, on either side of Corton Hill – one above Corton (formerly Corfetone) Farm, the other in the hamlet of Coryates, just beyond the Corfe Gate House B&B.

It may be a sign of civilization (or its decline) that the main cultural attraction of the region is now felt to be its literary representation. For the purposes of tourism, the kings of Wessex have been supplanted by a scribe and his favourite mount, *la petite reine*, as the French still call the bicycle. The characters of Thomas Hardy and the novelist himself are the inescapable guides to a realm which is neither entirely real nor entirely fictitious. By a happy coincidence, Hardy's Wessex (primarily Dorset, Devon, Somerset, Hampshire and Wiltshire) is the richest area of cols in southern England. In Dorset alone, there are thirteen, of which eleven are on a road.

Unlike his contemporary Edward Elgar, whose approach to bicycle maintenance consisted of buying a new one whenever anything went wrong with the old one, Hardy remained faithful to his Rover Cob, which he purchased in Weymouth in 1896 for £20. Two years later, he told a friend:

> The advantage [the bicycle] has for literary people is that you can go out for a long distance without coming in contact with another mind, – not even a horse's – & dissipating any little mental energy that has arisen in the course of a morning's application.

One consequence of this is that the bicycle itself, being the instrument but not the object of imagining, is absent from Hardy's Wessex. Famously, no Thomas Hardy character is ever seen with or on a bicycle. This hardly matters, since the place to go looking for a writer's imagination is in his books.

There is, however, a cheerful irony in the fact that one of those Dorset cols – a tree-shrouded meeting of ancient trackways on the Wessex Ridgeway called the Dorset Gap – has a book at its centre, a collective work of pleasant monotony written by visitors to the Gap, who, since 1972, have been invited to record their impressions in spiral notebooks contained in a blue plastic box (replacing the original biscuit tin).

After a long trek through the works of Thomas Hardy, I did eventually pick up the faint trace of a cyclist. In the short story 'The Honourable Laura' the landlord of a forlorn hotel on the North Devon coast glances idly at the visitors' book: 'Not a name had been entered there since the 19th of the previous November, and that was only the name of a man who had arrived on a tricycle, who, indeed, had not been asked to enter at all.'

Apart from Corvsgate, cols in Hardy's Wessex seemed to be as scarce as cyclists. His characters skulk in dank dells, lurch along hollow ways, march purposefully but vainly across moors and stand enigmatically on hill tops. But in some of the remoter corners of his work, in poems and short stories, the cols of Wessex exert their quiet influence. As the sun rises over the col of Dogbury Gate on the North Dorset Downs, 'a horseman from off the hill-tip / Comes clapping down into the dip' to meet a wagon bearing a coffin which 'creaks up from the fog'. In *The Hand of Ethelberta*, the heroine and her borrowed donkey pass through the Ulwell Gap on their way to Corvsgate Castle, and in 'A Trampwoman's Tragedy', which was written after a bicycle trip to Glastonbury, the tramp-woman remembers the 'lone inns we loved, my man and I' – 'the cosy house at Wynyard's Gap', and the inn 'far-famed as Marshal's Elm', with its view of the Mendip Hills and 'the western sea'.

The inn at the Marshall's Elm col has long since disappeared, but there is still a country pub at Winyard's Gap, where the Somerset hills are visible from the greensward of a beer garden. A traveller heading north on Hardy's route to Glastonbury would do well to stop at the col, if only to discover in a tankard of ale as 'luminous as an autumn sunset' the shortest route to a writer's imagination.

## The Malvern Hills

The geology of the Malvern Hills is extremely complex, made even more inscrutable by quarrying and, ironically, by the digging of geologists. Faults and fissures slice at almost regular intervals through some of the oldest rocks in England. The early geo-political significance of these gaps in the ridge is apparent in the ziggurat-shaped Iron Age hill fort known as British Camp, which guards one of the two trans-Malvern passes now served by an A road. The hills were sometimes referred to as 'the English Alps', not just because they had the classic triangular shape of mountains ('in a Pirramidy fashion on ye top', as the traveller Celia Fiennes noted in the 1690s), but also because they seemed to rise up between one country and the next.

For three years in the 1970s, I had a view of the Malvern Hills from my bedroom window, four miles away across the fields and hedges. I did not know that the 'U' shapes on the horizon were cols. The word was familiar to me only from the title of one of my father's books on Everest, and there was nothing obvious to connect the Tibetan Plateau with the Worcestershire plain. I did know, however, that, like the Himalayas, the Malvern Hills were a cultural and political frontier.

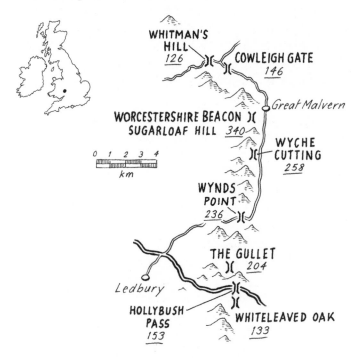

WHITMAN'S HILL *126*

COWLEIGH GATE *146*

*Great Malvern*

WORCESTERSHIRE BEACON
SUGARLOAF HILL *340*

WYCHE CUTTING *258*

0 1 2 3 4
km

WYNDS POINT *236*

THE GULLET *204*

*Ledbury*

HOLLYBUSH PASS *153*

WHITELEAVED OAK *133*

In the pub up the lane – a haunt of agricultural labourers whose conditions and outlook were not dissimilar to those of serfs – there were men who thought of Malvern as a different world and who had rarely even been there. The land beyond the hills on which the sun set was an ambiguous buffer zone inhabited by 'strangers'. Officially known as Herefordshire, it was, in their mental geography, a part of Wales.

The human fauna of the Malverns was almost as varied as the species of rare plant and animal which thrive in that transitional zone. Unlike the more homogeneous settlements of the plain, Great Malvern had something of the leery cosmopolitanism of a border town: an enclave of youth culture sheltered under the skirts of its genteel predecessor, the Victorian spa of grand guest houses and Winter Gardens. I did not then associate the Malverns with the local composer Edward Elgar who had found inspiration there on his cycling expeditions but with a specifically Malvernian blend of yokelish folk and German acid rock. The tea rooms of Malvern were patronized by hippies and bikers, retired ladies of leisure, scientists from the Radar Establishment and escapees from the high-security public schools.

Seven cols can be identified along the Malvern ridge which divides Herefordshire from Worcestershire. Most of those cols now have innocuously decorative names which say little of their ancient importance: Whiteleaved Oak, Hollybush Pass, the Gullet, Wynds Point, the Wyche Cutting, Cowleigh Gate. Their older names – Baldyate, Brustenyate, Shakellyate, Swyneyate, etc. – contain the medieval word for 'gate' or 'gateway'. These were the passages which cut through the hills to the lands beyond and, although few people now see them as portals to another world, these cols still mark an ineradicable boundary.

A tour of the seven Malvern cols is an ideal introduction to this magical realm. This is the most concentrated group of cols in England south of the Peak District, and the entire route is barely eighteen miles long. There are four railway stations in the immediate area, two of them postcard pretty and all with regular services. No other col route is better connected. This is probably also the only col route for which a description exists in medieval Latin.

*… usque Baldeyate, et de Baldeyate per fossatum [the Shire Ditch] usque Brustenyate, et de Brustenyate usque Swyneyate, et de Swyneyate usque Shakellyate, et de Shakellyate usque Dead orle [etc.]*

These were the boundaries of the hunting forest known as Malvern Chase. Such was the importance of cols that their names are older than those of the hills themselves, which are referred to in the document only as 'the mountain's ridge'.

With the prevailing south-west wind, the best itinerary would be the same, but in reverse, beginning with Dead Orle, now known as Whiteleaved Oak. A tiny hamlet in a hobbity hole at the southernmost col of the Malvern Hills, Whiteleaved Oak stands at the intersection of three counties. No sign reveals its significance, but when I visited the col in 2014 a man at the gate of a flint cottage kindly served as a talking signpost. He raised a finger and pointed at a tree, a hedge and then his feet: 'That's Gloucestershire, that's Herefordshire, and this is Worcestershire.' The oak itself was already a distant memory a century and a half ago, but another oak, not too far away, has been pressed into service as a Druid shrine and is permanently festooned with votive ribbons.

After Shakellyate (renamed Hollybush Pass in the nineteenth century) and Swyneyate (the Gullet Pass), which is reachable by a road and then a track, views of the sunny Worcestershire plain appear through the hedgerows. At this point, the percussion of boots and walking stick or the murmuring tyres and a chain running on sprockets may begin to perform melodies from the works of Elgar – a stately march for the downhill stretches, allegros for the uphill (assuming efficient rhythms). The route then descends into the plain only to rise again steeply on an 8 per cent gradient to the ridge at Brustenyate (Wynds Point).

Some people may find this descending and reascending irksome, but it provides an instructive interlude. From the broad heath of Castlemorton Common, there are superb views of the cols already crossed and those yet to come: the entire range seems to have been cut out and pasted on to the sky like a computer-generated col profile. At Castlemorton Common, with the tune of 'Nimrod' from the *Enigma Variations* playing in the bicycling brain, it struck me that the plunging intervals of that mysterious piece on an unknown theme exactly mirror the profile of the hills and that, although the work was completed in 1899, and Elgar did not acquire his first bicycle (a Royal Sunbeam) until the following year, he might already have been contemplating the hills with future exploits in mind …

Following one of Elgar's own cycling maps, on which he traced his favourite rides in red ink, the route continues along the western side of the ridge by the wooded corniche called Jubilee Drive. After little more than two miles, it reaches Baldeyate, which is now called the Wyche Cutting. The place is well worth a linger. From the picturesque chalet-style public toilet the view extends to the Black Mountains of Wales, and if the Countenance Divine is shining forth, it may seem inappropriate that it was Sir Hubert Parry and not Sir Edward Elgar who set Blake's 'Jerusalem' to music. A few steps to the east, just over the saddle of the col, with the roofs and priory of Great Malvern below, and the rutted 'Pixie Path' descending to the south-east, the Worcestershire Plain and the vale of the Severn are as beautiful a sight as the Welsh panorama.

Skirting the Worcestershire Beacon and Sugarloaf Hill – between which an unnamed col lies at the top of the gully called the Dingle – the col sequence reaches the northern boundary of Malvern Chase at Cowelsyate (Cowleigh Gate). A mile beyond, there is another, almost unnoticeable and nameless col by Whitman's Hill in Storridge. But perhaps the best course would be to turn around at Cowleigh Gate and complete the route in the other direction so that no view will have remained unseen and no melody unhummed. Cowleigh Gate lies across the county boundary, and the last col of all is on a busy road which leads to Hereford – whence come strangers – and Wales, which is a different country altogether.

## Wales BC

Every unexplored subject is full of mysteries. Before beginning a systematic search for every col in the British Isles, I imagined that a certain number of them might be located quite easily by following Roman roads. With nothing but muscle and coercion at their disposal, ancient road builders must have used whatever help nature had to offer. I found to my surprise that Roman roads in England and Scotland very rarely cross cols. They sidle across hill slopes and head straight for the top of steep ridges. Only when absolutely necessary – as in the English Lake District – do they pass through the gaps between hills.

I then tried looking for cols on drove roads. These are the tracks along which sheep and cattle were moved from highland

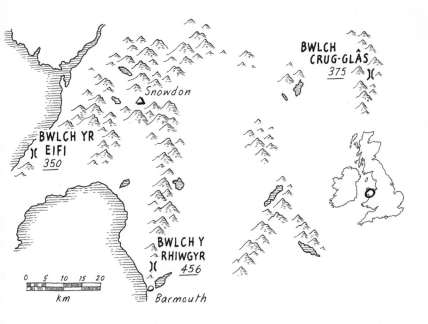

pastures to markets in the lowlands. Some of the drove roads which have been reincarnated as long-distance walking routes do occasionally cross well-known cols such as Cauldstane Slap in the Pentland Hills. But here, too, there appeared to have been a curious reluctance on the part of the drovers to take advantage of these natural gateways.

Finally, I found a rich seam of cols in the nationwide network of turnpike roads, and this provided a solution to the second, though not to the first mystery. As a report on 'Turnpike Trusts' to the Houses of Parliament in 1866 explained:

> The drovers of sheep and cattle to the several fairs and places where they are driven for sale, seek other routes and avoid this turnpike road on account of the high rate of such toll on such sheep and cattle, which ... they can readily do, although at the costs of travelling further and by more circuitous routes.

It is only comparatively recently that speed has been considered important. The turnpike roads of the eighteenth century were designed for the modern traveller, impatient with discomfort and delay. Gradients steeper than 5 per cent came to seem unacceptable, which is why a road's age can often be gauged by measuring the angle of its slope: the steeper the road, the more likely it is to be ancient. Naturally, turnpike roads made use of cols, and it is this that accounts for their scarcity on drove roads.

When I came to Wales, with its well-charted network of drove roads, other mysteries emerged. There are no obvious signs that Welsh drovers avoided cols as the English did; one col above Barmouth is even called Pass of the Drovers (Bwlch y Rhiwgyr). In fact, there is no sign that the Romans avoided them either. Col-baggers in Wales are quite likely to find themselves following the course of a Roman road. But they might find, too, that a col-tour of Wales takes them on a journey to an even more distant age.

Far more than in other parts of Britain, cols in Wales are dominated by major Iron Age hill forts and served by Roman roads which followed the earlier native tracks. These lofty citadels were also towns where the Celtic tribes lived more comfortably than we might suppose. They were still an impressive feature of the landscape in the late eighteenth century when the antiquarian Thomas Pennant travelled through Wales. At the col of Bwlch yr Eifl, he was astonished to find the remains of a huge settlement: 'Across this hollow, from one summit of the Eifl to the other, extends an immense rampart of stones, or perhaps the ruins of a wall, which effectually blocked up the pass.'*

Wales has much the same variety of terrain as the rest of the British Isles, yet there is something peculiarly and mysteriously Welsh about the presence of cols in the inhabited countryside. Not only are they often distinguished by major hill forts, they also seem to have imposed their preeminence on Welsh society. Farms, villages and towns are named after these passages through the hills, rather than the other way about, as though the cols had been an organizing principle of the landscape. The same phenomenon is even more noticeable in Ireland, where dozens of townlands bear the name of the local col.

Perhaps this reflects the Irish settlement of Wales in the early Middle Ages; perhaps, too, it contains an explanation of the other mystery of Welsh cols. Welsh is a rich and nuanced language, and yet, while the rest of Britain has almost one hundred words for 'col', all but seven of the 232 cols in Wales whose names have survived are called *bwlch*. Did the ubiquitous word *bwlch*, which

---

* Another example is the Bwlch Crug-glâs (the Col of the Blue Barrow or Mound) which Pennant, believing it to be pronounced *Bwlch Agricla*, associated with the Roman general Agricola.

can refer to any kind of opening, have a metaphorical value for
the people who named the land? Was there a Welsh Hercules
who, like his mythical Greek and Roman counterpart, dented
and demolished ridges and made it possible for mortals to pass
safely from one side of the mountains to the other by using these
gateways, breaches or portals? The original significance of the
word may never be known, but it is often more profitable to
travel in the wide-open spaces of ignorance than in the familiar,
upholstered surroundings of received knowledge. In historical
geography, nothing can replace the journey itself and the exhilarating exercise known to archaeologists as 'ground-proofing'.

While cycling through France and Britain on the trail of the
ancient Celts, I occasionally toyed with the idea of a useful
thought experiment. Given the surprising ingenuity and pre-
cision of their metalwork and the high-quality engineering of
their wheeled vehicles, could the ancient Celts have invented
the bicycle? If a reconstructive archaeologist ever builds such a
machine, employing the appropriate materials and techniques,
it should be taken on a tour of Welsh cols, and perhaps then
those dark mysteries will vanish in the light that comes through
the gap in the hills.


## North Wales

A few miles west of Llangollen, in the Berwyn Mountains
of North Wales, an unmarked road runs alongside the River
Ceiriog. As the valley narrows, the little road bends to the west
and begins to climb coaxingly into the hills. After the last human
habitation on the right, it turns into a surly track – manageable
on a road bike but becoming ever more obstructive, until the
hedgerows give way to stone walls and a windy moor. Up ahead
lies the col called Pen Bwlch Llandrillo ('pen' denoting the head
or top), from where the valley of the Dee opens up and the mountains of Snowdonia appear on the horizon. There at the summit,
set into a rocky outcrop, is a shiny metal plaque 'erected by the
R.S.F. [the 'Rough Stuff Fellowship')]' It commemorates a certain
'Wayfarer (1877–1956)', identified only as 'a lover of Wales'.

As thousands of British cyclists used to know, 'Wayfarer'
was the pen name of an insurance clerk in Liverpool, Walter
MacGregor Robinson. 'Robbie', whose many admirers included
the R.S.F. , was a formidably cheerful man. As tough and spindly

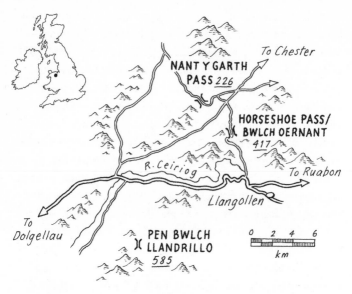

as a steel frame, he survived the trenches of the First World War – where he continued to write his cycling column – with only the pain of a leg wound to remind him of the horror. As soon as the snows began to melt, he would cycle out of Liverpool to the west, along the treacherous tramlined roads, equipped with acetylene lamps for the beginning and end of a long ride. Once over the border, he headed for the big passes of the Berwyn and Clwydian Mountains – the Horseshoe, Penbarras, Bwlch Arthur, Nant y Garth and Bwlch Llandrillo, where a stone memorial (later replaced by the stainless-steel plaque) was unveiled in the year after his death.

Wayfarer's *Three Men in a Boat*-style account of a weekend excursion to the col of Bwlch Llandrillo was published in *Cycling* magazine in March 1919. It is widely considered to be the founding text of all-terrain cycling. It perfectly expresses the pleasures of pushing a bike for several miles through a snowdrift at 1,500 feet and that meteorological optimism which can make a 'rough stuff' cyclist a nightmare companion for the more common fair-weather variety.

*The little window of my bedroom stood wide open (which was as it should be) and the snow was blowing in. I knelt on the broad casement and looked out. It was still snowing – but feebly. … Right opposite to me 1,500 feet of mountain upraised itself, clad in ermine.*

*… I took a walk up the hillside before breakfast and returned to find*

*the Old Gentleman looking over our machines. He at once began to pump his views into me. 'I think', he said, 'that they're exaggerating the condition of affairs on the mountain. Things aren't as bad as they say ... I think we might venture. What do you say?' I decided that what was good enough for him was good enough for me, 'and anyhow', I added, "twill be an adventure.'*

This article was titled 'Over the Top' (in memory of the trenches). Though it is often cited as a harbinger of mountain biking, it should be said that there was not as much difference then as there is today between on- and off-road cycling. In 1919, the road 'repairs' encountered by Wayfarer consisted of 'numerous patches of stones ... dumped down in higgledy-piggledy fashion'. According to a fellow member of the Anfield Bicycle Club, the Bwlch Penbarras was 'in those days rough and overgrown, much as it had been left, following the decay of coaching'. It was because of campaigning cyclists that a national programme of road-building and resurfacing began, paving the way for the motoring boom ... And therein lies the other, crucial difference, of which Wayfarer saw the early portents, and which must have him spinning his pedals in the grave.

It was in the hills near Llangollen, not far from Wayfarer's Col, that I had my first adult experience of off-road cycling. A friend had given me the key to an almost derelict house on the side of the Eglwyseg Mountain, where I intended to devote the long, quiet hours to writing. Half-way up the Horseshoe Pass, a small road between high hedges led to a ferociously steep track which resembled the bed of a dried-up torrent in a slate quarry. In repeated ascents of this track, I made three important discoveries about rough-stuff cycling.

First, it is extremely difficult to control a loaded bicycle on a rubbly track while swatting the notoriously swat-resistant horse-fly. Second, the regular shopping trip down and back up the mountain required exactly the amount of energy supplied by the food transported in the panniers: in effect, the food consumed itself. Third, and, in retrospect, most annoying of all, it was impossible to admire the view while concentrating on the micro-terrain of stone-sized hills and puddle-sized lakes. Living as I now do at the end of half a mile of vertiginous stony track, I can appreciate the video-game intensity of hurtling along a natural surface. But this is not at all what Wayfarer had in mind.

Some rough-stuff cyclists consider a ride half wasted if the bicycle is still in one piece at the end of it, depriving them of another engrossing day in the workshop putting it back together. Wayfarer was never a cycling fetishist. 'Cycles are for riding, not for cleaning!' he liked to say. Another motto was 'As little bicycle as possible.' The bicycle was simply the vehicle of discovery, however it was propelled:

> And is this cycling? Per se, possibly not altogether. Some of the way over the mountains was ridden, but for the most part it was a walking expedition ... At least, it is cycling as I understand it, for my conception of the pastime includes much besides main roads and secondary roads and much beyond the propelling of a bicycle ...
>
> I fling wide the boundaries of that pastime and include whatever is incidental thereto. Some of the best of cycling would be missed if one always had to be in the saddle or on a hard road.

Off-road cycling now tends to involve a great deal of on-road motoring, even in mainland Britain, where no col is more than a day's ride from a railway station. This has given rise to the depressing concept of 'a two-car expedition' (arriving in one car, being picked up at the end of the ride by another and returned to the first one). The bicycle becomes a tiny moon-lander which has to be delivered to its dusty trail by huge, expensive machines. In the far north of England, which has some of the best road-cycling country in Europe, at certain times of the year bicycles on car roofs are a more common sight than bicycles on the road.

Wayfarer's scathing jollity at this pointless extinction of all the 'incidentals' of cycling can easily be imagined. He witnessed only the first skirmishes of the great invasion, but he was already 'over the top' and ready for the battle, as his friend from the Anfield Bicycle Club remembered:

> One afternoon, 'Robbie' and I were approaching the top of Horseshoe Pass, when the window of a stationary car opened and out came some screwed-up papers and other rubbish onto the side of the road. 'Wayfarer' immediately dismounted, picked the papers up, knocked at the car window, and handed all the rubbish back, with the curt comment, 'I think you have dropped these!'

## The Pennine Way

Deliberate trespassing became a popular weekend activity in the industrial north of England in the late nineteenth century. To an increasingly confident, health-conscious middle class and a proletariat stuck for most of the week in smoky valleys with a view of green hills, a landowner's 'Keep Out' sign was like a red rag to a bull, even if the land so marked was occupied by one.

The first recorded mass trespass took place in 1896 on the eastern flank of Winter Hill near Bolton, above the col of Hordern Stoops. To prevent disturbance to his grouse, the local tyrant had barricaded the ancient footpaths over Smithills Moor, depriving Bolton's weavers and coal miners of their Sunday recreation for the sake of a few days' shooting. On four successive Sundays, inspired by the local Socialist Club and its poet, ten thousand men and women swarmed indignantly over the moorland, pushing through a thin line of policemen and gamekeepers and smashing the recently erected gate on Coal Pit Road. 'Must poor folk stroll in cinders while the rich cop all the green? / Is England but the landlord's who locks up each pretty scene?'

Thirty-six years later, the mass trespass on Kinder Scout, a grouse-shooting preserve of the Duke of Devonshire in the high Derbyshire Pennines, became the political battering ram which eventually opened the way to National Parks and 'right to roam' legislation. It also provided Britain's first long-distance trail with its symbolic starting point. The Pennine Way was the idea

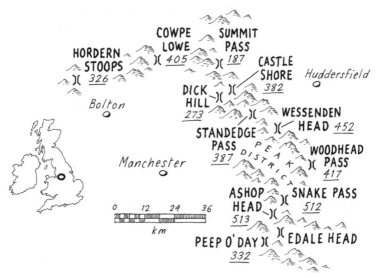

of journalist and rambling campaigner Tom Stephenson, who pictured it as 'a faint line on the Ordnance Maps which the feet of grateful pilgrims would, with the passing years, engrave on the face of the land' (*Daily Herald*, 22 June 1935). His wish would be granted in more ways than one.

The last section of the 256-mile trail was opened in 1965. By that time, even more land had been fenced off from the general public by the War Ministry, the Air Ministry, the Water Board, the Forestry Commission and the Nature Conservancy. Alfred Wainwright, the council clerk whose affably grumpy 'pictorial guides' to the Lake District express his continual delight at escaping from sooty Blackburn, found the Pennine Way a depressing trudge through wastelands created by civil servants:

> *Yorkshire folk used to build stone towers on their hilltops, but now all kinds of fancy contraptions in wire enclosures desecrate the skylines … The former much-abused private landowners, who at least knew and loved their countryside, were saints compared with the present autocrats who dictate their threats from city offices … The old landowners did at least wear tweeds and heavy boots, and listened to reason, but you can't argue against these gents in pin stripes and patent shoes. (Pennine Way Companion (1968), p. xxi)*

As Wainwright pointed out, the name of the trail is misleading. The 'backbone of England' ends at the Tyne Valley, but the 'Pennine' path continues regardless along Hadrian's Wall, and then, still without changing its name, across the Cheviot Hills, where it joins the national border, eventually leaving it near the col of Pete Swire (last mentioned in 1543 and never shown on a map). The Pennine Way finally calls it a day (or three weeks of hard slog) at Kirk Yetholm in Scotland, sixty miles from the nearest Pennine.

No other long-distance trail in Britain includes so many cols. But nineteen of the twenty-six are on the Pennine appendices of Hadrian's Wall and the Border. Of the remaining seven, four are indicated indirectly by 'Head' names – referring to the headwaters of a river – two are unnamed, and one, Castle Shore (from the Old English *sheard*, meaning 'gap' or 'cleft'), has only now had its name restored to it. (It had survived in the names of a gully and a hill.) The summit of Castle Shore lies on the central reservation of the M62 motorway, on the boundary of Lancashire and Yorkshire.

The Pennine Way itself now crosses the col further east, on a motorway footbridge.

The fact that these cols have either lost their names or were never named in the first place suggests that the permanent inhabitants of the Pennines were sensible enough to avoid these squelchy dips and gaps between the hills. Cols can be a godsend to level-headed walkers who prefer convenience to conquest, but in the softer parts of Britain, they can be a boggy nuisance, as Wainwright repeatedly discovered: 'Well, I'm glad it's finished, I must say. I mean the walking, not the making of the book, which has been very enjoyable. No, I mean the walking, the floundering in glutinous peatbogs, the stumbling in soggy heather, the squelching in muddy fields.'

On Kinder Scout, the success of the trail was its undoing. The line which 'grateful pilgrims' would 'engrave on the face of the land' became a broad, shallow trench in which nothing could live because there was no season when it was untrodden. Thousands of booted feet compacted the peat, creating an ever-widening swathe of devastation, which is why the Pennine Way now avoids the top of Kinder Scout and heads for the nameless col to the east of Edale Cross. As penny-pinching councils cut public transport, 'access' to the Pennines became the privilege of car drivers, whose subsidies were less easily computed. When Wainwright wrote, 'Nature creates; man destroys,' he can have had little idea of the millions of car miles that the Pennine Way would generate.

Perhaps the land is learning to defend itself. So many Pennine pilgrims may eventually be sucked into the bog or stuck in sinkholes and collapsing mine shafts that the entire Pennine route will be declared off limits. The nameless cols will be left to their murky devices and Wainwright's guide will become what it already is for thousands of armchair explorers – a luminous treasure map to a writer's imagination and the world he re-created among the smokestacks of sooty Blackburn.

## The Yorkshire Dales

In 2014, the Tour de France came to Yorkshire. Stage 1 ran from Leeds to Harrogate, stage 2 from York to Sheffield. The official song for the Grand Départ in Leeds was Alistair Griffin's 'The Road (Will Take You Home)'. The video shows him and his co-star, the singer Kimberley Walsh, sitting in an Aston Martin parked on top of a Yorkshire moor not far east of Blubberhouses Pass. Kimberley, a native of Bradford, gazes in wonder at the blasted heath, which she must have seen a thousand times from the city, a sombre horizon painted at the end of a brick street. 'No wonder I never came up here,' she seems to be thinking. There appears to have been some difficulty in persuading her out of the car. When she emerges from the metallic cocoon, a wool coat covers her beautiful frock, which has the grey sheen of a space blanket. Yet as the thrilling notes pour out of the insulated songbird, there can be no doubt that she has the lungs to power a bicycle up the steepest of Yorkshire cols.

Half-way through the song, an expression of bemused delight appears on her face as she sees a most peculiar sight. A posse of normal-looking folk – male and female, young and old – are gliding past on funny contraptions made of tubes and wheels. All those pushbikes that were languishing unused in dusty Bradford garages have taken to the hills; the magic of the Tour de France has cast its spell even over those satanic, rain-drenched moors.

The wonderment of the car-borne city-dwellers depicted in the video perfectly expresses the amazed reaction of much of the

British media whenever a cycling event attracts a huge audience. It sounds strange to anyone who cycles to work alongside thousands of other cyclists, but the fact is, as the CTC's 'SMIDSY' campaign pointed out ('Sorry, Mate, I Didn't See You'), cyclists are invisible until they unexpectedly materialize under the wheels of a truck or on the inside of a car door, or, in this case, all over the Yorkshire Dales. On July 5 2014, the country was amazed, as usual, to see remote hillsides literally covered with spectators and their bicycles – 2.5 million of them, according to the police; 5 million according to the organizers of the Tour de France.

The gruelling passes over which the peloton was to fly like a swarm of transhumant bees were revealed to be a gigantic commercial opportunity. In the 1930s, special trains were provided for holiday-makers, with customized carriages for bicycles, bound for popular resorts such as Scarborough and Whitby. In the summer of 2014, anticipating the sudden demand, regional train companies effectively banned bicycles from all their services. If the butchers, bakers and cheese-makers of Yorkshire had had the same foresight, they could have shut up shop before the hordes arrived to buy their Tour de France-themed produce. Knowing how quickly accommodation is booked up as soon as a Tour route is announced, we had telephoned a hotel in Ilkley in February. It lay close to the route on both of the Yorkshire stages. 'It's a long time ahead,' said the receptionist. 'Yes, but we were thinking that, because of the Tour de France, there might be a problem.' 'Let me see ... No, there's no problem at all. There's a cycling thing going on, but that won't make any difference ...'

On the day itself, French journalists, stunned by the enormous crowds, were even more astonished to see them just as dense on the downhill sections: the English waited all day to watch the peloton flash by in under fifteen seconds. Even on the stiffest climbs – Kidstones Pass and Buttertubs Pass – the riders were a blur. On a lone break, the veteran rider Jens Voigt skimmed up the Buttertubs Pass at 15 mph, and there were several near-accidents as amateur photographers stood in the road, assuming, as British drivers usually do, that bicycles travel no faster than a pedestrian in a hurry.

In England, these climbs are lauded by weekend cyclists as flesh-eating giants, worthy of epithets such as 'brutal', 'lung-busting' and 'ball-breaking'. The Kidstones climb is less than three miles long with an average gradient of 4.6 per cent, while the Buttertubs is just over three miles with an average gradient of 5.5 per cent. One French newspaper called them *bosses* ('bumps'). The big cols of the Continent average a gradient of 7 or 8 per cent and can stretch for thirty miles. The Yorkshire cols are a hasty pie and chips to be consumed at lightning speed; the Alpine cols are ten-course meals made to last for most of a long day. Henri Desgrange, who launched the Tour de France in 1903, once said of the mighty Col du Galibier in the French Alps that other cols were 'gnat's piss' by comparison. It is fortunate for English pride that the Tour de France never came to Yorkshire while Desgrange was in charge.

Both passes – the Kidstones and the Buttertubs – are bona fide cols, but the Tour organizers refused to grant them the *appellation d'origine contrôlée* and instead called them the Côte de Cray and the Côte de Buttertubs. (A *côte* is a hill or an incline.) Even some British commentators were therefore unaware that the famous Kidstones Pass was on the route. The hamlet of Cray, half-way up the climb, might have been chosen for ease of pronunciation, but the French commentators had no problem with *Beutaireteubse*, and it is likely that this was a deliberate, technical demotion.

The organizers were probably right to downplay the importance of these cols in the context of the Tour de France, which always includes both the Alps and the Pyrenees. In harsh weather, the desolation of the Yorkshire cols is impressive but, as cols, they offer a comparatively easy way in which to enjoy the Yorkshire Dales. The Kidstones Pass is the most convenient gateway from Wharfedale to Wensleydale, and the Buttertubs Pass the easiest route from Wensleydale to Swaledale. Unless they are provoked by lung-busting aggression or antagonized by the weather, these cols are friendly giants, and there is nothing inherently implausible in the video director's fantasy of normal-looking folk on normal bikes pedalling serenely across the blasted heath.

## Shap Fell

It is hard to believe that a col or a pass can disappear, and that it can do so within a few generations. It seems particularly incredible when the col or pass used to lie on a major route which crossed a natural frontier.

In the days before cars became virtually infallible, and communicated a sense of that virtue to their drivers, the word 'Shap' evoked the same heroic images as 'Khyber' or 'Karakoram'. Properly speaking, 'Shap' is the name of the mile-long village on the A6 north of Shap Fell.* For most people, it refers to the long ascent after which the road from the south runs down to Penrith and the border city of Carlisle. Once over Shap, a traveller was virtually in Scotland. Many never made it that far. The old crossing lies on the A6. A few yards south of the summit, a monolith in a lay-by bears a plaque commemorating the days when 'Shap' was synonymous with downpours, delays and mechanical failure:

*This memorial pays tribute to the drivers and crews of vehicles that made possible the social and commercial links between North and South on this old and difficult route over Shap Fell before the opening of the M6 Motorway.*

*Remembered, too, are those who built and maintained the road and the generations of local people who gave freely of food and shelter to stranded travellers in bad weather.*

The old pass on the A6 is now a delightful climb (in good weather) on a wonderfully quiet three-lane highway. The motorway crossing which replaced it is drab by comparison. The summit comes as a gradual realization and would be easy to miss without a blue sign marked 'M6 Shap Summit 1,036 feet'. In effect, the motorway has abolished the pass. For countless centuries, tracks never disappeared completely. Once created, even the spindliest trail was practically immortal. It might eventually mutate into a tarmacked road or survive only as the whisper of a path, but something remained to bear witness to its ancient usefulness. Then, in the 1960s, an alien species landed in Britain. It created what appeared to be extremely long runways for airplanes without brakes. The terrain was almost irrelevant. On the north–south trajectory of the motorway where it crosses Shap Fell, there was once nothing at all, not even a path. In their blankness, the earlier maps offer no inkling of the future. Uniquely in the history of British roads, the motorways represent a final break with the past.

---

* The Shap Fells are the rolling moorland south-west of Shap village; 'Shap Fell' is usually reserved for the ridge crossed by the A6.

To
Penrith

Shap

SHAP (M6)
316

A6

M6

Orton

WAIN GAP
263

SHAP (A6)
426

BREASTHIGH
PASS

HORSEHOUSE
303

431

Gaisgill

Tebay

To
Kendal

0  1  2  3  4
km

The whole area between the Lake District and the North
Pennines is something of a Bermuda Triangle of cols. Two miles
south of Shap Summit on the old A6, where the road curves
up and on to the ridge above Borrowdale, there is a col which
vanished a century and a half ago when it failed to appear on the
first Ordnance Survey map. It had been shown quite clearly, along
with its name, on several charts, though never identified as a col
or a pass. The earliest of all is a strip map in John Ogilby's *Britannia*
(1675). It was captioned with the peculiar name 'Horse House',
and so it appeared on one map after another until the Ordnance
Survey expunged it.

Ogilby had presumably obtained his information, as map-
makers inevitably did, from a local inhabitant, perhaps from the
postmistress or the coach driver himself. In north-west England,
the commonest term for a col or a pass is 'hause', pronounced
'*haws*' in some parts, '(h)*ows*' in others. The Horse House was
probably a col or the crossing of a ridge which could be negotiated
by horse-drawn vehicles. (Another 'horse hause', thus spelled, is
shown three miles to the west on a map of 1695.) But to Ogilby's
ear, or to that of his informant, the notion of an equine residence

sounded quite plausible, and so he drew a little house on his map with doors, windows and a chimney and labelled it Horse House, never wondering at the eccentric arrangement which stabled horses at the top rather than at the foot of a climb. The absurdity remained until it was removed by the Ordnance Survey. The col itself, of course, has been there all along.*

Shap Fell belongs to a region of undulating moorland in which cols and passes may well go unremarked until people find a use for them. Less than a mile from Ogilby's Horse House, an old track called Breasthigh Road crosses Borrowdale Edge. At its summit, on a parish boundary, is a col. This nameless feature has never been shown on a map but a few years ago, the track was discovered (and partially destroyed) by drivers of 4x4s, and now the track and its col are commonly referred to as Breasthigh Pass.

A few miles further on, a nebulous col called Wain Gap (a gap or pass suitable for a carriage) is now attested only in the name of a ruined building which serves as an animal pen and in 'Waingap Lane', while Black Hause near the eastern border of Cumbria is so indistinct that it has never settled in one place on the map. In view of these shadowy comings and goings of cols and passes, I came to wonder about Shap itself, which looms so large in the national geographical psyche and yet has no specific name. Perhaps it once did... A quarter of a mile from Shap Summit on the M6, I had noticed a farm on the modern Ordnance Survey map called 'Hause Farm'. It was recorded in 1719 as 'th'Hause House'. Another 'Hause Farm' in the Lake District sits at the foot of a certified col called Howtown Hause, but I assumed that, since 'hause' can mean ridge as well as col, the 'hause' near Shap referred to the nearby ridge of Hardendale Fell.

From the window of the Carlisle to London train, I had seen the white track winding up from Hause Farm to the motorway. From that point of view, it had the faint but detectable features of a col running north-east between Hardendale Fell and Coalpit Hill. Months later, I cycled up the diminishing, slaty track towards the roaring two-way river of cars and trucks. At the barbed-wire fence, I could read the sign on the far side of the motorway: 'Buried structure M60//440.20/Q/'. The structure is a square concrete tunnel with a gate in the middle which makes it possible to pass safely (though muddily) under the motorway.

---

* Horse House is the last col on the Lake District route: see p. 55.

These unphotogenic culverts which preserve the ancient path-ways of shepherds and their animals are known by the inglorious name of 'sheep creep'.

Thanks to the nomadic instincts and stubborn appetites of sheep, the original pass – which was perhaps once known as Shap Hause or Hardendale Hause – can still be crossed by human beings. Beyond the sheep creep, the path last shown on the Ordnance Survey map of 1899 wanders invisibly off to the north-east, avoiding the sinkholes, towards the concentric stone circles of Oddendale. These circles and the path that led to them belong to an age beyond history. Crossing the lost col of Shap through the gloom of the sheep creep, unobserved by the drivers above, a walker may well have a sympathetic sense of belonging to a primitive tribe which has somehow hung on into the age of motorways and machines.

## The Lake District

Everyone responds to beauty in a different way. Some people sink into passive contemplation; others roll up their sleeves and engage in energetic, even self-destructive acts. Almost as soon as it became famous for its wild beauty in the late eighteenth century, the Cumbrian Lake District attracted masochists as well as dreamers. Thousands of visitors now arrive every year, determined to subject themselves to punishing 'challenges' in a beautiful setting.

For £170 per person, fell walkers can 'push their physical and mental fitness to its limit' in the Lakeland 24 Peaks Challenge – twenty-four mountains in twenty-four hours over two days, featuring almost vertical ascents and the additional attraction of 'morale-crushing descents'. Those who prefer to run uphill can tackle the Bob Graham Round, named after a Keswick hotelier who celebrated his forty-second birthday by trotting over forty-two peaks in twenty-four hours. The dogs who take part in the Cumbrian sport of hound trailing have a comparatively easy time of it: a typical trail covers ten miles and crosses cols rather than summits.

The only human challenge based on cols is the Fred Whitton Challenge (commemorating a popular secretary of the Lakes Road Club). 'The Fred', as pain-loving road cyclists know the 112-mile event, claims to be 'the hardest one-day ride in the UK' and to include 'all the Lakeland passes': Kirkstone, Honister, Newlands, Whinlatter, Hardknott and Wrynose, in that order. In fact, though it misses out five other cols and two passes, the route does unwittingly include another road col. The place is unnamed except on the largest-scale Ordnance Survey map. It is hardly surprising that this obscure col has escaped the organizers' attention, especially since cols are assumed to be the same as climbs, and this col occurs on a descent. The two thousand annual participants who go whizzing down to Coldfell Gate on the western edge of the Lake District National Park, clattering over the cattle grid and surging up the opposite slope, can now add a seventh col to the tally.

Physical challenges of this sort used to be associated with betting. Financial gain is still the main object, but now, the money goes to charity. For some riders, this supplies a morally defensible excuse for eluding weekend chores: a challenge of this severity clearly demands at least three months of hard training… Participants in 'the Fred' are overwhelmingly male – twenty men for every woman – and in the not-yet-quite-over-the-hill age group. In view of the £1 million that have been raised for charity, no one could say that their time is misspent, but sponsored bike rides, like doping in professional cycling, have the unfortunate

effect of suggesting that riding a bicycle must be an unusually arduous and perilous activity. It surely takes a great deal of courage to sign up for the Fred Whitton after reading the official advice:

> The road has a poor surface, so take care and don't block traffic. ... Modern cars often fill the whole width of the road. ... Be careful and considerate to traffic. ... Please don't block people. ... Don't let your speed build up, or you'll be straight off the road and down the hillside, and we don't want to have to call out the ambulance to pick up the pieces.

The organizers have to be cautious. Inexperienced cyclists raising money for charities – including the British Heart Foundation – have been known to die of heart attacks. Some riders in the Fred Whitton have raised money for mountain rescue teams, while others have benefited personally from the service. For this reason, the following, entirely new Lake District challenge is proposed with the understanding that no one should attempt it. If anyone *does* attempt it, the only stipulation is that it should be completed without the help of a motorized vehicle, especially one of those which 'fill the whole width of the road'.

I did not cycle over every road col and pass in the Lake District in a single day. The severity of the challenge depends in any case on the definition of 'day'. Some riders move directly from bed to bike and then breakfast on the road. For such people, the course might be completed between 7 a.m. and 7 p.m. at a reasonable average speed of 12.5 miles per hour. For others, the cycling itself begins only after a leisurely conference with a mug of coffee in one hand and a set of Allen keys in the other. The actual ride will be an interlude between bouts of maintenance, and if the bike proves hard to reassemble, it may not take place at all.

There are precisely 101 cols and three passes in the Lake District National Park. Twelve cols and two passes are on roads. This produces a tally twice the size of the Fred Whitton list, though the complete course is only thirty-eight miles longer. It runs from Windermere railway station to Kendal railway station (or, adding another five miles, back to Windermere station). Fortunately, the hardest cols occur within the first twelve miles. They include the fearsome Hardknott Pass, reputed to be the steepest climb in the British Isles (p. 88).

An article in the British *Medical Magazine* in 1899 explained that the bicycle is so efficient because it makes use of the disproportionately enormous leg and bottom muscles we inherited from our quadrupedal ancestors. A cyclist is, in effect, a re-created ape.* At Hardknott Pass, the trick is to revert for a moment to humanity: apply the brakes, swing the leg over the saddle and, with both feet on the ground, walk the bicycle up the hill, admiring the beautiful view. As far as we know, apes are incapable of this, but an ape has the advantage of common sense and is unlikely to be seen tackling the Hardknott Pass.

## Hadrian's Wall

A peculiar optical illusion greets the traveller who approaches the central section of Hadrian's Wall from the south. A steep road leaves the little station of Haydon Bridge in the valley of the Tyne. After about seven kilometres of rolling moorland, the great barrier of the Whin Sill cliffs rises up, and there, on the skyline, unnaturally tall figures appear like carnival giants projected on to the landscape. Despite the distance, they can be seen quite clearly with their sticks and burdens, striding or stumbling along the ridge. As they descend into the gaps and wind among the crags, singly and in groups, they trace the exact line of the otherwise invisible Roman wall.†

The illusion is caused by the abruptness of the doleritic outcrop called the Whin Sill on which Hadrian's Wall was built. The eye sees towering cliffs which, in fact, rise less than fifty metres above the surrounding terrain. The ridge is notched at several points where the sedimentary rock has been eroded and where it is still being quarried away by floodwater, sheep's hooves and hikers' boots. The smaller notches are known locally as 'nicks', the greatest concentration being the Nine Nicks of Thirwall. This elastic name, originally applied to the uncountable fangs of the Walltown Crags to the west, is sometimes extended to the entire central section of the wall.

The larger gaps in the Whin Sill are significant enough to have names of their own. Even before the Romans, they were used as gateways by merchants, drovers and thieves passing through the wall to north or south, unlike the modern wall-walkers, who

---

* The words 'Go Ape' on the Ordnance Survey map just below Whinlatter Pass – the fifth col on the course – are not advisory but refer to a 'forest adventure' park.
† Something of this effect can be seen in figure 2 (p. 10)

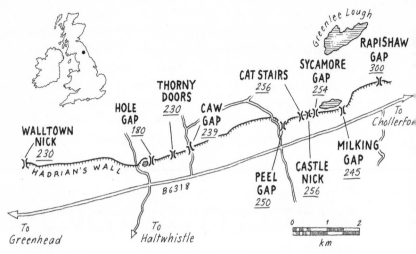

follow it to east or west. The easternmost col, known as Busy Gap, was notorious for centuries as the portal through which cattle rustlers came from the region of Newcastle. Today, spates of burglaries and acts of drunken vandalism are invariably blamed on people from 'the North-East'. In older times, the usual expression was 'the Busy Gap Rogues'.

After several weeks of research and a day of historical discovery, it became apparent that eleven of these gaps can be identified as cols. They occur in the most spectacular section – the eight miles between Sewingshields Crags and Haltwhistle Common – which means that a col-bagging tour of Hadrian's Wall is one of the best possible ways in which to discover this wonder of the ancient world. It sounds simple, but, as an Australian couple who flagged me down near Walltown had discovered, the wall can be quite hard to locate. They had to fly home that evening and were desperate to see at least a section of the Great Wall of England.

'Is this the wall?' they asked, pointing to a rubble-strewn hillside. Since practically everything referred to as the wall is a reconstruction, the correct but slightly disappointing answer was 'Quite possibly, yes.' Their other request for information – 'Why was it built?' – was, I assured them, an excellent question. No one knows the answer: Emperor Hadrian had a fondness for physical frontiers, and the wall was built because he commanded it. Its obvious purpose was to guard the shortest route from sea to sea. But in view of the towering crags along which the wall meanders, the proper answer to the question 'Why was it built?' is 'Because it was already there.'

I reconnoitred the eleven cols of Hadrian's Wall a few days before the Scottish referendum in 2014. It was the kind of weather commonly described in that part of far-northern England as 'not bad at all', which is to say damp, chilly if you stand still, but not actually raining, and with a fair chance of being able to work out more or less where the sun is in the sky. The shabby train which lurches along the valley of the Tyne joins Carlisle to Newcastle, or the Irish Sea to the North Sea. There is plenty of room for bicycles, even when the carriages are full, as they were that day, with dressed-up locals bound for the big city, wall-walkers and railway enthusiasts with thermos-bearing wives in support.

The best route for cyclists is the Military Way which runs along the foot of the Wall. This is the road along which the Romans travelled, unlike the illusory giants who skitter down the almost vertical slopes of the wall itself. The Military Way is part of the B6318, which happens to be the longest B road in England. This makes navigation extremely simple. Beyond the wall to the west, it tacks about over the mosses and moors like a fleeing Pict, retaining the same number, all the way to Liddesdale and the Scottish border. It is often said to be a dangerous road for cyclists, but HGVs or war chariots can be seen at a distance of a mile or more.

The section running parallel to the wall consists of a series of troughs and long climbs. Even ignoring its straightness, it is noticeably exotic. A cyclist's leg muscles experience the ancient road as precisely and evocatively as a gramophone needle in the grooves of a disc. It may be a roller-coaster, but each steep descent offers a discount of at least 50 per cent on the ensuing climb. The largest vehicle I encountered was a fuel tanker with 'Scottish Fuels' painted on its side and an enormous flag of St George covering the back of the driver's cab. Observing a local custom which cyclists from the south might find alarming, the driver waited patiently behind while I reached the top of a climb, then pulled out so far that his tyres sloughed through the opposite verge, and passed with a cheery wave and a winking of his red lights.

From this road, the eleven cols of Hadrian's Wall pass on the skyline in a scrolling panorama. Only one lies on a road – Caw Gap, which was marked that day, as cols so often are in France, by the white bulk of a camper van. But another col, Milking Gap, where black-faced sheep stare down from the crags like sentries, can easily be reached by a cyclable track, and three others are within a few yards of a road. One of these is Peel Gap, with its tumbling staircase of rock: the col is close enough to the road (National Cycle Route 68) for the bicycle to be left on the verge without worrying about a Busy Gap bicycle thief. The other cols are nicely visible in silhouette from the Military Way – notably Castle Nick and its neighbour, Sycamore Gap, sometimes called 'Robin Hood Gap' since it was temporarily immortalized by Kevin Costner in *Robin Hood: Prince of Thieves*.

Only a mountain bike fitted with a jet pack would be capable of traversing these cols in the modern fashion, to west or east, and the task of crossing them all as nature intended, to north or south, would be almost as tedious. But there is no reason why col-bagging should be the only col-related activity with certifiable results. Many cols are best enjoyed at a distance and in a meditative rather than triumphalist frame of mind. An exponent of the as yet unpractised sport of col-spotting could do worse than begin with the eleven nicks and gaps of Hadrian's Wall. This would have the additional advantage of re-creating the view of a Roman traveller trundling along the Military Way, eyeing the great barrier and wondering whether those gigantic figures on the skyline were Roman soldiers or barbarians from the dreaded north-east.

## Galloway

A vast peninsula of whose existence many English people are unaware bulges out into the Irish Sea. It belongs to Scotland, though its southernmost point lies eighty-four miles south of the English border near Berwick-upon-Tweed. On a bicycle, it takes as long to cross it from east to west as it does to go from London to Bristol. By car or by train, the journey is proportionately longer, for there are no motorways, and since the closure of much of the railway network in the 1960s, a train traveller has to head north-west to Glasgow or Ayr, then south-west towards Stranraer, describing the two longest sides of an isosceles triangle.

In the early Middle Ages, almost the entire peninsula was the kingdom of Galloway. Turning its back on Scotland, it looked to the Celtic 'Mediterranean' of the Hebrides, the Isle of Man, the kingdom of Dublin and the parts of north-western England that were settled by Norsemen. Of its language, Galwegian Gaelic, which was extinct by 1800, almost nothing has survived, and what little has survived is partially incomprehensible, containing as it does words that no etymologist has ever been able to decipher.

The obscurity of the ancient tongue that was muddled and enriched by conquest and migration is especially noticeable in col names, since these are older than most other place names. Unlike villages and towns whose names are modernized by use, the cols are like ruined moorland cottages in which lives long since extinguished seem to linger on among quaint and faded furnishings. A map of the Galloway cols would resemble the illustrated chart of an invented world, decorated with names that might have issued from the lips of a wizard or an elf: the Nick of Whirstone, the Nick of Curleywee, Neive of the Spit, Buittle Slot, the Nick of Knock, the Deep Nick of Dromore.

Even the names which seem intelligible evoke a world of peril and gloom. The Nick of the Dungeon, also known as the Wolf's Slock, lies near the reputedly bottomless loch of Murder Hole in a treacherous landscape of granite and bog. The Nick of the Dead Man's Banes might have been the site of prehistoric burials, or it might owe its name to a more recent event. The surveyors who recorded it in 1848 had only this to say: 'A hollow between Craigwhinnie and Benmeal in which human bones have at

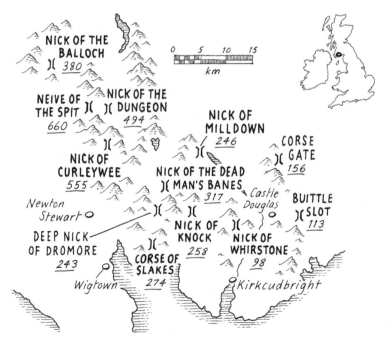

different times been found'. It is appropriate that the attraction on which the Galloway Tourist Board concentrates its resources is darkness: 'Scotland has some of the darkest skies in Europe and Galloway Forest Park is one of the darkest places in Scotland, which is why it's the UK's first Dark Sky Park. So few people live within the Forest Park that the nights really are inky black...'

In that inky black forest, from which the tiny lanterns of the heavens shine as brightly as a shepherd's fire, the largest group of Galloway cols is to be found – twenty-six in all, from the Nick of Milldown in the south-east to the Nick of the Balloch in the north-west. The last of these, marked 'Old Road very Hilly' on a map of 1828, is one of only three road cols in all of Galloway: the spectacular single-track road leads steeply out of the forest into Ayrshire, its former importance as a turnpike road evident only in its inclusion in National Cycle Route 7. Another road col, which has been entirely forgotten, lies beyond the forest to the east: almost immediately after the col, the road comes to an end, as though to confirm the disappearance of Corse Gate from recorded history.

Of the third road col, however, a great deal was written until it, too, became as silent as the abandoned railway which ran from the Solway Firth to the Irish Sea. The name of the col – which was also that of the road – is Corse of Slakes, meaning 'col of the cols' or 'crossing of the slacks', the latter word being a common term for a shallow, watery depression between two hills. The Ordnance Survey map still shows it as the start of the western section of the Old Military Road.

The military roads of Scotland, which are marked on all modern maps, are usually associated with the reconquest of the Highlands after the crushing of the Jacobites, but the Corse of Slakes road was built between 1763 and 1765 to enable troops to reach Ireland by the most direct route 'whenever the exigency of Affairs may require it'. Before then, the only coach known to have made the journey was able to do so only because it was accompanied by a party of labourers 'to lift the vehicle out of the ruts and put on the wheels when it got dismounted'.

When the army surveyors arrived in 1763, the 'Corse o' Slakes' was already an ancient route. The old Ordnance Survey map shows the area littered with Druidical Circles and the detritus of ancient burials and battles. In spite of the British army, the road continued to be used as it had been for centuries. 'In Galloway

there are no roads so wild as the one which leads over the celebrated pass of the above name,' wrote the author of *The Scottish
Gallovidian Encyclopedia* (1824), whose intention was evidently not
to attract visitors to Galloway. 'It is a perfect Alpine pass, and
was a haunt of Billy Marshall and his gang in the days of yore;
even yet it is frequently selected, as a suitable station for the
"bludgeon tribe".' No sooner had the road been completed with
'a top dressing of slaty gravel' than the thieves and smugglers
returned, along with the black cattle that could destroy a road
within a season. Twenty years later, the Corse of Slakes was still
'impassable in winter'.

For cyclists bound for the Irish ferries which sail from
Cairnryan, this is one of the quickest and quietest routes across
the wild expanse. The Corse of Slakes road is a thin strip of
tarmac laid over the endless bog, patched to the point of obliter-
ation like a beggar's cloak and almost swallowed by the landscape. There are no road markings and few signs other than an
occasional corroded 'Cattle Grid'. In such conditions, it is easy to
picture the old land in which roads were barely distinguishable
from the natural terrain.

Along this route, a few of the Galloway Forest cols can be spotted in low hills to the north. Six miles east of the Corse of Slakes
col, a rocky saddle in the worn velvet of the high moors is the
Nick of Knock. A track leads off the road in the general direction
of the col. On a recent expedition, there was no evidence of any
habitation or even the remnants of it apart from a small green
sign on a wooden post indicating that somewhere up there in the
vicinity of the Nick of Knock was to be found a place or a person
called 'Grobdale of Girthon'.

At the watershed itself, on Glenquicken Moor, a pearly sheen
glimmered on the western horizon and the sky was filled with an
army of sea-clouds, so vast that its vanguard must still have been
sailing over Ireland. The road descending from the col seems to
head straight for a large hill which blocks part of the view. This
was formerly the hill called Noggin – now shown on maps as
Knockeans Hill. This name at least can be confidently interpret-
ed as *cnocin*, a diminutive of *cnoc* or 'hill', but the incomprehensi-
bility of Galwegian names is an advantage not to be given up too
quickly. It serves to remind us how little we can know of this vast
peninsula and its vanished kingdom, and how far its quiet roads
might lead us into the unfathomable past.

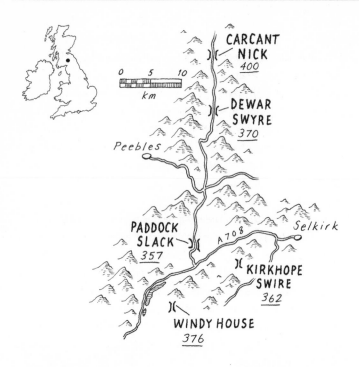

## The Scottish Borders

Some people think that hills are the traveller's worst natural
enemy. This may be true over short distances, but on long
journeys, nothing can match the malevolence of a deafening,
muscle-deadening wind. The hardest day I ever spent on a bike
was on the Beauce plain in northern France heading for Chartres
when the wind was heading in the other direction. One of the
easiest was spent riding through the Scottish Borders towards
Edinburgh with the broad hand of a southerly gale on my back.
Now and then, a south-bound cyclist would pass, as though in a
different dimension, grimacing like a soul in torment under the
curse of the heaven-sent wind.

I wondered at the time whether some of the passes through
which the wind propelled me were cols. The exhilarating sense of
being funnelled into a dark defile, then rocketed out on the other
side, reminded me of certain moorland passes in the southern
Massif Central. But when I looked at the map, there was nothing
but contour lines, field boundaries and 'sheepfolds'. It was only
ten years later, while compiling this catalogue, that I discovered
that they were indeed cols, and that they had names. One of
them, Carcant Nick, was shown on the first Ordnance Survey

map in 1854, and then never again. Another, Dewar Swyre, has not been seen on a map since 1821. The roads of the Scottish Borders were almost eerily deserted, and it was as though the names, too, had been removed from the landscape, along with all the people.

The deletion of what were once familiar features marking parish and county boundaries seemed particularly odd since the road to Edinburgh forms part of National Cycle Route 1. This M1 of the cycling world, which runs all the way from Dover to Shetland (with the aid of two ferries), might just as well have been the abandoned highway of a vanished race. The Border cols are well known to local cycling clubs and are included on the routes of their weekend rides and races, yet most of them are unrecognized as cols, and nearly all have lost their original identity.

Paddock Slack, on the old route to Edinburgh, is now humor-ously known as 'the Paddy's Slacks', as though in commemora-tion of an Irishman's trousers. (A slack is a gully or a watery col, while a paddock was a small farm or, as a variant of 'puddock', a frog.) Two other cols in the area have been christened Top Swire and Bottom Swire, their original names being quite forgotten. The first was either Hart Leap or Windy Hause. The second was known – but not to map-makers – as Kirkhope or Kershope Swire. (It featured in a ballad of 1909: 'The sun was setting on Kirkhope Swire, / The sky in the West was a field of fire.') A third, which is not a col at all, has been named Middle Swire, and the local council appears to have adopted the factitious name.

It is tempting to see this rechristening as the latest phase in a long, continuous tradition, but the casual misidentification of geographical features is something quite different. An erasure rather than an evolution, it brings the process of transmission to an end. The highly mobile tribes of the twenty-first century occupy a land whose original inhabitants departed long ago, and the old place names they left behind are food for jocularity and speculation. 'Square Nick', it is now supposed, must refer to a carpenter's square, whereas 'square' was merely a synonym of 'sware' or 'swyre'. This curious incuriosity about the past begs the question: are we really interested in our heritage, or only in our own reinvention of it?

Dewar Swyre, over which I sailed in wind-blown obliviousness ten years ago, stands on the former boundary of Edinburghshire and Peebles-shire. Though the col was named on a reputable map of 1821, the Ordnance Survey in 1853 retained only a quaint caption, which is still on the map today: 'Piper of Peebles Grave'. The piper's gravestone stood at the col on the old county boundary. For some reason, it now stands where the modern map places it, 150 metres to the south. The stone itself is modern and sits in the verge next to a heavily littered lay-by.

The Piper of Peebles is typical of the microhistorical characters one encounters at cols: real people rooted to a particular spot but half dissolved in legend. The piper was evidently a versatile fellow, or perhaps several fellows, since he crops up in various tales in various guises. He performed in a red costume with an antique cocked hat and, as an exponent of the world's least ignorable instrument, charged 'a shilling for beginning to play, and two to leave off'. According to one of the best-known tales, he accepted a bet that he could blow his infernal bagpipes all the way from Peebles to Lauder. By the time he reached Dewar Swyre, he was out of puff, collapsed and died, and was buried at the col.

There are cyclists – even some professional cyclists – who blame any poor performance on mechanical rather than physiological failure. The Piper of Peebles actually did have an excuse, though he never knew it. One of the punters who bet against him pricked his bag with a needle, thus effectively reducing his lung power and precipitating his demise. It is an odd tale in some respects but slightly more luminous when set alongside another story from the same period (the 1790s). An impoverished laird had made a pact with the Devil. When the Devil returned years later to claim his due, the laird shot him dead. The body turned out to be that of the Piper of Peebles, who had died a fortnight before the shooting…

This sounds like a genuine folk legend, centred on the comically antiquated figure of the piper. The Devil of popular myth was often undone by his own inept stratagems and foolish pride. But the question then arises: who lies buried at the col of Dewar Swyre? Since the original stone has gone, exhumation and autopsy are probably out of the question. However, there is an intriguing clue on the first Ordnance Survey map of Peebles-shire.

A short distance from the cross which marks the piper's grave another small cross is labelled 'Friar's Grave'. It first appeared on a map of 1773, identified as 'Fryars Grave'. In 1856, the man from the Ordnance Survey was told by local people of a friar who, in days gone by, having 'incurred the displeasure of the church', was buried at the swire in unconsecrated ground. The next time the Ordnance Survey visited the spot was in the winter of 1962. On that occasion, the surveyor noted in his name book: 'No feature marks the site of this grave. Enquiries at the nearby farm of Dewar produced no further information.'

The mysterious lost graves at Dewar Swyre may have been the last surviving evidence of a ritual (and not always entirely ritual) interment of the Devil. At many cols, the corpses of malefactors swung from gibbets before being consigned to the bog. Criminals and witches who were considered to be beyond the pale of society were deposited there like the rubbish which often marks these sites today. For the friar and the piper, as well as for the living traveller, the swire was a gateway to another world.

The wind that dried their corpses usually blows from the south-west, and then, for a traveller bound for Edinburgh, the col routes of the Scottish Borders are among the pleasantest anywhere in wild Britain. But these were once grim and lonely places of suffering and retribution, and it is not surprising that we pick and choose from the past and reinvent our heritage. One should linger at a col just long enough to enjoy the view and the sense of achievement. A traveller who arrives at the summit out of breath will soon grow cold, and the descent may be colder still.

If the col itself was the goal of the journey, and if, as often happens, a tailwind has been mistaken for fitness, the return journey will be nearly twice as long. As the British *Cycling Manual* of 1917 warned: 'Do not be tempted to ride too far afield when helped by a following wind. It will be slower and harder work coming back.' The solution, of course, is to accept the gift of the wind and to keep going in the same direction, towards the comfort and warmth of the city, where the Devil is treated less unkindly.

## Edinburgh

Was it the act of a specifically Scottish providence that endowed the capital of Scotland with one of the loveliest cols in the British Isles? The other capital cities have nothing to compare with the Hawse. Cardiff and Dublin are ten miles from their nearest col and London's only col is in a suburb near the end of a bus-line. Four nameless cols look down towards Belfast from the Belfast

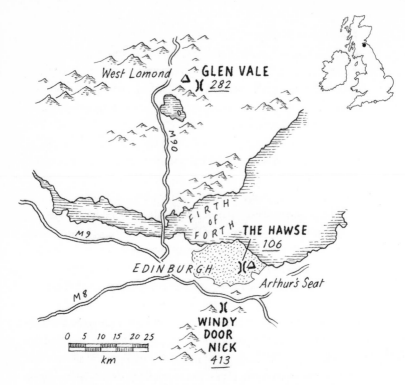

Hills, but only Edinburgh has a col at its very heart. It stands in the miniature mountain landscape of Holyrood Park, at the foot of the volcanic plug of Arthur's Seat where the Salisbury Crags disappear underground. The final ascent begins at Powderhouse Corner on Queen's Drive, which means that the 'drop', in mountaineering parlance, is less than thirty feet, making this, technically, one of the lowest cols in Scotland.

The dual view from the Hawse is the sort of vision that appears in momentous dreams and allegorical illustrations: on one side, the city, on the other, the sea. The spires of Edinburgh are a magnificent sight, but the revelation of the blue beyond is a thrilling surprise. For many visitors, a herring gull in Princes Street Gardens or a slim view of the Firth of Forth from Dundas Street are the only reminders that Edinburgh is a maritime city. From the fulcrum of the Hawse, the Pentland Hills are a silhouette on the southern horizon. The cradle at their centre is the col called Windy Door Nick, from which a sequence of mutually visible cols stretches to the borders of England. To the north, across the estuary, is the prominent peak of West Lomond, at the foot of which is the col of Glen Vale, or Gleann a' Bhealaich.

Aesthetically, if not geologically, the Hawse of Holyrood Park is a point of juncture between the austere but companionable cols of the Borders and the craggy eccentricities of the Highlands.

The place is well known, but not for what it is: an undercover col in full view, trampled by thousands of feet every day, a few yards from National Cycle Route 1 and only ten minutes' walk from the Scottish Parliament. It is missing from all but the largest-scale Ordnance Survey maps. The spelling of the name, unusual in Scotland, is an efficient disguise: it suggests the nautical term (the hole through which the anchor cable runs) rather than a 'hass' or a 'hause', especially since the gully next to it is called the Gutted Haddie (the filleted haddock). This slithering scree chute was created by a landslide in 1744 which exposed the volcanic rock and set the father of modern geology, James Hutton, thinking about erosion and igneous intrusions.

It is curious that the natural viewing platform of the Hawse, so close to half a million people and the seat of kings and First Ministers, has played almost no role in fiction.* Robert Louis Stevenson might have brought a hunted man to heel at that very spot, where several paths meet and the only means of escape lies far above on the crags of Arthur's Seat. John Buchan, who set many of his adventure tales in the Scottish Lowlands, might have had a German pleasure yacht anchored in the Firth of Forth and a boat rowed ashore to Portobello while an Eton-educated spy impeccably dressed in rags shambled convincingly up from the slums of the Grassmarket to receive a coded message on which the future of the civilized world depended.

Any col, especially one which lies at the heart of a metropolis, is likely to set the cerebellum racing. When I first knowingly crossed the Hawse on foot in 2014, there was a steady stream of joggers and festival-goers, students from the nearby Pollock Halls of Residence and groups of Edimbourgeois out for a walk. Just as David Livingstone seems not to have suffered disappointment when he found the distant object of his quest, the Victoria Falls, swarming with people, a crowd does not diminish the excitement, because even the most famous and populous of cols conveys the sense of uncovering a secret.

........................................................................................................................

* The only exception is a reference in James Hogg's *Confessions of a Justified Sinner* (1824) to 'the swire at the head of the dell, – that little delightful verge from which in one moment the eastern limits and shores of Lothian arise on the view'.

After photographing the angles and panoramas of the Hawse and its naturally cobbled pavement, I left to visit two other sites nearby whose names suggested that they, too, were cols. They turned out to be red herrings. Cat Nick is just a gap in the teeth of the Salisbury Crags, and Windy Gowl, though it shares a name with a col in the Pentland Hills, is a brief ravine which cuts through the south-eastern slope of Arthur's Seat.

It may not be a col, but Windy Gowl is exactly the sort of place that John Buchan chose for his chase scenes. The road descending into the gully has a blind corner. On the right, there is a sudden drop to Duddingston Loch, where a stolen Daimler might have plunged invisibly to its doom while its driver scrambled up over the haunch of Arthur's Seat to reach his rendezvous at the Hawse, predestined by 350 million years of igneous intrusions and erosion to play its role in the drama of nations. There, between the city and the North Sea, a stone's throw from the Scottish Parliament, the future of the United Kingdom hangs in the balance.

## The Highland Boundary Fault

On north-bound trains from Birmingham and Manchester, after the crossing of the border, foreign tourists can often be seen staring out of the window, looking for Scottish scenery as depicted in their guide books. But apart from the modest Pentland Hills to the east, there are few signs of 'rugged beauty' until the train pulls into Waverley Station under the giant crag of Arthur's Seat. The region through which the train has passed is one of the largest 'col deserts' in northern Britain – two thousand square miles without a single col. Four hundred million years ago, a rift valley formed between two faults which ran the entire width of the island. The valley was gradually raised up and became the area known as the Central Lowlands. Two-thirds of Scotland's 5 million inhabitants live there, apparently indifferent to its unphotogenic flatness.

If the tourists pursue their journey to Aberdeen and the north-east, they will see still more flat farmland and eventually find themselves in one of the least rainy parts of the British Isles, barely one hundred miles from the northern tip of Great Britain. If, on the other hand, they head west from Edinburgh instead of north, snowy peaks with Gaelic names will soon reveal the whereabouts of the advertised wildness.

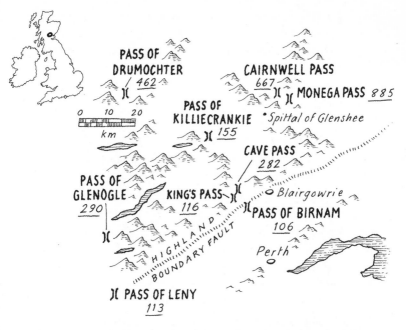

The geography of Scotland can come as a baffling surprise even to well-informed visitors. The elongated rectangle of Great Britain suggests a topography organized like a tall office building in which everything goes either from side to side, like the Cotswolds and the Chilterns, or up and down, like the Pennines. It seems reasonable, therefore, to suppose that the Scottish Lowlands will be lower down and the Highlands higher up. In reality, one half of Scotland – and one of its languages – is divided from the other by a great diagonal. This is the Highland Boundary Fault, whose north-eastern terminus is near Stonehaven on the North Sea.

For the last two hundred years, tourism beyond the Lowland cities has been concentrated on the picturesque and relatively comfortable zone at the foot of the Highland Boundary Fault. Coach tours with a 'castles and distilleries' theme take parties from Glasgow and Edinburgh into the romantic, rocky glens and return in time for tea. In the Trossachs and in the region around Pitlochry, the Highlands come down to offer visitors a taste of their salmon rivers, peat bogs and purple-headed mountains.

The high cols, which are frequented mainly by deer, grouse and their human predators, lie further to the north, but some of the tarmacked gorges and defiles of the Boundary Fault are almost perfect miniatures of their Highland cousins. Many have lost their

Gaelic names, or were nameless until the age of tourism began. The foreign word 'pass' was imported to inspire adventurous visitors with visions of grandeur and to evoke the novels of Walter Scott and the mock-Celtic poetry of Ossian. In the Trossachs alone, there are five 'passes', none of which is a col. Further east, along National Cycle Route 77, which meets Route 7 just south of Pitlochry, there is a beautiful sequence of passes from Birnam and Dunkeld to the Pass of Killiecrankie and the Pass of Drumochter.

Between these two regions, on Route 7, lie the Pass of Leny and the Pass of Glenogle (previously known as Lairig Eala, or Pass of the Wild Swan). In 1842, an intrepid twenty-three-year-old tourist, who had been Queen of Great Britain and Ireland for less than five years, was appropriately delighted by the latter: 'The country we came to now was very wild ... *Glen Ogle* putting one in mind of the prints of the *Khyber Pass*.' Two years later, she returned to the gateways of the Highlands, hungry for more adventures:

> We passed Pitlochrie, a small village ... and then came to the Pass of Killicrankie, which is quite magnificent; the road winds along it, and you look down from a great height, all wooded on both sides; the Garry rolling below it. I cannot describe how beautiful it is. Albert was in perfect ecstasies.

The queen was to return several times, and on each occasion she ventured deeper into the Highlands. While Albert scurried off at the sight of the merest feathered or antlered creature, scrambling over hillsides on his hands and knees, clad from head to foot in camouflage grey, Victoria pushed ever onward into truly dangerous territory.

For all its signposted woodland walks and friendly tourist traps, this frontier zone is a deceptively alluring adventure playground. Every winter, at least one visitor will drive into a sunny glen, park in a passing place, and, while storm clouds are massing on the other side of the ridge, go jogging up a heather-scented glen wearing only shorts and a T-shirt, to return much later in a mountain rescue helicopter.

In 1849, Queen Victoria drove from Perth to Blairgowrie and from there, under a darkening sky, 'into completely wild Highland scenery, with barren rocky hills'. From Spittal of Glenshee – 'which can scarcely be called a village' – the royal party set off up 'a very bad, and at night, positively dangerous road ... with very abrupt

turns and steep ascents. One sharp turn is called *The Devil's Elbow*.'
They crossed the Cairnwell in a downpour – 'a very fine pass', she
called it in her journal, as appreciative of the mountains' black
savagery as of her nimble native guides, and never expecting the
Highland weather to change its habits on her account.

The Cairnwell is still an impressively Alpine col, complete
with a concrete ski station at its summit and a snow-ploughed
road which is often passable even in the harshest winter months.
Twelve years later, Victoria was back to tackle the mighty Month
Eigie (the Monega Pass). She rode a pony for part of the way
and walked for much of the slippery descent, falling only twice
and having a wonderful time. 'The moon rose and shone most
beautifully, and we returned [to Balmoral] at twenty minutes to
seven o'clock, much pleased and interested with this delightful
expedition. Alas! I fear our last great one!'

To any col-bagging walker or cyclist, this will seem entirely
appropriate behaviour for a British monarch. The Cairnwell is the
highest road col anywhere in the British Isles and the Monega
the highest pass. Victoria claimed to possess a 'very ungeographical' head, yet she clearly had a more accurate perception
of Scottish geography than most of her English subjects, and she
knew how deeply the physical experience of a country can etch
its characteristics in the mind. An empress who had fallen on the
Monega Pass while the sun was sinking behind the Cairngorms
was a perfect emblem of the late-Romantic Age, and when
her great-great-granddaughter crossed the Cairnwell in 1967,
smoothly negotiating the Devil's Elbow in a Daimler driven by her
husband, the Duke of Edinburgh, she, too, was an emblem of the
age in which she reigned, when tarmacked roads and concrete
made the cols and passes beyond the Highland Boundary Fault
more deceptively welcoming than ever.

## The West Highlands

A seventy-mile-long gash of lochs resembling broken sword
blades placed end to end cuts Scotland into two. The lochs – from
Loch Linnhe in the south-west to Loch Ness in the north-east –
are connected by the Caledonian Canal, which now provides a
useful walking, cycling and canoeing route along the Great Glen
between Fort William and Inverness. Reconnoitring the northern
section of a possible col-route from one end of Britain to the

other, I crossed this frontier at Gairlochy. There was nothing at the well-tended canal lock to show that another world begins on the other side, but a few miles further on, at the eastern end of the Mìle Dorcha, or Black Mile pass, where the road turns into a forest track, this sign appeared:

TAKE CARE

*You are entering remote, sparsely-populated,*
*potentially dangerous mountain country.*

*Please ensure that you are adequately experienced and*
*equipped to complete your journey without assistance.*

A hundred years ago, crossing to the north side of the Caledonian Canal called not only for experience and equipment but also for a passport. In the First World War, all of Scotland north of the Great Glen was a restricted zone. The lochs were patrolled by the British Navy, and the police had instructions to watch for strangers on the roads to Skye and the naval base at Kyle of Lochalsh. The military installations of two world wars – landing bays, pillboxes and bunkers – can be seen all over the West Highlands, though the only enemy attacks in Highland Scotland

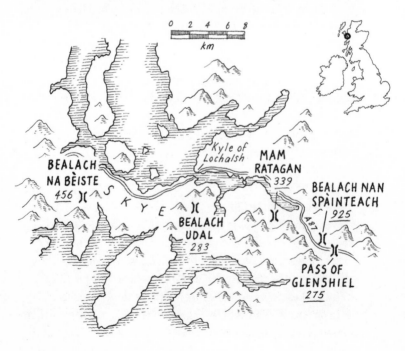

were the U-boat shelling of the radio station on St Kilda in 1918, and damage to the starboard bow of a naval motor launch on Loch Ness in 1943 by something which Lieutenant-Commander Flint described in his report to the Admiralty as 'a very large animal form' which 'disappeared in a flurry of water'.

By the peculiar logic of West Highland geography – deep lacerations of the sea pushing far inland and great tracts of bog and mountain intervening – the route to the north first runs west to Skye through the Pass of Glen Shiel, where the Bealach nan Spàinteach preserves the memory of an older war. It was by this slippery and precipitous col, the fifteenth-highest in Scotland, that the Spanish soldiers who fought in the Jacobite uprising of 1719 tried to flee from government troops.

Beyond Glen Shiel, the road staggers over the savage Mam Ratagan. In 1773, on a tour of the Highlands with his biographer, James Boswell, Dr Samuel Johnson, whose corpulence was an image of his enormous literary reputation, lumbered up the col, two horses taking turns to carry him – 'a terrible steep* to climb, notwithstanding the road is formed slanting along it'. On the other side of the col, the ruined hulk of Bernera Barracks, which guarded the route to the Skye ferry, is a bleak reminder of the repression of the Jacobites.

The manually operated Skye ferry (the only ferry still running) deposits its passengers at the foot of another forbidding but picturesque col, the Bealach Udal, whose name means Gloomy Pass or Pass of Distress. From here on, the land itself is a memorial to the unending war of the West Highlands, compared to which the political agitations of the Jacobites are mere episodes. This was always an occupied country in which even the natives were never at home. In the half-light of the long summer nights, the ancient enemy lurked in the black hills and the deep sea lochs. In 1923, a collector of place names on Skye learned that the Pass of Distress was 'haunted by a monster which appears in various shapes', though it had not been seen 'since the dead body of a man was found in the neighbourhood'. Below the pass, towards Lochalsh, derelict anti-aircraft batteries look down on the Loch na Bèiste (Loch of the Monster). To the west, the Bealach na Bèiste was on the regular route of a 'water horse'

---

* 'Steep' was used as a noun: 'Precipice; ascent or descent approaching to perpendicularity' (Johnson's *Dictionary of the English Language*, 1755).

which devoured the island's prettiest maidens, until it was killed by MacKinnon of Strath.

The further one travels into the West Highlands, the more *bèistes* there are, and the easier it is to recapture the constant fear of the Highlander. On the Applecross peninsula, the old drove road called Bealach na Bà (Cow Pass) is often appropriately described as 'a monster'. With black shrouds blowing in on a gale from the Atlantic, this single-track ascent into Hell is probably the most frightening road col in Britain. On the upper slopes, where the verges have collapsed, a violent gust that might have been mistaken for an invisible fist propelled me off the road and sent the pannier which contained the camera cartwheeling down into a torrential tributary of the Allt a' Chumhaing. A car descending through the mist with two bicycles on its roof drove past without stopping to identify the murky creature that was rising from the bog.

To the north, permanent traces of human life are increasingly sparse. The fissured granite rocks of the Archaean age predate organic life on earth, and it is almost a comfort to discover in that unhuman landscape the familiar evidence of conventional war. The road to the north follows the coast, where the pillboxes are like miniature concrete castles with tiny windows through which shivering soldiers scanned the sea for periscopes. The road turns to the east just south of another Loch na Bèiste – the home of a 'sea cow' which was said to resemble a large upturned boat. It was last spotted in the 1840s, shortly before the loch was partially drained by the estate-owner at his tenants' urgent request and chemically contaminated with fourteen barrels of lime.

This almost treeless route includes an unexpectedly lovely col: the Cadha Beag, or Little Pass, rises above Gruinard Bay, offering close-up views of a beautiful green island lying less than a mile offshore. A human being would be clearly visible with the naked eye, but the island is deserted. An anthrax experiment was conducted there in 1942: a flock of sheep died for the defence of the realm, and Gruinard Island became an image of what Germany might have been for most of the later twentieth century. The island was eventually decontaminated and declared safe in 1990. Serious doubts have been expressed, however, and, for present purposes, it is just as well that there are no cols on this eeriest of Highland war memorials.

## The Mourne Wall

The British Isles are full of mysterious monuments: Stonehenge, Silbury Hill, the Dorset Cursus and hundreds of other impenetrable temples, mounds and alignments. There are no records to tell us why they were built, which is not surprising since most of them are more than three thousand years old. Not the least enigmatic is a drystone wall of gigantic granite slabs which stretches for twenty-two miles over the Mourne Mountains of Northern Ireland. It was completed ninety-three years ago, yet its purpose is still a matter of conjecture. Despite the efforts of the Northern Ireland Tourist Board, and despite the thousands of people who walk along it every year, the second-longest continuous wall in the world (after the Great Wall of China) is absent from almost every list of 'the world's longest walls'.

The Mourne Wall was built by hand between 1904 and 1922. Work ended each year in November and started again in April, when the snow had melted. It follows the catchment boundary of the reservoirs which serve Belfast, tracing the watershed line exactly and crossing ten cols, making it virtually impossible to get lost. The reason is far from clear. It is almost as though the Works Department mistook a line on the Belfast Water Commissioners' map for an instruction.

According to one theory, the Water Commissioners wanted to exclude sheep and cattle from the catchment area; instead of erecting a livestock fence, which might have been completed in a matter of weeks, they decided to spend eighteen years building a wall which a single-minded sheep could easily jump in several places. The other most popular theory was nicely expressed by a local walker in 2007, when an Australian journalist asked him the obvious question:

> 'Foine wall dis', Dermott said, patting it. 'Built by de Belfast Water Commissioners, to mark de catchment area. Course, laybroors did the real work.'
>
> 'Why the rocks?' I asked, 'Couldn't they have used a line of coloured pegs?'
>
> 'Onemplayment schayme in the 1920s', Dermott said. 'Med the job last longer.'*

---

* Richard Tulloch, 'Pack Up Your Troubles', *Sydney Morning Herald*, 29 July 2007.

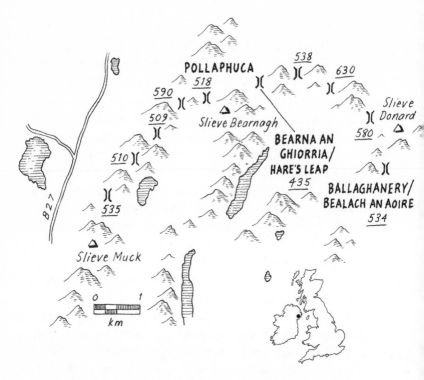

The unemployment scheme (which operated mostly in the 1900s and 1910s) now keeps thousands of walkers happily employed in walking along it, using it as a windbreak and a guide rail across the peaks and troughs of the Mountains of Mourne. This might justify proponents of the third main theory, according to which this most magnificent and labour intensive of col routes was built as a tourist attraction.

The other, unmentioned mystery of the Mourne Wall is harder to explain. In contrast to Hadrian's Wall, where even the tiniest 'nick' has a name, all but two of the Mourne Wall cols are nameless. The two which survive are Ballaghanery or Bealach an Aoire (Shepherd's Pass) and Bearna an Ghiorria, now known as Hares' Gap. Both cols lie on the old smugglers' path called the Brandy Pad. There is no doubt that the other cols were used, yet all their names have vanished. The Mourne Wall might as well be a prehistoric monument. Its many cols now have to be referred to cumbersomely, as though by outsiders, with circumlocutions such as 'the col between Carn Mountain and Slieve Muck'.

Since Ireland was mapped before the rest of the British Isles, the old names might be expected to have survived. But the original name of the Mourne Mountains – Beanna Boirche – was already passing out of use in the seventeenth century, and the men of the Ordnance Survey who mapped this region evidently thought that only the names of the summits were worth recording, thereby accelerating the disappearance of Gaelic from the landscape.

Just as Stonehenge and other prehistoric sites were subsequently occupied by tribes who probably had no notion of their original purpose, the Mourne Wall is being rebranded by the thousands who process along it every year. The name Pollaphuca, 'the hole of the *púca*' (a creature of folklore occasionally depicted with the ears of a rabbit), has been transferred from a gully to the otherwise anonymous col between Slieve Bearnagh and Slieve Meelmore. When the Mourne Wall Challenge (walking the entire wall in a day) was stopped in the 1980s to prevent erosion and accidents, the wall-walkers, like early humans, began to follow sheep tracks instead, creating what planners call 'desire lines' on either side of the wall. Even then, according to a report sponsored by the Environment Agency, the cols remained as 'key control points'.

This is one of several ways in which cols offer a glimpse of ancient forms of collective behaviour, and perhaps the Mourne Wall actually does have something to tell us about monuments such as Silbury Hill. Some archaeologists believe that these enormous, seemingly irrational projects were intended to reinforce the community and to serve as monuments to the cooperative spirit that built them: '"Foine wall dis", Dermott said, patting it … "Course, laybroors did the real work"'…

During the Troubles, the strong flow of wall-walkers dried to a trickle, and the Mourne Wall became a symbol of the diminishment of social life in Ulster. The blogs of walkers on the Mourne Wall today typically express as much delight in chance encounters and the conviviality of shared experience as in the landscape itself – or, as the official report put it, in a desk-bound idiom which will be as baffling to future generations as the monument itself, the Mourne Wall is 'an important deliverer for government agendas relating to economic development and health and wellbeing'.

## The Wicklow Mountains

The Wicklow Mountains, a forty-minute bus ride south of
Dublin, are practically a theme park of cols. There are twen-
ty-nine in all, including the highest road col in Ireland. Some
are on quiet roads, others on walking trails. Few major cities
have such wildness on their doorstep. At the deserted moorland
crossroads of Sally Gap, a sign indicating that Dublin is less than
twenty-four miles to the north looks like a practical joke. There
are so many 'secret' valleys in the Wicklows that even the most
jaded walker will have a sense of personal discovery. This is not
necessarily an illusion: despite their proximity to the capital,
many of these cols are nowhere to be found on the Ordnance
Survey 'Discovery' maps (5th edition, 2010).

In 1846, when the Ordnance Survey declared its work finished, Ireland was the most comprehensively mapped country
in Europe. This might surprise anyone who has peered at the
original six-inch sheets. A pallid quilt of dotted lines thickened
with pink, the map is curiously devoid of detail, especially in the
hills. The pink lines are the boundaries of the townlands (the
smallest administrative unit), the main purpose of the survey
being to regularize local taxation, which was based on land
valuations. This was a map to gladden a functionary's soul and
to leave a traveller in the dark.

The men of the Ordnance Survey who tried to fill the gaps
with place names have often been vilified, sometimes quite cyn-
ically, as haughty imperialists who conspired to eradicate Irish
culture. Most of them (unlike half the population of Ireland
in 1841) were Gaelic speakers, determined to rescue what little
remained of the ancient toponymy of Ireland. Once the initial
triangulation had been completed in 1832, they were sent out
to interview as many natives as possible – literate and illiterate,
peasant and noble – and to compare the physical reality with the
documentary evidence.

The most energetic and scholarly of the Ordnance Survey's
Topographical Branch was John O'Donovan, born in County
Kilkenny in 1806. Incensed at the 'mangling' of old Irish names
by generations of English settlers, O'Donovan wanted the map
to make room for 'all the rhymes and rags of history'. To the
discomfiture of his superior officer, he was unhampered by
the delicacy of the age: 'In the present artificial state of society

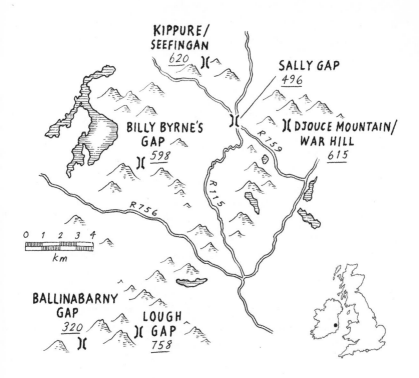

it is curious to observe that one word is filthy, while another that expresses the same identical idea is honourable, as arse, backside, bottom, etc.' This was an important virtue in a man who wanted to record the traditional landscape in which every mound, pinnacle and cleft had been seen as a part of the great body of Nature and named accordingly.

To cover the entire county of Wicklow, O'Donovan and his two colleagues were given only two months in the winter of 1838–9, which happened to be the winter when Ireland was hit by the most violent hurricane on record. To make matters worse, at least one of the surveyors was not, as he might have put it, upwardly mobile:

> We ascended the Sugar Loaf Mountain this day and though anxious I may be for elevation in this world I hope never again will have occasion to rise so high in it. (Eugene Curry, 17 December 1838)

With so little time at their disposal, they were unable to scale all the Wicklow peaks and were forced to rely on hearsay. 'The top of Kippure Mountain over which the boundary line of Dublin and Wicklow runs' being enveloped in 'heavy mist', the attempt was immediately abandoned:

> To the sportsman, the geologist, or the artist, this might afford
> a pleasing enough excursion but the Antiquary finds nothing
> there but rocks, cliffs, water and bogs, as old, and apparently as
> untouched by the fashioning hand of man, as the foundations of the
> earth. (Eugene Curry, 13 December 1838)

As a result, we shall probably never know the name of the col below Djouce Mountain which looks down to Bray and its harbour, nor the name of the broad saddle between Kippure and Seefingan which offers a panoramic view of Dublin.

Despite the efforts of O'Donovan and his colleagues, most of the blank spaces on the map were never filled. A few years later, the Great Famine began, after which thousands of old names survived only in the memories of emigrants. But without the Topographical Branch and its battle against time, weather, 'soft and spewy bog' and 'infernally' rude inn-keepers, many more would have vanished.

It is frightening to think how much of a country's heritage depended on the work of a handful of men, and astonishing to discover that the most detailed maps of the Wicklow Mountains available today are the work of a small private company based in County Wexford between the Wicklow and the Blackstairs Mountains. Several of the cols in the Wicklow section of this catalogue are named only on the maps produced by EastWest Mapping. They include Lough Gap, which is identified for the first time in this book as the highest col in Ireland outside the far south-west.

Like O'Donovan and his colleagues, the EastWest Mapping team used the work of earlier place-name collectors and interviewed people who had grown up in the area. Both teams were aware that local informants could be seriously ill-informed. A word which some applied to a hollow or a valley might be applied by their neighbours to a mountain top. Billy Byrne's Gap in the western Wicklows, for example, is usually associated with a leader of the Irish Rebellion of 1798, but locals who were interviewed in the 1930s swore that it referred to a different, more recent Billy Byrne. In fact, like Ballinabarny Gap in the southern Wicklows, the name probably has a much earlier origin in 'Baile na Bearna', or 'the place of the pass'.

High above the Wicklow Mountains, flying at an altitude of ten thousand feet, a modern surveyor occasionally updates the Ordnance Survey map as though scanning enemy territory or an inhospitable planet. This is why walkers will sometimes encounter features on the ground, for example in dense woodland, which are missing from the Ordnance Survey map. The terrestrial 'Survey Team' of EastWest Mapping is depicted in two small photographs on the map of Wicklow East (2011) – Barry Dalby with a dog and Clive Dalby with a bike. We have to hope that this active remembrance of the weather-beaten expeditions of O'Donovan and his colleagues is also the future of Irish mapping.

## South-west Ireland

In a world congested with clamorous novelties, the past can appear too plain and bare to be of much interest. The names that were given to the gaps between hills tend to suggest an age of uncluttered innocence whose basic, material truths could be adequately expressed by the vocabulary of a child: 'little', 'big', 'red', 'black', 'narrow', 'steep', 'cold', 'windy', etc. 'Windy' in particular seems a naive statement of the obvious. All cols have a funnelling effect and there are many that are windier than the 'windy' cols.

Wondering whether something lay behind this artless word, I examined all seventy cols of the British Isles which have 'wind' in their name (or its Welsh and Gaelic equivalents) and found nothing of note until I came to Ireland. There are nineteen 'windy' cols in Ireland, from Donegal to the Mountains of Mourne and from the Wicklow Mountains to the far south-west. All without exception turn out to have something quite particular in common. Whereas the cols of Ireland, as one would expect, are oriented in all directions, every single 'windy' col faces the north-west wind.

This consistency is hard to explain. The prevailing wind in Ireland blows from the south-west, but when Gerald of Wales was compiling his *Topographia Hibernica* in the late twelfth century, he was told that 'a wind blowing transversely from the north-west, and more frequent and violent than any other

winds, prevails here, the blast either bending or uprooting all
the trees standing on high ground'. Perhaps the name was just a
useful warning not to cross these cols when a storm was brewing.
Or perhaps, like so many other natural phenomena for which
we have our own, scientific explanations, the nor-wester had a
special significance in Irish mythology.

If we knew more about the earlier inhabitants of Ireland, other
names, too, might surprise us with their precise connotations.
The word 'dearg' is attached to several Irish cols. It is always
translated as 'red', but in this case, our simplified visual perception of the natural world has erased its multiple implications.
'Dearg' can refer to the bedrock exposed by feet or hooves, to
the ploughed earth of fallow land, to the red hue of vegetation
seen from a distance, to the blood of a battle or to the blood of a
serpent slain by Saint Patrick.

Eight of the nineteen 'windy' cols of Ireland are in the far
south-west. This tattered fringe of westernmost Europe, with its
five peninsulas reaching out into the Atlantic, has always been
separate culturally as well as geographically. In no other part of
the British Isles are so many cols marked by religious monuments.

At the summit of the Coomakesta Pass, a cement-grey Virgin Mary guards the parking area. At the Healy Pass between Cork and Kerry, a crucified Christ looks down on the cyclists who struggle up the hairpin bends. At Keam-a-gower (The Goat's Path), ignoring the sublime views of the rolling waves, a marble Mary stares at the body of her dead son. The faithful or the superstitious place coins in her open palm. These monuments are all quite recent, but there are others which predate Christianity itself. At Mám na hAltóra on the Dingle Peninsula, where pilgrims used to perform penitential rituals, the 'altar' is a flagstone which covers a prehistoric burial.

Cols with religious names are found all over Catholic Europe but they seem remarkably rare in Ireland. Apart from the Pass of the Altar, only two col names in the south-west are obviously religious: Priest's Leap Pass and Coomanaspig (the Bishops' Hollow). But many others may once have had a sacred connotation. On the waymarked 'Pilgrims' Route', the 'liag' or 'stone' of Com an Liaigh is a prehistoric menhir. Three miles to the east, one of the 'gilded' stones which gave its name to Mám an Óraigh bears an early Christian ogham inscription commemorating 'Colman the Pilgrim'. Perhaps all the 'stony' cols of Ireland once had metaphysical depths of which we see only the rough surface.

The medieval mind perceived the earth as a world between two other worlds. Every living or inanimate thing corresponded to something in heaven or hell. Our mental geography now tends to be horizontal rather than vertical, and what we take to be the transparency of the past may be only the mirror of our ignorance. To us, these childish names are like crude chess pieces whose blank expressions tell us nothing of the complicated rules that governed their movements.

Why were Irish cols never explicitly named after Mary or the saints? Why are so many geographical features in all parts of the British Isles named after the Devil? It may be that this reflects a popular belief that the 'black' hills are Satan's domain, that the physical world itself is inherently evil and that the tortured earth with its scars and tumours is in a state of sin. According to the Bible, the earth will be transformed by the coming of God – 'Every valley shall be exalted, and every mountain and hill shall be made low: and the crooked shall be made straight, and the rough places plain' (Isaiah 40:4) – which means that there will be no cols in heaven.

It would be nice to believe that, even when speed has flattened every landscape, the road to a col still represents the path of wisdom, and that all these ways are Pilgrim Ways, rising above the miasma of humanity but shunning the egotistical peaks. Wisdom, however, proverbially comes only at the end of the endless journey, and there are many other, more practical matters to consider when climbing to a col and especially when descending on the other side – the heavenly reward of food and drink, the restorative sleep and the long day yet to come.

# Superlatives

## The highest

Identifying the highest col in each country of the British Isles implies an overly literal conception of height. For more than a century, cyclists have been conquering what they believed to be the highest road col in Wales by struggling up the heart-stopping Bwlch y Groes (454 metres), while others have celebrated the same feat after crossing the gentler Gospel Pass (459 metres). Ideally, one would also identify the highest-seeming cols. In a high mountain massif a few extra metres here or there make little difference, whereas a walker or a cyclist who leaves a coastal plain for a towering peak may well have a greater sense of giddy altitude.

Ben Nevis, Snowdon, Scafell Pike and Carrauntoohil in MacGillycuddy's Reeks are known to be the highest peaks in Britain and Ireland. The highest cols, on the other hand, unlike their famous French counterparts, are strangely obscure. How many people have heard of The Blue Pass (Bwlch Glas in Snowdonia) which is the highest col in Wales? Ill Crag Col, the highest col in England, is unnamed on maps, and Lough Gap, the highest col in Ireland beyond the far southwest, is shown on only one map. The highest col anywhere in the British Isles is in the Cairngorms.

I have had to call it An Lairig ('The Pass'), since this unsung giant is named only implicitly in the nearby Sròn na Lairige, the 'nose' or 'headland of the pass'.

## The lowest

The col of Tayvallich, from the foot of which a ferry boat sails to the Isle of Jura, is only twelve metres above sea level, and very nearly in the sea. This makes it the lowest col anywhere in the British Isles. The original name is lost, but this Lilliputian climb is indeed a *bealach*. 'Tayvallich' means 'house of the pass', and the name also survives in Loch a' Bhealaich and Dùn a' Bhealaich, the Iron Age fort which guarded the pass. The climb begins on the edge of the village with the knoll of the fort straight ahead. The road kicks up almost at once, but there is some respite after twenty metres as it levels out next to a rock garden built out of the col's western slope. The descent begins at the second bungalow on the right and ends eighty-six metres later at the loch side.

This tiny but certifiable col with an average gradient of 3 per cent and a total length of 350 metres would make an ideal training ground for an infant cyclist contemplating a future career in professional racing.

It covers a wide range of cycling skills, including general road awareness in a built-up area and smooth braking after a descent. If an over-confident or limp-fingered tot overshoots the finish line by ten metres, missing the road sign and the floral tubs, they will have to be fished out of Loch a' Bhealaich and encouraged to consider an alternative career.

### The steepest

Strange to say, the steepest col (or, rather, the steepest climb to a col) is almost impossible to determine. Some have ridiculously steep sections but a piffling average gradient. Others are uniformly steep but quite cooperative if climbed at a steady pace. The steepest roads in Britain are all in cities and do not cross cols. In such cases, the descent gives a more accurate sense of unusual declivity than the climb, fear being more sharply focussed than despair.

Steepness is endlessly discussed in cycling forums. Everyone's personal experience is necessarily limited, and so a consensus has arisen, as in a democratic dictatorship, to elect a supreme leader – Hardknott Pass in the Lake District – which seems to have a name to match its hard and knotty incline. Its thirteenth-century name, however – Wainscarth, or 'cart gap' – shows that it was used by vehicles, and the steepest section, west of the col, lasts for only (so to speak) 1.9 kilometres and has an average gradient of 15.7 per cent. The road sign at the western foot

marked '30%' indicates the maximum gradient and applies only to very brief sections of the climb.

A new leader is sometimes installed with inaccurate profiles as its credentials. The Bealach na Bà on the Applecross Peninsula (a pass with a col 800 metres before the summit) is one of the longest climbs in Britain – almost ten kilometres from Tornapress. A kilometre-long section near the top averages 10.8 per cent (rather than 21.9 per cent, as the Climbbybike website has it). But a truly accurate expression of steepness would have to combine so many different factors that the concept is effectively subjective. For every cyclist who bears the scars of an extraordinarily arduous climb, there is another who is disappointed to have reached the same fabled summit so quickly.

### The riskiest

Mountain-rescue statistics suggest that the higher the col, the more dangerous it is. Lingmell Col and Mickledore in the Lake District – on the slopes of England's highest mountain, Scafell Pike – are regularly cited in incident reports. The other main danger areas in Britain are Snowdonia and the Cairngorms, but the bwlchs and bealachs are safer than the summits. Lost walkers with mobile phones are often talked down to cols, where they can be met by rescue teams and helicopters.

Some col names are a warning: Bealach Garbh (Rough Pass), Bealach Sneachda (Snowy Pass), Cadh' an Amadain (Fool's Pass), etc., though it is some time since anyone had to be rescued from a *bèiste* (a 'monster': see p. 75–6). The most dangerous col in Scotland is the Rest and Be Thankful on the A83, where cars and coaches frequently collide. In 2007, the Cat and Fiddle Pass and the Woodhead Pass came first and fifth in a list of the most dangerous roads in England. It is almost a shame to have to include them in the catalogue. The best safety advice would be to stick to cols, which tend to be less trafficky than passes.

### The tastiest

Almost anything tastes good at a col. After cycling for years with a

firm believer in the virtues of the peanut-butter-and-jelly (i.e. jam) sandwich, I finally tried one on the Col du Tourmalet in the Pyrenees, being unable to face another energy bar, and found it delicious, though I have never tried one since.

Tea stops are still the primary goal of many cycling and walking clubs, but are now very thin on the ground. Only seven col summits in the British Isles have regular food outlets. They include a pub once celebrated by Thomas Hardy (see p. 34), and, at Moll's Gap in County Kerry, a respectable descendant of the illegal brewhouse where Moll Kissane provided liquid solace to the men who built the road through

| Col | Establishment | Length of climb (kms) | Gradient (%) | Calories | Sample meal (corresponding to calorie consumption) |
|---|---|---|---|---|---|
| Sydenham Rise | Horniman Museum Café | 1.6 | 2.4 | 195 | Half a goat's cheese salad |
| Wicklow Gap | The Gap Pub | 4.8 | 2.4 | 568 | 3 pints Guinness |
| Winyard's Gap | Winyard's Gap Inn | 5.5 | 2.1 | 613 | 1 packet crisps + ½ pint bitter |
| Rest & Be Thankful | Catering van | 6.8 | 3.7 | 1,025 | 4 hotdogs + trimmings |
| Carter Bar | Catering van | 8.0 | 2.9 | 1,044 | 1 deep-fried Mars Bar (unfinished) |
| Moll's Gap | Moll's Gap Store & Café | 15.6 | 1.2 | 1,480 | 4 scones with jam & cream |
| Hartside Cross | Hartside Top Café | 9.0 | 4.7 | 1,606 | 1 orange juice, 1 plate fish & chips w/ mushy peas, 1 sticky bun, 3 cups tea (full milk and sugar), 1 last sticky bun |

NB: The sample meals assume that the journey will end at the col. I have excluded Kirkstone Pass Inn (Lake District) because it lies 200 m. below the col summit.

the pass in the 1820s. In accordance with the precept expressed above, I have arranged these seven col establishments (see previous page) in ascending order of theoretical tastiness, based on the energy consumption of a moderately fit male cyclist on a road bike. Female cyclists, walkers, runners and horse riders will have to adjust the figures accordingly, but the order will remain the same.

## The remotest

Nature has placed this impediment in the way of anyone who sets out to cross every col in the British Isles. Am Blaid ('The Mouth') is a magnificent saddle on the central ridge of Hirta, the largest of the islands which make up the archipelago of St Kilda, one hundred miles from the Scottish mainland. A ribbon of tarmac, misleadingly shown as a track on the Ordnance Survey map, rises from the ghostly remains of St Kilda's only street to the radio masts on Mullach Mòr, crossing Am Blaid at 239 metres. Two other St Kildan cols, both trackless, can be reached on foot: they teeter on the cliff-edge and are patrolled by the fearless and belligerent great skua – one of the few situations in which a bicycle helmet is essential.

The last permanent inhabitants left St Kilda in 1930, and there is no record of the first person to cycle over Am Blaid. In 2012, a Revd David Post from Lincolnshire, who was raising money for a church in Baghdad, cycled up to Mullach Mòr, presumably crossing Am Blaid on the way. Someone may have crossed

it on a bike in the early 1900s. The son of a St Kildan who lived in Paris returned every year, bringing items that were unobtainable on the island. Once, he brought a tree and, on another occasion, a bicycle. But as his daughter points out, 'They couldn't ride much on St Kilda: there was no surfaced road.'

The word 'remote' begs the question 'Remote from what?' Am Blaid is the furthest from any other col or inhabited place, but perhaps the correct term would be 'inconvenient', in which case there are several other candidates. The Gap lies at the very bottom of the Mull of Kintyre on a dead-end road which leads only to the Mull Lighthouse. There are also cols on the islands of Lismore, Barra and Raasay (served by ferries), Rona and Sandray (chartered fishing boat) and Garbh Eileach, which is almost split in two by its col ('water taxi'). In Ireland, there are cols on the Atlantic islands of Aranmore and Inisturk. The latter was sold in 2013 for about 3 million euros. The relatively low asking price did not take account of the col, which had yet to be identified.

If all other islands are included – Orkney and Shetland, the other Hebrides, the Isle of Man and the Isle of Wight (the Channel Islands, the Scillies and Anglesey are col-less), the total number of inconveniently insular cols rises to 221. But since this is the British Isles, every col in the catalogue is on an island. In any case, a ferry crossing can be a relaxing break on a long journey.

Other inconvenient cols are Bealach na Muic (Sutherland),

which is the furthest from a road (9.4 miles), and Bealach Coire a' Chuidhe (also Sutherland), which is the furthest from a railway station in the mainland British Isles (40.4 miles). If the range is extended to cover all British territories, the scale of inconvenience must be recalibrated. There is a beautiful col on Sandy Bay Ridge on St Helena, which the exiled Napoleon crossed, partly on horseback and partly in a carriage, one morning in October 1820. Perhaps on that occasion, as he recovered over breakfast and three glasses of champagne, he remembered his crossing of the St Bernard Pass. The Falkland Islands have as many cols as a comparable area in the French Alps, but the most remote of all are on South Georgia, where cols are still being formed by glaciers. The north col of Mount Paget is not only the remotest but also, at 2,220 metres, the highest col on British territory. It is therefore less than half the height of the highest col in the French Alps, the Col Major, which had no name until it was christened in 1927 by the Scottish mountaineer Thomas Graham Brown.

### The earliest recorded

Cols first appeared in documents as boundary markers or place names, for example Swuran Tune (c. 970), Swyn Geat (972), and Corfes Geat (after 979), where Edward the Martyr met his end: 'Hér wæs Eádweard cyning ofslægen æt Corfes geate'.*

The first known written references to cols as natural gateways are the sixteenth-century lists of 'ingates and passages' by which Scottish raiders crossed the Border.

The earliest cartographic record of a British col dates from the same period. In about 1583, with nothing but his own meagre resources, a student of St Andrews University called Timothy Pont set out to map Scotland. According to the cartographer and antiquarian Robert Gordon of Straloch:

> ... he traversed on foot the whole kingdom (as no one had done previously); he saw all the islands, for the most part inhabited by hostile and barbarous peoples, with a language different from ours; he listened; he was often robbed (as he used to tell me) by cruel bandits, and not infrequently experienced a total loss of the results of a dangerous journey; yet he was never overcome by the difficulties and reduced to despair.

Pont died in 1614 or 1615, before his maps could be published. Moths and bookworms munched at the priceless sheets, obliterating the inky scrawls on them. It was not until 1654 that the legible remains of Pont's work became known to the wider world, in the fifth volume of Joan Blaeu's *Atlas novus*. No other country had ever been so thoroughly mapped.

Pont's sketches are the first British maps on which cols are recorded. One is labelled 'Ruynavey Bhellach'

---

* Sourton (Devon) contains the word 'swyre'; Swyn Geat, or Swyneyate, is the Gullet Pass (Malvern Hills); Corfes Geate is Corfe Gate at Corfe Castle (Dorset).

('The Pass of Runavey'). Four centuries later, this distinct col on the boundary of Angus and Perthshire has yet to appear on any other map. Another col is in the far north-west, labelled 'Bhellach maddy, or Woolfs Way'. To its left, Pont has noted 'Extreem Wilderness' (the wilderness at the extremity of the land) and, a little below, 'Many Woolfs in this country'.

It sounds like the figment of a medieval imagination, but the unprecedented accuracy of Pont's mapping makes it possible to pinpoint the Bhellach Maddy (or Bealach a' Mhadaidh). The Woolfs Way is the col beside the road to Durness which has been shown on Ordnance Survey maps since 1878 as 'Am Bealach' ('the pass'). Pont places the col precisely where it is in relation to Strath Dionard and the hill called Farrmheall.*

It might seem strange that some of the first cols to be recorded should lie at the obscure extremities of Britain, but these were often the only guide-posts in the wolves' wide domain. The *bealachs* showed the way into and out of the wilderness and, although their role in the creation of modern Britain is almost imperceptible today, it is fitting that they first appear in this shining, misty dawn of scientific cartography.

### The oldest and the youngest

Several cols in the Hebrides and north-western Scotland cut through some of the oldest rocks on the planet. When the granite called Lewisian gneiss formed, nothing else that we now see on the face of the Earth existed. There is an exposed section north of Laxford Bridge on the A838, but the tidy grooves of the road builders' rock drill make it hard to picture it in its primordial chaos. Not far away, a single-track road leaves the A838 and runs alongside the Loch na Bèiste Brice ('Loch of the Spotted Monster') into an oddly claustrophobic landscape of low granite protrusions and shivering lakelets to a col called simply An Cadha ('the pass'). The road comes to a dead end shortly after the col. On a dreary day, the faint Archaean sun which shone dimly on those rocks that were bare of all life is only too easy to imagine.

Until a few months ago, the youngest col in Britain appeared to be Sydenham Rise in South London. When the clay of the Norwood Ridge began to form in a tropical sea, hominids were already walking the Earth, and when glacial meltwater cut through the ridge, creating the col, our own species was spreading north towards the Thames Basin. This happened ten thousand years ago, at the end of the last Ice Age. However, in 2014, a team of scientists found evidence that glaciers survived in the Cairngorms as recently as the eighteenth century, during the 'Little Ice Age'. The evidence came from the vicinity of An Lairig (1134 m.), which is the highest and perhaps, it now seems, the youngest col in the British Isles.

---

* Sometimes misidentified as the Bealach Coir' a' Choin ('Dogs' Corrie Pass').

## The ugliest and the loveliest

Nothing in the names of British and Irish cols suggests that they were ever considered for their aesthetic qualities. Some names might strike us as pleasantly poetic – the 'glittering' Bwlch-lluan or the 'tinkling' Bealach Gliogarsnaich – but they are, almost without exception, bluntly realistic. Colours (most often black) describe the shade of the rock or the vegetation. The common Gaelic term 'fionn' ('fair') refers to paleness, not to prettiness. When a name implies a subjective reaction, the impression is always physical rather than mental: 'rough', 'difficult', 'cold' and – commonest of all – 'windy'. Imagination is rarely in evidence and, when it is, it tends to the nightmarish: a few names refer to the fairies, but many more to a 'monster' or the Devil.

In the twenty-first century, landscapes have become contestants in a national beauty pageant and are rated according to their visual charm. There are Areas of Outstanding Natural Beauty and official viewpoints from which to observe them. The focus of a beautiful view is often provided by the cleavage of a col, the dip and curve of the hills suggesting another, unseen world beyond. Even with AONB committees to establish firm criteria, natural beauty is subjective and, therefore, changeable. There might, however, be some consensus on the following.

The Gospel Pass in the Black Mountains of Wales is reached from the south through a tunnel of hedges. For the last mile, there is only the sheep-cropped moor and the sky framed in the gunsight of the V-shaped col. But then, at the summit of the col, a thousand square miles of mid-Wales explode into view. To the east are the cols of the Malvern Hills, the highest of which – the unnamed col below the Worcestershire Beacon – might be called the most beautiful in England, despite the more obviously stunning passes of the Lake District. Surrounded as it is by plains, its beauty is unchallenged by any other.

In Scotland, the choice is too wide but, if convenience is the deciding factor, the most beautiful col might be the Bealach na Searmoin ('Pass of the Sermon'), previously known as Bealach na Searbhaig ('Pass of the Struggle'). It forms a narrow plateau below Ben Vrackie. From this wind-blasted Shangri-la, the distant white sentry of Blair Castle to the north-west and Pitlochry and the Tummel Valley to the south are like the peaceful visions of a departing spirit.

The ugliest cols are easy to identify. Two English cols can be crossed only on a motorway bridge; another now lies underneath the M6 (see p. 53). Several cols have rubbish dumps, official or not. The Caha Pass on the boundary of Cork and Kerry has its summit in the middle of an unlit road tunnel. This gloomiest of cols presents its magnificent views through the windows of a prison. On the other hand, if, as Stendhal said, 'Beauty is the promise of happiness,' this dark passageway with a light at both ends must also be one of the most beautiful.

The south-west of Ireland probably has the greatest concentration of beautiful cols. The forgotten col of Mám Clasach ('The Furrowed Pass'), at the tip of the Dingle Peninsula is the westernmost col in the British Isles. At its summit, the ocean appears on either side and a radio mast conveys a sense of distant connections. The road from the east slopes down towards green fields dotted with white houses, towards the foaming breakers and the islands, which look like unmoored mountains floating out to sea, towards the broadest col of all, whose summit is the highest wave in the mid-Atlantic and whose opposite slope lies somewhere in the Allegheny Mountains.

# References

### Prologue

The 'col' of Snowdon: John Barnard, Myrddyn Phillips and Graham Jackson, 'Defining the Summits and Cols of Hills', version 3 (2015), p. 6: http://www.hills-database.co.uk/summits_and_cols.pdf

The Nick o' Thungs: John A. Clayton, *Cotton and Cold Blood: East Lancashire 1867–1897* (Barrowford, Lancs: Barrowford Press, 2008), p. 158–9.

Whithaugh Swire: 'A breife of the Bounderes, Wayes and Passages of the Midle March', in *The Border Papers*, ed. Joseph Bain, II (Edinburgh: H. M. General Register House, 1896), pp. 469–70; Joan Blaeu, 'Lidalia vel Lidisdalia regio, Lidisdail' (Amsterdam: Blaeu, 1654), based on an earlier map by Timothy Pont.

Hardhaugh or Hindhaugh Swire: 'Jamie Telfer o' the Fair Dodhead', in Herbert Maxwell, *The Story of the Tweed* (London: James Nisbet, 1909), p. 158; Walter Scott, *The Lay of the Last Minstrel* (London: Longman, 1806), p. 110.

Hethouswyre: James Morton, *The Monastic Annals of Teviotdale* (Edinburgh: W. H. Lizars, 1832), p. 267 (from the 'Chartulary of Melros').

### London

Camille Pissarro's *Lordship Lane Station*: In the Courtauld Institute of Art, London.

Émile Zola lived in a hotel on the Norwood Ridge: Photographs in The Norwood Society, *Émile Zola – Photographer* (London: Norwood Society, 1997).

Moved to Margate for an exhibition: http://advisor.museumsandheritage.com/features/museums-heritage-awards-2014-award-winners-review-horniman-museum-and-garde/

### Wessex

'On corf getes westran cotan': *Codex diplomaticus aevi Saxonici*, IV (London: English Historical Society, 1846), p. 31.

'The advantage [the bicycle] has for literary people': Letter to Sir George Douglas, 3 March 1898, in *The Collected Letters of Thomas Hardy*, ed. R. Purdy and M. Millgate (Oxford University Press, 1978–2012), II, p. 118.

'Not a name had been entered there': Thomas Hardy, 'The Honourable Laura', in *A Group of Noble Dames* (1891), p. 258.

In some of the remoter corners of his work: 'Life and Death at Sunrise (Near Dogbury Gate, 1867)', in *Human Shows, Far Phantasies, Songs, and Trifles* (1925); *The Hand of Ethelberta* (1876), chap. 31; 'A Trampwoman's Tragedy', in *Time's Laughingstocks* (1909).

'Luminous as an autumn sunset': Thomas Hardy, *The Trumpet Major* (1880), chap. 16.

### The Malvern Hills

'In a Pirramidy fashion on ye top': Celia Fiennes, *Through England on a Side Saddle*

*In the Time of William and Mary* (London: Field & Tuer, 1888), p. 33.

*Usque Baldeyate, et de Baldeyate per fossatum: A Roll of the Household Expenses of Richard de Swinfield, Bishop of Hereford*, ed. J. Webb (London: The Camden Society, 1855), p. cviii (quoting a survey of 1577–8).

Elgar's own cycling maps: In the Elgar Birthplace Museum, Broadheath, Worcestershire.

## Wales

'Turnpike Trusts. Presented to Both Houses of Parliament', in *Reports from Commissioners*, XX (London: The House of Commons, 1866), p. 16.

'Across this hollow': Thomas Pennant, *A Tour in Wales MDCCLXXIII*, part 2 (London: Henry Hughes, 1781), p. 205.

'Bwlch Agricla': T. Pennant, *A Tour in Wales MDCCLXXIII*, part 1 (London: Henry Hughes, 1778), p. 388.

## North Wales

'The little window of my bedroom': 'Wayfarer' (Walter MacGregor Robinson), 'Over the Top: Crossing the Berwyn Mountains in March', *Cycling*, 8 May 1919; reproduced in http://www.cyclingnorthwales.co.uk/pages/wayfarer.htm

'In those days rough and overgrown': Cyril R. Rowson, tribute to 'Wayfarer' in *Cycling* magazine, 1972; reproduced in http://www.cyclingnorthwales.co.uk/pages/wayf_1st_rough.htm

'And is this cycling?': 'Wayfarer', art. cit.

'One afternoon, "Robbie" and I': Rowson, art. cit.

## The Pennine Way

'Must poor folk stroll in cinders': quoted in Paul Salveson, 'Bolton Moors

"Liberated", 1896', *Tribune*, 27 August 1982.

'A faint line on the Ordnance Maps': Tom Stephenson, 'Wanted – A Long Green Trail', *Daily Herald*, 22 June 1935.

'Yorkshire folk used to build stone towers': Alfred Wainwright, *Pennine Way Companion: A Pictorial Guide* (Kendal: Westmorland Gazette, 1968), p. xxi.

'Well, I'm glad it's finished': A. Wainwright, *Pennine Way Companion*, p. xv.

## The Yorkshire Dales

2.5 million of them: West Yorkshire Police, 'Yorkshire Grand Départ': http://www.westyorkshire.police.uk/tour-defrance; Sylvain Mouillard, 'Chiens, selfies et indépendance', *Libération*, 7 July 2014.

Regional train companies: Chris Marshall-Bell, 'Tour de France in Yorkshire: Avoid Taking Your Bike on a Train', *Cycling Weekly*, 23 May 2014.

'Gnat's piss': Henri Desgrange, in *L'Auto*, 10 July 1911; translating '*bibine*'.

## Shap Fell

Another 'horse hause' ... on a map of 1695: Robert Morden, 'Westmorland', first published in William Camden's *Britannia* in 1695.

It was recorded in 1719 as 'th'Hause House': Parish register, cited in The Historical Gazetteer of England's Place Names: http://placenames.org.uk/id/placename/43/007981

## The Lake District

'Morale-crushing descents': http://www.lakelandmountainguides.co.uk/#!24-peaks-challenge-in-24-hours/c1cz

'All the Lakeland passes': http://www.fredwhittonchallenge.co.uk/

'The road has a poor surface': http://www.fredwhittonchallenge.co.uk/the-route/

'An article in the British *Medical Magazine*': Dr Sydney S. Buckman, 'Cycling: Its Effect on the Future of the Human Race', *The Medical Magazine*, VIII (1899), pp. 128–135.

## Hadrian's Wall

The 'Busy Gap Rogues': Jim Crow, 'Tracing the Busy Gap Rogues', *International Journal of Historical Archaeology*, XI, 4 (December 2007), pp. 322–35.

## Galloway

'A hollow between Craigwhinnie and Benmeal': Canmore record, quoting Ordnance Survey Name Book, 1848: http://canmore.org.uk/site/63762/nick-of-the-dead-mans-banes

'Scotland has some of the darkest skies in Europe': Forestry Commission Scotland, 'Dark Skies in Galloway Forest Park': http://scotland.forestry.gov.uk/forest-parks/galloway-forest-park/dark-skies

'Old Road very Hilly': John Thomson and William Johnson, 'Northern Part of Ayrshire. Southern Part' (Edinburgh: J. Thomson, 1828).

'Whenever the exigency of Affairs may require it': William Taylor, *The Military Roads in Scotland*, revised ed. (Colonsay: House of Lochar, 1996), p. 95.

'To lift the vehicle out of the ruts': Samuel Smiles, *The Life of Thomas Telford, Civil Engineer*, new ed. (London: John Murray, 1867), p. 56.

'In Galloway there are no roads so wild...': John Mactaggart, *The Scottish Gallovidian Encyclopedia* (London: Printed for the author, 1824), p. 142.

'A top dressing of slaty gravel': W. Taylor, *The Military Roads in Scotland*, p. 99.

'Impassable in winter': W. Taylor, *The Military Roads in Scotland*, p. 102.

## The Scottish Borders

'The sun was setting on Kirkhope Swire': Will Ogilvie, *Whaup o' the Rede: A Ballad of the Border Raiders* (Dalbeattie: Thomas Fraser, 1909), p. 15.

The local council appears to have adopted the factitious name: Ettrick and Yarrow Community Council, *Resilient Community Plan* (Scottish Borders Council, 2013), p. 6.

'A shilling for beginning to play, and two to leave off': John Gordon Smith, *Santarem* (London: Fisher, 1832), p. 272.

According to one of the best known tales: For example, John Sinclair, *The Statistical Account of Scotland*, *XVI* (Edinburgh: William Creech, 1795), p. 57.

An impoverished laird had made a pact with the Devil: William Anderson, *The Piper of Peebles: A Tale* (Dundee: T. Colvill, 1794).

On a map of 1773: Andrew Armstrong, 'Map of the Three Lothians' (Edinburgh: n. p., 1773).

'Incurred the displeasure of the church': Canmore record, quoting Ordnance Survey Name Book, 1856: http://canmore.org.uk/site/53226/friars-grave-gill-rig

'No feature marks the site of this grave': Ibid., quoting Ordnance Survey report, 22 February 1962.

'Do not be tempted to ride too far afield': H. H. England, *Cycling Manual* (London: Temple Press, 1917; 1954), p. 13.

## Edinburgh

A landslide in 1744: Jack Repcheck, *The Man Who Found Time: James Hutton and the*

*Discovery of the Earth's Antiquity* (New York: Basic Books, 2009), p. 64.

'The swire at the head of the dell': James Hogg, *The Private Memoirs and Confessions of a Justified Sinner* (London: Longman, 1824), p. 59.

## The Highland Boundary Fault

'The country we came to now was very wild': Queen Victoria, *Leaves from the Journal of Our Life in the Highlands* (1868; Cambridge University Press, 2010), p. 20 (10 September 1842).

'We passed *Pitlochrie*...': Ibid., p. 32 (11 September 1844).

'Into completely wild Highland scenery': Ibid., p. 193 (15 August 1849).

'The moon rose and shone most beautifully': Ibid., p. 171 (16 October 1861).

A 'very ungeographical' head: Ibid.

Her great-great-granddaughter crossed the Cairnwell: Contemporary postcard reproduced in http://www.bbc.co.uk/scotland/landscapes/devils_elbow/ The double bend of the Devil's Elbow has since been straightened.

## The West Highlands

A restricted zone: Trevor Royle, *The Flowers of the Forest: Scotland and the First World War* (Edinburgh: Birlinn, 2006), p. 177.

Radio station on St Kilda: T. Royle, *The Flowers of the Forest*, p. 178.

A naval motor launch on Loch Ness: Nicholas Witchell, *The Loch Ness Story*, revised ed. (London: Corgi, 1989), p. 80.

'A terrible steep to climb': James Boswell, *The Journal of a Tour to the Hebrides, with Samuel Johnson* (London: Henry Baldwin, 1785), p. 159.

'Haunted by a monster': Alexander Forbes, *Place-Names of Skye and Adjacent Islands* (Paisley: Gardner, 1923), p. 352.

The Bealach na Bèiste was on the regular route of a 'water horse': A. Forbes, *Place-Names of Skye*, p. 62; Peter Drummond, *Scottish Hill and Mountain Names* (Glasgow: Scottish Mountaineering Trust, 1991), p. 181.

Loch na Bèiste – the home of a 'sea cow': John H. Dixon, *Gairloch in North-West Ross-Shire* (Edinburgh: Co-operative Printing Company, 1886), p. 162.

An anthrax experiment: Richard M. Swiderski, *Anthrax: A History* (Jefferson, North Carolina: McFarland, 2004), pp. 131–2.

## The Mourne Wall

An Australian journalist: Richard Tulloch, 'Pack Up Your Troubles', *Sydney Morning Herald*, 29 July 2007.

'Key control points': Dafydd Davis, *The Mournes and Slieve Croob Strategic Path Review* (Annalong: Mourne Heritage Trust, 2012), 2.2.

'An important deliverer for government agendas': D. Davis, *The Mournes*, 2.4.

## The Wicklow Mountains

The men of the Ordnance Survey: Rachel Hewitt, *Map Of A Nation: A Biography Of The Ordnance Survey* (London: Granta, 2010), chap. 11.

John O'Donovan: R. Hewitt, ibid.

'In the present artificial state of society': Quoted by R. Hewitt, ibid.

'We ascended the Sugar Loaf Mountain': *The Ordnance Survey Letters: Wicklow*, ed. Christiaan Corlett and John Medlycott (Roundwood & District Historical & Folklore Society, Wicklow Archaeological Society and Kestrel Books, 2000), p. 14.

'To the sportsman, the geologist, or the artist': *The Ordnance Survey Letters: Wicklow*, p. 2.

'Soft and spewy bog' and 'infernally' rude inn-keepers: *The Ordnance Survey Letters: Wicklow*, pp. 7 and 65.

Walkers will sometimes encounter features on the ground: EastWest Mapping, 'Thoughts on Navigation – Maps and their Makers', 16 March 2015: https://www.facebook.com/permalink.php?story_fbid=954498881228185&id=693816783963064&substory_index=0

#### South-West Ireland

*Topographia Hibernica*: Giraldus Cambrensis, *The Topography of Ireland*, trans. T. Forester, rev. ed. T. Wright (Cambridge, Ontario: Medieval Latin Series, 2000), pp. 12–13.

'Colman the Pilgrim': Description, photograph and bibliography at http://www.ucl.ac.uk/archaeology/cisp/database/stone/mauig_1.html

#### Superlatives

A list of the most dangerous roads in England: 'Cat and Fiddle road tops crash league', *Manchester Evening News*, 17 February 2007.

Revd David Post from Lincolnshire: 'David Post's Long Bike Ride' (8 July 2012): http://bike4baghdad.tumblr.com/

'They couldn't ride much on St Kilda': Joujou Ferguson Mitchell, in Timothy Neat, *When I Was Young: Voices from Lost Communities in Scotland: the Islands* (Edinburgh: Birlinn, 2000), p. 192.

Breakfast and three glasses of champagne: Dr F. Antommarchi, *The Last Days of the Emperor Napoleon By … His Physician*, 2 vols (London: Henry Colburn, 1825), I, 336.

'Hér wæs Eádweard cyning ofslægen æt Corfes geate': In the *Anglo-Saxon Chronicle* under the date 979.

'He traversed on foot the whole kingdom': Translation from the Latin by Ian C. Cunningham, in the National Library of Scotland's introduction to Blaeu's Atlas: http://maps.nls.uk/atlas/blaeu/page.cfm?id=897

A team of scientists found evidence: Martin Kirkbride, Jez Everest, Doug Benn, Delia Gheorghiu and Alastair Dawson, 'Late-Holocene and Younger Dryas Glaciers in the Northern Cairngorm Mountains, Scotland', *The Holocene*, XXIV, 2 (2014), pp. 141–8.

'Beauty is the promise of happiness': Henri Beyle (Stendhal), *De l'amour* (Paris: Mongie, 1822), I, 63.

# The Catalogue

The catalogue is organized by country (England, Wales, Scotland, Northern Ireland, Republic of Ireland), then by county or, in Scotland, council area. Since the Highland council area is vast and contains almost half the Scottish cols, I have sub-divided it into the 'lieutenancy areas', which partly reflect older county boundaries. Inverness and Argyll and Bute are further sub-divided into Mainland and Islands.

Cols and passes are listed alphabetically by county – cols first, then passes. Anonymous cols (set in italics) are listed either by the hills on either side (e.g. *Beacon Hill – Steps Hill*) or by a feature at the col itself (e.g. the tumulus called *Giant's Grave*). Anonymous cols are included only when they are commonly recognized as cols (in the geological rather than technical, mountaineering sense: see p. 17) or distinct enough to be a conspicuous feature of the landscape.

If the col or pass stands on a county boundary, it is listed under each county or, in the case of Whiteleaved Oak in the Malvern Hills, under all three counties. Thirteen cols and one pass also stand on national borders, which explains why the sum of cols in each country is greater than the total number of cols.

Bold type indicates a col or a pass which stands on a road. The uneven distribution of road cols (about one-third of English but only one-thirteenth of Scottish cols) reflects the size of the road networks: England has 3.73 miles of paved road for every square mile; in Scotland the ratio is only 1:22.

The table below shows the total number of cols and passes in each part of the British Isles. The number of road cols is given in parentheses. On the distinction between cols and passes, see p. 17.

| | Cols (on road) | Passes (on road) |
|---|---|---|
| England | 308 (123) | 21 (17) |
| Wales | 268 (90) | 14 (14) |
| Scotland | 1158 (87) | 49 (34) |
| Northern Ireland | 51 (19) | 2 (2) |
| Republic of Ireland | 230 (112) | 20 (18) |
| Total (counting the thirteen cols and one pass on national borders only once) | 2002 (429) | 105 (84) |

Each entry has eight headings: name, elevation, surface, nearest place, region, latitude and longitude coordinates, National Grid coordinates, notes.

## Name

Named cols and passes are in regular type, anonymous ones in italics. Passes are listed within a three-sided box after the cols in each county section.

If the name appears on an Ordnance Survey map, this is the preferred form, except in cases of obvious error (but ignoring minor deviations in spelling). Other forms of the name which are still in use are also cited. Historical forms are given in the notes.

Where the col has both an English and a Welsh or Gaelic name, the English name comes first if the Welsh or Gaelic equivalent has been deduced from the English but is not recorded on a map or other document.

## Elevation

This is the height of the col in metres above sea level. About half of these are Ordnance Survey spot heights (© Crown copyright 2016. All rights reserved). Spot heights are scarce on Irish Ordnance Survey maps and indicate the summit of a col in only fourteen cases. The remainder are derived from contour lines at five- and ten-metre intervals and refined by other altimetric data.

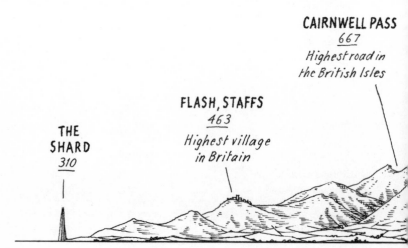

THE SHARD
*310*

FLASH, STAFFS
*463*
*Highest village in Britain*

CAIRNWELL PASS
*667*
*Highest road in the British Isles*

On British Ordnance Survey maps, the orange-brown dots at cols tend to indicate the summit; the black dots belong to later, occasional surveys and are, in effect, more arbitrary. These heights should be considered conventional rather than literal. Several cols lie on lung-like bogs which regularly lose or gain a metre or more in height. Walkers who have struggled over the tussocky terrain of the English–Scottish border will know that 'ground level' is a concept rather than a solid reality.

## Surface

This is the terrain (road, track or path) indicated on Ordnance Survey 1:25,000 ('Explorer') maps and Irish equivalents (see p. 104) in 2016. Where no indication is given, the col is considered trackless.

Parentheses indicate proximity – usually within one hundred metres, occasionally a little more on easy terrain.

Maps, especially when updated from the air, are not infallible guides to terrain. The differences between roads, tracks, paths and open country are neither absolute nor permanent. Many tracks are easier to negotiate than narrow, potholed roads. A path which experienced walkers might follow quite happily may not even be visible to some.

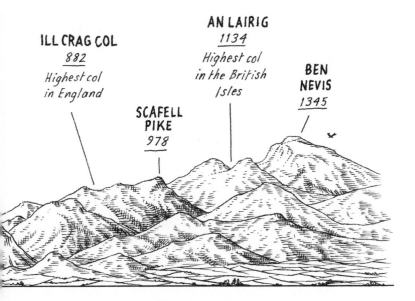

## Nearest place

For consistency, this is the nearest place shown on 1:100,000 Ordnance Survey maps (not necessarily the nearest inhabited place).

## Area

The 'region' is the hill range, river basin or other natural area to which the col belongs. Snowdonia is the traditional region (Eryri), not the enormous National Park. Because it has such a high concentration of cols, Lake District is divided into northern (N), north-western (NW), western (W), southern (S), eastern (E) and central (C), following the boundaries defined by Alfred Wainwright.

## Latitude and longitude coordinates and National Grid coordinates

The maps of reference are the British Ordnance Survey 'Explorer' series on a scale of 1:25,000, the Northern Irish 'Activity' (1:25,000) and 'Discoverer' series (1:50,000), and the Irish 'Adventure' (1:25,000) and 'Discovery' series (1:50,000). (On Irish maps, see pp. 80–85).

The latitude and longitude coordinates refer to the WGS 84 system used by GPS units and most online maps. The equivalent National Grid coordinates (British and Irish) are also provided. For practical purposes, these define the location to the nearest square metre. Some computer applications may place the point several metres from its true position, but no serious ambiguities result, except at vertiginous cols such as The Gap on St Kilda, which Google Earth (in 2016) displays half-way down a sheer cliff.

The position given for the col is usually the summit of the lowest route between the heights on either side. In geometry, this would be the 'saddle point' (fig. 5).

Some cols, however, are broad, flattish areas with no tidy summit. By definition, a col is subject to erosion. The terrain on a watershed can change from year to year. Paths come and go; they migrate to higher or lower ground or disappear altogether. A firm, wide forest track that can support heavy machinery may be engulfed by the new plantation within a few seasons.

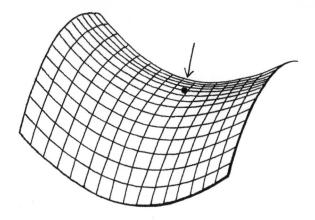

Fig. 5 A saddle point

Where no path exists, the coordinates are those of the geographical summit or the centre of the plateau. The point so defined may lie only a few steps from an existing path or track, in which case the words 'path' or 'track' appear between parentheses. No one who sets out to 'bag' these cols should feel obliged to match the twelve-digit coordinates in the catalogue to those on a GPS device and to position themselves on the exact spot, which could turn out to be occupied by a sinkhole, a thorn bush or the home of an animal. The last place anyone should want to stare at a tiny screen (I have been told) is at a col.

Roads, on the other hand, are likely to remain where they are, and so the coordinates for road cols identify the highest point on the road which crosses the col. There are some rare exceptions to the rule. For example, the quiet road which winds gently up out of Liddesdale to Billhope Hass continues to rise after the col identified in the catalogue, adding five metres to the climb. The geographical col is slightly lower, along the sheep fence, in a trackless patch of marshy ground. But the hass itself is historically inscribed on the landscape, where the road crosses the fence line on the county boundary, at the 'Welcome to Scottish Borders' sign.

Only in a few cases (indicated in the Notes column) would a geographer disagree with the location identified by tradition. Wherever there is a doubt, I have erred, so to speak, on the side of accuracy, which is why the summit of the Caha Pass which leads from Cork to Kerry in south-western Ireland is located at the only part of the climb without a magnificent view, since it occurs inside a tunnel. Occasionally, practicality dictates a compromise. The unnamed gap in the Failand Ridge near Norton's Wood in Somerset was once marked by a meeting of prehistoric paths associated with the hill fort of Cadbury Castle. Now that the M5 motorway sprawls obliquely across the ridge, the only reasonable crossing of the col is on the footbridge above the motorway.

## Notes

The notes contain some or all of the following information in this order:

| Information | Example |
| --- | --- |
| The boundary or border on which the col or pass stands | Derbyshire boundary |
| The long-distance trail or cycle route on which the col or pass stands | Pennine Way; (NCR 68)<br><br>The col lies on the Pennine Way and just off National Cycle Route 68. |
| Its earlier name(s) | 'Wyndeyaterigg', 1338 |
| Its absence from or misplacement on Ordnance Survey maps | Not on OS 25 or 50<br><br>The col is missing from Ordnance Survey 1:25,000 ('Explorer') and 1:50,000 ('Landranger') maps. |
| Other maps or documents which record the col or pass with significant differences | 'Wild Mares Loup' on W. Garden, 'A Map of Kincardineshire' (1797) and OS 1st edn. |
| English translation of the name | 'Pass of the White Waterfall' |
| Any other notable features | The third-highest road col in England; café at summit |
| Historical importance | Battle site, 4 August 1642 |

## Corrections and additions

In a work of this complexity, total accuracy is a mirage, and any corrections and additions will be gratefully and solemnly received. To save time, the following questions should be asked. Does the putative col have a name suggestive of a col, and, if so, does it have the geographical features of a col? If the col is nameless, is it commonly referred to as a col (in the geological rather than technical, mountaineering sense: see p. 17), and is it a conspicuous feature of the landscape? In Ireland, a *bearna* is more often a path or a track than a col; in Scotland, fewer than two-thirds of sites named *bealach* are cols. A road which climbs out of one valley and descends into the next is only rarely a col.

*Attested names are given in the 'Name' column, while definitions and translations of names are given in the 'Notes' column.*

| Name | Elevation (m) | Surface | Nearest place | Region |
|---|---|---|---|---|

# England

## Berkshire · 1 col

| *Gallows Down – Walbury Hill* | 263 | **road** | Upper Green | Inkpen Hill |
|---|---|---|---|---|

## Buckinghamshire · 1 col

| *Beacon Hill – Steps Hill* | 204 | **road** | Ivinghoe | Chiltern Hills |
|---|---|---|---|---|

## Cheshire · 5 cols 1 pass

| **Charles Head** | 344 | **B road** | Kettleshulme | Peak District |
|---|---|---|---|---|
| **Golden Slack / Goldenslack** | 340 | **A road** | Wincle | Peak District |
| **Nick i' th' Hill** | 219 | **road** / track | Biddulph | Congleton Edge |
| Oldgate Nick | 499 | path | Fernilee | Peak District |
| **Peckforton Gap** | 160 | **road** / track | Bulkeley | Peckforton Hills |
| **Cat and Fiddle Pass** | 514 | **A road** | Cat and Fiddle Inn | Peak District |

## Cumbria · 127 cols 5 passes

| The Bad Step | 802 | path | Cockley Beck | Lake District S |
|---|---|---|---|---|
| Barrow Door | 384 | path | Stair | Lake District NW |
| Beck Head | 621 | path | Wasdale Head | Lake District W |
| **Black Hause / Blackhause** | 415 | **A road** / track | North Stainmore | North Pennines |
| Black Sail Pass | 544 | path | Wasdale Head | Lake District W |
| **Blea Tarn (or Bleatarn)** | 224 | **road** | Little Langdale | Lake District S |
| Boredale Hause | 399 | path | Patterdale | Lake District E |
| Bouscard / Bowesscard *see* Three Tarns Gap | | | | |
| Bowderdale Head | 431 | path | Low Haygarth | Howgill Fells |
| Bracken Hause | 335 | path | Grasmere | Lake District C |
| Bradscarth *see* Gillercomb Head | | | | |
| Bram Rigg Top – The Calf | 641 | path | Low Haygarth | Howgill Fells |
| Breasthigh Pass / Breast High Pass | 431 | track | Bretherdale Head | Lake District E |
| Broadcrag (or Broad Crag) Col | 878 | path | Wasdale Head | Lake District S |
| Brownber Hill – Rossgill Edge | 483 | | Knock | North Pennines |
| Burnbank Fell – Carling Knott | 456 | | Lamplugh | Lake District W |
| Burnbank Fell – Owsen Fell | 387 | | Lamplugh | Lake District W |
| Carlside Col | 715 | path | Little Crosthwaite | Lake District N |
| **Coldfell Gate / Red Gate** | 212 | **road** | Wilton | Lake District E |
| Coledale Hause (or Pass) | 605 | path | Loweswater | Lake District NW |
| **Cross** | 413 | **road** | Ravenstonedale | Howgill Fells |
| Deepdale Hause (or Hass) | 685 | path | Wythburn | Lake District E |
| Dodd Pass | 412 | (path) | High Lorton | Lake District NW |
| Doe Hause *see* Fairfield Col | | | | |

| Latitude, Longitude | National Grid | Notes |
|---|---|---|
| 51.35669, -1.47114 | SU3692262090 | Wayfarer's Walk; 500 m east of Combe Gibbet |
| 51.83731, -0.60742 | SP9604416327 | Icknield Way Trail / Ridgeway |
| 53.30772, -2.03931 | SJ9747878976 | 'Chorleshede', 1466; attached on OS 1st, 2nd and 3rd edn to the col rather than the hill |
| 53.20343, -2.09085 | SJ9402967377 | Gritstone Trail; 'Top o' th' Hill', 1831 |
| 53.13600, -2.18649 | SJ8762159888 | Staffordshire boundary; Gritstone Trail / Staffordshire Way |
| 53.28373, -2.00821 | SJ9955076306 | Derbyshire boundary; earlier name perhaps 'Holegate'; often misattributed by cyclists to the summit of the B road 500 m north of the col |
| 53.09793, -2.70912 | SJ5261555872 | Sandstone Trail; on a salt route known as Walesmonsway or Walchmonstreet; not on OS 1st edn |
| 53.24407, -1.99997 | SK0009971894 | From the name of the inn; see p. 89 |
| 54.43237, -3.15906 | NY2491004724 | Former Cumberland–Westmorland boundary; only on OS 10; 200 m south of Mickle Door (which is not a col; cf. Mickledore below); the relatively recent origin suggests a translation of the common French toponym *mauvais pas*, which also occurs as 'Malpas' |
| 54.58434, -3.20529 | NY2220221684 | 'Barrow' is the hill to the east |
| 54.48519, -3.22705 | NY2060310676 | The source of Gable Beck |
| 54.50964, -2.19238 | NY8764212720 | The name 'Blackhause' has slipped downhill on modern maps; the col is near the source of Blackhause Sike; coordinates are for the paved track beside the A66; see p. 53 |
| 54.49169, -3.24965 | NY1915211425 | 'Le Blacksayl', 1322; distinct from Sail Pass |
| 54.43645, -3.09710 | NY2893705114 | Not on maps; names in common use since c. 1875; 'Side Gates' on OS 1st edn |
| 54.53392, -2.91432 | NY4093315790 | 'Burdale', 1250; 'Boardale', 1787 |
| 54.37610, -2.49177 | SD6815397956 | Former Westmorland–Yorkshire boundary |
| 54.47655, -3.04418 | NY3243609523 | Name self-explanatory |
| 54.36536, -2.51142 | SD6686896770 | Dales High Way |
| 54.43161, -2.67492 | NY5631504231 | Local name; on maps only as 'Breasthigh Road'; see p. 53 |
| 54.45625, -3.20882 | NY2172907436 | Not on maps; named by Wainwright; the second-highest col in England |
| 54.64312, -2.45631 | NY7064927652 | |
| 54.57328, -3.37622 | NY1113120656 | |
| 54.57626, -3.38757 | NY1040421002 | |
| 54.64387, -3.15447 | NY2559528252 | Not on maps; named by Wainwright |
| 54.47739, -3.45922 | NY0554510095 | Not on OS 25 or 50; both names attached to the same crossing but positions switched between OS 1st edn and OS 10 |
| 54.58008, -3.25657 | NY1887921268 | 'The Moon now hangs midway over Cowdale Halse [sic] – in a line, & resting on each of the divergent Legs of its Triangle a fish-head-shaped Cloud': S. T. Coleridge, *The Notebooks*, edn K. Coburn, I (1957), p. 525. |
| 54.40221, -2.44029 | NY7151500839 | 'Cross' is a place name, not a reference to a monument |
| 54.50417, -2.98915 | NY3604512545 | 'Deepdale Hoss', 1860 |
| 54.59525, -3.28632 | NY1698722990 | Not on maps; named by Wainwright from Dodd (a hill) |

| Name | Elevation (m) | Surface | Nearest place | Region |
|---|---|---|---|---|
| Dore Head | 485 | (path) | Wasdale Head | Lake District W |
| Dove Crag – Hart Crag | 742 | path | Hartsop | Lake District E |
| Drum House | 530 | path | Gatesgarth | Lake District W |
| Dufton Pike – Bluethwaite Hill | 318 | | Knock | North Pennines |
| Dunmail Raise see Raise Gap | | | | |
| Esk Hause / Eskhals | 759 | path | Seathwaite (Borrowdale) | Lake District S |
| Fairfield Col | 695 | path | Cockley Beck | Lake District S |
| Fell Head – Linghaw | 465 | path | Lowgill | Howgill Fells |
| Fellbarrow – Smithy Fell | 367 | | Low Lorton | Lake District NW |
| Flag Pots | 664 | path | Applethwaite | Lake District N |
| Floutern Pass | 410 | (path) | Croasdale | Lake District N |
| Flue Scarth | 639 | | Aisgill | Yorkshire Dales |
| Fothergill Head | 451 | (path) | Croasdale | Lake District W |
| Froswick | 633 | path | Hartsop | Lake District E |
| Garburn Pass / Garburn (or Garbourn) Nook | 447 | (path) | Kentmere | Lake District E |
| Gatescarth (or Gate Scarth) Pass | 583 | path | Sadgill | Lake District E |
| Gillercomb Head | 654 | path | Seathwaite (Borrowdale) | Lake District W |
| Goat's Hawse (or Hause) | 649 | path | Coniston | Lake District S |
| Green Castle – Knock Fell | 746 | track | Knock | North Pennines |
| Greenup Edge Pass | 610 | path | Stonethwaite | Lake District C |
| Grisedale Hause (or Hass) / Hause Gap / Horse Gap | 592 | path | Wythburn | Lake District E |
| **Hardknott (or Hard Knott) Pass** | 393 | **road** | Cockley Beck | Lake District S |
| **Hartside Pass / Hartside Cross** | 575 | **A road** | Haresceugh | North Pennines |
| Hause | 548 | (path) | Longlands | Lake District N |
| Hause | 471 | path | Bayles | North Pennines |
| The Hause | 310 | track | Oddendale | Shap Fells |
| **The Hause / Hause Head** | 383 | **road** | Wreay (Ullswater) | Lake District E |
| Hause Gap see Grisedale Hause | | | | |
| Hause Gate | 364 | path | Little Town | Lake District NW |
| Hause (or Hawse) Mouth | 508 | | Row | North Pennines |
| Haycock – Scoat Fell | 703 | (path) | Wasdale Head | Lake District W |
| High Crag – Dollywaggon Pike | 808 | path | Wythburn | Lake District E |
| High House | 662 | (path) | Seathwaite (Borrowdale) | Lake District S |
| High Raise – Rampsgill Head | 751 | (path) | Hartsop | Lake District E |
| Hindscarth | 656 | path | Gatesgarth | Lake District NW |
| Hobcarton Crag | 673 | (path) | Stair | Lake District NW |
| **Honister Hause** | 361 | **B road** | Seatoller | Lake District W/NW |
| **Horse House / Horsehouse** | 303 | **A road** | Forest Hall | Lake District E / Shap Fells |
| **Howtown Hause / The Hause** | 226 | **road** | Sandwick | Lake District E |
| Ill Crag Col | 882 | (path) | Wasdale Head | Lake District S |
| Keasgill Head | 655 | (path) | Dale Head | Lake District E |
| Kentmere Pike – Brown Howe | 691 | (path) | Sadgill | Lake District E |

| Latitude, Longitude | National Grid | Notes |
|---|---|---|
| 54.47432, -3.27481 | NY1748709522 | 'Le Mikeldor de Yowberg', 1322; 'Le Durre de Youbergh', 1338; sometimes written 'Door Head' |
| 54.48905, -2.97310 | NY3706110848 | |
| 54.51034, -3.21417 | NY2148613460 | The 'house' is not a 'hause' but the building which housed the winch of the slate quarry tramway |
| 54.63408, -2.45899 | NY7046926647 | |
| 54.46257, -3.18542 | NY2325808113 | 'Eskhals', 1242; 'Long Eske Hawse', 1540; 'Esk Horse', 1821 |
| 54.39623, -3.13272 | NY2655500675 | 'Fairfield' on maps; named by Wainwright; earlier name may survive in 'Doe House Gill' |
| 54.38056, -2.55621 | SD6397198483 | |
| 54.60294, -3.34334 | NY1332023915 | |
| 54.63565, -3.11673 | NY2801627298 | The 'pots' are deep pools |
| 54.54212, -3.36098 | NY1204917170 | Name in common use; not on maps |
| 54.35842, -2.37201 | SD7592295941 | Name survives in Flue Scarth Nick (the gully beneath the col) |
| 54.55835, -3.37014 | NY1149218987 | The source of Fother Gill |
| 54.47169, -2.87643 | NY4329908834 | Col name attributed to mountain?; see 'wick' in the Glossary |
| 54.43162, -2.87120 | NY4358204372 | 'Garburne Pass', 1719 |
| 54.47628, -2.81362 | NY4737509296 | 'Gate Scarth' on OS 1st edn; 'Goatscar, summit of the road from Hawes-water to Kendal' in T. West, A Guide to the Lakes (1778; 1821) |
| 54.49282, -3.21345 | NY2149911510 | Perhaps earlier 'Bradscarth' ('brad' = 'broad'): Transactions of the Cumberland & Westmorland Antiquarian & Archaeological Society (1920), p. 244 |
| 54.37452, -3.13143 | SD2660098258 | |
| 54.67668, -2.43986 | NY7046926647 | (Pennine Way); 'Green Castle' (a possible medieval earthwork) is closer to the col on OS 1st edn |
| 54.48517, -3.10392 | NY2858010542 | Name in common use; 'Greenup Edge' on maps; 'Grenehope', 1211 |
| 54.49628, -3.00649 | NY3490911683 | 'Grisedale Hass / Horse Gap' on OS 1st edn; sometimes 'Grizedale' in 19th c. |
| 54.40285, -3.18597 | NY2311001469 | (Roman road); 'Hardecnuut', c. 1210 ('hard craggy hill'); 'Wainscarth', 1242 ('wagon Gap') |
| 54.77041, -2.55137 | NY6462641860 | NCR 7 (C2C); the third-highest road col in England; café at summit |
| 54.68143, -3.10724 | NY2870932382 | Unnamed on maps; deduced from Hause Gill, which rises at the col |
| 54.80204, -2.47846 | NY6934045345 | Maiden Way (Roman road); deduced from Horse Edge (see Glossary) |
| 54.49904, -2.64467 | NY5834611715 | Not on maps; deduced from Hause Farm ('th'Hause House', 1719); coordinates are for the 'sheep creep' under the motorway (see p. 54) |
| 54.60366, -2.89411 | NY4234023533 | 'The Hawse' on OS 1st edn; second name attested 1741 |
| 54.56223, -3.17019 | NY2442919185 | |
| 54.72664, -2.54783 | NY6481536988 | |
| 54.48657, -3.31546 | NY1487910933 | |
| 54.51079, -3.01525 | NY3436513306 | Former Cumberland–Westmorland boundary |
| 54.47368, -3.17296 | NY2408509335 | Deduced from High House Tarn; not on 19th-c. OS; in view of the col, 'house' is probably a 'hause' rather than a ruined building |
| 54.51009, -2.85751 | NY4457613091 | (High Street Roman road) |
| 54.53059, -3.21409 | NY2153015713 | Not specifically named on maps; col name ('Pass of the Deer') attributed to the mountain |
| 54.58626, -3.25391 | NY1906421952 | |
| 54.51145, -3.19831 | NY2251513566 | 'Unnisterre', 1751; the summit of 'Honister Pass' |
| 54.42490, -2.69144 | NY5523603495 | See p. 52–3 |
| 54.56518, -2.87381 | NY4359819235 | 'The Horse' on OS 1st edn |
| 54.45723, -3.20314 | NY2209907538 | Not on maps; named by Wainwright; the highest col in England |
| 54.53609, -2.84748 | NY4526115977 | (High Street Roman road) |
| 54.46473, -2.82892 | NY4636908023 | |

| Name | Elevation (m) | Surface | Nearest place | Region |
|------|---------------|---------|---------------|--------|
| **Killhope Cross** | 623 | **A road** | Nenthead | North Pennines |
| **Kirkstone (or Kirk Stone) Pass** | 455 | **A road** | Ambleside | Lake District E |
| Leathgill Bridge | 518 | (track) | Low Haygarth | Howgill Fells |
| Levers Hawse | 682 | path | Cockley Beck | Lake District S |
| Lingmell Col | 735 | | Wasdale Head | Lake District S |
| Link Hause | 775 | path | Hartsop | Lake District E |
| Little Dun Fell – Great Dun Fell | 781 | (path) | Kirkland | North Pennines |
| Little Scoat Fell – Black Crag | 794 | path | Wasdale Head | Lake District W |
| Littledale Edge | 576 | path | Gatesgarth | Lake District NW |
| Long Doors | 399 | track | Little Crosthwaite | Lake District N |
| Lord's Seat – Ullister Hill | 491 | (path) | Thornthwaite | Lake District NW |
| Low Fell – Sourfoot Fell | 380 | path | Loweswater | Lake District NW |
| Lower Man – Whiteside Bank | 792 | path | Wythburn | Lake District E |
| Mickledore / Mickle Door | 831 | path | Wasdale Head | Lake District S |
| Moss Hause | 617 | | Wythburn | Lake District C |
| Mousthwaite Col | 435 | path | Scales | Lake District N |
| Nan Bield Pass | 629 | path | Sadgill | Lake District E |
| Nenthead Pass  see Killhope Cross | | | | |
| **Newlands Hause (or Pass)** | 333 | **road** | Buttermere | Lake District NW |
| Nick Head | 584 | path | Glenridding | Lake District E |
| Ore Gap / Ure Gap | 773 | path | Seathwaite (Borrowdale) | Lake District S |
| Pots of Ashness | 499 | path | Wasdale Head | Lake District W |
| Raise – Whiteside Bank | 821 | path | Wythburn | Lake District E |
| **Raise Gap / Pass of Dunmail Raise** | 238 | **A road** | Wythburn | Lake District C/E |
| Randygill Top – Kensgriff | 509 | | Low Haygarth | Howgill Fells |
| Rest Dodd – The Knott | 585 | | Hartsop | Lake District E |
| Roman Fell – Long Fell | 534 | | Hilton | North Pennines |
| Rossett Pass | 610 | path | Seathwaite (Borrowdale) | Lake District S |
| Saddle | 493 | (path) | Low Haygarth | Howgill Fells |
| The Saddle | 621 | path | Buttermere | Lake District W |
| Saddle Gate | 624 | path | Buttermere | Lake District NW |
| Saddle of Fells | 604 | | Deepdale | Whernside |
| Sail – Ard Crags | 462 | (path) | Little Town | Lake District NW |
| Sail Pass | 617 | path | Little Town | Lake District NW |
| Scandale Pass | 518 | path | Hartsop | Lake District E |
| The Scar | 755 | path | Little Town | Lake District NW |
| Scarth Gap | 445 | path | Gatesgarth | Lake District W |
| Seatallan – Middle Fell | 465 | (path) | Wasdale Head | Lake District W |
| Side Gates  see Blea Tarn Pass | | | | |
| Skiddaw – Little Man | 804 | | Millbeck | Lake District N |
| Spengill Head | 560 | track | Ravenstonedale | Howgill Fells |
| Stake Pass | 475 | path | Seathwaite (Borrowdale) | Lake District C |

| Latitude, Longitude | National Grid | Notes |
|---|---|---|
| 54.78351, -2.31356 | NY7993243224 | Co. Durham boundary; occasionally 'Nenthead Pass'; the highest road col in England and third-highest road col in the British Isles |
| 54.46607, -2.92486 | NY4015208249 | 'Kirkestain', 1184; 'The Rayse of Kyrkestone', 16th c.; 'Kirkstone Yeat', 1630; 'Kirkston-pass', 1778; 'the fork/Of these fraternal hills:/Where, save the rugged road, we find/No appanage of human kind,/No hint of man' (Wordsworth, 'The Pass of Kirkstone', 1820) |
| 54.39851, -2.48395 | NY6867800446 | 'Bridge' in the sense of 'col' |
| 54.38524, -3.12454 | SD2706699444 | Name from Levers Water and Leversdale |
| 54.46028, -3.21963 | NY2103607896 | Not on OS 50; the only col named 'col' on OS maps of England |
| 54.49396, -2.97933 | NY3666511400 | Not on OS 1st or 2nd edn; from Link Cove, the corrie to the north-east |
| 54.68884, -2.45466 | NY7078932739 | (Pennine Way) |
| 54.49234, -3.29424 | NY1626511549 | |
| 54.53416, -3.22687 | NY2071016124 | |
| 54.63590, -3.16418 | NY2495427376 | The name refers to Long Side fell |
| 54.62576, -3.22864 | NY2077326318 | |
| 54.59512, -3.33653 | NY1374323036 | |
| 54.53651, -3.02396 | NY3384316176 | Former Cumberland–Westmorland boundary |
| 54.45136, -3.21963 | NY2101906904 | 'Great Pass'; 'The two elevations of Scawfell and Scawfell Pike ... are separated by a fearful chasm, called Mickle-dore': *Black's Picturesque Tourist and Road-book of England and Wales* (1843), p. 255 |
| 54.51443, -3.08831 | NY2964113782 | Not on maps; deduced from Mosshause Gill |
| 54.64223, -3.01339 | NY3469627929 | Not on maps; named by Wainwright from Mousthwaite Comb |
| 54.47869, -2.84672 | NY4523309590 | 'Nan' may be 'nant' (valley); 'bield' (Scots) = 'shelter' or 'cattle fold'; it can also refer to the shelter provided by a hill |
| 54.54721, -3.24934 | NY1928217602 | 'Newland Hose', 1783 |
| 54.55498, -2.98751 | NY3623018197 | Not on OS 1st edn; 'The Nick' is a stream |
| 54.45433, -3.17277 | NY2406207182 | 'Orscarth', 1242; 'Pass of the Ore' (from the red stains of haematite) |
| 54.47077, -3.32403 | NY1429009185 | The 'pots' are deep pools |
| 54.54282, -3.02245 | NY3395116876 | Former Cumberland–Westmorland boundary |
| 54.49689, -3.04058 | NY3270211783 | Former Cumberland–Westmorland boundary; the 'raise' is a heap of stones said to mark the grave of Dunmail, the last king of Cumberland |
| 54.39241, -2.47784 | SD6907099764 | |
| 54.51139, -2.87595 | NY4338513251 | |
| 54.57499, -2.37041 | NY7615220038 | |
| 54.45783, -3.16335 | NY2467907562 | Former Cumberland–Westmorland boundary; not on maps; name in common use, referring both to the route and to the col summit |
| 54.38518, -2.48405 | SD6866198963 | |
| 54.52924, -3.29452 | NY1632215655 | |
| 54.56093, -3.26763 | NY1812619150 | |
| 54.23772, -2.45941 | SD7015582544 | Lancashire boundary; 'Saddle Fells' on OS 1st edn ('Yorkshire', 1853); the name has drifted away from the col on modern OS maps |
| 54.56874, -3.23231 | NY2042519978 | |
| 54.57323, -3.23249 | NY2042220478 | Not on maps; named by Wainwright; below Sail (a fell); distinct from Black Sail Pass |
| 54.47773, -2.94617 | NY3878809565 | Neither col nor pass on old OS |
| 54.57110, -3.24504 | NY1960720255 | |
| 54.50886, -3.25348 | NY1893813340 | 'Scarf Gapp', 1821; 'Scarf Gap', 1843 |
| 54.46086, -3.31522 | NY1484108072 | |
| 54.64237, -3.14025 | NY2651028070 | |
| 54.40088, -2.47133 | NY6949900704 | The main col might also be located to the south-west, at the head of Stockless Gill |
| 54.46890, -3.13535 | NY2651408764 | Former Cumberland–Westmorland boundary; Cumbria Way; 'The Stakes', 1823; 'Pass of the Stake', 1835 (Wordsworth); 'The Stake', mid 19th c.; the name probably refers to guide posts or snow poles |

| Name | Elevation (m) | Surface | Nearest place | Region |
|---|---|---|---|---|
| Standard Brow – Swarth Fell | 602 | | Aisgill | Yorkshire Dales |
| Starling Dodd – Little Dodd | 560 | path | Buttermere | Lake District W |
| Sticks Pass | 748 | path | Glenridding | Lake District E |
| Stile End Pass | 345 | track | Sadgill | Lake District E |
| Stone Hause / The Hause | 435 | (path) | Wythburn | Lake District C |
| Straits (or Straights) of Riggindale | 714 | path | Hartsop | Lake District E |
| Sty Head (or Styhead) Pass / The Sty / The Stee | 477 | path | Wasdale Head | Lake District S/W |
| Swallow Scarth | 862 | path | Wythburn | Lake District E |
| Sware | 423 | | High Lorton | Lake District NW |
| Swirl Hawse | 618 | path | Cockley Beck | Lake District S |
| Tees Head | 772 | (path) | Kirkland | North Pennines |
| Three Tarns Gap | 724 | (path) | Cockley Beck | Lake District S |
| Threshthwaite Mouth | 592 | path | Hartsop | Lake District E |
| Uskdale Gap | 255 | path | Little Langdale | Lake District S |
| **Wain Gap** | 263 | **road** | Kelleth | Lune Valley |
| Wainscarth  *see* Hardknott Pass | | | | |
| *Wandope Moss* | 722 | path | Buttermere | Lake District NW |
| **Whinlatter Pass** | 318 | **B road** | Thornthwaite | Lake District NW |
| *White Oak / Whiteoak* | 418 | | Croasdale | Lake District W |
| *Whoap – Lank Rigg* | 438 | (path) | Ennerdale Bridge | Lake District W |
| Widow Hause | 378 | | High Lorton | Lake District NW |
| *Wilson's Bield* | 505 | path | Seatoller | Lake District NW |
| Wind Gap | 755 | path | Wasdale Head | Lake District W |
| Windscarth Wyke | 554 | path | Lowgill | Howgill Fells |
| Windy Gap | 471 | track | Row | North Pennines |
| Windy Gap / Wind Yatt | 751 | path | Seathwaite (Borrowdale) | Lake District W |
| **Wrynose Pass (or Hawse)** | 393 | **road** | Cockley Beck | Lake District S |
| **Pass of Borrowdale** | 91 | **B road** | Grange | Lake District NW |
| **Shap** | 426 | **A road** | Bretherdale Head | Lake District E / Shap Fells |
| **Shap** | 316 | **motorway** | Oddendale | Shap Fells |
| **Stainmore Pass** | 439 | **A road** | Clove Lodge | North Pennines |
| Walna Scar Pass | 605 | path | Seathwaite (Furness) | Lake District S |

# Derbyshire · 10 cols 3 passes

| Name | Elevation (m) | Surface | Nearest place | Region |
|---|---|---|---|---|
| Ashop Head | 513 | path | Moorfield | Peak District |
| **Back Dale – North Cliff** | 206 | **B road** | Calver | Peak District |
| Backtor Nook | 400 | path | Edale | Peak District |
| **Chadwick Nick** | 217 | **road** | Crich | Amber Valley |
| **Curbar Bar Head / Curbar Gap** | 309 | **road** | Curbar | Peak District |

| Latitude, Longitude | National Grid | Notes |
|---|---|---|
| 54.37166, -2.38006 | SD7535697396 | |
| 54.52933, -3.32068 | NY1463015697 | |
| 54.55471, -3.01836 | NY3423518196 | Former Cumberland–Westmorland boundary; probably the same origin as Stake Pass (*see above*) |
| 54.43746, -2.80950 | NY4759204974 | Not on maps; 'Stile End Pass' attested 1929; 'Steel End', 1836; 'stile' is used for 'col' in Ireland |
| 54.52014, -3.07656 | NY3041214405 | Probably named for an erratic boulder |
| 54.50175, -2.86661 | NY4397612171 | High Street Roman road; 'Regendale', 1522 |
| 54.47495, -3.20676 | NY2189809514 | 'Edderlanghals', 1209–10 (meaning of 'edder' obscure); 'sty' from Old English 'stigan', 'to ascend' |
| 54.52109, -3.01669 | NY3428914453 | Former Cumberland–Westmorland boundary; the third-highest col in England |
| 54.62792, -3.28085 | NY1740726619 | Not on maps; deduced from Sware Gill |
| 54.39717, -3.11328 | NY2781900760 | At the foot of Swirl How; 'swirl' is obscure |
| 54.69813, -2.46782 | NY6994733778 | (Pennine Way); former Cumberland–Westmorland boundary; source of the Tees |
| 54.44429, -3.16025 | NY2485606052 | Former Cumberland–Westmorland boundary; not on maps; attested 1918; formerly Bowesscard, Bouescarth or Bouscard ('The Col of Bow Fell') |
| 54.48454, -2.88786 | NY4257610273 | Pronounced 'threshet' |
| 54.39883, -3.05297 | NY3173700884 | Caption at the col on OS 1st edn ('Lancashire', 1850) |
| 54.44889, -2.53480 | NY6541906075 | 'Gap (or pass) suitable for a carriage' |
| 54.57019, -3.26051 | NY1860520172 | 'Wanlope Moss' on OS 1st edn |
| 54.60949, -3.23158 | NY2055224511 | NCR 71 (C2C); 'Whynlater', 1505; 'Passes of Whinlate', 1794; 'whin' is 'gorse', or 'furze'; 'latter' is from Gaelic 'leitir', 'hillside' |
| 54.54700, -3.36493 | NY1180417718 | |
| 54.49807, -3.39746 | NY0959212315 | |
| 54.63034, -3.27128 | NY1803026877 | Perhaps on a 'corpse road', or 'coffin road' |
| 54.52771, -3.18648 | NY2331115362 | 'Bield' (Scots) = 'shelter' or 'cattle fold'; it can also refer to the shelter provided by a hill |
| 54.49412, -3.28595 | NY1680611738 | 'Wyndeyaterigg', 1338; 'Windy Gap' on Bartholomew, 'The Lake District' (1903) |
| 54.37925, -2.52948 | SD6570698324 | Former Westmorland–Yorkshire boundary; *see* 'wick' in Glossary |
| 54.71338, -2.54889 | NY6473635513 | Earlier name perhaps in nearby Hawse (or Hause) Crag |
| 54.48419, -3.21425 | NY2143010550 | Second name not on maps; 'yatt' = 'gate' |
| 54.41455, -3.11551 | NY2770402696 | (Roman road); by the Three Shire Stone (meeting of Lancashire and the former counties of Westmorland and Cumberland); 'Wreineshals' ('Raven Pass'), 1157–63 |
| 54.53999, -3.15814 | NY2516716697 | First attested 1778 |
| 54.45143, -2.68998 | NY5536006446 | Name in common use; memorial in lay-by; this crossing predates the following; earlier name perhaps in Hause Foot, 1000 m to the south; *see* p. 51 |
| 54.50192, -2.64510 | NY5832112036 | Name of village commonly applied to the pass; summit sign; coordinates are for 'Shap Summit', a name also applied to the railway summit; see also 'The Hause' (Shap Fells), and p. 53–4 |
| 54.50662, -2.16351 | NY8951012380 | Co. Durham boundary; Roman road; name in common use; 'Stainmore Gap' is a broad term used by geographers |
| 54.35834, -3.14270 | SD2583896470 | Name in common use; attested 1899 (Karl Baedeker, *Grossbritannien*); 'Walna' (once 'Walney') is the name of the fell |
| 53.40773, -1.90476 | SK0642890105 | Pennine Way; the source of the River Ashop |
| 53.25859, -1.64759 | SK2360673567 | |
| 53.36032, -1.78533 | SK1438484849 | Below Back Tor |
| 53.07505, -1.48181 | SK3481453216 | Name on sign in sewage treatment plant |
| 53.26854, -1.60795 | SK2624574688 | Not on maps; car park sign 'Curbar Gap'; earlier name attested 1933 ('bar' indicates the turnpike) |

| Name | Elevation (m) | Surface | Nearest place | Region |
|---|---|---|---|---|
| Edale Head (east of) | 533 | path | Barber Booth | Peak District |
| Hollins Cross | 392 | path | Edale | Peak District |
| **Mam Nick** | 455 | road | Barber Booth | Peak District |
| Oldgate Nick | 499 | path | Fernilee | Peak District |
| **Peep o Day** | 332 | **A road** | Chinley Head | Peak District |
| **Holme Pass (Holme Moss)** | 524 | **A road** | Holme | Peak District |
| **Snake Pass** | 512 | **A road** | Glossop | Peak District |
| **Winnats Pass** | 390 | **road** | Castleton | Peak District |

## Devon · 10 cols

| Name | Elevation (m) | Surface | Nearest place | Region |
|---|---|---|---|---|
| **Blackmoor Gate** | 278 | **A road** | Blackmoor Gate | Exmoor |
| **County Gate / Cosgates Feet** | 323 | **A road** | Malmsmead | Exmoor |
| Cox Tor – Great Staple Tor | 393 | (path) | Merrivale | Dartmoor |
| **Hallshot** | 202 | **road** | Cadbury | Exe Valley |
| Headland Warren | 427 | (path) | Warren House | Dartmoor |
| **Hemsworthy Gate** | 394 | **B road** | Widecombe in the Moor | Dartmoor |
| Hollow Head Cross | 219 | track | Coombe | Otter Valley |
| **Mockham Down Gate** | 267 | **A road** | Benton | Exmoor |
| Swyre? / Sourton Tors – Corn Ridge | 423 | track | Sourton | Dartmoor |
| **Yar Tor – Yartor Down** | 355 | **B road** | Dartmeet | Dartmoor |

## Dorset · 14 cols

| Name | Elevation (m) | Surface | Nearest place | Region |
|---|---|---|---|---|
| **Bare Cross / White Crossways / Cocknowle Gap** | 113 | **road** | East Creech | Purbeck Hills |
| **Corfe** | 85 | **road** | West Milton | Mangerton Valley |
| **Corfe Gate** | 97 | **road** | Portesham | South Dorset Downs |
| **Corfe Gate** | 89 | **road** | Portesham | South Dorset Downs |
| **Corfe Gate / East Gap** | 21 | **A road** | Corfe Castle | Purbeck Hills |
| **Corfe Gate / West Gap** | 15 | **road** | Corfe Castle | Purbeck Hills |
| **Dogbury Gate** | 190 | **A road** | Lyon's Gate | North Dorset Downs |
| Dorsetshire Gap / Dorset Gap | 225 | track | Folly | North Dorset Downs |
| **Eype Down – Quarry Hill** | 91 | **A road** | Symondsbury | Dorset Coast |
| **Lawford Sheard Gate** | 157 | **road** / track | Tyneham | Purbeck Hills |
| The Saddle | 141 | (path) | Seatown | Dorset Coast |
| **Swyre** | 70 | **B road** | Swyre | Dorset Coast |
| **Ulwell Gap / Forked Down End / Forked Down Bottom** | 62 | **road** | Ulwell | Isle of Purbeck |
| **Winyard's Gap** | 182 | **A road** | Chedington | North Dorset Downs |

| Latitude, Longitude | National Grid | Notes |
|---|---|---|
| 53.37181, -1.88006 | SK0807886112 | (Pennine Way); the cross and the unnamed col 350 m to the east both lie on a parish boundary |
| 53.35735, -1.79730 | SK1358884516 | The name may originally have referred to the crossing of the ridge on the 'coffin road' to Hope Church; no cross survives |
| 53.34771, -1.81373 | SK1249883440 | Not on maps, though some show 'Mam Nick Car Park' |
| 53.28373, -2.00821 | SJ9955076306 | Cheshire boundary; earlier name perhaps 'Holegate'; often misattributed to the summit of the B road 500 m to the north |
| 53.36204, -1.92838 | SK0486485021 | (Pennine Bridleway); 'Hills House' on OS 1st and 2nd edn; perhaps an echo of earlier name in Highgate Road to the north |
| 53.52961, -1.85623 | SE0962803671 | West Yorkshire boundary; 'Holme Pass' is commonly used but shown only on Michelin maps; Tour de France 2014, Stage 2 |
| 53.43290, -1.86891 | SK0880792910 | Pennine Way; 'Snake Road' on OS 25 (1955) |
| 53.34254, -1.80493 | SK1308582867 | 'Le Wyndeyates', 1330; 'The Winyate Mouth', 1688; the coordinates are for Winnats Head |
| 51.17189, -3.93699 | SS6468343189 | 'Blackmire Yatt', 1782 |
| 51.22405, -3.72884 | SS7937048627 | Somerset boundary; also 'Cosgate' and 'Cosgates Feet Gate'; 'Corsnestake', 1279; 'Corneseyete', 1298 |
| 50.56746, -4.06784 | SX5365476232 | 'Cockestorre', 1618: the prefix 'cock' is occasionally associated with a col (see Glossary) |
| 50.83367, -3.53691 | SS9186604919 | Not on modern OS; 'Halsholte', 1291, from Old Norse 'hals' (see Glossary) |
| 50.61304, -3.85386 | SX6893380899 | |
| 50.57101, -3.77825 | SX7417076095 | 'Aylmesworthy', 1379 |
| 50.71696, -3.25896 | SY1121891571 | East Devon Way; 'Berrdescumbes Heafod', 1061 |
| 51.11039, -3.90813 | SS6652336298 | 'Mockam Down Gate' on OS 1903 revision |
| 50.68786, -4.05961 | SX5460989603 | 'Swuran Tune', c. 970; 'Sourton' preserves the name 'swyre' |
| 50.54461, -3.86289 | SX6810373307 | Spot height on OS 10 (376 m) incorrect |
| 50.63846, -2.09932 | SY9307382090 | 'Bere Cross', 1888; 'White Crossways' used in 1768; for 'Cocknowle' see 'cock' in Glossary; OS shows only 'Bere Cross' or 'Bare Cross'; not on OS 25 or 50; 'Cocknowle Gap' is a geographers' term |
| 50.75802, -2.71498 | SY4966595624 | Deduced from Corfe Farm; see 'corfe' in Glossary |
| 50.66859, -2.51594 | SY6363585563 | Jubilee Trail; see note to Corfe Gate below |
| 50.66938, -2.52488 | SY6300485655 | Jubilee Trail; deduced from Corfe Gate House and Coryates ('on corf getes westran cotan', 1024), and Corton ('Corfetone', 1086); one side of a twin col; see 'corfe' in Glossary, and p. 33 |
| 50.64046, -2.05739 | SY9603882309 | (NCR 2); (Purbeck Way); see note to Corfe Gate/West Gap below; 'East Gap' attested 1860; see p. 32 |
| 50.64084, -2.06063 | SY9580982352 | (NCR 2); (Purbeck Way); not on maps; 'Corfes Geat', 10th c.; also deduced from name of Corfe Castle between the two 'cuts'; see 'corfe' in Glossary; 'West Gap' attested 1860; see p. 32; the lowest col in England |
| 50.84564, -2.48993 | ST6560305239 | See p. 34 (Thomas Hardy, 'Life and Death at Sunrise, near Dogbury Gate, 1867') |
| 50.82711, -2.36553 | ST7435103127 | Wessex Ridgeway; there is a 'visitors' book' at the col: see p. 34 |
| 50.73185, -2.79963 | SY4353992679 | |
| 50.62911, -2.16869 | SY8816581059 | 'Lawford Share Gate', 1888; not on OS 25 or 50; 'sheard' is from Old English 'sceard' ('gap', 'cleft'); 'Lawford' may contain Old English 'hlaw' ('hill') and 'ford' in the sense of 'col' or 'crossing' |
| 50.72748, -2.83832 | SY4092792325 | South West Coast Path; not on maps; 'The Saddle, a col between Golden Cap and Langdon Hill' (National Trust purchase, 1974) |
| 50.69136, -2.67028 | SY5275188182 | 'Suere', 1086; 'Swuore', 1280; the village is named after the col |
| 50.63068, -1.97578 | SZ0180981220 | Purbeck Way; not on OS 25 or 50; name 'from the twin-spurred shape of the chalk ridge where it dips to form a Gap': A.D. Mills, The Place-Names of Dorset (1977) |
| 50.85277, -2.72411 | ST4912406167 | Monarch's Way; 'Winiards Gap', 1811; 'Wynyard's Gap' (Thomas Hardy, 'A Trampwoman's Tragedy' (1902)); see p. 34 |

| Name | Elevation (m) | Surface | Nearest place | Region |
|------|---------------|---------|---------------|--------|

## Durham · 3 cols  2 passes

| Name | Elevation (m) | Surface | Nearest place | Region |
|------|---------------|---------|---------------|--------|
| **Killhope Cross** | 623 | **A road** | Nenthead | North Pennines |
| **Scarsike Head** | 539 | road | Rookhope | Teesdale |
| **Swinhope Head** | 609 | road | Forest-in-Teesdale | Weardale |
| **Harthope Head / Harthope Pass** | 627 | road | St John's Chapel | Weardale |
| **Stainmore Pass** | 439 | **A road** | Clove Lodge | North Pennines |

## Gloucestershire · 3 cols

| Name | Elevation (m) | Surface | Nearest place | Region |
|------|---------------|---------|---------------|--------|
| **Freezinghill Lane** | 164 | road | Beach | Cotswold Hills |
| **Hydegate** | 143 | road | Uley | Cotswold Hills |
| **Whiteleaved Oak** | 133 | road | Chase End Street | Malvern Hills |

## Hampshire · 3 cols

| Name | Elevation (m) | Surface | Nearest place | Region |
|------|---------------|---------|---------------|--------|
| Beacon Pass | 188 | track | Old Burghclere | Hampshire Downs |
| **Butser Hill** | 152 | **A road** | Buriton | South Downs |
| Khyber Pass | 127 | (track) | The Common | Broughton Down |

## Herefordshire · 13 cols

| Name | Elevation (m) | Surface | Nearest place | Region |
|------|---------------|---------|---------------|--------|
| **Cockyard** | 143 | road | Whitfield | Grey Valley |
| *Coldridge* | 144 | (track) | Lea | Forest of Dean |
| **Cowleigh Gate** | 146 | **B road** | Storridge | Malvern Hills |
| **Dinedor Cross** | 102 | road | Twyford Common | Dinedor Hill |
| The Gullet / The Gullet Pass | 204 | track | Hollybush | Malvern Hills |
| **Harley's Mountain – The Warren** | 295 | road | Stapleton | Welsh Borders |
| *Hergest Ridge – Hanter Hill* | 347 | track | Dolyhir | Hergest Ridge |
| **Hollybush Pass** | 153 | **A road** | Hollybush | Malvern Hills |
| **Kerry's Gate** | 156 | road | Kerry's Gate | Golden Valley |
| *Whiteleaved Oak* | 133 | road | Chase End Street | Malvern Hills |
| **Whitman's Hill** | 126 | **A road** | Storridge | Malvern Hills |
| **Wyche Cutting** | 258 | **B road** | Upper Wyche | Malvern Hills |
| **Wynds Point** | 236 | **A road** | Little Malvern | Malvern Hills |

## Isle of Man · 11 cols

| Name | Elevation (m) | Surface | Nearest place | Region |
|------|---------------|---------|---------------|--------|
| **Baarney Skeddan / Round Table** | 308 | **A road** | Ronague | Isle of Man |
| **Black Hut / Stonebreakers' Hut** | 420 | **A road** | Glen Mona | Isle of Man |
| **Braaid** | 138 | **A road** | Braaid | Isle of Man |
| **The Braaid** | 345 | **B road** | Injebreck | Isle of Man |
| **Bungalow** | 410 | **A road** | Laxey | Isle of Man |
| *Carn Vuel* | 320 | track | Ravensdale | Isle of Man |
| **Carnane Bane** | 425 | **A road** | Injebreck | Isle of Man |
| **Injebreck Hill – Slieau Maggle** | 399 | **B road** | Injebreck | Isle of Man |
| *Sartfell – Slieau Freoaghane* | 407 | track | Barregarrow | Isle of Man |

| Latitude, Longitude | National Grid | Notes |
|---|---|---|
| 54.78351, -2.31356 | NY7993243224 | Cumbria boundary; the highest road col in England and third-highest road col in the British Isles |
| 54.76698, -2.13981 | NY9110341348 | In view of the col, 'scar' was perhaps 'scarth' (*see* Glossary) |
| 54.69361, -2.15883 | NY8986033186 | A Pennine Journey; below Dora's Seat, which was probably 'Dore's Seat', 'hill of the Pass'; the second-highest road col in England and fourth-highest road col in the British Isles |
| 54.70997, -2.21501 | NY8624435016 | |
| 54.50662, -2.16351 | NY8951012380 | Cumbria boundary; Roman road; name in common use; 'Stainmore Gap' is a broad term used by geographers |
| | | |
| 51.43615, -2.39818 | ST7241870869 | |
| 51.68682, -2.32027 | ST7795698722 | Below Uley Bury hill fort; from Old English 'hid' (a land measure); 'gate' in the sense of 'pass' |
| 52.02119, -2.35105 | SO7600835922 | Herefordshire and Worcestershire boundaries; (Three Choirs Way); 'Whiteleaf'd Oak', 1830; *see* p. 37 |
| | | |
| 51.31605, -1.35183 | SU4527057637 | Between Beacon Hill and Sidown Hill; first attested 1877 (OS 1st edn) |
| 50.97404, -0.97235 | SU7224819905 | The cutting predates the A road |
| 51.10286, -1.60748 | SU2757933802 | 'Khyber Pass Plantation' first shown on OS in 1910; earlier name unknown |
| | | |
| 52.00095, -2.85797 | SO4119633959 | For the name, *see* 'cock' in Glossary |
| 51.89391, -2.47408 | SO6747321812 | |
| 52.13105, -2.35889 | SO7553048144 | Earlier name 'Cowelsyate' survives in 'Cowleigh Gate Farm'; the northern limit of Malvern Chase; 'yate' in the names of other Malvern cols suggests 'pass' rather than 'gate'; *see* p. 36 |
| 52.01891, -2.70138 | SO5196535842 | Perhaps originally referring to the col or 'crossing' rather than to a cross |
| 52.04002, -2.35654 | SO7564138018 | Three Choirs Way; 'Swyn geat', 972; 'Swyneyate', 1577–8; 'The Gullet' on OS; 'Gullet Pass' in common use since 1884 |
| 52.31050, -2.98229 | SO3312868497 | (Herefordshire Trail) |
| 52.20451, -3.09296 | SO2540656817 | Welsh border (Powys) |
| 52.02980, -2.35154 | SO7597936879 | Three Choirs Way; 45 m from Worcestershire boundary; 'Shakellyate', 1577–8; modern name first attested 1865 |
| 51.99538, -2.88605 | SO3926133363 | Roman road |
| 52.02119, -2.35105 | SO7600835922 | Gloucestershire and Worcestershire boundaries; (Three Choirs Way); 'Whiteleaf'd Oak', 1830; *see* p. 37 |
| 52.13383, -2.37440 | SO7447048458 | |
| 52.09136, -2.33828 | SO7692043722 | Worcestershire boundary; 'Baldeyate', 1577–8; the col is natural but exaggerated by the cutting; *see* p. 38 |
| 52.06155, -2.34706 | SO7630340409 | Worcestershire boundary; Three Choirs Way; misplaced on OS 25; 'Windiat' (i.e. 'Windgate'), 1278; 'Brustenyate', 1577–8; 'Wind's Point', 1865 |
| | | |
| 54.14849, -4.68619 | SC2466175853 | On maps as 'Bayr ('road') ny Skeddan' but probably 'baarney' ('gap') |
| 54.26741, -4.44903 | SC4060688518 | TT Course |
| 54.15456, -4.57446 | SC3198276257 | NCR 1; 'Gullet' |
| 54.24815, -4.54086 | SC3455086588 | 'The Gullet' |
| 54.25124, -4.46309 | SC3962886752 | TT Course |
| 54.27726, -4.54695 | SC3427089839 | Cairn thus captioned on OS 1st edn |
| 54.24266, -4.47199 | SC3901585818 | TT Course |
| 54.24404, -4.53247 | SC3508086110 | |
| 54.25597, -4.54772 | SC3413487473 | |

| Name | Elevation (m) | Surface | Nearest place | Region |
|---|---|---|---|---|
| **The Sloc** | 205 | **A road** | Lingague | Isle of Man |
| **Windy Corner** | 372 | **A road** | Injebreck | Isle of Man |

## Isle of Wight · 1 col

| Name | Elevation (m) | Surface | Nearest place | Region |
|---|---|---|---|---|
| *Cheverton Shute – Shorwell Shute* | 106 | **B road** | Shorwell | Isle of Wight |

## Lancashire · 10 cols 1 pass

| Name | Elevation (m) | Surface | Nearest place | Region |
|---|---|---|---|---|
| **Castle Shore** | 382 | **motorway** | Lydgate | South Pennines |
| *Cowpe Lowe – Black Hill* | 405 | track | Cowpe | South Pennines |
| Hard Hill Top | 416 | track | Botton Head | Forest of Bowland |
| **Hordern Stoops** | 326 | road | Belmont | South Pennines |
| **Nick O' Thungs / Annel (or Hannell) Cross** | 323 | road | Twiston | Forest of Pendle |
| **Nick of Pendle** | 305 | road | Sabden | Forest of Pendle |
| Saddle of Fells | 604 | | Deepdale | Whernside |
| **Trough Gate** | 295 | **A road** | Trough Gate | South Pennines |
| **Trough of Bowland** | 295 | road | Sykes | Forest of Bowland |
| **Widdop Gap / Widdop Cross** | 392 | road | Thursden | South Pennines |
| **Cross of Greet** | 427 | **road** | Botton Head | Forest of Bowland |

## Greater London · 1 col

| Name | Elevation (m) | Surface | Nearest place | Region |
|---|---|---|---|---|
| **Sydenham Rise** | 77 | **A road** | Forest Hill | Norwood Ridge |

## Greater Manchester · 4 cols 2 passes

| Name | Elevation (m) | Surface | Nearest place | Region |
|---|---|---|---|---|
| **Cherry Top** | 344 | **A road** | Denshaw | South Pennines |
| *Dick Hill – Town Hill* | 273 | path | Newhey | South Pennines |
| Low Gate | 339 | track | Denshaw | South Pennines |
| **Roe Cross** | 256 | road | Roe Cross | South Pennines |
| **Standedge Pass** | 387 | **A road** | Bleak Hey Nook | Peak District |
| **Summit Pass (or Gap)** | 187 | **A road** | Summit | South Pennines |

## Northumberland · 33 cols

| Name | Elevation (m) | Surface | Nearest place | Region |
|---|---|---|---|---|
| Aucopswire | 477 | path | Sourhope | Cheviot Hills |
| Bittlestonegate | 463 | | Byrness | Redesdale Forest |
| Black Halls / Black Hass / Black Haus | 446 | path | Makendon | Cheviot Hills |
| Blakehope Nick | 457 | track | Byrness | Redesdale Forest |

| Latitude, Longitude | National Grid | Notes |
|---|---|---|
| 54.12521, -4.73063 | SC2166073375 | 'Gully' or 'defile': see Glossary |
| 54.23080, -4.47003 | SC3909684494 | TT Course |
| | | |
| 50.65169, -1.35402 | SZ4576483755 | Worsley Trail; a 'shute' is a steep hill |
| | | |
| 53.62918, -2.03095 | SD9805014739 | West Yorkshire boundary; (Pennine Way); for historical accuracy, the coordinates indicate the central reservation of the M62 motorway, on the county boundary; this was the original route of the Pennine Way, now shifted east to cross the motorway on a footbridge at 53.62934, -2.02650; original name deduced from Castle Shore Hill and Castle Shore Clough, which rises at the col (as Red Shore in Wiltshire, a gap in the Wansdyke, formerly Reddscherd and Read Geat); see 'sheard' in Glossary |
| 53.67991, -2.26278 | SD8274020415 | Pennine Bridleway / Rossendale Way |
| 54.01163, -2.50824 | SD6679157410 | Roman road; caption closer to col on OS 1st edn and OS 50 |
| 53.63807, -2.52335 | SD6549415855 | A 'staup' (from Old Norse) is a steep drop |
| 53.87938, -2.27678 | SD8190242612 | First name not on maps; col name 'Nick o' Thungs' later attributed to a gathering on the first Sunday in May; see p. 24 |
| 53.84291, -2.34851 | SD7716638575 | On the old pack-horse trail from Clitheroe to Sabden; 'I opine that the drovers from the forest [of Pendle] – the drivers of strings of gals [Galloway ponies] with lime sacks o'er the nick of Pendle – are better customers to Betty than tramps and poachers': J. P. Kay-Shuttleworth, Scarsdale, I (1860), 117. |
| 54.23772, -2.45941 | SD7015582544 | Cumbria boundary; 'Saddle Fells' on OS 1st edn ('Yorkshire', 1853); the name has drifted away from the col on modern OS maps |
| 53.68929, -2.17440 | SD8858021441 | 'Le Trogh' or 'Troghbrok', 14th c. |
| 53.97207, -2.57693 | SD6225453043 | 'Trogh', 1343; at the Grey Stone of Trough (on the former boundary of Lancashire and the West Riding) |
| 53.80008, -2.13070 | SD9148933761 | NCR 68; Burnley Way; not on modern OS; a nearby stream, Yoke Syke, may preserve an earlier name; before it was used for road repairs in the 19th c., the cross marked the col summit and the Yorkshire–Lancashire boundary, which now lies a short distance to the east |
| 54.04252, -2.48661 | SD6823260837 | Probably referring to the 'crossing' rather than the boundary cross (a local name is 'Top of t' Cross'); 'The Cross of Grete' on J. Speed, 'The Countie Pallatine of Lancaster' (1610) |
| | | |
| 51.44059, -0.06201 | TQ3479173070 | (Green Chain Walk); see pp. 31, 92 |
| | | |
| 53.59703, -2.05721 | SD9631111163 | (Oldham Way); on modern OS only as 'Cherry Top Farm' |
| 53.61631, -2.07392 | SD9520713309 | Pennine Bridleway / Rochdale Way |
| 53.58847, -2.01779 | SD9892010210 | Oldham Way |
| 53.46604, -2.02283 | SJ9858296589 | On the adjacent A road, the col (247 m) is at 53.46617, -2.02373 |
| 53.58309, -1.97027 | SE0206609612 | West Yorkshire boundary; Standedge Trail / Pennine Way; attested 1891; name in common use |
| 53.66591, -2.08235 | SD9465618828 | NCR 66; Pennine Bridleway; unnamed on maps but commonly used in reference to canal and railway |
| | | |
| 55.47443, -2.19214 | NT8795220084 | Scottish border; Pennine Way; not on maps; identified from 'The passages of the Scottes all along Rydsdayle' (1597), and from place names Auchope Cairn and Auchope Rig |
| 55.30268, -2.41698 | NT7362501033 | Deduced from Bittlestonegate Cairn |
| 55.38989, -2.33494 | NT7888010710 | Scottish border; (Roman road: Dere Street); (Pennine Way); shifted south on OS 10 and 25; 'Black Haus' on Roy's Military Survey of Scotland (1752–5); 'Black Hass' on OS 1st edn |
| 55.27860, -2.45419 | NY7124598368 | Spot height on OS 25 (434 m) incorrect; name on stone monument; pronounced 'blackup' |

| Name | Elevation (m) | Surface | Nearest place | Region |
|------|---------------|---------|---------------|--------|
| Broadhope Hill – Preston Hill | 420 | track | Langleeford | Cheviot Hills |
| Busy Gap | 271 | path | Thorngrafton | Hadrian's Wall |
| Busy Gap | 248 | | Raechester | Wansbeck Valley |
| Carter Bar *see Redeswire* | | | | |
| Castle Nick | 256 | track | Henshaw | Hadrian's Wall |
| Cat Stairs | 256 | track | Henshaw | Hadrian's Wall |
| **Caw Gap** | 239 | **road** | Melkridge | Hadrian's Wall |
| Foulstep | 468 | (path) | Langleeford | Cheviot Hills |
| Harpath | 583 | (path) | Langleeford | Cheviot Hills |
| Hetha Swyre / Hethouswyre | 228 | track | Hethpool | Cheviot Hills |
| Hole Gap | 180 | track | Haltwhistle | Hadrian's Wall |
| Humbleton Swyre | 315 | | Yetholm Mains | Cheviot Hills |
| Kingscrag Gate | 263 | track | Thorngrafton | (Hadrian's Wall) |
| Maiden Cross | 536 | path | Sourhope | Cheviot Hills |
| Midway Nick | 320 | | North Yardhope | Cheviot Hills |
| Milking Gap | 245 | track | Thorngrafton | Hadrian's Wall |
| Peel Gap | 250 | path | Henshaw | Hadrian's Wall |
| Randy's Gap | 506 | path | Sourhope | Cheviot Hills |
| Rapishaw Gap | 300 | path | Thorngrafton | Hadrian's Wall |
| **Redeswire / Carter Bar** | 418 | **A road** | Huntford | Cheviot Hills |
| Robb's Cross | 477 | | Singdean | Wauchope Forest |
| Salters Road (Bush Knowe – Shill Moor) | 423 | track | Prendwick | Cheviot Hills |
| Spithope Nick (or Neuk) | 427 | (track) | Catcleugh | Cheviot Hills |
| Swinlaw Gap | 430 | (path) | Blindburn | Cheviot Hills |
| Sycamore Gap | 254 | path | Henshaw | Hadrian's Wall |
| Thorny Doors | 220 | track | Haltwhistle | Hadrian's Wall |
| Walltown Nick | 230 | track | Greenhead | Hadrian's Wall |
| Whitelaw Nick / White Swire | 385 | path | Kirk Yetholm | Cheviot Hills |
| Wideopen Head | 358 | path | Hethpool | Cheviot Hills |
| Windy Gyle | 540 | path | Blindburn | Cheviot Hills |

| Latitude, Longitude | National Grid | Notes |
|---|---|---|
| 55.50624, -2.11526 | NT9281823613 | |
| 55.01973, -2.31649 | NY7986269511 | Pennine Way; not on OS 25 or 50; 'King's Wicket' nearby on OS 25; see p. 58 |
| 55.17780, -2.02542 | NY9847987056 | Perhaps originally 'Bushy Gap' |
| 55.00367, -2.37585 | NY7605767743 | Pennine Way; not on OS 25 or 50; the 'castle' is Roman milecastle 39; see pp. 10, 60 |
| 55.00335, -2.37893 | NY7586067708 | Pennine Way; not on OS 25 or 50; sometimes 'Cat's Stairs' |
| 54.99588, -2.42824 | NY7270166895 | Pennine Way |
| 55.43541, -2.15238 | NT9045615735 | (Salter's Road); deduced from 'Foulstep Sike ', the name of two streams, one on either side of the col |
| 55.46282, -2.14466 | NT9095118784 | Deduced from Harpath Sike; perhaps 'army road'; 'path' as in Windy Path col, also in the Cheviots |
| 55.53578, -2.19680 | NT8767726913 | Not on maps; identified from boundary description in Chartulary of Melros (13th c.); name survives in Hetha Burn and Great Hetha |
| 54.99371, -2.44617 | NY7155266661 | Pennine Way |
| 55.54483, -2.23225 | NT8544327927 | Scottish border |
| 55.03144, -2.32455 | NY7935370817 | Misplaced to east on modern OS |
| 55.43537, -2.21331 | NT8660115741 | Scottish border; Pennine Way; not on modern maps; location uncertain, deduced from surveys (e.g. 'ingates and passages forth of Scotland', 1543) and maps (from 1633); 'Mayden Crosse', 1543 (probably 'meadhon', 'middle') |
| 55.31338, -2.13953 | NT9124202153 | The col stands on a parish boundary; there is no other obvious reason for the name |
| 55.00558, -2.35955 | NY7710167950 | Pennine Way; not on OS 25 or 50; name from former milking sheds |
| 55.00142, -2.38701 | NY7534267496 | (NCR 68); Pennine Way; not on OS; name from a medieval pele tower; the two 'slacks' to the west – Green Slack and Lodhams Slack – are shallow gullies rather than cols (see Glossary) |
| 55.44551, -2.19414 | NT8781716866 | Scottish border; Pennine Way; probably from Scots 'randy' or 'randie' ('rough', 'aggressive', used especially of beggars) |
| 55.01174, -2.34411 | NY7809268630 | Pennine Way; not on OS 25 or 50; name obscure |
| 55.35434, -2.47764 | NT6981306806 | Scottish border; 'Rid Square' (or 'Squire'), 'The Read Squire', 'Reidswire', 'Reed Swire', 'Red Swire' or 'Redswire'; 'Carter Barr' on N. Tennant, 'Map of the County of Roxburgh' (1840); 'Carter Bar' on Bartholomew, 'Cheviots' (1912) and OS 1 (1926); 'bar' indicates the turnpike; battle site, 1400 and 7 July 1575 |
| 55.31761, -2.55794 | NT6468902757 | Scottish border; not on modern maps; location uncertain, deduced from surveys (e.g. 'Ingates and passages forth of Scotland', 1543) and maps (from 1633); 'Robbes Crosse', 1543; 'Robb' is unknown and there is no cross (and perhaps never was); see 'cross' in Glossary |
| 55.42582, -2.09091 | NT9434414661 | Also 'Salter's Road' |
| 55.35698, -2.36665 | NT7685207057 | Scottish border; 'Spitthope Nick' on Roy's Military Survey of Scotland (1752–5), and on no other map; 'Spitupunk' in 'The passages of the Scottes all along Rydsdayle' (1597); 'Spiddop Nuke' in 'Survey of the Debatable and Border Lands' (1604); the col summit lies 18 m south of the present border |
| 55.40819, -2.32069 | NT7979212742 | Scottish border; (Pennine Way); not on OS; the col and its name are recorded only on Roy's Military Survey of Scotland (1752–5) |
| 55.00356, -2.37394 | NY7617967730 | Pennine Way; not on OS; attested late 19th c.; see pp. 11, 60 |
| 54.99522, -2.43650 | NY7217266825 | Pennine Way |
| 54.99333, -2.50150 | NY6801266642 | Pennine Way; not on OS; sometimes counted as one of the Nine Nicks of Thirlwall |
| 55.52961, -2.23323 | NT8537626233 | Scottish border; Pennine Way; 'White Swire' not on maps but in various surveys of the border, e.g. 'White Swyer' in 1543 |
| 55.53225, -2.22220 | NT8607326525 | Former Scottish border; 'Wide Open' is the name of the burn which rises at the col |
| 55.43153, -2.23909 | NT8496815319 | Scottish border; Pennine Way; the name, shown as 'Windygyle' in W. Crawford, 'Map Embracing Extensive Portions [...]' (1843), is misattached to the hill – correctly 'Windgate Fell' (N. Tennant, 'Map of the County of Roxburgh', 1840) or 'Windygate Hill' (OS, 'Roxburghshire', 1863); the col is near the head of Gyle Burn and Windy Rig; 'Windy Gyle Swire', 1604; sometimes confused with Cocklawgate or Hexpethgate |

| Name | Elevation (m) | Surface | Nearest place | Region |
|------|---------------|---------|---------------|--------|

## Shropshire · 10 cols

| Name | Elevation (m) | Surface | Nearest place | Region |
|------|---------------|---------|---------------|--------|
| Burwarton Pole | 449 | track | Burwarton | Clee Hills |
| Barrister's Plain | 405 | path | Minton | The Long Mynd |
| **Bwlch** | 299 | **road** | Purlogue | Teme Valley |
| Bwlch | 291 | track | Llawnt | North Shropshire |
| **Bwlch** | 275 | **road** | Llanfair Waterdine | Teme Valley |
| Cefn Gunthly – Heath Mynd | 353 | (track) | Linley | Shropshire Hills |
| **Dog and Duck** | 356 | **road** | Mainstone | Edenhope Hill |
| Grindle Hollow | 368 | (path) | Minton | The Long Mynd |
| **Holloway Mouth** | 115 | **A road** | Wixhill | North Shropshire |
| Yearlet | 411 | path | Church Stretton | The Long Mynd |

## Somerset · 18 cols 1 pass

| Name | Elevation (m) | Surface | Nearest place | Region |
|------|---------------|---------|---------------|--------|
| **Buncombe Hill** | 225 | **road** | Courtway | Quantock Hills |
| **Comer's Cross** | 351 | **B road** | Withypool | Exmoor |
| **County Gate / Cosgates Feet** | 323 | **A road** | Malmsmead | Exmoor |
| Court Hill – Norton's Wood | 102 | track | Walton in Gordano | Failand Ridge |
| **East Clevedon Gap / Cleve** | 16 | **B road** | Clevedon | Failand Ridge |
| Exe Head | 457 | path | Simonsbath | Exmoor |
| **Girt (or Gurt) Goyle** | 131 | **road** | Sutton Montis | South Somerset |
| Halsway / Halsway Post | 316 | track | Halsway | Quantock Hills |
| Limebreach Wood – Cadbury Camp | 93 | track | Tickenham | Failand Ridge |
| **Marshall's Elm crossroads** | 63 | **B road** | Compton Dundon | Polden Hills |
| **Park End** | 251 | **road** | Cothelstone | Quantock Hills |
| **The Rhodyate** | 53 | **A road** | Banwell | Mendip Hills |
| **Rhodyate Hill** | 66 | **A road** | Congresbury | North Somerset |
| **Shipham Gorge** | 174 | **road** | Shipham | Mendip Hills |
| **Shute Shelve** | 76 | **A road** | Winscombe | Mendip Hills |
| Tickenham Hill – Cadbury Camp | 88 | track | Tickenham | Failand Ridge |
| **Triscombe Stone** | 321 | **road** / track | Triscombe | Quantock Hills |
| **West's Grave Batch** | 27 | **road** | Yarley | Axe Valley |
| **Pass of St Kew** | 84 | **road** / path | Kewstoke | Worlebury Hill |

## Staffordshire · 3 cols

| Name | Elevation (m) | Surface | Nearest place | Region |
|------|---------------|---------|---------------|--------|
| **Nick i' th' Hill** | 219 | **road** / track | Biddulph | Congleton Edge |
| **Rednick / Red Nick** | 210 | **road** / track | Freehay | Staffordshire Moorlands |
| Windygates / Windygates Gap | 343 | path | Upper Hulme | The Roaches |

## Surrey · 1 col

| Name | Elevation (m) | Surface | Nearest place | Region |
|------|---------------|---------|---------------|--------|
| Windy Gap / Cockshot Hollow | 250 | track | Coldharbour | Leith Hill |

## Sussex · 4 cols

| Name | Elevation (m) | Surface | Nearest place | Region |
|------|---------------|---------|---------------|--------|
| Beacon Hill – Pen Hill | 191 | (track) | Elsted | South Downs |
| **Clayton Gap** | 141 | **A road** | Clayton | South Downs |

| Latitude, Longitude | National Grid | Notes |
| --- | --- | --- |
| 52.46452, -2.59482 | SO5968585342 | Shropshire Way; *see* 'pole' in Glossary |
| 52.52951, -2.84769 | SO4259192742 | |
| 52.38491, -3.07457 | SO2696076863 | Name attributed to farm (now Bwlch Farm) |
| 52.86007, -3.10727 | SJ2554729750 | (Offa's Dyke Path) |
| 52.39302, -3.11804 | SO2401677810 | |
| 52.54499, -2.98496 | SO3330294582 | |
| 52.49902, -3.07854 | SO2687989559 | Welsh border (Powys); 'Dog and Duck Cottage' on modern OS |
| 52.52444, -2.84047 | SO4307492173 | |
| 52.84823, -2.66230 | SJ5549328064 | Roman road?; not on OS; 'Holloway-mouth', 1829 |
| 52.53819, -2.83539 | SO4343693698 | |

| Latitude, Longitude | National Grid | Notes |
| --- | --- | --- |
| 51.08986, -3.13349 | ST2071232894 | |
| 51.10758, -3.62962 | SS8601135517 | 'Cross' referring to the col or 'crossing', perhaps to the crossroads |
| 51.22405, -3.72884 | SS7937048627 | Devon boundary; also 'Cosgate' and 'Cosgates Feet Gate'; 'Cornestake', 1279; 'Cornesyete', 1298 |
| 51.44619, -2.81300 | ST4359672225 | The Gordano Round; on bridge over M5 motorway |
| 51.44537, -2.84102 | ST4164872156 | NCR 410; from Old English 'cleafa' ('cleft') rather than 'clif' ('cliff') |
| 51.15911, -3.78696 | SS7513641503 | Tarka Trail / Two Moors Way |
| 51.01050, -2.52822 | ST6303923590 | NCR 26; not on maps; perhaps originally a 'corfe' (*see* Glossary), at intersection of Corton Hill and Corton Ridge, near Corton Denham ('Corfetone', 1086); *see* 'goul' in Glossary |
| 51.13955, -3.23047 | ST1401338529 | Macmillan Way West; 'Healswege', 1080 ('the way between hills'); from Old Norse 'hals' (*see* Glossary) |
| 51.45130, -2.78456 | ST4557972772 | The Gordano Round |
| 51.10710, -2.73760 | ST4845734459 | Battle site, 4 August 1642; 'Marshal's Elm' (Thomas Hardy, 'A Trampwoman's Tragedy' (1902)); *see* p. 34 |
| 51.09142, -3.15944 | ST1889833096 | Macmillan Way West |
| 51.32418, -2.86112 | ST4009358694 | The name is obscure – perhaps 'rood' ('cross' or 'pole') and 'yate' ('gate' or 'pass'); the two 'Rhodyates' are cols and have very similar features |
| 51.38101, -2.79601 | ST4469864963 | *See* 'The Rhodyate' above |
| 51.30271, -2.79576 | ST4462156255 | |
| 51.30045, -2.82930 | ST4228056030 | (NCR 26); (Strawberry Line); name attached to col on OS 1st edn; *see* 'shelve' in Glossary |
| 51.44809, -2.79481 | ST4486372422 | The Gordano Round |
| 51.11635, -3.19608 | ST1637735910 | Macmillan Way West; the stone is a menhir at the col |
| 51.20151, -2.70188 | ST5105844933 | |
| 51.36380, -2.95469 | ST3363063181 | Also known as Monk's Steps; 'St Kew's Steps' on OS 1st and later edn; name attested 1843 |

| Latitude, Longitude | National Grid | Notes |
| --- | --- | --- |
| 53.13600, -2.18649 | SJ8762159888 | Cheshire boundary; Gritstone Trail / Staffordshire Way |
| 52.96055, -1.96805 | SK0224340354 | Not on OS 25 or 50 |
| 53.15509, -1.99032 | SK0074561995 | Misattributed on modern OS to Windygates Farm ('Windygates Hall Farm' according to sign on gate) |

| Latitude, Longitude | National Grid | Notes |
| --- | --- | --- |
| 51.17643, -0.36859 | TQ1413743175 | Greensand Way; col name transferred to Windy Gap Cottage (OS, 1898) and more recently to Windy Gap car park; *see* 'cock' in Glossary |

| Latitude, Longitude | National Grid | Notes |
| --- | --- | --- |
| 50.95854, -0.84797 | SU8100718311 | South Downs Way |
| 50.90526, -0.15799 | TQ2961113369 | Roman road?; above Clayton Tunnel; name used by geographers and historians |

| Name | Elevation (m) | Surface | Nearest place | Region |
|------|--------------|---------|---------------|--------|
| **Cocking Gap** | 107 | **A road** | Cocking | South Downs |
| **Pyecombe / Dale Hill** | 103 | **road** / track | Pyecombe | South Downs |

## Wiltshire · 2 cols

| | | | | |
|------|--------------|---------|---------------|--------|
| **Knap Hill – Walkers Hill** | 217 | road | Alton Priors | Marlborough Downs |
| **Savernake Station** | 154 | road | Durley | Vale of Pewsey |

## Worcestershire · 7 cols

| | | | | |
|------|--------------|---------|---------------|--------|
| **Corfe** | 209 | **B road** | Cofton Hackett | Lickey Hills |
| **Hallhouse** | 130 | road | Alfrick | Suckley Hills |
| **St Kenelm's Pass** | 259 | road | Clent | Clent Hills |
| **Whiteleaved Oak** | 133 | road | Chase End Street | Malvern Hills |
| **Wyche Cutting** | 258 | **B road** | Upper Wyche | Malvern Hills |
| **Wynds Point** | 236 | **A road** | Little Malvern | Malvern Hills |
| *Worcestershire Beacon – Height of Hazely* | 340 | path | Great Malvern | Malvern Hills |

## Yorkshire, North · 17 cols  6 passes

| | | | | |
|------|--------------|---------|---------------|--------|
| **Butter Tubs (or Buttertubs) Pass** | 526 | road | Thwaite | Yorkshire Dales |
| The Devil's Leap | 160 | track | High Kilburn | Hambleton Hills |
| Donna Cross | 305 | path | Kirkby | North York Moors |
| **Fairy Cross** | 212 | road | Street | North York Moors |
| Garfit Gap | 303 | path | Urra | North York Moors |
| **Gribdale Gate** | 229 | road | Little Ayton | North York Moors |
| **Hagg's Gate** | 265 | **B road** | Urra | North York Moors |
| *Harland Hill – Height of Hazely* | 485 | path | West Burton | Yorkshire Dales |
| Highcliff Gate | 295 | path | Guisborough | North York Moors |
| **Kidstones Pass** | 425 | **B road** | Kidstones | Yorkshire Dales |
| **Moor Gate** | 220 | road | Hawnby | North York Moors |
| Newby Head Pass  *see Widdale Head* | | | | |
| **Oxnop Beck Head** | 498 | road | Oxnop Ghyll | Yorkshire Dales |
| **Robinson's Cross** | 286 | road | Osmotherley | North York Moors |
| **Saltergate** | 260 | **A road** | Saltergate | North York Moors |
| **Scarth Nick** | 222 | road | Swainby | North York Moors |
| Swire | 150 | path | West Marton | Aire Gap |
| **Widdale Head / Newby Head Pass** | 438 | **B road** | Stone House | Yorkshire Dales |
| **Blubberhouses Pass / Kex Gill Pass** | 300 | **A road** | West End | Yorkshire Dales |
| Clapdale Pass | 320 | path | Newby Cote | Yorkshire Dales |
| **Fleet Moss Pass** | 588 | road | Oughtershaw | Yorkshire Dales |
| Horse Head Pass | 596 | track | Halton Gill | Yorkshire Dales |
| **Park Rash Pass** | 503 | road | Starbotton | Yorkshire Dales |
| Stockdale Pass | 514 | path | Malham | Yorkshire Dales |

| Latitude, Longitude | National Grid | Notes |
|---|---|---|
| 50.94273, -0.75528 | SU8754616658 | Name used by geographers; *see* 'cock' in Glossary |
| 50.90035, -0.17419 | TQ2848612795 | NCR 20; 'Picumba', 1180–2014; coordinates are for the cycle path; the col is also crossed by the A23 and by Pyecombe Street |
| 51.37339, -1.83515 | SU1157163828 | NCR 45; Tan Hill Way |
| 51.36714, -1.66362 | SU2351463173 | NCR 4; (Mid Wilts Way); (Kennet and Avon Canal) |
| 52.38103, -2.00502 | SO9975575888 | (North Worcestershire Path); deduced from Cofton Hackett ('Corfton', 1431); *see* 'corfe' in Glossary |
| 52.16699, -2.39406 | SO7313652160 | 'House' is a coincidental echo of 'hause' |
| 52.42192, -2.08953 | SO9400880440 | North Worcestershire Path; only on modern OS; leads to St Kenelm's Church and Well |
| 52.02119, -2.35105 | SO7600835922 | Gloucestershire and Herefordshire boundaries; (Three Choirs Way); 'Whiteleaf'd Oak', 1830; *see* p. 37 |
| 52.09136, -2.33828 | SO7692043722 | Herefordshire boundary; 'Baldeyate', 1577–8; the col is natural but exaggerated by the cutting; *see* p. 38 |
| 52.06155, -2.34706 | SO7630340409 | Herefordshire boundary; Three Choirs Way; misplaced on OS 25; 'Windiat' (i.e. 'Windgate'), 1278; 'Brustenyate', 1577–8; 'Wind's Point', 1865 |
| 52.10883, -2.33995 | SO7681545665 | At the top of The Dingle |
| 54.35652, -2.20337 | SD8688195685 | The 'butter tubs' are limestone swallow holes; name attested 1853; Tour de France 2014, Stage 1; *see* pp. 49–50 |
| 54.22527, -1.22252 | SE5078681340 | Not on maps; 'the vale ... dividing Roulston Crag from Hood Hill is called "The Happy Valley" but the intermediate distance is less auspiciously named "The Devil's Leap"' (T. Gill, *Vallis Eboracensis* (1852), p. 224); *see* 'loup' in Glossary |
| 54.42315, -1.16156 | NZ5449903403 | Cleveland Way; boundary stone; not on OS 25 or 50 |
| 54.43547, -0.89441 | NZ7181105013 | Deduced from Fairy Cross Plain and Cottage |
| 54.42365, -1.14513 | NZ5556503471 | Cleveland Way; attested 1857 |
| 54.49137, -1.08887 | NZ5911711052 | (Cleveland Way); not on modern OS |
| 54.42220, -1.11860 | NZ5728803331 | Cleveland Way; not on modern OS; 'Haggesgate', *c.* 1175–89 |
| 54.26064, -1.94817 | SE0347484998 | |
| 54.51554, -1.05039 | NZ6157413775 | (Cleveland Way) |
| 54.22281, -2.08309 | SD9468080791 | 'Kydestanes', 1270; 'Kidstones Pass' in common use, attested early 20th c.; not specifically named on maps; renamed 'Côte de Cray' by the Tour de France in 2014 (Stage 1); *see* pp. 49–50 |
| 54.31791, -1.17195 | SE5396391685 | NCR 656 |
| 54.34348, -2.09258 | SD9407994218 | A Pennine Journey |
| 54.35393, -1.25449 | SE4855195633 | NCR 656; the 'cross' is a boundary stone at the col |
| 54.33519, -0.69484 | SE8496294077 | Tabular Hills Walk; 'Saltergate' is applied to various features in the vicinity of the col |
| 54.39281, -1.27479 | SE4718799946 | NCR 65; (Cleveland Way); the 'nick' may indicate the road or a characteristic of the 'scarth'; misplaced on OS 50, but placed at the col on OS 1st and 2nd edn |
| 53.94358, -2.17515 | SD8860149733 | Deduced from Swire Hill |
| 54.25433, -2.31318 | SD7969484340 | First name only on maps; both attested 19th c. |
| 53.99054, -1.79901 | SE1327654963 | 'Bluberhous', 1172 (origin obscure); Tour de France 2014, Stage 2 |
| 54.14044, -2.37717 | SD7545771688 | A Pennine Journey; attested late 19th c. |
| 54.25466, -2.21258 | SD8624884352 | |
| 54.19441, -2.17142 | SD8891377641 | A Pennine Journey; summit marked 'Horse Head Gate' on all OS maps |
| 54.17806, -2.02149 | SD9869575809 | Name in common use |
| 54.07164, -2.19311 | SD8746163985 | Dales High Way / Pennine Bridleway; attested 1892 |

| Name | Elevation (m) | Surface | Nearest place | Region |
|------|---------------|---------|---------------|--------|

## Yorkshire, South · 1 col

| Woodhead Pass | 417 | **A road** | Dunford Bridge | Peak District |
|---|---|---|---|---|

## Yorkshire, West · 5 cols 3 passes

| *Brown Wardle Hill – Little Middle Hill* | 351 | path | Facit | South Pennines |
|---|---|---|---|---|
| **Castle Shore** | 382 | **motorway** | Lydgate | South Pennines |
| **Pule Nick** | 281 | **road** | Halifax | South Pennines |
| *Tom Stell's Seat* | 299 | road | Stanbury | South Pennines |
| **Wessenden Head** | 452 | **A road** | Holme | Peak District |
| **Buckstones Pass** | 451 | **A road** | Marsden | South Pennines |
| **Holme Pass (Holme Moss)** | 524 | **A road** | Holme | Peak District |
| **Standedge Pass** | 387 | **A road** | Bleak Hey Nook | Peak District |

# Wales

## Bridgend · 4 cols

| Bwlch gwyn | 308 | track | Pontycymer | Garw Valley |
|---|---|---|---|---|
| **Bwlch y Clawdd** | 450 | **A road** | Nant-y-moel | Ogmore Vale |
| Bwlch yr Afan | 533 | track | Nant-y-moel | Ogmore Vale |
| Pant Blaenhirwr | 332 | (path) | Ogmore Vale | Ogmore Vale |

## Caerphilly · 1 col

| Pegwn-y-bwlch | 300 | track | Pontywaun | Ebbw Valley |
|---|---|---|---|---|

## Carmarthenshire   20 cols

| **Bwlch** | 188 | **road** | Plas | Tywi Valley |
|---|---|---|---|---|
| **Bwlch** | 118 | **road** | Tre-vaughan | Tywi Valley |
| **Bwlch** | 78 | **road** | Abernant | Cywyn Valley |
| **Bwlch blaen-corn** | 322 | **road** | Llanycrwys | Twrch Valley |
| Bwlch Blaen-Twrch | 656 | (path) | Llanddeusant | The Black Mountain |
| **Bwlch Cae Brîth** | 202 | **road** | Penrherber | Teifi Valley |
| **Bwlch Caermalwas** | 289 | **B road** | Rhydcymerau | Teifi Valley |
| **Bwlchcefnsarth** | 231 | **A road** | Aberbowlan | Tywi Valley |
| **Bwlch-Cynnant** | 251 | **road** | Rhandirmwyn | Cambrian Mountains |
| **Bwlchgwynt** | 268 | **road** | Cwrt-y-cadno | Cambrian Mountains |
| **Bwlch-tre-banau / Bwlchdrebannau** | 223 | **road** | Porthyrhyd | Tywi Valley |
| **Bwlch-y-ffin** | 368 | **road** | Llanycrwys | Twrch Valley |

| Latitude, Longitude | National Grid | Notes |
|---|---|---|
| 53.50132, -1.78907 | SE1408800534 | NCR 68; Trans Pennine Trail; attested 1946; Tour de France 2014, Stage 2 (not mentioned in official route); *see* p. 89 |
| 53.66777, -2.15271 | SD9000719043 | 50 m from Lancashire boundary |
| 53.62918, -2.03095 | SD9805014739 | Lancashire boundary; (Pennine Way); for historical accuracy, the coordinates indicate the central reservation of the M62 motorway, on the county boundary; this was the original route of the Pennine Way, now shifted east to cross the motorway on a footbridge at 53.62934, -2.02650; original name deduced from Castle Shore Hill and Castle Shore Clough, which rises at the col (as Red Shore in Wiltshire, a gap in the Wansdyke, formerly Reddscherd and Read Geat); *see* 'sheard' in Glossary |
| 53.74112, -1.86131 | SE0924527202 | Not on maps; in common use until early 20th c. |
| 53.82274, -1.97445 | SE0177936274 | Millennium Way / (Brontë Way); labelled 'Stanbury Height' on OS 1st edn; memorial dated 1932; Tour de France 2014, Stage 2 (not mentioned in official route) |
| 53.56039, -1.89006 | SE0738007091 | (Pennine Way) |
| 53.61934, -1.97483 | SE0176213644 | Name in common use |
| 53.52961, -1.85623 | SE0962803671 | Derbyshire boundary; 'Holme Pass' in common use but shown only on Michelin maps; Tour de France 2014, Stage 2 |
| 53.58309, -1.97027 | SE0206609612 | Greater Manchester boundary; Standedge Trail / Pennine Way; attested 1891; name in common use |
| 51.60360, -3.60509 | SS8893590638 | Deduced from Croes y Bwlch gwyn; 'White Gap' |
| 51.63911, -3.53358 | SS9397194481 | Rhondda Cynon Taff boundary; 'Pass of the (Earthen) Bank'; fourth-highest road col and highest point on an A road in Wales (not, as sometimes stated, Britain) |
| 51.64239, -3.56534 | SS9178194893 | Neath Port Talbot boundary; 'Pass of the River Afan'; 'Avan' on OS 1st edn |
| 51.60322, -3.56204 | SS9191690531 | 'Pant' = 'hollow' or 'depression' |
| 51.62959, -3.10266 | ST2377492885 | Raven Walk; 'pegwn' = 'pole' ,'axis' or 'beacon'; below Twmbarlwm hill fort; *see* 'pole' in Glossary |
| 51.90238, -4.21468 | SN4773224967 | Deduced from Pen-y-bwlch-uchaf |
| 51.87546, -4.35261 | SN3814722271 | Deduced from Bwlch Farm |
| 51.86472, -4.44211 | SN3194721280 | 'Bwlch Farm' on modern OS |
| 52.10531, -3.98614 | SN6407047081 | 'Summit Cairn Pass' |
| 51.88116, -3.72131 | SN8161621689 | Powys boundary; (Beacons Way); shifted east on OS 25; 'Pass at the head of the (river) Twrch' |
| 52.02112, -4.47570 | SN3022638750 | 'Speckled Field Gap', or related to 'brith y cae' ('pied wagtail')? |
| 52.04446, -4.09914 | SN5613640532 | 'Bwlch-cae'r-malwas' on OS 1st edn; 'caer' = ''fort', but earlier form suggests 'cae' ('field'); 'malwas', 'malwod' = 'snail', 'slug' |
| 52.02161, -3.92672 | SN6789237663 | 'Bwlch-cefn-sarth' on OS 1st edn; name attributed to farm; 'cefn' = 'ridge'; 'sarth' = 'service tree' |
| 52.06967, -3.74741 | SN8032442697 | 'Pass of the River Cynnant' |
| 52.08928, -3.92400 | SN6827845183 | 'Wind Gap'; 'Bwlch-y-gwynt' on OS 1st edn; name attributed to farm |
| 52.01937, -3.86570 | SN7207337305 | Roman road?; name attributed to several neighbouring features; 'bannau' = 'hills', 'peaks' |
| 52.11283, -3.97877 | SN6459847904 | Roman road (Sarn Helen) and watch tower; not on modern OS; 'boundary Gap' (the county boundary now runs 200 m from the col) |

| Name | Elevation (m) | Surface | Nearest place | Region |
|---|---|---|---|---|
| **Bwlch-y-ffin** | 240 | **road** | Ystradffin | Cambrian Mountains |
| **Bwlch-y-gilwen** | 213 | **road**/track | Llandre | Cambrian Mountains |
| Bwlch y Gors | 336 | track | Capel Gwynfe | The Black Mountain |
| **Bwlch-y-gwynt** | 248 | **road** | Llwyn-y-brain | Tywi Valley |
| **Blwch-yr-adwy / Bwlchyradwy** | 139 | **road** | Felingwmisaf | Cothi Valley |
| **Bwlch-y-rhew** | 227 | **road** | Glanbran | Cambrian Mountains |
| **Bwlch-y-rhiw** | 258 | **road** | Garthynty | Cambrian Mountains |
| Bylchau Rhos-fain | 525 | | Upper Brynamman | The Black Mountain |

## Ceredigion · 18 cols

| Name | Elevation (m) | Surface | Nearest place | Region |
|---|---|---|---|---|
| Bwlch | 224 | path | Wenallt | Cambrian Mountains |
| Bwlch | 115 | track | Capel Seion | Rheidol Valley |
| **Bwlch-castell** | 249 | **road** | Cilcennin | Aeron Valley |
| **Bwlch-cefn** | 107 | **road** | Gilfacherda | Cardigan Bay |
| Bwlch-Dihewyd | 249 | track | Dihewyd | Aeron Valley |
| **Bwlch Esgair Gelli** | 472 | **road** | Abergwesyn | Cambrian Mountains |
| Bwlch-glâs | 265 | track | Bont-goch | Cambrian Mountains |
| **Bwlch-heble (Pen-y-bwlch-heble)** | 193 | **A road** | Aberffrwd | Cambrian Mountains |
| **Bwlch Nant-yr-arian** | 313 | **A road** | Cwmbrwyno | Cambrian Mountains |
| Bwlch Rhyd-y-meirch | 481 | track | Strata Florida | Cambrian Mountains |
| Bwlchwernen | 210 | (path) | Llwyn-y-groes | Dulas Valley |
| Bwlchyddwyallt | 266 | track | Pontrhydfendigaid | Cambrian Mountains |
| Bwlch-y-ddwyallt | 258 | (path) | Talybont | Cambrian Mountains |
| **Bwlch-y-groes / Bwlchygroes** | 242 | **road** | Ffostrasol | Teifi Valley |
| Bwlch y Maen | 294 | track | Bont-goch | Cambrian Mountains |
| Bwlch yr Adwy | 394 | track | Cwmsymlog | Cambrian Mountains |
| Bwlch yr Oerfa | 382 | track | Cwmystwyth | Cambrian Mountains |
| **Plynlimon Pass / Pass of Plynlimon** | 410 | **A road** | Eisteddfa-Gurig | Cambrian Mountains |

## Conwy · 26 cols 2 passes

| Name | Elevation (m) | Surface | Nearest place | Region |
|---|---|---|---|---|
| Bwlch | 594 | | Llanbedr-y-cennin | Snowdonia |
| Bwlch | 450 | track | Cefn-brith | Alwen Valley |
| Bwlch | 405 | path | Pentre-bont | Snowdonia |
| **Bwlch** | 312 | **road** | Plasisaf | Aled Valley |
| Bwlch | 211 | track | Capel Garmon | Snowdonia |
| Bwlch Blaen-y-cwm | 429 | (track) | Ty-Mawr | Snowdonia |
| Bwlch clorad | 526 | | Pen-y-Gwryd | Snowdonia |
| Bwlch Cyfryw-drum | 933 | path | Pont Pen-y-benglog | Snowdonia |
| Bwlch Ehediad *see* Bwlch y Rhediad | | | | |
| Bwlch Eryl Farchog | 748 | path | Pont Pen-y-benglog | Snowdonia |
| Bwlch Goleuni | 441 | (path) | Capel Curig | Snowdonia |
| Bwlch Rhiw'r Ychen | 510 | | Pen-y-Gwryd | Snowdonia |
| Bwlch Tryfan | 730 | (path) | Pont Pen-y-benglog | Snowdonia |
| Bwlch y Cŵm | 492 | | Rhiwbryfdir | Snowdonia |
| Bwlch y Ddeufaen | 431 | track | Nant-y-Pandy | Snowdonia |
| Bwlch y Ddwy-Glyder | 919 | path | Pen-y-benglog | Snowdonia |

| Latitude, Longitude | National Grid | Notes |
|---|---|---|
| 52.11779, -3.76354 | SN7934848075 | Name attributed to farm; 'boundary gap' |
| 52.07386, -3.94463 | SN6681943507 | 'Gilwen' is probably a personal name |
| 51.88653, -3.89894 | SN6940622590 | (Beacons Way); 'Marsh Gap' |
| 51.99358, -3.87112 | SN7162734446 | 'Wind Gap'; name attributed to farm 500 m to south-west |
| 51.89450, -4.15466 | SN5183523967 | 'Pass of the Gap' |
| 52.04675, -3.77558 | SN7833040194 | 'Frost Gap'; name attributed to farm |
| 52.10045, -3.86125 | SN7260946314 | 'Pass of the Hill Slope' |
| 51.84592, -3.81631 | SN7498017929 | Beacons Way; 'Moor Stone Pass'? ('faen' on OS 1st edn, thus probably mutation of 'maen', 'stone') |

| Latitude, Longitude | National Grid | Notes |
|---|---|---|
| 52.31871, -3.94749 | SN6735470742 | Deduced from Tynbwlch / Ty'n-y-bwlch |
| 52.39524, -4.04667 | SN6083679440 | Between Bwlch-bâch and Bwlch-mawr ('little' and 'great') |
| 52.20993, -4.15401 | SN5292059044 | 'Hill Fort Gap'; the col is at the hill fort but its name is attributed to the farm 500 m north-west |
| 52.20083, -4.33849 | SN4028458423 | 'Ridge Gap' |
| 52.17954, -4.19677 | SN4989655752 | 'Bwlch' on modern OS |
| 52.20331, -3.78152 | SN7835057616 | Esgair Gelli is the spur to the north-east |
| 52.47126, -3.90983 | SN7037087640 | 'Blue Gap'; name attributed to farm |
| 52.38096, -3.94221 | SN6790177656 | Labelled 'Pen-y-bwlch-heble' ('Head of the Pass') on OS 1st edn |
| 52.41451, -3.88512 | SN7188381285 | Borth to Devil's Bridge to Pontrhydfendigaid Trail; road sign; 'Silver (money) Brook Pass': streams so named are associated with markets held in times of plague, when coins were deposited in the water, not passed from hand to hand |
| 52.25031, -3.79395 | SN7763162865 | 'Bwlch' on modern OS; 'Horse Ford Pass' (the ford is further east) |
| 52.18229, -4.04573 | SN6023155756 | 'Alder Pass'; between Bwlch-wernen-fawr and -fâch on OS 1st edn |
| 52.25143, -3.88555 | SN7138163148 | 'Two Hills Gap'; name attributed to farm |
| 52.47259, -3.96598 | SN6656087891 | 'Two Hills Gap'; name attributed to farm |
| 52.09134, -4.36743 | SN3790946310 | 'Cross Gap' |
| 52.45694, -3.91388 | SN7005286055 | 'Stone Gap'; not on OS 1st edn |
| 52.46389, -3.88784 | SN7184286781 | 'Pass of the Gap' |
| 52.36065, -3.81230 | SN7668575168 | 'Cold Place Gap'; misplaced to south on OS 25 |
| 52.43976, -3.77238 | SN7963183927 | 200 m from Powys boundary; name in common use |

| Latitude, Longitude | National Grid | Notes |
|---|---|---|
| 53.20280, -3.91874 | SH7193869020 | Deduced from Tan-y-bwlch, which may refer to Bwlch-y-gaer (Conwy) |
| 53.05586, -3.58638 | SH9377352133 | Implied by Tan-y-bwlch ('Below the Bwlch') |
| 53.03181, -3.89463 | SH7304449960 | Implied by Tan-y-bwlch ('Below the Bwlch') |
| 53.20352, -3.53712 | SH9742768486 | The name might also have been applied to the gap 450 m to the south between Moel Fodiar and Pengwern |
| 53.07771, -3.78093 | SH8079554870 | Implied by Ty'n-y-bwlch ('House of the Bwlch') |
| 53.00523, -3.68110 | SH8729346646 | 'Pass at the Head of the Coomb' |
| 53.06975, -3.97135 | SH6801654319 | 'Bwlch cloron' on OS 1st edn ('Potato Pass') |
| 53.15310, -3.97481 | SH6804063596 | Probably 'cyfrwy', in which case, 'Saddle of the Ridge'; the equal second-highest col in Wales |
| 53.15116, -3.95367 | SH6944763341 | 'Pass of the Hunting Knights'; sometimes conflated with Bwlch y Tri Marchog |
| 53.10411, -3.94802 | SH6968358098 | 'Pass of Light' |
| 53.06892, -3.97706 | SH6763154237 | Gwynedd boundary; 'Rhiw-yr-ychain' on OS 1st edn; 'Oxen Slope Pass' |
| 53.10991, -4.00048 | SH6618958840 | Not on OS 1st edn; 'Pointed Pass' |
| 53.01837, -3.95050 | SH6925748565 | 'Pass of the Coomb'; the bwlch lies above the Blaenau railway tunnel |
| 53.22831, -3.92998 | SH7126371880 | Roman road; 'Two Stones Pass'; the stones are menhirs |
| 53.10353, -4.01387 | SH6527358155 | Gwynedd boundary; 'Gap of the Two Heaps of Stone' (the two mountains called 'Glyder') |

| Name | Elevation (m) | Surface | Nearest place | Region |
|---|---|---|---|---|
| Bwlch-y-gaer | 358 | track | Llanbedr-y-cennin | Snowdonia |
| **Bwlch y Gorddinan / Crimea Pass** | 385 | **A road** | Rhiwbryfdir | Snowdonia |
| Bwlch y Groes | 432 | (path) | Pentre-bont | Snowdonia |
| Bwlch y Gwryd | 725 | (path) | Nant-y-Pandy | Snowdonia |
| Bwlch y Pentre | 541 | | Ty-Mawr | Snowdonia |
| **Bwlch-yr-haiarn** | 241 | **road** | Llanrwst | Snowdonia |
| Bwlch y Rhediad | 378 | path | Blaenau Dolwyddelan | Snowdonia |
| Bwlch y Tri Marchog | 620 | | Capel Curig | Snowdonia |
| **Bylchau** | 329 | **A road** | Bylchau | Aled Valley |
| **Bylchau Isa** | 302 | **B road** | Bylchau | Aled Valley |
| Carnedd Uchaf – Foel Grach | 884 | (path) | Gerlan | Snowdonia |
| Crimea Pass  *see* Bwlch y Gorddinan | | | | |
| **Ogwen Pass** | 303 | **A road** | Pen-y-benglog | Snowdonia |
| **Sychnant Pass** | 160 | **road** | Capelulo | Snowdonia |

# Denbighshire · 19 cols 3 passes

| Name | Elevation (m) | Surface | Nearest place | Region |
|---|---|---|---|---|
| **Adwy-wynt** | 153 | **road** | Sodom | Clwydian Range |
| Bwlch | 307 | track | Waen | Clwydian Range |
| **Bwlch** | 302 | **road** | Llangollen | Berwyn Range |
| **Bwlch Arthur** | 336 | **road** | Llangwyfan | Clwydian Range |
| Bwlch Côch | 330 | track | Carrog | Clwydian Range |
| Bwlch Crug-glâs | 375 | path | Llanbedr-Dyffryn-Clwyd | Clwydian Range |
| Bwlch Cynwyd | 562 | track | Plas Nantyr | Berwyn Range |
| Bwlch Maen Gwynedd | 711 | path | Tan-y-pistyll | Berwyn Range |
| **Bwlch Penbarras (or Pen Barras) / The Old Bwlch** | 358 | **road** | Llanbedr-Dyffryn-Clwyd | Clwydian Range |
| Bwlch y Fedw | 530 | (track) | Llandrillo | Berwyn Range |
| Bwlch y Gaseg | 519 | (track) | Corwen | Berwyn Range |
| **Bwlch-y-parc / Clwyd Gate** | 286 | **A road** | Llanbedr-Dyffryn-Clwyd | Clwydian Range |
| Cadair Bronwen / Bwrdd Arthur | 685 | (path) | Llandrillo | Berwyn Range |
| Croes-y-wernen | 525 | path | Plas Nantyr | Berwyn Range |
| **Drŵs-y-buddel** | 353 | **road** | Cader | Vale of Clwyd |
| Moel Gyw – Moel Llanfair | 395 | track | Llanarmon-yn-Ial | Clwydian Range |
| Horseshoe Pass  *see* Bwlch Oernant (pass) | | | | |
| Moel Llêch – Moel y Plâs | 354 | track | Gelli Gynan | Clwydian Range |
| Moel y Gamelin – Moel y Gaer | 435 | track | Ty-mawr | Clwydian Range |
| Pen Bwlch Llandrillo | 585 | track | Cynwyd | Berwyn Range |
| **Bwlch Oernant / Horseshoe Pass** | 417 | **A road** | Pentredwr | Clwydian Range |
| **Milltir Gerrig (or Cerrig) Pass** | 489 | **B road** | Pennant Melangell | Berwyn Range |
| **Nant y Garth Pass** | 226 | **A road** | Ty-mawr | Clwydian Range |

| Latitude, Longitude | National Grid | Notes |
|---|---|---|
| 53.20540, -3.88247 | SH7436769247 | 'Pass of the Fort' |
| 53.01944, -3.93927 | SH7001448664 | 'Pass of the Impulsive (River)'; English name from an inn |
| 53.04441, -3.85565 | SH7569451293 | 'Pass of the Cross' |
| 53.20284, -3.93757 | SH7068069060 | Gwynedd boundary; 'Bwlch y Gwrhyd' on OS 1st edn; 'gwryd' or 'gwrhyd' = 'fathom' (measurement) but can also mean 'battle' or 'miracle' |
| 52.99630, -3.66530 | SH8833045628 | Gwynedd boundary; 'Pass of the Village'; misplaced on OS 50 |
| 53.11780, -3.82682 | SH7783559407 | 'Iron Pass' |
| 53.05199, -3.99108 | SH6663952380 | Gwynedd boundary; 'Bwlch Ehediad' on OS 1st edn; 'Pass of the Birds' or 'Flight' |
| 53.14529, -3.93102 | SH7094462647 | 'Pass of the Three Knights'; sometimes conflated with Bwlch Eryl Farchog |
| 53.15446, -3.53269 | SH9760663023 | 'Bylchau' is the plural of *bwlch*, perhaps referring to the meeting of ways or the proximity of two cols |
| 53.15735, -3.51986 | SH9847063325 | 'Bylchau-isaf' ('lower') on OS 1st edn; see previous note |
| 53.17961, -3.96433 | SH6882166525 | Gwynedd boundary |
| 53.12341, -4.01863 | SH6501760375 | Gwynedd boundary; NCR 82; not on maps; name in common use, attested 1826; named after Llyn Ogwen |
| 53.27531, -3.87647 | SH7497277013 | North Wales Path; 'Dry Stream Pass'; 'Bwlch Sychnant' is modern |
| 53.23010, -3.35602 | SJ0957971198 | Offa's Dyke Path / Clwydian Way; 'Wind Gap' |
| 53.21078, -3.31751 | SJ1211069001 | Flintshire boundary; Offa's Dyke Path / Clwydian Way; name attributed to farm |
| 52.96616, -3.19353 | SJ1993641644 | Name attributed to farm |
| 53.18205, -3.27812 | SJ1468365758 | Flintshire boundary; Offa's Dyke Path / Clwydian Way; name in common use (sometimes 'Arthur's Pass'), between Moel Arthur and Moel Llys-y-coed |
| 52.99079, -3.31391 | SJ1190144525 | Clwydian Way; 'Red Pass' |
| 53.12695, -3.24725 | SJ1663959592 | Offa's Dyke Path; the 'blue barrow' or 'mound' refers to the Iron Age hill fort; on the spurious 'Bwlch Agricla' (*sic*), *see* p. 40 |
| 52.94282, -3.31731 | SJ1157539194 | Wrexham boundary; North Berwyn Way; Cynwyd is the village to which the col leads |
| 52.89625, -3.37494 | SJ0760334086 | Wrexham boundary; North Berwyn Way; Roman road?; 'Gwynedd Stone Pass' (referring to a boundary stone 500 m to the east) |
| 53.13567, -3.25472 | SJ1615660571 | Offa's Dyke Path; Roman road?; road sign; 'Bwlch-pen-Barres' on OS 1st edn; 'Bwlch Penbarra' on OS 50; name may refer to a boundary; second name in common use |
| 52.91267, -3.40227 | SJ0580035948 | 'Birch Pass' |
| 52.95395, -3.34953 | SJ0943340471 | 'Mare's Pass' |
| 53.11428, -3.24856 | SJ1652758184 | Offa's Dyke Path; name attributed to farm; 'Pass of the Field' or 'Park' |
| 52.90396, -3.36355 | SJ0838534929 | 30 m from Wrexham boundary |
| 52.93238, -3.32673 | SJ1092038043 | Wrexham boundary; 'Alder cross'; the path along the Nant Croes-y-wernen continues to the col except on modern OS |
| 53.12907, -3.46782 | SJ0188560107 | Name attributed to farm; 'drŵs' = 'door', 'buddel' = 'post' or 'stake' |
| 53.10409, -3.24057 | SJ1704157041 | (Offa's Dyke Path) |
| 53.09353, -3.24381 | SJ1680455870 | Offa's Dyke Path |
| 53.00944, -3.23717 | SJ1708846508 | Clwydian Way |
| 52.91894, -3.35354 | SJ0909036583 | 80 m west of Wrexham boundary; 'Pen y Bwlch' on OS 1st edn; name means 'Head of Llandrillo Pass'; a memorial at the summit to the cycling writer, 'Wayfarer' (*see* pp. 41–2); the climb was also known as 'Over the Top' and is sometimes called 'The Wayfarer' |
| 53.01966, -3.20207 | SJ1946247605 | 'Cold Stream Pass'; English name from the bend in the road; *see* p. 17 |
| 52.86303, -3.46157 | SJ0170030505 | Powys boundary; attested 1843; 'Siglen y Bwlch' ('Marsh of the Pass') nearby, on OS 10; 'Stoney Mile' |
| 53.04828, -3.24871 | SJ1638950842 | 'Stream of the Mountain Ridge' |

| Name | Elevation (m) | Surface | Nearest place | Region |
|------|---------------|---------|---------------|--------|

## Flintshire · 2 cols

| | | | | |
|------|------|------|------|------|
| Bwlch | 307 | track | Waen | Clwydian Range |
| **Bwlch Arthur** | 336 | **road** | Llangwyfan | Clwydian Range |

## Gwynedd · 97 cols  7 passes

| | | | | |
|------|------|------|------|------|
| **Bwlch** | 298 | **road** | Llanuwchllyn | Snowdonia |
| **Bwlch** | 269 | **road** | Glan-yr-afon | The Arenigs |
| Bwlch | 266 | | Llandderfel | The Arenigs |
| **Bwlch** | 206 | **road** / track | Penhelig | Dovey Estuary |
| **Bwlch** | 138 | **road** | Nefyn | Lleyn Peninsula |
| **Bwlch** | 73 | **B road** | Maentwrog | Snowdonia |
| **Bwlch** | 63 | **road** | Rhoslefain | Dysynni Valley |
| Bwlch Blaen Cwm Idwal | 711 | (path) | Pen-y-benglog | Snowdonia |
| Bwlch Cau | 716 | path | Minffordd | Cadair Idris Range |
| Bwlch Ciliau | 744 | (path) | Plas Gwynant | Snowdonia |
| Bwlch-coch | 229 | track | Bontddu | Mawddach Estuary |
| Bwlch-coediog | 280 | path | Abercywarch | Dyfi Hills |
| Bwlch Cwm-breuan  see Bwlch Cwmmaria | | | | |
| Bwlch Cwm Brwynog | 500 | (path) | Nant Peris | Snowdonia |
| Bwlch Cwm Cesig | 598 | (path) | Salem | Snowdonia |
| Bwlch-cwm-Cewydd | 255 | (track) | Dinas-Mawddwy | Dyfi Hills |
| Bwlch Cwmdulyn | 535 | path | Pant Glas | Snowdonia |
| Bwlch Cwmmaria | 417 | | Cutiau | Mawddach Estuary |
| Bwlch Cwm-orthin  see Bwlch y Rhosydd | | | | |
| Bwlch Cwm-trwsgl | 340 | path | Rhyd-Ddu | Snowdonia |
| Bwlch Cwm-y-llan | 515 | (path) | Plas Gwynant | Snowdonia |
| Bwlch Cwm-ystradllyn | 357 | path | Nantmor | Snowdonia |
| **Bwlch-cyfyng** | 68 | **B road** | Abergynolwyn | Cadair Idris |
| Bwlch Dros-bern | 513 | | Nantlle | Snowdonia |
| Bwlch Drws-Ardudwy | 359 | path | Bronaber | The Rhinogs |
| Bwlch Ehediad  see Bwlch y Rhediad | | | | |
| Bwlch Glas | 998 | path | Gwastadnant | Snowdonia |
| Bwlch Goriwared | 388 | track | Llanfachreth | Coed y Brenin |
| Bwlch Gwylim | 564 | | Eisingrug | Snowdonia |
| Bwlch Gwyn | 375 | (path) | Llanfachreth | Coed y Brenin |
| **Bwlch Gwynt** | 162 | **road** | Pistyll | Lleyn Peninsula |
| **Bwlchgylfin / Bwlch Gylfin** | 251 | **B road** | Rhyd-Ddu | Snowdonia |
| **Bwlch Llyn Bach** | 285 | **A road** | Cross Foxes Inn | Cadair Idris Range |
| Bwlch Maesgwm | 467 | path | Salem | Snowdonia |
| Bwlch Mawr | 365 | (path) | Gyrn Goch | Lleyn Peninsula |

| Latitude, Longitude | National Grid | Notes |
|---|---|---|
| 53.21078, -3.31751 | SJ 1211069001 | Denbighshire boundary; Offa's Dyke Path / Clwydian Way; name attributed to farm |
| 53.18205, -3.27812 | SJ 1468365758 | Denbighshire boundary; Offa's Dyke Path / Clwydian Way; name in common use (sometimes 'Arthur's Pass'), between Moel Arthur and Moel Llys-y-coed |
| 52.87051, -3.71701 | SH 8452531718 | CR 13; deduced from Ty'n-y-bwlch |
| 52.96909, -3.47985 | SJ 0071342329 | 225 m from Conwy boundary; deduced from Tyn-y-bwlch |
| 52.92377, -3.53006 | SH 9723437358 | Deduced from Ty'n-y-bwlch |
| 52.56264, -4.00209 | SN 6438597973 | Wales Coast Path; not on modern OS (Bwlch-y-llan, in the gully below the col, is shown as a distinct location on OS 1st edn); road continues as paved track after gate |
| 52.92849, -4.50197 | SH 3192139718 | CR 41; deduced from Cae'r-Bwlch |
| 52.94922, -4.00143 | SH 6562640968 | Wales Coast Path; NCR 82; deduced from Tan-y-bwlch |
| 52.62760, -4.11029 | SH 5726305407 | Wales Coast Path |
| 53.10608, -4.03902 | SH 6359758486 | 'Pass of the Head of Cwm Idwal'; on OS 1901 revision but not 1st edn, 25 or 50 |
| 52.69447, -3.91175 | SH 7089812469 | Misplaced on OS 25; named after mountain and lake |
| 53.06265, -4.06136 | SH 6196353699 | (Watkin Path); 'Nook Gap'; below Snowdon summit |
| 52.76123, -3.99415 | SH 6553520046 | Deduced from Bwlch-coch-uchaf; 'Red Gap' |
| 52.72476, -3.66051 | SH 8795315417 | 'Woody Gap' |
| 53.08045, -4.10550 | SH 5906455764 | 'Pass of the Rushy Coomb'; 'The ascent becomes very difficult, on account of its vast steepness. People here usually quit their horses.' (T. Pennant, *A Tour in Wales* (1773)) |
| 53.09149, -4.15328 | SH 5590157087 | 'Pass of the Mares' Coomb' |
| 52.71703, -3.67354 | SH 8705314578 | 'Cewydd' is the name of the river |
| 53.01567, -4.22316 | SH 5096048798 | 'Pass of the Coomb of the Black Lake' |
| 52.74749, -4.04127 | SH 6231318607 | 'Bwlch Cwm-breuan' on OS 1st edn ('Pass of the Raven's Coomb') |
| 53.02465, -4.15835 | SH 5533749663 | Roman road?; first shown on OS in 1901; the 'clumsy coomb' refers to a giant who missed his footing and formed a bridge with his fallen body |
| 53.04817, -4.08350 | SH 6043352131 | 'Bwlch Cwm Llan' on modern OS; 'Pass of the Coomb of the Church' |
| 52.98305, -4.12274 | SH 5758844965 | 'Pass of the Lake in the Vale'; not on OS 25 or 50 |
| 52.63932, -3.96603 | SH 6706206434 | 'Narrow Gap'; at Abergynolwyn Station on the Talyllyn Railway |
| 53.03376, -4.19188 | SH 5312050745 | 'Bwlch Drosbern' on OS 1st edn; 'Pass above the Burn' |
| 52.83456, -3.98485 | SH 6638828184 | Misplaced on OS 25; 'the door of Ardudwy, formed by nature through the sterile mountains, which separate the districts. I was tempted to visit this noted pass, and found the horror of it far exceeding the most gloomy idea that could be conceived of it' (T. Pennant, *A Tour in Wales* (1773)) |
| 53.07272, -4.07955 | SH 6077754854 | Llanberis Path, Pyg Track, Snowdon Ranger Path; 'Blue Gap'; below Snowdon summit; the highest col in Wales |
| 52.80466, -3.83401 | SH 7646324589 | 'Sloping Gap' |
| 52.87770, -3.99945 | SH 6553833010 | Personal name (as 'Guillaume') |
| 52.80088, -3.84835 | SH 7548624193 | 'White Gap' |
| 52.94398, -4.48980 | SH 3279941412 | 'Wind Gap' |
| 53.05812, -4.15727 | SH 5552253384 | 'Gylfin' = 'beak' or 'snout' (perhaps from the shape of the crag to the north) |
| 52.70890, -3.84134 | SH 7569713950 | 'Little Lake Pass'; misplaced on OS 25 and 50; not on earlier OS |
| 53.08081, -4.13288 | SH 5723155859 | 'Bwlch y Maes-cwm' on OS 1st edn |
| 52.99364, -4.36417 | SH 4142146650 | Col name attributed to mountain ('Great Pass'); identification uncertain |

| Name | Elevation (m) | Surface | Nearest place | Region |
|---|---|---|---|---|
| Bwlch Meillionen | 540 | path | Beddgelert | Snowdonia |
| **Bwlch Oerddrws / Bwlch Oer-drŵs** | 363 | **A road** | Cross Foxes Inn | Dyfi Hills |
| Bwlch Pen-y-feidiog | 529 | | Bronaber | Snowdonia |
| Bwlch Rhiw'r Ychen | 510 | | Pen-y-Gwryd | Snowdonia |
| Bwlch Siglen | 340 | path | Minllyn | Dyfi Hills |
| Bwlch Sirddyn | 500 | (path) | Ty-nant | Aran Range |
| Bwlch Stwlan | 586 | (path) | Tanygrisiau | Snowdonia |
| Bwlch Sycan | 437 | | Abercywarch | Aran Range |
| Bwlch Trwst-y-llan  see Bwlch Stwlan | | | | |
| Bwlch Tyddiad | 440 | path | Bronaber | The Rhinogs |
| Bwlch y Battel | 379 | path | Croesor | Snowdonia |
| Bwlch y Brecan | 710 | path | Pont Pen-y-benglog | Snowdonia |
| Bwlch y Cribwr | 444 | (path) | Rhyd-wen | Berwyn Range |
| Bwlch y Ddwy-Glyder | 919 | path | Pont Pen-y-benglog | Snowdonia |
| Bwlch y Dŵr | 591 | path | Pennant Melangell | Berwyn Range |
| **Bwlch y Fenni (or Feni)** | 422 | **road** | Pale | Berwyn Range |
| Bwlch y Fign | 614 | | Rhydymain | Aran Range |
| Bwlch-y-fwlet | 408 | path | Pentre-piod | Berwyn Range |
| Bwlch y Garnedd | 382 | path | Cwm-Cewydd | Dyfi Hills |
| Bwlch y Gesail | 567 | (track) | Dinas-Mawddwy | Aran Range |
| Bwlch y Greigwen | 469 | path | Gellioedd | The Arenigs |
| Bwlch y Groes | 545 | **road** | Ty-nant | Aran Range |
| Bwlch-y-groes | 375 | track | Llanberis | Snowdonia |
| Bwlch y Gwryd | 725 | (path) | Nant-y-Pandy | Snowdonia |
| Bwlch-y-maen | 171 | (track) | Dolgoch | Cadair Idris |
| **Bwlch-y-maen** | 153 | **B road** | Rhyd | Snowdonia |
| Bwlch y Marchlyn | 740 | path | Dinorwig | Snowdonia |
| Bwlch y Mawn | 343 | track | Mynydd Llandygai | Snowdonia |
| Bwlch ym Mhwll-le | 364 | (path) | Llanllechid | Snowdonia |
| Bwlch y Moch | 569 | path | Pen-y-Gwryd | Snowdonia |
| Bwlch y Moch | 251 | path | Rhyd-Ddu | Snowdonia |
| **Bwlch-y-mynydd** | 153 | **road** | Rhedyn | Lleyn Peninsula |
| Bwlch-yn-horeb | 317 | (track) | Rhos-y-gwaliau | Berwyn Range |
| Bwlch y Pawl | 559 | (path) | Ty-nant | Aran Range |
| Bwlch y Pentre | 541 | | Ty-Mawr | Snowdonia |
| Bwlch yr Anges | 445 | | Abercywarch | Aran Range |
| Bwlch-y-ddwy-elor | 410 | path | Ffridd Uchaf | Snowdonia |
| Bwlch yr Eifl | 350 | track | Trefor | Lleyn Peninsula |
| Bwlch y Rhediad | 378 | path | Blaenau Dolwyddelan | Snowdonia |

| Latitude, Longitude | National Grid | Notes |
|---|---|---|
| 53.00536, -4.14746 | SH5600347496 | 'Clover Pass'; below the Cave of Owain Glyndwr |
| 52.73746, -3.77471 | SH8027617014 | 'Cold Door Pass'; 'This pass is noted for being one of the three places, in which were assembled, six years after the wars of Glyndwr, all the great men of certain districts, in order to enforce the observation of justice' (T. Pennant, *A Tour in Wales* (1773)) |
| 52.88212, -3.80943 | SH7833733162 | 'Feidiog' is the name of several plants, including ground-ivy and wormwood; the col lies 200 m from the road (CR 13) in trackless terrain |
| 53.06892, -3.97706 | SH6763154237 | Conwy boundary; 'Rhiw-yr-ychain' on OS 1st edn; 'Oxen Slope Pass' |
| 52.70857, -3.72341 | SH8366213716 | 'Bog Gap' |
| 52.79289, -3.65542 | SH8847122987 | 'Bwlch Maes-yr-hirddyn' on OS 1st edn; 'Ram Pass' |
| 52.97749, -3.99618 | SH6606744103 | 'Bwlch Trwst-y-llon' on OS 1st edn; named after the lake; name changed between 1888 and 1899 |
| 52.74383, -3.66483 | SH8771117545 | 'Bwlch y Sygn' on OS 1st edn |
| 52.85053, -3.99264 | SH6591229975 | The summit of 'The Roman Steps' (a medieval trackway formed of stone slabs); 'tyddiad' = 'spreading out'? |
| 53.00209, -4.03212 | SH6373146907 | Slightly misplaced on modern OS; the 'battle' is unknown |
| 53.13267, -4.05568 | SH6256761476 | Misplaced on modern OS; 'brecan' = 'blanket' or 'breeches', but perhaps from 'bre' ('peak') and 'can' ('white', 'shining') |
| 52.85890, -3.60140 | SH9227730247 | 'Wool Carder Pass' |
| 53.10353, -4.01387 | SH6527358155 | Conwy boundary; 'Gap of the Two Mounds of Stone' (the two mountains called 'Glyder') |
| 52.85663, -3.50051 | SH9906429848 | 'Water Gap' |
| 52.88696, -3.52938 | SH9719233263 | 'Cart Gap'; road shown as track on OS |
| 52.75224, -3.74684 | SH8219718612 | 'Bog Gap' |
| 52.85688, -3.62681 | SH9056130061 | 'Cannon Ball Gap'?; name attributed to farm |
| 52.71325, -3.65002 | SH8863214121 | 'Pass of the Mound / Tumulus' |
| 52.74656, -3.71769 | SH8414917932 | The name, 'nook' or 'recess' (also 'armpit' or 'bosom'), describes the col; caption closer to the col on OS 1st edn |
| 52.97108, -3.59169 | SH9320942711 | 40 m from Conwy boundary; 'Bwlch y Graig-wen' on OS 1st edn; 'Greigwen' is the name of the nearby farm |
| 52.79614, -3.61328 | SH9132123284 | CR 16; the second-highest road col in Wales; nicknamed 'Hellfire Pass' by test drivers in mid-20th c; 'the pass of The Cross, one of the most terrible in North Wales. The height is gained by going up an exceedingly steep and narrow zig-zag path' (T. Pennant, *A Tour in Wales* (1773)) |
| 53.11691, -4.15783 | SH5568159924 | 'Pass of the Cross'; site of the Bwlch-y-groes slate quarry |
| 53.20284, -3.93757 | SH7068069060 | Conwy boundary; 'Bwlch y Gwrhyd' on OS 1st edn; 'gwryd' or 'gwrhyd' = 'fathom' (measurement) but can also mean 'battle' or 'miracle' |
| 52.63829, -3.99361 | SH6519306371 | 'Stone Gap'; name attributed to farm |
| 52.95727, -4.02467 | SH6409041908 | 'Stone Gap'; NCR 82 |
| 53.13305, -4.06418 | SH6200061534 | 'Horse Lake Pass' |
| 53.16658, -4.10882 | SH5912465351 | 'Peat Gap' |
| 53.19357, -4.04071 | SH6376268221 | 'Step Pass'? |
| 53.07700, -4.04165 | SH6332955257 | Pyg Track; 'Pig Pass' |
| 53.06394, -4.14855 | SH5612554014 | 'Pig Pass' |
| 52.86441, -4.52090 | SH3039932636 | 'Mountain Pass' |
| 52.90234, -3.54011 | SH9650734988 | 'Bwlch-hannerob' on OS 1st edn; 'Bacon Pass' |
| 52.82389, -3.60185 | SH9216026354 | 'Stake Pass'; once a place where legal disputes were settled, and considered to lie on the Gwynedd–Powys boundary |
| 52.99630, -3.66530 | SH8833045628 | Conwy boundary; misplaced on OS 50; 'Pass of the Village' |
| 52.73969, -3.70064 | SH8528217141 | 'Bwlch yr Henfaes' on OS 1st edn; 'henfaes' = 'uncultivated land' |
| 53.03156, -4.15956 | SH5527950434 | Roman road?; 'Two Biers Pass' (indicating a corpse road) |
| 52.98048, -4.44195 | SH3615245361 | Llŷn Coastal Path (pilgrim route); Roman road?; the name is that of the mountain; *see* p. 40 |
| 53.05199, -3.99108 | SH6663952380 | Conwy boundary; 'Bwlch Ehediad' on OS 1st edn; 'Pass of the Birds' or 'Flight' |

| Name | Elevation (m) | Surface | Nearest place | Region |
|---|---|---|---|---|
| Bwlch yr Henfaes  *see Bwlch yr Anges* | | | | |
| Bwlch y Rhiwgyr | 456 | path | Caerdeon | Mawddach Estuary |
| Bwlch y Rhosydd | 460 | track | Tanygrisiau | Snowdonia |
| Bwlch yr Ole Wen | 933 | path | Pont Pen-y-benglog | Snowdonia |
| **Bwlch-yr-ysgol** | 146 | **road** | Caerdeon | Mawddach Estuary |
| Bwlch-y-Sygyn | 250 | (path) | Beddgelert | Snowdonia |
| *Caergribin – Mynydd Carnguwch* | 255 | **B road** | Llithfaen | Lleyn Peninsula |
| *Carnedd Uchaf – Foel Grach* | 884 | (path) | Gerlan | Snowdonia |
| *Craig Portas (east)* | 550 | | Minllyn | Dyfi Hills |
| *Craig Portas (west)* | 550 | | Minllyn | Dyfi Hills |
| *Cribin Fawr – Waun Oer* | 566 | (path) | Brithdir | Dyfi Hills |
| *Cwm Dwyfor – Cwmuffynnon* | 602 | | Rhyd-Ddu | Snowdonia |
| Drws Bach | 731 | path | Llanymawddwy | Aran Range |
| *Drysgol – Gwaun Lydan* | 615 | | Llanymawddwy | Aran Range |
| *Foel Gron – Foel Goch* | 513 | path | Salem | Snowdonia |
| *Gyrn – Moel Wnion* | 496 | path | Llanllechid | Snowdonia |
| *Gyrn Goch – Gyrn Ddu* | 429 | | Gyrn Goch | Lleyn Peninsula |
| Hirnant Pass  *see Bwlch yr Hŵch* | | | | |
| *Llyn Hywel* | 560 | (path) | Ganllwyd | The Rhinogs |
| *Moel-ddu – Ffridd Bach* | 508 | path | Prenteg | Snowdonia |
| *Moelfre – Moelyblithcwm* | 427 | path | Dyffryn Ardudwy | The Rhinogs |
| *Moel Llyfnant – Llechwedd Erwent* | 542 | | Parc | The Arenigs |
| *Moel Ogof – Moel Lefn* | 576 | | Beddgelert | Snowdonia |
| Nant Llaeron | 486 | path | Pantperthog | Cadair Idris |
| Pant Gwyn | 442 | path | Pennal-isaf | Cadair Idris |
| *Trum y Ddysgl – Mynydd Drws-y-coed* | 638 | | Rhyd-Ddu | Snowdonia |
| Pen-y-bwlch | 263 | | Llanaelhaearn | Lleyn Peninsula |
| **Pen-y-bwlch-uchaf** | 53 | **A road** | Penrhyndeudraeth | Snowdonia |
| **Pen-y-pass** | 359 | **A road** | Pen-y-Gwryd | Snowdonia |
| The Roman Steps  *see Bwlch Tyddiad* | | | | |
| **Bwlch yr Hŵch / Hirnant Pass** | 320 | **road** | Rhyd-wen | Berwyn Range |
| **Drws-y-coed / Drws-y-coed Pass** | 144 | **B road** | Rhyd-Ddu | Snowdonia |
| **Drws-y-nant** | 143 | **A road** | Drws-y-nant | Aran Range |
| **Nant Ffrancon Pass** | 232 | **A road** | Pont Pen-y-benglog | Snowdonia |
| **Ogwen Pass** | 303 | **A road** | Pen-y-benglog | Snowdonia |
| **Pass of Aberglaslyn** | 14 | **A road** | Pont Aberglaslyn | Snowdonia |
| **Pass of Llanberis** | 194 | **A road** | Gwastadnant | Snowdonia |

## Monmouthshire · 1 col

| | | | | |
|---|---|---|---|---|
| **Bwlch** | 231 | **road** | Trewyn | Black Mountains |

## Neath Port Talbot · 5 cols

| | | | | |
|---|---|---|---|---|
| **Bwlch** | 231 | **road** | Cwmafan | Afan Valley |
| **Bwlch** | 106 | track | Cwmafan | Afan Valley |

| Latitude, Longitude | National Grid | Notes |
|---|---|---|
| 52.76036, -4.03618 | SH6269720028 | 'Rhiw' = 'slope', 'climb'; 'gyr' = 'flock', 'herd', 'drove'; sometimes called 'Pass of the Drovers' |
| 52.99712, -3.99539 | SH6618046285 | 'Bwlch Cwm-orthin' on OS 1st edn, now shifted to the north-east; 'Rhosydd' is the name of the slate quarry; the col is crossed by the remains of a tramway |
| 53.13991, -4.01260 | SH6547262199 | Not on OS 1st edn; later 'Oleu-wen' (the name of the mountain); 175 m from Conwy boundary; the equal second-highest col in Wales |
| 52.74995, -4.00194 | SH6497518806 | 'Ladder Gap'; 'ysgol' is probably 'ladder' rather than 'school' (no school is shown on OS 1st edn) |
| 53.01215, -4.08437 | SH6025848126 | 'Sygyn' or 'Sygun' is the name of the nearby copper mine |
| 52.96400, -4.43042 | SH3686343502 | |
| 53.17961, -3.96433 | SH6882166525 | Conwy boundary |
| 52.71235, -3.77002 | SH8052314213 | |
| 52.71363, -3.77611 | SH8011614365 | |
| 52.71981, -3.79376 | SH7894115082 | |
| 53.03959, -4.18097 | SH5387051371 | The two 'cooms' form the col |
| 52.77692, -3.68141 | SH8667721252 | 'Little Door' |
| 52.77635, -3.66529 | SH8776321163 | |
| 53.08512, -4.14232 | SH5661356357 | |
| 53.20172, -4.02501 | SH6483669097 | |
| 52.99753, -4.37506 | SH4070547107 | |
| 52.82010, -3.98189 | SH6654226570 | |
| 52.97596, -4.12193 | SH5761944175 | |
| 52.80165, -4.02251 | SH6374824594 | |
| 52.90337, -3.76097 | SH8165535444 | |
| 53.01103, -4.15622 | SH5543548144 | On the other side of the hill from Bwlch Meillionen |
| 52.63115, -3.89676 | SH7172505400 | Close to col on OS 1st edn |
| 52.61747, -3.93080 | SH6945503919 | 'White Hollow'; perhaps the 'hard strait' of the neighbouring Mynydd Rhyd-galed, though this could refer to the small, unnamed saddle north-east of Pant Gwyn |
| 53.04213, -4.16802 | SH5472451607 | 'Trum' = 'ridge'; 'Drws-y-coed' refers to the Drwys-y-coed Pass (*see* below), not to this col |
| 52.98889, -4.39474 | SH3935246190 | 'Head of the Pass' |
| 52.93755, -4.06296 | SH6145639787 | (Wales Coast Path); NCR 82; not on modern OS; 'Top of the Head of the Pass'; the lowest col in Wales |
| 53.08072, -4.02081 | SH6473755631 | 'Miners' Track', 'Pyg Track'; Roman road?; summit of Pass of Llanberis |
| 52.85836, -3.55923 | SH9511530125 | 'Pig Pass'; 'Hirnant' is the name of the river |
| 53.05836, -4.17329 | SH5444953443 | 'Door to the Wood' |
| 52.79095, -3.75533 | SH8160922991 | Not on OS 25 or 50; 'Drws Nant' on J. Cary, 'North Wales' (1804); 'Pass of the Stream' |
| 53.13987, -4.02942 | SH6434762227 | 'Beaver Stream' or 'Gorge'; continued to the south and east as Ogwen Pass; 'Nant Frangon' on J. Cary, 'Part of North Wales' (1794); the Khyber Pass in *Carry On up the Khyber* (1968) |
| 53.12341, -4.01863 | SH6501760375 | Conwy boundary; NCR 82; not on maps; name in common use, attested 1826; named after Llyn Ogwen |
| 52.99653, -4.09484 | SH5950546409 | 'Pass of Aber Glaslyn' on OS 1st edn |
| 53.08967, -4.04951 | SH6284356681 | *See* Pen-y-pass |
| 51.89560, -2.98849 | SO3207722357 | Offa's Dyke Path; between Bwlch Trewyn (not a col) and Dan-y-bwlch |
| 51.62699, -3.77543 | SS7720293512 | Not on modern OS |
| 51.61587, -3.79009 | SS7615792300 | Wales Coast Path |

| Name | Elevation (m) | Surface | Nearest place | Region |
|---|---|---|---|---|
| Bwlchgarw / Bwlch Garw | 464 | path | Abergwynfi | Ogmore Vale |
| Bwlch Nant-gwyn | 480 | track | Blaengwynfi | Ogmore Vale |
| Bwlch yr Afan | 533 | track | Nant-y-moel | Ogmore Vale |

## Pembrokeshire · 8 cols

| | | | | |
|---|---|---|---|---|
| **Bwlch** | 284 | **B road** | Tafarn-y-bwlch | Preseli Hills |
| Bwlch-giden | 340 | (path) | Mynachlog-ddu | Preseli Hills |
| **Bwlch-gwynt** | 405 | **B road** | Tafarn-y-bwlch | Preseli Hills |
| Bwlch Pennant | 412 | path | Tafarn-y-bwlch | Preseli Hills |
| Bwlch Ungwr | 317 | (path) | Mynachlog-ddu | Preseli Hills |
| **Bwlch-wyniad** | 254 | **B road** | Morvil | Preseli Hills |
| **Bwlchygroes / Bwlch-y-groes** | 195 | road | Bwlch-y-groes | Cneifa Valley |
| **Bwlch-y-pant** | 272 | **road** | Rosebush | Preseli Hills |

## Powys · 76 cols 4 passes

| | | | | |
|---|---|---|---|---|
| Adwy'r Graig | 468 | | Pencraig | Berwyn Range |
| Blaen-llymwynt Gate | 430 | path | Llanbadarn Fynydd | Beacon Hill uplands |
| **Bryn – Middletown Hill** | 271 | **road** | Middletown | Breiddin Hill |
| Bryn Gwyn | 421 | track | Pentre | Caersws Basin |
| Bwlch | 406 | track | Felindre | Beacon Hill uplands |
| **Bwlch** | 372 | **road** | Colva | Arrow Valley |
| **Bwlch** | 358 | **road** | Cefn Canol | Berwyn Range |
| **Bwlch** | 226 | **A road** | Bwlch | Black Mountains (Brecon Beacons) |
| **Bwlch Aeddan** | 231 | **road** | Cloddiau | Vyrnwy Valley |
| Bwlch ar y Fan / The Gap | 599 | track | Abercynafon | Brecon Beacons |
| Bwlch Bach | 411 | (path) | Abergwesyn | Cambrian Mountains |
| Bwlch Bach a'r Grib | 470 | track | Pengenffordd | Black Mountains (Brecon Beacons) |
| Bwlch Blaen-Twrch | 656 | (path) | Llanddeusant | The Black Mountain |
| **Bwlch Bryn-rhudd** | 385 | **A road** | Cnewr | The Black Mountain |
| Bwlch-cae-Griffyd | 235 | track | Aberangell | Dyfi Forest |
| Bwlch Carn | 588 | | Alltforgan | Berwyn Range |
| Bwlch-chwyrn | 347 | track | Pentre-llwyn-llŵyd | Cambrian Mountains |
| Bwlchciliau | 312 | track | Llanafan-fawr | Cambrian Mountains |
| Bwlch Cilgwyn | 425 | path | Dolfach | Cambrian Mountains |
| Bwlch Du | 438 | (track) | Penybontfawr | Berwyn Range |
| Bwlch Duwynt | 810 | path | Libanus | Brecon Beacons |
| Bwlch Giedd | 718 | (path) | Llanddeusant | The Black Mountain |
| **Bwlch-glâs** | 278 | **road** | Abertridwr | Vyrnwy Valley |
| **Bwlch Glynmynydd / Glyn mynydd** | 303 | **road** | Bont Dolgadfan | Cambrian Mountains |
| Bwlch Greolen | 415 | track | Penygarnedd | Berwyn Range |
| **Bwlch-gwyn** | 457 | track | Brynmelyn | Beacon Hill uplands |
| Bwlch Gwyn | 327 | path | Pandy | Cambrian Mountains |
| Bwlch-gynffyrch | 160 | track | Cemmaes | Dyfi Valley |
| Bwlch-hafod-y-gôg | 356 | track | Cwmbelan | Cambrian Mountains |
| Bwlch Hyddgen | 460 | track | Angler's Retreat | Cambrian Mountains |
| Bwlch-lluan | 255 | track | Esgairgeiliog | Dyfi Forest |
| **Bwlch-llwyn** | 345 | **road** | Betws Disserth | Edw Valley |
| Bwlch Main | 295 | track | Aberangell | Dyfi Forest |

| Latitude, Longitude | National Grid | Notes |
|---|---|---|
| 51.64105, -3.59759 | SS8954694792 | 150 m from Bridgend boundary; 'Rough Gap' |
| 51.66160, -3.57656 | SS9105197046 | 'White Stream Pass' |
| 51.64239, -3.56534 | SS9178194893 | Bridgend boundary; 'Pass of the River Afan'; 'Avan' on OS 1st edn |
| | | |
| 51.96821, -4.79074 | SN0838833650 | Deduced from 'Tafarn-y-bwlch' ('The Gap Inn') |
| 51.95785, -4.73567 | SN1202332409 | Not on modern OS; name attributed to farm (now a ruin); 'Goat Pass' |
| 51.95481, -4.80296 | SN0749132192 | 'Wind Gap'; 'Windy Yete': J. Johnston, *The Place-names of England and Wales* (1916), p. 179 (in 'old charter', undated) |
| 51.95444, -4.78722 | SN0857132110 | 'Pass at the Head of the Valley' |
| 51.96352, -4.70852 | SN1401632915 | 'One Man Pass' |
| 51.94797, -4.86582 | SN0314331600 | 'Shining Pass' |
| 51.99474, -4.56485 | SN2400736029 | 'Cross Gap' |
| 51.93097, -4.75685 | SN1055829420 | NCR 47; 'Pass of the Hollow' |
| | | |
| 52.83687, -3.40377 | SJ0553527518 | 'Rock Gap' |
| 52.39738, -3.26935 | SO1372878465 | 'Cold Wind Head Gate'; 'llynwynt' on OS 1st edn |
| 52.71036, -3.04203 | SJ2969813042 | A 'bryn' is a hill, bank or mound |
| 52.47411, -3.40192 | SO0487487166 | 'White Hill' |
| 52.40295, -3.22428 | SO1680579032 | Glyndŵr's Way |
| 52.16866, -3.17715 | SO1958852920 | NCR 825; name attributed to farm |
| 52.86862, -3.15411 | SJ2240930751 | Name attributed to farm and wood |
| 51.89099, -3.23961 | SO1478922108 | (Beacons Way); Roman road; 'Bwlch'r allwys' ('purging', 'flowing') on OS 1st edn |
| 52.68641, -3.22951 | SJ1698710567 | Glyndŵr's Way; 'Aeddan' is a personal name |
| 51.87488, -3.40807 | SO0316220527 | Beacons Way; The Gap Road; 'Pass on the Peak' (the hill called 'Fan y Big') |
| 52.16704, -3.64251 | SN8775853358 | Misspelt 'Bwich' on OS 25; 'Little Pass' |
| 51.96974, -3.18506 | SO1868630804 | 'Little Pass of (the ridge called) Y Grib' |
| | | |
| 51.88116, -3.72131 | SN8161621689 | Carmarthenshire boundary; 'Pass at the Head of the (River) Twrch' |
| 51.86333, -3.64128 | SN8708019579 | NCR 43; 'Bwlch Pen Rhûdd' on OS 1st edn; 'Pass of the Red Hill'; partly contiguous with a tramroad causeway |
| 52.67089, -3.72808 | SH8324609533 | 'Bwlch-cae-griffin' on OS 1st edn; 'cae' ('field') and personal name |
| 52.83381, -3.52308 | SH9749127342 | 'Cairn / Mound Pass'; Bwlch Cam on modern OS |
| 52.18075, -3.53844 | SN9490854727 | 'Chwyrn' = 'rapid', 'harsh', 'violent'; the reason for the col's name is unclear |
| 52.19141, -3.52904 | SN9557655899 | 'Nook Gap' |
| 52.39363, -3.55562 | SN9424278429 | 'Pass of the White Nook' |
| 52.79283, -3.36033 | SJ0836822564 | 'Black Pass' |
| 51.87731, -3.44620 | SO0054320849 | 'Black Wind Pass' |
| 51.87787, -3.70282 | SN8288021293 | (Beacons Way); 'Bwlch y Giedd' on OS 1st edn; 'giedd' for 'gledd' ('turf')? |
| 52.74566, -3.43883 | SJ0297017420 | Glyndŵr's Way; 'Blue Gap'; not on modern OS |
| 52.57911, -3.67490 | SN8660599240 | 'Pass of the Mountain Glen' |
| 52.79729, -3.35055 | SJ0903723047 | 'Greolen' = 'white bryony' |
| 52.38059, -3.26151 | SO1422976589 | 'White Gap'; name attributed to farm |
| 52.61850, -3.60400 | SH9150603512 | Glyndŵr's Way; 'White Gap' |
| 52.64559, -3.72991 | SH8305506722 | 'Pass before the Fork'; name attributed to farm |
| 52.41686, -3.57340 | SN9308881038 | 'Gap of Cuckoo Shieling' (summer pasture) |
| 52.52718, -3.82189 | SN7650093706 | 'Deer-skin Pass' |
| 52.63966, -3.79306 | SH7876606167 | 'Glittering Gap' |
| 52.22814, -3.29919 | SO1136059678 | NCR 825; 'Grove Gap' |
| 52.66702, -3.74075 | SH8237909123 | 'Stone Pass' ('maen') |

| Name | Elevation (m) | Surface | Nearest place | Region |
|---|---|---|---|---|
| **Bwlch-mawr** | 365 | **road** | Nantmel | Camlo Hill |
| **Bwlchmawr / Bwlch mawr** | 283 | **road** | Llwyn-Madoc | Cambrian Mountains |
| Bwlch-serth | 337 | track | Merthyr Cynog | Mynydd Epynt |
| Bwlch Sych | 448 | path | Hirnant | Berwyn Range |
| Bwlch Tri-Arglwydd | 399 | path | Aberllefenni | Dyfi Forest |
| Bwlchtuathre / Bwlch-tua-thre | 332 | path | Llanwrtyd | Cambrian Mountains |
| Bwlchybryngolan / Blwch y Bryn-golan | 505 | (track) | Llanfihangel Rhydithon | Radnor Forest |
| Bwlch-y-cefn | 350 | track | Llandegley | Edw Valley |
| **Bwlch-y-cibau** | 151 | **A road** | Bwlch-y-cibau | Vyrnwy Valley |
| Bwlch y Crogfa | 300 | | Meifod | Vyrnwy Valley |
| **Bwlchyddar / Bwlch-y-ddâr** | 282 | **road** | Bwlch-y-ddar | Tanat Valley |
| Bwlch y Ddau Faen | 530 | (path) | Llwyn-Madoc | Cambrian Mountains |
| **Bwlch-y-dderwen** | 281 | **road** | Tycrwyn | Vyrnwy Valley |
| **Bwlch-y-diarth** | 315 | **road** | Llanyre | Cambrian Mountains |
| Bwlch y Duwynt | 570 | (track) | Cnewr | Fforest Fawr |
| **Bwlchyfan / Bwlch y Fan** | 355 | **road** | Y Fan | Cambrian Mountains |
| **Bwlch y Fedwen** | 292 | **A road** | Nant-y-dugoed | Dyfi Hills |
| **Bwlch-y-garnedd** | 227 | **road** | Meifod | Vyrnwy Valley |
| **Bwlch-y-gle** | 285 | **B road** | Y Fan | Cambrian Mountains |
| **Bwlch-y-gorllwyn** | 333 | **road** | Abergwesyn | Cambrian Mountains |
| Bwlch y Groesen | 279 | track | Cwmyrhaiadr | Cambrian Mountains |
| Bwlch y Main | 385 | track | Pentre | Berwyn Range |
| Bwlch-y-Plain | 274 | (track) | Lloyney | Teme Valley |
| **Bwlch yr Efengyl / Gospel Pass** | 549 | **road** | Capel-y-ffin | Black Mountains (Brecon Beacons) |
| **Bwlch-y-sarnau (Pen-y-bwlch / Penbwlch)** | 395 | **road** | Bwlch-y-sarnau | Clywedog Valley |
| **Bwlch-y-waun** | 411 | **road** | Wern | Brecon Beacons |
| **Castell Dinas** | 395 | path | Pengenffordd | Black Mountains (Brecon Beacons) |
| **Clwyd Bwlch-y-groes** | 410 | **road** | Llandeilo'r-Fan | Mynydd Epynt |
| **Cockit Hill** | 354 | **road** | Pengenffordd | Black Mountains (Brecon Beacons) |
| Cwm Sere | 665 | (path) | Libanus | Brecon Beacons |
| **Dog and Duck** | 356 | **road** | Mainstone | Edenhope Hill |
| The Gap  see Bwlch ar y Fan | | | | |
| Garneddwen – Rhos | 473 | (path) | Tyn-y-ffridd | Berwyn Range |
| Giant's Grave | 447 | track | Glascwm | Radnorshire Hills |
| **Gore** | 225 | **A road** | Walton | Arrow Valley |
| Gospel Pass  see Bwlch yr Efengyl | | | | |
| Gwern-y-Bwlch | 213 | (path) | Commins Coch | Cambrian Mountains |
| Hergest Ridge – Hanter Hill | 347 | track | Dolyhir | Hergest Ridge |
| **Llaethbwlch** | 298 | **road** | Tycrwyn | Vyrnwy Valley |
| Pen Trumau – Mynydd Llysiau | 618 | path | Pengenffordd | Black Mountains (Brecon Beacons) |
| Pen y Bwlch | 358 | path | Llwyn-Madoc | Cambrian Mountains |
| Pwll Brwynog | 434 | track | Rhulen | Radnorshire Hills |
| Rocky Wood | 299 | track | Pentre | Radnor Forest |

| Latitude, Longitude | National Grid | Notes |
|---|---|---|
| 52.29950, -3.40720 | SO0413767752 | 'Great Gap' |
| 52.14473, -3.61847 | SN8934750840 | 'Great Gap' |
| 52.02229, -3.45386 | SO0033836984 | 'Steep Gap'; the col lies 100 m from the road on a cyclable track |
| 52.79635, -3.44236 | SJ0284523063 | Pererindod Melangell Walk; 'Dry Gap' |
| 52.67018, -3.76824 | SH8052909520 | 30 m from Gwynedd boundary; 'Three Lords' Pass' |
| 52.13051, -3.63081 | SN8846749277 | 'Homewards Gap' |
| 52.28197, -3.20323 | SO1801465552 | 'Hill-slope Pass' |
| 52.23918, -3.27962 | SO1271960882 | 'Ridge Gap'; name attributed to farm |
| 52.74826, -3.21888 | SJ1782217435 | 'Cibau' = a measure (four gallons or half a bushel), 'bowl', 'husk' |
| 52.73155, -3.28010 | SJ1365715648 | 'Hanging Pass' |
| 52.79105, -3.23121 | SJ1707122209 | Roman road?; 'Oak Tree Pass' |
| 52.21196, -3.62081 | SN8935458321 | 'Two Stones Pass' |
| 52.73498, -3.29927 | SJ1236916052 | 'Oak Gap' |
| 52.24557, -3.43537 | SO0209861792 | 'Pass of the Stranger'; name attributed to farm |
| 51.86394, -3.59828 | SN9004219581 | 'Pass of the Black Wind' |
| 52.48959, -3.56302 | SN9397089113 | 'Pass of the Peak' |
| 52.71155, -3.58166 | SH9324613828 | 'Birch Pass' |
| 52.73582, -3.25903 | SJ1508816098 | 'Pass of the Mound / Tumulus' |
| 52.48176, -3.58994 | SN9212388282 | Meaning uncertain; on modern OS only in the name of the dam |
| 52.16972, -3.65364 | SN8700453674 | 'Pass of the Escort' or 'convoy'; located between Bwlch-y-gorllwyn-isaf and -uchaf ('lower' and 'upper') |
| 52.54403, -3.81981 | SN7668895576 | Glyndŵr's Way; Bwlch y Groes on OS 1st edn; 'Pass of the Cross' |
| 52.81200, -3.40509 | SJ0539224754 | 'Stone Pass' ('maen') |
| 52.37021, -3.11869 | SO2393275274 | Name obscure (English, applied to flattish area at summit?) |
| 52.01003, -3.11552 | SO2353235210 | NCR 42; the highest road col in Wales; traditionally associated with Peter and Paul, or with fundraising for the Third Crusade, though 'efengyl' ('gospel') may derive from 'y fingel' or 'y fan cul', referring to the narrow notch in the ridge |
| 52.36082, -3.42664 | SO0294674599 | Glyndŵr's Way; the col summit is 'Pen-y-bwlch' on OS 1st edn; 'Pass of the Causeway' or 'Paved Road' |
| 51.86058, -3.29406 | SO1098218791 | Beacons Way; 'Bwlch-y-waen' on OS 1st edn; name attributed to farm; road ends at col; 'waun' or 'gwaun' = 'moorland', 'heath', 'marshy meadow' |
| 51.96527, -3.19471 | SO1801430317 | (Three Rivers Ride); the 'castell' is the site of an Iron Age hill fort and the highest castle in Wales |
| 52.01442, -3.64181 | SN8742236383 | 'Cross Gap Gate'; caption at the col on OS 1st edn; misspelt 'Clwud' on OS 25 |
| 51.94715, -3.22248 | SO1607328334 | Three Rivers Ride; the prefix 'cock' is sometimes associated with a col (related to Old Norse 'kok', 'gullet' or 'throat'?) |
| 51.88024, -3.42613 | SO0193121148 | (Beacons Way); 'Cwm Seri' on OS 1st edn |
| 52.49902, -3.07854 | SO2687989559 | English border (Shropshire); 'Dog and Duck Cottage' on modern OS |
| 52.87341, -3.29361 | SJ1302831443 | Wrexham boundary |
| 52.18113, -3.25877 | SO1403054400 | The 'Giant's Grave' is a tumulus |
| 52.22545, -3.08567 | SO2593859138 | From Old English 'gara', a triangular piece of land, a cape or a promontory, perhaps here referring to the 'necks' of land on either side of the col |
| 52.62503, -3.70346 | SH8479004393 | (Glyndŵr's Way); 'Alders of the Pass'; not on OS 1st edn |
| 52.20451, -3.09296 | SO2540656817 | English border (Herefordshire) |
| 52.74025, -3.30972 | SJ1167416651 | 'Milk Gap'; name attributed to farm |
| 51.95031, -3.15904 | SO2043828614 | The meeting of five paths; frequently referred to as a col but unnamed |
| 52.17238, -3.61703 | SN8951453913 | 'Head of the Pass' |
| 52.14841, -3.23481 | SO1560650732 | The 'pwll' is a small pool |
| 52.29626, -3.10883 | SO2447767038 | The meeting of five paths; no other place name survives |

| Name | Elevation (m) | Surface | Nearest place | Region |
|---|---|---|---|---|
| Waun Bwlch | 394 | | Llanafan-fawr | Cambrian Mountains |
| Whimble – Whinyard Rocks | 514 | (track) | New Radnor | Radnor Forest |
| **Abergwesyn Pass** | 475 | **road** | Abergwesyn | Cambrian Mountains |
| **Bwlch Cerrig Duon** | 480 | **road** | Cnewr | The Black Mountain |
| **Milltir Gerrig (or Cerrig) Pass** | 489 | **B road** | Pennant Melangell | Berwyn Range |
| **Storey Arms Pass** | 435 | **A road** | Libanus | Brecon Beacons |

## Rhondda Cynon Taff · 2 cols

| Name | Elevation (m) | Surface | Nearest place | Region |
|---|---|---|---|---|
| **Bwlch y Clawdd** | 450 | **A road** | Nant-y-moel | Ogmore Vale |
| Bwlch y Lladron | 496 | (track) | Hirwaun | Rhondda Valley |

## Wrexham · 5 cols

| Name | Elevation (m) | Surface | Nearest place | Region |
|---|---|---|---|---|
| Bwlch Cynwyd | 562 | track | Plas Nantyr | Berwyn Range |
| Bwlch Maen Gwynedd | 711 | path | Tan-y-pistyll | Berwyn Range |
| Bwlch y Dolydd | 445 | path | Plas Nantyr | Berwyn Range |
| Croes-y-wernen | 525 | path | Plas Nantyr | Berwyn Range |
| Garneddwen – Rhos | 473 | (path) | Tyn-y-ffridd | Berwyn Range |

# Scotland

## Aberdeenshire · 42 cols 3 passes

| Name | Elevation (m) | Surface | Nearest place | Region |
|---|---|---|---|---|
| A' Chuingeal  *see* The Fungle | | | | |
| Am Braid | 765 | | Glenlee | Cairngorms |
| Am Braid | 698 | | Auchronie | Cairngorms |
| An Cadha Mor  *see* Camore | | | | |
| An Lairig | 1134 | (path) | Feshiebridge | Cairngorms |
| An Slugan | 600 | path | Allanaquoich | Cairngorms |
| An Slugan | 600 | | Gairnshiel Lodge | Cairngorms |
| An Slugan | 519 | | Easter Balmoral | Cairngorms |
| Bealach Dearg | 651 | path | Inver | Cairngorms |
| Black Sneck | 485 | track | Rinmore | Don Valley |
| Cairnagour Hill – Mona Gowan | 663 | | Fleuchats | Mona Gowan |
| **Cairnwell Pass** | 667 | **A road** | Spittal of Glenshee | Cairngorms |
| Camore / Ca Mor / An Cadha Mor | 694 | | Blairnamarrow | Ladder Hills |
| Charsk | 562 | (track) | Fleuchats | Mona Gowan |
| Corse of Garbet | 446 | (track) | Elrick | Strathbogie |
| **Corsedardar Hill / Corse Dardar** | 225 | **B road** | Finzean | Lower Deeside |
| Craws Nest | 443 | (track) | Lumsden | Correen Hills |
| Cross | 560 | path | Bracklach | Mount Meddin |
| The Eag | 587 | (path) | Dalestie | Cairngorms |
| The Fungle / A' Chuingeal / Slochd | 602 | track | Ballochan | Forest of Birse |
| Glac na Mòine | 450 | track | Kirkton of Glenbuchat | Cairngorms |
| Glac of Barns | 310 | track | Mains of Glenbuchat | Cairngorms |

| Latitude, Longitude | National Grid | Notes |
|---|---|---|
| 52.21735, -3.51598 | SN9652958765 | 'Heath Pass' |
| 52.25798, -3.16136 | SO2082762837 | |
| 52.19207, -3.72072 | SN8247656266 | Unnamed on OS 1st edn |
| 51.89073, -3.66318 | SN8564122661 | 'Pass of the Black Stones' |
| 52.86303, -3.46157 | SJ0170030505 | Denbighshire boundary; attested 1843; 'Siglen y Bwlch' ('Marsh of the Pass') nearby, on OS 10; 'Stoney Mile' |
| 51.87102, -3.47580 | SN9849120190 | From the name of a drovers' inn |
| 51.63911, -3.53358 | SS9397194481 | Bridgend boundary; 'Pass of the (Earthen) Bank'; fourth-highest road col and highest point on an A road in Wales (not, as sometimes stated, Britain) |
| 51.71858, -3.52605 | SN9467703308 | 'Thieves' Pass' |
| 52.94282, -3.31731 | SJ1157539194 | Denbighshire boundary; North Berwyn Way; Cynwyd is the village to which the col leads |
| 52.89625, -3.37494 | SJ0760334086 | Denbighshire boundary; North Berwyn Way; Roman road?; 'Gwynedd Stone Pass' (referring to a boundary stone 500 m to the east) |
| 52.92472, -3.28286 | SJ1385337138 | 'Pass of the Meadows' |
| 52.93238, -3.32673 | SJ1092038043 | Denbighshire boundary; 'Alder Cross'; the path along the Nant Croes-y-wernen continues to the col except on modern OS |
| 52.87341, -3.29361 | SJ1302831443 | Powys boundary |
| 56.96805, -2.96031 | NO4171186725 | Angus boundary; deduced from Braid Cairn; 'The Horse-collar' |
| 56.97230, -2.93145 | NO4347387173 | Angus boundary; deduced from Braid Cairn; 'The Horse-collar' |
| 57.08174, -3.71175 | NH9634500272 | Inverness boundary; deduced from Sròn na Lairige ('Sròn na Leirg' on OS 1st edn); 'The Pass'; the highest col in the British Isles |
| 57.04308, -3.45823 | NO1161895611 | Deduced from Allt Gleann and Meall an t-Slugain; see 'slug' in Glossary |
| 57.11380, -3.17664 | NJ2883903154 | Deduced from Coire an t-Slugain; see 'slug' in Glossary |
| 56.99540, -3.19963 | NO2721589999 | Deduced from Coire an t-Slugain; see 'slug' in Glossary |
| 57.06695, -3.35492 | NO1793998139 | 'Red Pass' |
| 57.25510, -2.96499 | NJ4187918681 | See 'sneck' in Glossary |
| 57.13739, -3.10656 | NJ3312505708 | |
| 56.88082, -3.41072 | NO1412877491 | Perth & Kinross boundary; from 'Càrn Bhalg' ('Hill of Bags'), perhaps referring to the rounded hills; the highest road col in the British Isles; see p. 73 |
| 57.19639, -3.27785 | NJ2288212457 | Moray boundary; 'The Great Pass' |
| 57.15072, -3.09737 | NJ3370507183 | From 'crasg' (see Glossary) |
| 57.33277, -2.97282 | NJ4153027334 | Moray boundary; 'Rough Place Crossing' |
| 57.03510, -2.66836 | NO5953593977 | 'Corse' may be 'cross' or 'crossing'; Birse parish war memorial (1921) |
| 57.28391, -2.82428 | NJ5040721777 | Craw's Nest on OS 1st edn; a common term for a robbers' den |
| 57.27163, -2.99829 | NJ3989720550 | Moray boundary; deduced from Burn of Cross and Hillock of Cross |
| 57.17495, -3.35545 | NJ1814610161 | Moray boundary; 'The Notch' |
| 56.96211, -2.81895 | NO5029885951 | Angus boundary; 'chuingeal' = 'defile' |
| 57.22450, -3.05558 | NJ3636115356 | 'Peat Hollow' |
| 57.20701, -2.98879 | NJ4036513349 | From 'beàrn' ('gap', 'breach') |

| Name | Elevation (m) | Surface | Nearest place | Region |
|---|---|---|---|---|
| Glac of Bunzeach | 555 | | Fleuchats | Mona Gowan |
| Glac of Skellater | 497 | track | Colnabaichin | Cairngorms |
| Glac Riach | 379 | | Waterside | Cairngorms |
| Glack | 216 | (track) | Invery House | Lower Deeside |
| Glack of Tillyminnate | 300 | track | Clashindarroch | Strathbogie |
| **Glackhead** | 355 | **A road** | Bruntland | Strathbogie |
| Glacks of Balloch | 228 | track | Davoch of Grange | Strath Isla |
| Glac-na-far | 281 | (track) | Cairnargat | Strathbogie |
| The Ladder | 732 | path | Chapeltown | Ladder Hills |
| Làirig Ghrù / Learg Ghruamach | 836 | (path) | Glenmore | Cairngorms |
| **Lecht Pass / The Lecht** | 645 | **A road** | Milltown | Ladder Hills |
| Màm nan Carn | 910 | | Dalmunzie House | Cairngorms |
| Meall Tarsuinn – Meall nan Eun | 785 | | Glenceitlein | Black Mount |
| Slack | 191 | track | Rorandle | Garioch |
| Slack of Dye | 385 | path | Glendye Lodge | Glen Dye |
| Slacks of Glencarvie | 627 | | Fleuchats | Mona Gowan |
| Slochd Chaimbeil | 745 | | Chapeltown | Ladder Hills |
| **The Slug / Slochd / Pass of the Mountains** | 235 | **A road** | Darnford | Durris Forest |
| Smart's Cairn | 329 | | East Cairnbeg | Strath Finella |
| The Sneck | 970 | | Inchrory | Cairngorms |
| Snowy Slack | 577 | | Bracklach | Mount Meddin |
| Wild Mare's Leap | 340 | | Tipperty | Fetteresso Forest |
| **Birkhill Pass / (The) Birk Hill** | 363 | **A road** | Tillypronie | Cairngorms |
| **Cairn O' Mounth (or Mount) Pass** | 449 | **B road** | Clatterin Brig | Strath Finella |
| **Pass of Ballater** | 225 | **B road** | Ballater | Deeside |

## Angus · 40 cols 2 passes

| | | | | |
|---|---|---|---|---|
| A' Chuingeal  *see* The Fungle | | | | |
| Am Braid | 765 | | Glenlee | Cairngorms |
| Am Braid | 698 | | Auchronie | Cairngorms |
| **An Lairig / Lumley Den** | 251 | **A road** | Milton | Sidlaw Hills |
| Balkello Hill – Balluderon Hill | 333 | track | Nether Handwick | Sidlaw Hills |
| Balloch | 745 | | Glen Lee | Spittal of Glenmuick |

| Latitude, Longitude | National Grid | Notes |
|---|---|---|
| 57.12958, -3.06409 | NJ3568204798 | Glac of Bunnsach on OS 1st edn; 'Hollow of the place where osiers grow' |
| 57.19015, -3.14042 | NJ3117411615 | Above Wester Skellater |
| 57.19148, -3.06475 | NJ3575011689 | From 'riabhach' ('brindled' or 'grey') |
| 57.03065, -2.47687 | NO7115393384 | Col name suggested by Glack's Well 500 m north-east |
| 57.38610, -2.84454 | NJ4932733168 | Above Tillyminnate Farm |
| 57.33893, -2.92544 | NJ4439227980 | 'Glack' = 'hollow'; 'head' derived from 'cuid' (cattle-fold) |
| 57.52858, -2.87166 | NJ4790049049 | Below the Balloch (a hill); from 'glacan' (a small 'glack') and *bealach* |
| 57.43297, -2.89086 | NJ4661138421 | 'Glack-na-far' on OS 1st edn; 'Hollow of the ridge' |
| 57.25766, -3.19382 | NJ2807919185 | Moray boundary |
| 57.09145, -3.69515 | NH9737801327 | Inverness boundary; name obscure; second name, perhaps speculative, on OS 1st edn ('Gloomy' or 'Forbidding Pass'); also known locally as An Làirig Shuas, 'The Western Pass', the eastern being Learg an Laoigh; (A. Diack, *Place-Names of the Cairngorms National Park*) |
| 57.20069, -3.24744 | NJ2472812902 | Moray boundary; 'The Lecht' on Roy's Military Survey of Scotland (1747–52); Leac a' Ghobhainn on OS 1st edn (caption shifted west on modern OS); 'Hill Slope of the Smith' (from the legend of a blacksmith banished from Inverness-shire); 'leac' can also be a hill summit or a flat stone; the geographical summit is at 57.20032, -3.24887 (636 m) on the other side of the Lecht Ski Centre building; the original col name (perhaps 'lairig' or 'learg') has not survived; the second-highest road col in the British Isles |
| 56.88757, -3.56493 | NO0474878446 | Perth & Kinross boundary; name attributed to mountain; 'Pass of the Cairns' |
| 56.56194, -4.95729 | NN1837045023 | Inverness boundary; 'Tarsuinn' contains the notion of 'crossing' |
| 57.25795, -2.58969 | NJ6452418740 | Deduced from Slack Burn and Slack Wood |
| 56.97262, -2.62428 | NO6214786996 | 'Slock of Glendye' on W. Garden, 'A Map of Kincardineshire' (1797) |
| 57.13649, -3.08120 | NJ3465905584 | 'Slocks of Glencarvy' in *The New Statistical Account of Scotland*, XII (1845), p. 536 |
| 57.23534, -3.23250 | NJ2570116742 | Moray boundary; deduced from Grains of Slochd Chaimbeil; 'Campbell's Hollow' |
| 57.01535, -2.37287 | NO7745791641 | 'Pass of the Mountains' in *The Traveller's Guide through Scotland* (1824) and *Leigh's New Pocket Road-Book of Scotland* (1829) |
| 56.89193, -2.50424 | NO6937877954 | The cairn is above the col to the south; associated in folklore with the slaying of a huge serpent; personal name unexplained; 'The traditions relative to this Cairn are so extravagant, and wild, that none of them can with propriety be given here.' (OS name book, 1863) |
| 57.09160, -3.45678 | NJ1182101010 | Moray boundary; not on OS 1st edn |
| 57.27736, -2.98221 | NJ4087621174 | Col summit 130 m from Moray boundary |
| 56.96644, -2.47305 | NO7132986223 | 'Wild Mares Loup' on W. Garden, 'A Map of Kincardineshire' (1797) and OS 1st edn; 'loup' = 'leap' |
| 57.16504, -2.96877 | NJ4151308659 | Not on OS, except as hill name; I. Murray and A. Watson, *Place Names Discoveries on Upper Deeside and the Far Highlands* (2015); there is another Birkhill Pass on the Borders / Dumfries & Galloway boundary |
| 56.91671, -2.57732 | NO6494980748 | 'The Mounth' = the Grampian Mountains; 'Cairn O' Mont' on W. Garden, 'A Map of Kincardineshire' (1797) and J. Thomson, 'Kincardine Shire' (1822) |
| 57.05967, -3.04548 | NO3668996999 | Name attested 1819; first mapped 1869 (OS 1st edn); Ballater (perhaps containing *bealach*) is the town to the south of the pass |
| | | |
| 56.96805, -2.96031 | NO4171186725 | Aberdeenshire boundary; deduced from Braid Cairn; 'The Horse-collar' |
| 56.97230, -2.93145 | NO4347387173 | Aberdeenshire boundary; deduced from Braid Cairn; 'The Horse-collar' |
| 56.56327, -2.97648 | NO4008641683 | First name deduced from Finlarg Hill |
| 56.54563, -3.03427 | NO3650539772 | |
| 56.90425, -3.08722 | NO3388379739 | Name attributed to a burn and two hills; from *bealach* |

| Name | Elevation (m) | Surface | Nearest place | Region |
|---|---|---|---|---|
| Bealach of Runavey | 438 | | Auchavan | Glen Beanie |
| Clash Cairny | 518 | (track) | Redheugh | Hill of Garbet |
| Clash of Dullet | 499 | | Tarfside | Glen Esk |
| Clash of Wirren | 369 | (track) | Cairncross | Glen Esk |
| Corse | 603 | (track) | Redheugh | Glen Lethnot |
| Corse | 571 | (track) | Runtaleave | Glen Prosen |
| *Corwiry / Coire Fhuaraidh* | 622 | | Rottal | Glen Clova |
| *Cowie Hill – Garlet* | 409 | track | Cairncross | Glen Esk |
| Craig of Balloch | 328 | path | Glenhead Farm | Glenisla Forest |
| Cross / An Gobhal | 340 | track | Nether Handwick | Sidlaw Hills |
| Deep Sneck of Creag Leacachd | 919 | | Auchavan | Cairngorms |
| Farquharson's Sneck / Easter Glacanbuidhe | 668 | | Auchavan | Cairngorms |
| Flobbit | 595 | | Tarfside | Glen Esk |
| The Fungle / A' Chuingeal / Slochd | 602 | track | Ballochan | Forest of Birse |
| Glack of Balquhader | 586 | (track) | Auchavan | Glen Prosen |
| Glack of Barny | 387 | path | Glenhead Farm | Glenisla Forest |
| Glack of Corraich / Sneck o Corraich | 470 | track | Easter Lednathie | Glen Prosen |
| Glack of Glengairney / The Glack | 608 | | Auchavan | Cairngorms |
| Glack of the Barnetts | 532 | | Alrick | Glen Shee |
| *Hayston Hill – Whyrnny Hill* | 283 | (track) | Kincaldrum | Sidlaw Hills |
| Little Glack an Buidhe | 735 | | Auchavan | Cairngorms |
| Lumley Den  *see* An Lairig | | | | |
| *Mount Sned – Hill of Mondurran* | 535 | (path) | Auchnacree | Glen Lethnot |
| Slack of Barna | 444 | track | Auchmull | Glen Esk |
| Slack of Forbie | 518 | | Fernybank | Glen Esk |
| Slochd | 409 | track | Tillyarblet | Glen Esk |
| Slochd  *see* The Fungle | | | | |
| The Slug | 320 | (track) | Auchnacree | Glen Ogil |
| The Sneck o Arnagullan | 534 | (track) | Clachnabrain | Glen Clova |
| Sneck o Corraich  *see* Glack of Corraich | | | | |
| Sneck of Corinch | 422 | track | Glenarm | Glen Clova |
| Sneck of Cormuir | 485 | path | Runtaleave | Glen Prosen |
| Sneck of Farchal | 705 | | Braedownie | Glen Clova |
| Sneck of Inks | 562 | | Clova | Glen Clova |
| Sneck of Lapshalloch | 475 | path | The Drums | Glen Clova |
| Sneck of the Call | 686 | track | Auchavan | Cairngorms |
| The Sneck o the Barns | 554 | | Clova | Glen Clova |
| Windy Gates | 345 | path | Kirkton of Auchterhouse | Sidlaw Hills |
| **Glack of Newtyle** | 127 | **B road** | Newtyle | Sidlaw Hills |
| Monega Pass | 885 | track | Auchavan | Cairngorms |

| Latitude, Longitude | National Grid | Notes |
|---|---|---|
| 56.79918, -3.36341 | NO1683068345 | Perth & Kinross boundary; not on OS; 'Ruynavey Bhellach' on Pont, 28 (c. 1583–96) |
| 56.80809, -2.88868 | NO4583568860 | 'Stony Furrow' (see below) |
| 56.88067, -2.85693 | NO4787576914 | 'Clash' is from 'clais' ('furrow', 'trench', 'gutter', 'hollow'), 'dullet' from 'diollaid' ('saddle') |
| 56.86548, -2.83209 | NO4936875204 | For 'clais', see above; on a smugglers' and peddlers' route; Wirren is the hill to the east; 'Clash' on J. Ainslie, 'Map of the County of Forfar' (1794) |
| 56.83125, -2.91588 | NO4420971460 | Presumed location, deduced from Burn of Corscarie ('Crosg-choire') |
| 56.76818, -3.16957 | NO2860964676 | Deduced from Cairn Corse |
| 56.81412, -2.99276 | NO3949069619 | Name of burn ('Windward Corrie') |
| 56.88386, -2.84096 | NO4885277257 | |
| 56.73707, -3.19122 | NO2722561236 | 'Balloch' from bealach |
| 56.55310, -2.99993 | NO3862840572 | Deduced from Cross Den and Craigowl Hill above the col ('Creag Gobhal', 'Hill of the Fork' or 'Crotch') |
| 56.85788, -3.38349 | NO1573574903 | Perth & Kinross boundary; not on OS; A. Watson, Place Names (2013); Creag Leacach ('Flat Stone Rock') is the mountain to the south |
| 56.83657, -3.38214 | NO1577072530 | Perth & Kinross boundary; first name in A. Watson, Place Names (2013); second name on OS; Farquharson was Laird of Invercauld |
| 56.86796, -2.87941 | NO4648675517 | The name ('Flow Bog') is closer to the col on OS 1st edn |
| 56.96211, -2.81895 | NO5029885951 | Aberdeenshire boundary; 'chuingeal' = 'defile' |
| 56.82057, -3.25075 | NO2375370595 | Name obscure |
| 56.76058, -3.22610 | NO2513863890 | From 'beàrn' ('gap', 'breach') |
| 56.74887, -3.13150 | NO3090062488 | First name closer to col on OS 1st edn; second name only in A. Watson, Place Names (2013); 'Horse Corrie' |
| 56.82579, -3.35928 | NO1714171302 | Perth & Kinross boundary; at the head of Gleann Carnach |
| 56.74029, -3.36162 | NO1680961789 | Perth & Kinross boundary; 'Barnetts' is probably related to 'beàrn' (see Glossary) |
| 56.57863, -2.95872 | NO4120143377 | 'Whyrny Hill' on J. Ainslie, 'Map of the County of Forfar' (1794) |
| 56.84257, -3.39279 | NO1513473211 | Perth & Kinross boundary; not on OS but survives in 'Easter Glacanbuidhe' nearby; A. Watson, Place Names (2013); 'Little Yellow Hollow' |
| 56.81658, -2.89526 | NO4544669810 | |
| 56.88368, -2.68015 | NO5865277128 | From 'beàrn' ('gap', 'breach') |
| 56.87091, -2.75270 | NO5421575753 | Col name from 'burn' |
| 56.79795, -2.80866 | NO5070867671 | 'Sloc' = 'gully', 'defile' |
| 56.76751, -2.89132 | NO4561564345 | 'Slug' = 'gorge', 'narrow pass'' |
| 56.80062, -2.99451 | NO3936168118 | Not on OS; A. Watson, Place Names (2013); col name from 'burn' |
| 56.76679, -3.04775 | NO3605264401 | 'Corinch' is the neighbouring hillside ('Corrie of the Field') |
| 56.77984, -3.17334 | NO2840065978 | Not on OS; 'cormuir' = 'big corrie'?; A. Watson, Place Names (2013); earlier name perhaps in Cairn Corse Corrie to the south |
| 56.84800, -3.17851 | NO2821573570 | From 'faireachail' ('watching') |
| 56.82498, -3.13960 | NO3054670967 | Below Cairn Inks |
| 56.78724, -3.06078 | NO3529166689 | From 'Lub Seilich' ('Bend of the Willow'); A. Watson, Place Names (2013) |
| 56.83782, -3.30700 | NO2035772579 | 'The Call' is the hill to the south |
| 56.83046, -3.12298 | NO3157071560 | Not on OS (though name survives in Cairn of Barns); from beàrn ('gap', 'breach'); A. Watson, Place Names (2013) |
| 56.54259, -3.04289 | NO3597039441 | |
| 56.54927, -3.13432 | NO3036040274 | Commonly referred to as a pass (both road and railway); Newtyle is the village at the northern end |
| 56.86571, -3.34056 | NO1837075723 | The highest pass (as opposed to col) in the British Isles; 'Month Eigie' in Queen Victoria's Journal, 16 October, 1861; see p. 73; 'eagach' = 'notched', 'indented' |

| Name | Elevation (m) | Surface | Nearest place | Region |
|---|---|---|---|---|
| **Argyll and Bute – Islands** · 45 cols 2 passes | | | | |
| Am Bealach | 341 | track | Lussagiven | Jura |
| Am Feadan | 285 | | Ardmenish | Jura |
| An Eag | 206 | | Kinuachdrachd | Jura |
| An Fiar Màm | 293 | | Tenga | Mull |
| Bealach a' Bhearnain | 210 | | Bunnahabhain | Islay |
| Bealach a' Chruaidh-ghlinn | 330 | | Lussagiven | Jura |
| Bealach a' Ghrianain Mòr | 217 | | Glengarrisdale | Jura |
| Bealach a' Mhaim | 90 | | Kilcheran | Lismore |
| Bealach an Eisg | 154 | | Kinuachdrachd | Jura |
| Bealach an Fhir-bhogha | 430 | | Kinlochspelve | Mull |
| Bealach an Friodhain | 155 | path | Auchnacraig | Mull |
| Bealach an Tarabairt | 40 | | Garbh Eileach | Garbh Eileach |
| Bealach Àrd | 140 | | Killinallan | Islay |
| Bealach Bhriste Cnàimhe | 343 | | Glenbatrick | Jura |
| Bealach Cnoc nan Coileach | 132 | | Kinuachdrachd | Jura |
| Bealach Dearg | 58 | | Garrochty | Bute |
| Bealach Gaoithe | 209 | | Lealt | Jura |
| Bealach Gaoth' Niar | 250 | | Bunnahabhain | Islay |
| Bealach Loch Tigh-sealga | 310 | | Lussagiven | Jura |
| Bealach Mòr | 323 | | Glenbyre | Mull |
| Bealach Mòr | 187 | | Fellonmore | Mull |
| Bealach na Baintighearna | 113 | (track) | Glenbatrick | Jura |
| Bealach na Caillich | 84 | track | Kilchiaran | Islay |
| Bealach na h-Imriche | 232 | | Tarbert | Jura |
| Bealach nan Craobh | 275 | | Lagganulva | Mull |
| *Beinn nan Gabhar – An Cruachan* | 475 | | Knock | Mull |
| *Beinn nan Gabhar – Beinn a' Ghràig* | 405 | | Knock | Mull |
| *Beinn Shiantaidh – Corra Bheinn* | 367 | | Leargybreck | Jura |
| Eag an Fhir-bhogha | 269 | | Tarbert | Jura |
| Eag Fionna Mhàm | 440 | | Balmeanach | Mull |
| Glac an t-Saighdeir | 291 | | Leargybreck | Jura |
| Glac Mhearsamail / An Caolas | 395 | | Leargybreck | Jura |
| Glac nan Cruidhean | 120 | | Kilchoman | Islay |
| Imir an Aonaich | 454 | | Leargybreck | Jura |
| Màm a' Choir' Idhir | 574 | | Gortenbuie | Mull |
| Màm an Tiompain | 456 | | Craig | Mull |
| Màm an Trotanaich | 399 | (path) | Glenbyre | Mull |
| Màm an t-Sìob' | 374 | | Leargybreck | Jura |
| Màm Bhradhadail | 424 | | Ishriff | Mull |
| Màm Bhreapadail | 388 | path | Craig | Mull |
| Màm Chlachaig | 330 | path | Uluvalt | Mull |
| Màm Choireadail | 464 | | Craig | Mull |
| Màm Clach a' Bhadain | 373 | | Dererach | Mull |
| Màm Lìrein | 495 | | Ardura | Mull |
| Màm na Croise | 422 | | Balevulin | Mull |
| **Gleann Seilisdeir (or Seilisteir)** | 141 | **B road** | Balmeanach | Mull |

| Latitude, Longitude | National Grid | Notes |
|---|---|---|
| 56.02201, -5.87977 | NR5832587804 | Deduced from Lochan Barr a' Bhealaich; 'The Pass' |
| 55.91790, -5.91897 | NR5522676364 | 'The Whistle' (*see* Glossary) |
| 56.12700, -5.73317 | NR6808898976 | 'The Nick' |
| 56.51856, -6.08993 | NM4852143775 | Deduced from Meall an Fhìar Mhàim; 'The Crooked Pass' |
| 55.88090, -6.18139 | NR3859173212 | 'Pass of the Small Gap' |
| 56.04415, -5.85169 | NR6021290168 | 'Hard Valley Pass' |
| 56.09389, -5.79979 | NR6374795520 | 'Bealach a' Ghrianain Mhòir' on OS 1st edn; 'Pass of the Great Peak' |
| 56.47007, -5.58343 | NM7937836640 | 'Pass of the Gap' |
| 56.13399, -5.70931 | NR6961299674 | 'Pass of the Fish' |
| 56.39055, -5.80932 | NM6498128545 | 'Archers' Pass' |
| 56.40424, -5.68931 | NM7246629663 | Not on OS 25 or 50; Fhiodhain on OS 1st edn; 'friodhan' = 'frioghan' ('bristle' or 'edge') |
| 56.24466, -5.76831 | NM6662212180 | 'Pass of the Isthmus' |
| 55.84004, -6.26596 | NR3302568992 | Not on OS 25 or 50; 'High Pass' |
| 55.91646, -5.98865 | NR5086676454 | 'Pass of the Broken Bone' |
| 56.12686, -5.70534 | NR6981698868 | 'Pass of the Hill of the Grouse' |
| 55.72751, -5.02801 | NS0994852388 | (West Island Way); deduced from Bealach-dearg Bog; 'Red Pass' |
| 56.07210, -5.81208 | NR6284993139 | 'Wind Pass' |
| 55.91845, -6.15224 | NR4066477277 | 'Pass of the West Wind' |
| 56.03752, -5.85708 | NR5983589450 | 'Pass of Hunting House Loch' |
| 56.34631, -5.94032 | NM5661824081 | 'Great Pass' |
| 56.35201, -5.78921 | NM6598524190 | Not on OS 25 or 50; misplaced on other OS maps on a steep slope to the west; 'Great Pass' |
| 55.99598, -5.96719 | NR5271585219 | 'Lady's Pass' |
| 55.76351, -6.45897 | NR2040261246 | 'Old Woman's (or 'Nun's') Pass' |
| 56.00898, -5.89688 | NR5717886415 | 'Pass of the Flitting' (transhumance) |
| 56.50578, -6.09412 | NM4817842369 | 'Pass of the Trees' |
| 56.44760, -5.98476 | NM5452735503 | |
| 56.45428, -5.98017 | NM5485336229 | |
| 55.90615, -5.96779 | NR5210375232 | |
| 55.99208, -5.90975 | NR5627084581 | 'Archers' Nick' |
| 56.39537, -6.13806 | NM4473630254 | 'Eag Fiona Mham' on OS 1st edn; 'Nick of the Fair Pass' |
| 55.87618, -5.98962 | NR5054771978 | 'Soldier's Hollow' |
| 55.88631, -6.00750 | NR4949473169 | Below Beinn Mhearsamail; the caption is closer to the col on OS 1st edn; 'An Caolas' ('narrow' or 'strait') deduced from Beinn a' Chaolais to the west |
| 55.77114, -6.44307 | NR2145262030 | 'Horseshoe Hollow' |
| 55.90214, -5.99035 | NR5066874867 | 'Imir' = 'ridge', or 'furrow'; 'aonach' = 'moor', or 'hill' |
| 56.42536, -5.94258 | NM5698332880 | 'Pass of the Dun-coloured Corrie' |
| 56.41279, -5.88877 | NM6022031293 | 'Tiompan' = 'timbrel' or 'harp'; also applied to a rounded hill with a steep drop on one side |
| 56.36171, -5.94743 | NM5627825819 | 'Trotting Pass' |
| 55.89390, -6.00796 | NR4951574015 | The river of Gleann an t-Siob' rises at the col |
| 56.43289, -5.84773 | NM6287633386 | 'Pass of the Upland Meadow'? |
| 56.41822, -5.92264 | NM5816732015 | Source of Allt Bhreapadail |
| 56.42750, -5.96899 | NM5537033212 | Not on OS 25 or 50; 'Stone Pass' |
| 56.41046, -5.90168 | NM5941031079 | 'Meadow Corrie Pass' |
| 56.41646, -6.04314 | NM5072832251 | 'Pass of the Stone of the Grove', or 'thicket' |
| 56.44697, -5.77839 | NM6723434714 | 'Lìrein' is the name of the river which rises at the col |
| 56.41643, -6.06419 | NM4943032324 | 'Pass of the Cross' (either a cross or a crossing, on an old route from Kilfinichen Bay to Dhiseig) |
| 56.41322, -6.11742 | NM4612832162 | Commonly referred to as a pass; 'seilisdeir' = 'sedge' or 'flag', ('iris') |

| Name | Elevation (m) | Surface | Nearest place | Region |
|---|---|---|---|---|
| Nuns' Pass | 168 | | Carsaig | Mull |

## Argyll and Bute – Mainland · 83 cols 4 passes

| Name | Elevation (m) | Surface | Nearest place | Region |
|---|---|---|---|---|
| Am Bealach | 349 | | Rhonadale | Kintyre |
| Am Bealach | 120 | track | Ellary | Knapdale |
| **Am Bealach** | **12** | **road** | Tayvallich | Knapdale |
| An Màm | 178 | | Inverliver | Lorn |
| An Suidhe *see* Learg Mheuran / An Suidhe | | | | |
| An t-Sreang | 359 | | Ardmay | Arrochar Alps |
| Bealach a' Chabair | 577 | | Auchenvennel | Arrochar Alps |
| **Bealach a' Chaisteil** | **140** | **A road** | West Glen | Cowal |
| Bealach a' Choire Odhair | 802 | | Black Mount | Black Mount |
| Bealach a' Chraois | 244 | (track) | Ardanstur | Lorn |
| Bealach a' Chuirn | 401 | | Dubhchladach | Knapdale |
| Bealach a' Mhaim | 637 | (path) | Succoth | Arrochar Alps |
| Bealach a' Mhaim | 508 | | Ardtaraig | Cowal |
| Bealach a' Mhargaidh | 682 | | Succoth | Arrochar Alps |
| Bealach an Aoghlain | 813 | | Achallader | Beinn Dorain Range |
| Bealach an Doruis | 319 | | Stuckbeg | Arrochar Alps |
| Bealach an Dùin | 626 | | Doune | Arrochar Alps |
| **Bealach an Easain Duibh** | **247** | **A road** | Monevechadan | Arrochar Alps |
| Bealach an Lochain | 823 | path | Bridge of Awe | Lorn |
| Bealach an Lochain | 325 | | Corrow | Arrochar Alps |
| Bealach an Tobair | 418 | | Springfield | Cowal |
| Bealach an t-Sionnaich | 619 | | Ardnahein | Arrochar Alps |
| Bealach Bernice | 318 | | Bernice | Cowal |
| Bealach Buidhe | 696 | | Monevechadan | Arrochar Alps |
| Bealach Caol Creran | 449 | | Invercharnan | Bidean nam Bian Range |
| Bealach Carra | 465 | | Cadderlie | Benderloch |
| Bealach Coire a' Ghabhalach | 744 | | Bridge of Orchy | Beinn Dorain Range |
| Bealach Coire Laoghan | 900 | | Clashgour | Black Mount |
| Bealach Corrach | 385 | | Camquhart | Cowal |
| Bealach Cumhann | 465 | | Acharn | Lorn |
| Bealach Dearg | 645 | | Salachail | Appin |
| Bealach Dubh-lic | 384 | | Ardgartan | Arrochar Alps |
| Bealach Eas nan Cabar | 416 | | Clashgour | Glen Strae |
| Bealach Fraoch | 590 | | Kinlochetive | Lorn |
| Bealach Gaoith | 319 | | Craigendive | Cowal |
| Bealach Gaoithe | 165 | track | Caddleton | Lorn |
| Bealach Gaothach | 556 | | Invernoaden | Arrochar Alps |
| Bealach Gaothach | 395 | | Daltote | Knapdale |
| Bealach Gaothach | 360 | | Blairbuie | Cowal |
| Bealach Gaothach | 100 | | Ardchonnel | Lorn |
| Bealach Ghearran | 197 | track | Birdfield | Loch Fyne |
| Bealach Glas | 745 | | Lubreoch | Loch Lyon |
| Bealach Leathan | 673 | | Kinlochetive | Lorn |
| **Bealach Mòr / Pass of Kintraw** | **115** | **A road** | Kintraw | Loch Craignish |
| Bealach na Croidhich | 485 | | Stuck | Cowal |

| Latitude, Longitude | National Grid | Notes |
|---|---|---|
| 56.31109, -6.00964 | NM5210920412 | A notch in the cliffs, associated with nuns fleeing from Iona, but likely to be a translation of Gaelic 'cailleach' '('old woman', 'nun'), referring to a physical feature |
| 55.58071, -5.55897 | NR7578137646 | Deduced from Clach a' Bhealaich; 'The Pass' |
| 55.92532, -5.62718 | NR7349376195 | Deduced from Dùn and Loch a' Bhealaich; 'The Pass' |
| 56.02492, -5.62638 | NR7412487269 | Deduced from Dùn and Loch a' Bhealaich and Tayvallich (from 'tigh' and bealach, 'house of the pass'); 'The Pass'; the lowest col in the British Isles (see pp. 87–8) |
| 56.46536, -5.14319 | NN0645934788 | 'The Pass' |
| 56.17551, -4.73582 | NN3026501466 | See 'The String' (Ayrshire) |
| 56.08690, -4.74179 | NS2950291622 | 'Pass of the Antler' (perhaps figurative) |
| 55.92309, -5.21372 | NR9930174668 | NCR 75; 'Castle Pass' (the castle is invisible) |
| 56.57029, -4.83405 | NN2597945633 | Inverness boundary; deduced from Coire Odhar and Stob a' Choire Odhair; 'Dun Corrie Pass' |
| 56.26895, -5.54186 | NM8078414137 | 'Big Mouth Pass' |
| 55.88545, -5.51751 | NR8011571406 | Bealach Chàrn on OS 1st edn; 'Cairn Pass' |
| 56.22459, -4.80533 | NN2617407100 | 'Gap of the Pass' |
| 55.98563, -5.08324 | NS0776181254 | 'Gap of the Pass' |
| 56.23167, -4.82491 | NN2499207937 | 'Pass of the Market' (significance unknown) |
| 56.55429, -4.68081 | NN3532243475 | Perth & Kinross boundary; 'Bealach an Aoghlan' on OS 1st edn; name obscure |
| 56.12381, -4.87432 | NS2143096064 | Not on OS 1st edn; 'Door Pass' |
| 56.13748, -4.74521 | NS2951497258 | 'Pass of the mound' or 'Fortress' |
| 56.23775, -4.85323 | NN2326608686 | 'Pass of the Black Waterfall' |
| 56.42082, -5.13136 | NN0696229800 | 'Lochan Pass' |
| 56.15703, -4.98112 | NN1495300041 | 'Lochan Pass' |
| 55.95947, -5.22479 | NR9879978747 | 'Pass of the Spring' |
| 56.08565, -4.92265 | NS1824791945 | 'Pass of the Fox' |
| 56.08415, -5.02829 | NS1166992062 | 'Bernice' is related to 'beàrn' ('gap', 'breach') |
| 56.19954, -4.87811 | NN2154604499 | 'Yellow Pass' |
| 56.60947, -5.07998 | NN1107150643 | Inverness boundary; 'Pass of the Strait of the (River) Creran' |
| 56.48608, -5.20790 | NN0258237277 | Bealach Charragh on OS 1st edn; 'Pass of the Pillar' |
| 56.52078, -4.72404 | NN3251739851 | Deduced from Coire a' Ghabhalach; name perhaps from 'gabhal' or 'gobhal' '(fork', 'junction') |
| 56.56951, -4.90901 | NN2137245739 | Inverness boundary; 'Pass of Little Calf Corrie' |
| 56.03406, -5.23676 | NR9844187079 | 'Steep Pass' |
| 56.51016, -5.03133 | NN1356839462 | 'Narrow Pass' |
| 56.61514, -5.19623 | NN0396951600 | 'Red Pass' |
| 56.19654, -4.83646 | NN2411604058 | 'Black Stone Pass' |
| 56.49293, -4.91306 | NN2076237230 | 'Eas' = 'waterfall'; 'cabar' = 'staves', 'rafters' or 'antlers' |
| 56.52052, -4.97215 | NN1725840455 | 'Heather Pass' |
| 56.00896, -5.14191 | NS0422184014 | 'Wind Pass' |
| 56.27584, -5.57332 | NM7887715004 | 'Wind Pass' |
| 56.14769, -4.98805 | NS1447899021 | 'Windy Pass' |
| 55.98217, -5.56465 | NR7772482314 | 'Windy Pass' |
| 55.94056, -4.98282 | NS1380675964 | 'Windy Pass' |
| 56.42219, -5.41985 | NM8918330800 | 'Windy Pass' |
| 56.09942, -5.29430 | NR9520494518 | Not on OS 25 or 50; 'Horses Pass' |
| 56.57127, -4.57584 | NN4184345117 | Perth & Kinross boundary; not on OS 25 or 50; 'Grey Pass' |
| 56.52394, -4.99041 | NN1615240885 | 'Broad Pass' |
| 56.18460, -5.48325 | NM8393704570 | 'Great Gap'; English name attested 1885; Kintraw is the hamlet at the western end of the pass |
| 56.09055, -5.06213 | NS0959592867 | 'Dowry Pass'? |

| Name | Elevation (m) | Surface | Nearest place | Region |
|---|---|---|---|---|
| Bealach na Croise | 300 | | Lagalochan | Inverliever Forest |
| Bealach na Diollaide | 425 | | Stuckbeg | Arrochar Alps |
| Bealach na Gaoith | 340 | | Achaglass | Kintyre |
| Bealach na h-Imriche | 397 | | Glenlean | Cowal |
| Bealach na Srèine | 325 | (path) | Glenkin | Cowal |
| Bealach nan Airigh | 360 | path | Camquhart | Cowal |
| Bealach nan Cabrach | 445 | | Barran | Loch Awe |
| Bealach nan Gall | 327 | | Daltote | Knapdale |
| Bealach nan Sac | 499 | | Garrachra | Cowal |
| Bealach Odhar | 839 | | Clashgour | Black Mount |
| **Bealach Salach nan Airm** | 153 | **road** | Maolachy | Lorn |
| Bealachan Lochain Ghaineamhaich | 766 | path | Kinlochetive | Lorn |
| Cumhann Bhealach | 453 | | Craig | Benderloch |
| Drochaid an Droma | 536 | | Clifton | Ben Lui Range |
| Feadan Mòr | 341 | | Lochgoilhead | Arrochar Alps |
| Fliuch Learg | 473 | | Cononish | Ben Lui Range |
| **The Gap** | 360 | **road** | Feorlan | Kintyre |
| Glas Bhealach | 750 | | Succoth | Arrochar Alps |
| Lag Uaine | 490 | | Inveruglas | Arrochar Alps |
| Lairig Arnan / Làirig Àirnein | 382 | | Garabal | Glen Fyne |
| Làirig Dhochard | 632 | | Glenceitlein | Black Mount |
| Lairig Dhoireann | 612 | (path) | Duiletter | Lorn |
| Lairig Duirinnis | 306 | | Craig | Benderloch |
| Lairig Ianachain | 728 | | Acharn | Lorn |
| Lairig Inne | 282 | | Acharn | Lorn |
| Lairig Noe | 564 | track | Acharn | Lorn |
| Lairig Torran | 728 | | Lochawe | Lorn |
| Learg Mheuran | 733 | (path) | Coileitir | Lorn |
| Learg Mheuran / An Suidhe | 431 | | Achallader | Loch Lyon |
| Lòn na Cailliche | 638 | | Achallader | Beinn Dorain Range |
| Mam Hael | 570 | | Druimavuic | Benderloch |
| Màm Lorn | 546 | | Auch | Beinn Dorain Range |
| Màm nan Sac | 588 | | Clashgour | Black Mount |
| Meall Beag – Mon | 392 | | Achallader | Black Mount |
| Parlan Hill – Cruach | 425 | | Ardleish | Trossachs |
| Pass of Kintraw see Bealach Mòr | | | | |
| **Rest and Be Thankful** | 261 | **A road** | Monevechadan | Arrochar Alps |
| **Slochd an t-Seipine** | 315 | **A road** | Auch | Beinn Dorain Range |
| Stoineag | 897 | | Kinlochetive | Lorn |
| **The Summit / An Lairig** | 102 | **road** | Glencruitten | Lorn |
| **Pass of Brander / Pass of Awe / Cumhang a' Bhrannraidh** | 42 | **A road** | Shellachan | Lorn |
| **Pass of Craigenterrive** | 45 | **B road** | Carnassarie | Loch Awe |
| **Pass of Glencroe** | 86 | **A road** | Ardgartan | Arrochar Alps |
| Pass of Melfort | 95 | track | Melfort | Lorn |

| Latitude, Longitude | National Grid | Notes |
|---|---|---|
| 56.22324, -5.41874 | NM8815208668 | The caption on modern OS maps has drifted away from the col; 'Pass of the Cross' |
| 56.13371, -4.85459 | NS2270297114 | 'Saddle Pass' |
| 55.62625, -5.58788 | NR7422242805 | 'Pass of the Wind' |
| 55.98979, -5.06188 | NS0911481657 | 'Pass of the Flitting' (transhumance) |
| 55.95604, -5.01978 | NS1157577787 | 'Bridle Pass' |
| 56.02686, -5.24016 | NR9819186288 | Bealach nan Airidh on OS 1st edn; 'Shieling Pass' |
| 56.36260, -4.97748 | NN1616922901 | 'Cabrach' = 'deer' or 'copse, thicket' |
| 55.97785, -5.55310 | NR7841981796 | 'Pass of the Lowlanders' |
| 56.07061, -5.08433 | NS0811690710 | 'Pass of the Burdens' |
| 56.57431, -4.92737 | NN2026746321 | Inverness boundary; 'Dun(-coloured) Pass' |
| 56.25369, -5.40986 | NM8887012027 | 'Foul Pass of the Weapons' |
| 56.53640, -5.02741 | NN1393842370 | Inverness boundary; 'Gravelly (or 'Sandy') Lochan Pass' |
| 56.47755, -5.20077 | NN0297636308 | 'Narrow Pass' |
| 56.43654, -4.75584 | NN3018630557 | Stirling boundary; 'drochaid' = 'bridge' (see Glossary); 'droma' = 'ridge' |
| 56.16603, -4.88100 | NN2121100778 | 'Big Whistle' (see Glossary) |
| 56.42927, -4.77535 | NN2895129796 | Stirling boundary; misplaced to north-west on modern OS; 'Wet Pass' |
| 55.30820, -5.78115 | NR6013508083 | The road ends at Mull Lighthouse |
| 56.24239, -4.81667 | NN2555209109 | 'Grey Pass' |
| 56.24744, -4.80424 | NN2634409638 | 'Green Hollow' |
| 56.32355, -4.78516 | NN2786918059 | Stirling boundary; 'Àirnein' is the name of the river |
| 56.57062, -4.95136 | NN1877645974 | Inverness boundary; name related to 'docha(i)r' ('injury', 'sorrow', 'pain')? |
| 56.46205, -4.98849 | NN1597033994 | 'Storm Pass' |
| 56.46758, -5.21005 | NN0235335225 | Below Beinn Duirinnis |
| 56.45002, -5.04029 | NN1272032796 | Lairig Ianachan on OS 1st edn; below Beinn Eunaich ('eunach' or 'ianach' = 'abounding in birds') |
| 56.47246, -5.07500 | NN1069435387 | 'Gutter Pass'? |
| 56.44153, -5.07630 | NN1045931950 | Larig Noe on OS 1st edn; source of the River Noe; W. Watson, *Celtic Place-names* (1926) has 'Làirig Nodha'; see pp. 9, 19 |
| 56.41316, -5.08894 | NN0953928829 | 'Thunder Pass' |
| 56.54593, -4.98900 | NN1634543327 | Inverness boundary; 'meuran' = 'thimble', 'little finger' or 'small branch' |
| 56.57001, -4.61865 | NN3920845076 | Perth & Kinross boundary; for 'meuran', see above; 'suidhe' = 'seat' (see Glossary) |
| 56.53851, -4.67776 | NN3544141712 | Perth & Kinross boundary; 'Old Woman's (or Nun's) Marsh' |
| 56.52312, -5.22270 | NN0186441440 | Col name shared with hill; see 'mam' in Glossary; 'Hael' is obscure |
| 56.50193, -4.67252 | NN3560537629 | Perth & Kinross boundary; 'Lorn' is the ancient name of the district to which the col is a gateway |
| 56.55696, -4.90670 | NN2145544337 | 'Pass of the Burdens' |
| 56.58692, -4.77068 | NN2994647325 | Inverness boundary |
| 56.31322, -4.67537 | NN3461216640 | Stirling boundary |
| 56.22629, -4.85632 | NN2302107419 | Gaelic name unknown but probably related to nearby Loch Restil |
| 56.45978, -4.71393 | NN3287133039 | Stirling boundary; (West Highland Way); deduced from Allt Slochd an t-Seipine; name from 'seipinn' (a liquid measure)? |
| 56.53136, -5.04274 | NN1297041851 | Name obscure; 'eag' = 'nick', 'notch'; first part perhaps 'staoin' ('juniper'): cf. Bealach na Staoineig (Inverness – Mainland) |
| 56.42319, -5.43687 | NM8814030964 | 'An Lairig' deduced from Achnalarig (Acha na Lairig on OS 1st edn) |
| 56.40442, -5.15738 | NN0527328049 | 'Cumhang' = 'narrow'; 'brannradh' = 'obstruction' (or 'snare' or 'gibbet' in Irish); battle site, c. 1308 |
| 56.15939, -5.44750 | NM8601301654 | Attested 1885; from Creag an Tairbh ('Bull Rock') |
| 56.20001, -4.81971 | NN2517004401 | Attested 1830 |
| 56.28183, -5.48490 | NM8438215390 | First shown on OS 1st edn (1875) |

| Name | Elevation (m) | Surface | Nearest place | Region |
|------|------|------|------|------|
| **Ayrshire** · 23 cols 1 pass | | | | |
| An t-Sreang  *see* The String | | | | |
| Alhang – Alwhat | 565 | | Craigdarroch | Carsphairn Hills |
| Bealach an Fharaidh | 574 | | Pirnmill | Arran |
| Bealach an Fhir-bhogha | 634 | (path) | Corrie | Arran |
| Bealach Coire Buidhe | 591 | path | Sannox | Arran |
| Bearradh Tom a' Muidhe | 263 | path | Lochranza | Arran |
| *Beinn Tarsuinn – Beinn Bhreac* | 408 | (path) | Lochranza | Arran |
| Carcow Hass | 431 | | Craigdarroch | Carsphairn Hills |
| Clashywarrant | 552 | | Craigdarroch | Carsphairn Hills |
| *Corsencon Hill – Ellergoffe Knowe* | 390 | (track) | Lagrae | Lowther Hills |
| Fionn Bhealach | 407 | | Lochranza | Arran |
| Glen Eis na Bearradh | 361 | path | Lochranza | Arran |
| How Nick | 420 | | Kames | Lowther Hills |
| Nick of Brecbowie | 375 | | Starr | Galloway Forest |
| Nick of Carclach | 628 | | Palgowan | Galloway Forest |
| **Nick of the Balloch** | 389 | **road** | South Balloch | Galloway Forest |
| Nick of the Liberty / Neck of the Liberty | 381 | | Balkissock | Luce Valley |
| Nick of the Loup | 342 | | Starr | Galloway Forest |
| Nick of the Mahm / Nick of the Mum | 374 | | Starr | Galloway Forest |
| Nick of the Nawin / Nick o' the Nawin | 195 | | Ardwell | Firth of Clyde |
| Nick of the Strand | 430 | | Starr | Galloway Forest |
| The Saddle | 432 | path | Sannox | Arran |
| **The String / An t-Sreang** | 234 | **B road** | Glencloy | Arran |
| *Windy Standard – Millaneoch Hill* | 583 | | Craigdarroch | Carsphairn Hills |
| **Kennedy's Pass** | 7 | **road** | Ardwell | Firth of Clyde |
| **Borders** · 100 cols 2 passes | | | | |
| Aucopswire | 477 | path | Sourhope | Cheviot Hills |
| Barn Corse | 514 | | Ericstane | Tweedsmuir Hills |
| **Billhope Hass** | 314 | **road** | Linhope | Liddesdale |
| *Birkscairn Hill – Stake Law* | 599 | path | Kirkburn | Manor Hills |
| Black Halls / Black Hass / Black Haus | 446 | path | Makendon | Cheviot Hills |
| Braidlie-swire  *see* Moss Patrick Swire | | | | |
| *Broomy Law – Coomb Hill* | 490 | | Oliver | Culter Hills |
| *Broomy Side – Hammer Head* | 388 | path | Broughton | Tweeddale |
| Bye Hass | 393 | | Linhope | Eskdale |

| Latitude, Longitude | National Grid | Notes |
|---|---|---|
| 55.28892, -4.13645 | NS6442301502 | East Ayrshire; Dumfries & Galloway boundary; the source of the Afton |
| 55.63640, -5.32362 | NR9090643105 | North Ayrshire; 'Ladder Pass' |
| 55.62522, -5.23634 | NR9633941602 | North Ayrshire; 'Archers' Pass' |
| 55.63667, -5.22996 | NR9680042856 | North Ayrshire; deduced from Coire Buidhe; 'Yellow Corrie Pass' |
| 55.70823, -5.24496 | NR9622850860 | North Ayrshire; 'Churn Hill Cutting' |
| 55.65541, -5.27474 | NR9408145073 | North Ayrshire; 'Tarsuinn' contains the notion of 'crossing' |
| 55.32864, -4.22681 | NS5882706101 | East Ayrshire; the source of Carcow Burn; 'Carcow' is probably 'Homestead in the Hollow' |
| 55.29815, -4.11982 | NS6551102497 | East Ayrshire; Dumfries & Galloway boundary; 'Clashwarrant' is the name of the burn which rises at the col between Alwhat and Meikledodd Hill; from Gaelic 'clais' (see Glossary) |
| 55.41194, -4.08961 | NS6780815099 | East Ayrshire; Dumfries & Galloway boundary |
| 55.69613, -5.21437 | NR9808849425 | North Ayrshire; 'Fair (White) Pass' |
| 55.66160, -5.26063 | NR9500045721 | North Ayrshire; in OS name book (1855–64); on OS as 'Gleann Easan Biorach'; see 'bearradh' in Glossary |
| 55.48453, -4.01402 | NS7282723035 | East Ayrshire; Lanarkshire boundary; not on OS; J. Thomson, 'Berwick-Shire' (1821); a 'how' (Scots) was a prehistoric burial mound or tumulus |
| 55.22777, -4.46668 | NX4321695392 | South Ayrshire; named after Loch Brecbowie |
| 55.17695, -4.49953 | NX4092489813 | South Ayrshire; name related to Irish 'carcair', 'narrow place' ? (see Glossary) |
| 55.20013, -4.59946 | NX3465892624 | South Ayrshire; NCR 7; here, 'balloch' comes from bealach |
| 55.06698, -4.91192 | NX1415978599 | South Ayrshire; probably 'liberty' in the sense of 'bounds' (the col lies 100 m from the Dumfries & Galloway boundary) |
| 55.23594, -4.42923 | NX4562996217 | East Ayrshire; 'loup' = 'leap' |
| 55.23514, -4.39346 | NX4790096050 | East Ayrshire; second name on J. Thomson, 'Northern Part of Ayrshire: Southern Part' (1828); 'mahm' = 'mam'? (see Glossary) |
| 55.18918, -4.90275 | NX1531092168 | South Ayrshire; misplaced on OS to north-east; related to 'neamhan' ('raven' or 'crow')? |
| 55.20945, -4.48845 | NX4175993403 | South Ayrshire; a 'strand' (Scots) is a small stream or gutter |
| 55.63832, -5.21159 | NR9796442986 | North Ayrshire; not on OS 1st edn |
| 55.57425, -5.20944 | NR9777035853 | North Ayrshire; on most modern maps, 'The String' is applied, perhaps erroneously, to the road, but on OS (1st edn and later) 'An t-Sreang' designates the col; in Argyll and Bute, the col called An t-Sreang is trackless |
| 55.29136, -4.16434 | NS6266101828 | East Ayrshire; Dumfries & Galloway boundary |
| 55.19731, -4.91134 | NX1480193095 | South Ayrshire; not on OS 1st edn; named after the 19th-c. road-builder |
| 55.47443, -2.19214 | NT8795220084 | English border (Northumberland); Pennine Way; not on maps; identified from 'The passages of the Scottes all along Rydsdayle', 1597, and from place names, Auchope Rig and Cairn |
| 55.42404, -3.43354 | NT0936715394 | Deduced from Barncorse Knowe; 'beàrn' ('gap', 'breach') and 'corse' ('crossing') |
| 55.27089, -2.88588 | NY4381197773 | Dumfries & Galloway boundary; Billhope is the valley to the east; see p. 105 |
| 55.58132, -3.15955 | NT2699932573 | |
| 55.38989, -2.33494 | NT7888010710 | English border (Northumberland); (Roman road: Dere Street); (Pennine Way); shifted south on OS 10 and 25; 'Black Haus' on Roy's Military Survey of Scotland (1752–5); 'Black Hass' on OS 1st edn |
| 55.52975, -3.46746 | NT0746827202 | |
| 55.63866, -3.38826 | NT1271039219 | (John Buchan Way) |
| 55.28734, -2.92537 | NY4132699636 | Deduced from Bye Sike and Bye Hill, and by analogy with the following |

| Name | Elevation (m) | Surface | Nearest place | Region |
|------|-----------|---------|---------------|--------|
| Bye Hass | 389 | (track) | Howpasley | Teviotdale |
| *Captain's Road* | 516 | path / track | Tibbie Shiels Inn | Ettrick Forest |
| **Carcant Nick** | 400 | **B road** | Middleton | Moorfoot Hills |
| Carter Bar *see* Redeswire | | | | |
| Cauldstane Slap | 435 | | Carlops | Pentland Hills |
| Clydes Nick | 489 | (track) | Glenbreck | Tweedsmuir Hills |
| Comb Hass | 384 | track | Langshawburn | Craik Forest |
| *Comb Hill – Wisp Hill* | 441 | | Linhope | Eskdale |
| Corse | 368 | path | Makendon | Cheviot Hills |
| Cowiemuir Hass | 425 | path | Broughton | Tweeddale |
| Craik Cross / Craykcorse | 387 | (track) | Langshawburn | Craik Forest |
| **Crosscryne** | 318 | **road** | Biggar | Hartree Hills |
| Deuchar (or Duchar) Swire | 433 | (path) | Mountbenger | Ettrick Forest |
| **Dewar Swyre (or Swire)** | 370 | **B road** | Dewar | Moorfoot Hills |
| Door Hass | 609 | | Kirkton Manor | Manor Hills |
| *Drumelzier Law – Glenstivon Dod* | 575 | | Stanhope | Tweeddale |
| Early Slack | 258 | | Walkerburn | Moorfoot Hills |
| *Eildon Hill North – Eildon Mid Hill* | 318 | path | Melrose | Eildon Hills |
| Ewes Doors | 338 | | Linhope | Eskdale |
| Faddon Nick *see* Whitrope Hass | | | | |
| Fanna Swire | 458 | | Singdean | Wauchope Forest |
| Fifescar | 785 | (track) | Stanhope | Tweeddale |
| Footman Hass / Footman's Hass | 503 | | Linhope | Liddesdale |
| *Four Lords Lands* | 400 | (path) | Broadmeadows | Ettrick Forest |
| Gatelaw Head | 445 | | Galabank | Moorfoot Hills |
| The Glack | 302 | path | Rachan | Tweeddale |
| Grieston Nick | 294 | | Traquair | Cardrona Forest |
| Guile Hass | 374 | | Linhope | Liddesdale |
| The Gyle | 527 | | Ericstane | Tweedsmuir Hills |
| *Gypsy Glen (Craig Head)* | 388 | path | Kirkburn | Cardrona Forest |
| Hare Swyre | 435 | path | West Linton | Pentland Hills |
| Hart Leap *see* Windy House | | | | |
| Hass | 325 | (track) | Hyndlee | Wauchope Forest |

| Latitude, Longitude | National Grid | Notes |
|---|---|---|
| 55.32518, -3.02351 | NT3515603935 | Below Byehass Fell |
| 55.45002, -3.17202 | NT2596717975 | The track or 'road' made by a Captain Napier on the old drovers' way runs most of the way to the col from the west |
| 55.77648, -3.03844 | NT3495954172 | Midlothian boundary; NCR 1; last shown on OS 1st edn; Carcant is the hamlet on the old road south-east of the col |
| 55.81297, -3.41189 | NT1161858647 | West Lothian boundary; (Cross Borders Drove Road); 'Coldstone Slap' on J. Ainslie, 'Map of the Southern Part of Scotland' (1821); 'Cauld Stane Slap' on OS 1st edn; a 'slap' or 'slop' is a gap or a breach |
| 55.43393, -3.53187 | NT0316816628 | Lanarkshire boundary; at the foot of Clyde Law, near the source of Clydes Burn |
| 55.33035, -3.07444 | NT3193304559 | The source of Comb Sike |
| 55.29116, -2.96037 | NT3910900091 | 150 m from Dumfries & Galloway boundary |
| 55.37779, -2.35931 | NT7733009371 | Deduced from Corse Slack |
| 55.63978, -3.39372 | NT1236939351 | John Buchan Way; 'Cowiemuir' is the extinct name of a small district |
| 55.32983, -3.09255 | NT3078304519 | Dumfries & Galloway boundary; the col, not specifically named, lies at the foot of Craik Cross Hill, which is crossed by a Roman road; an earlier name perhaps in Gowl Sike, which rises at the col; 'Craykcorse' marked one of the boundaries of the Middle March in 1550 |
| 55.59968, -3.50829 | NT0506135039 | In 1334, Crosscryne was on the boundary of Scottish territory ceded to Edward III |
| 55.56152, -3.11922 | NT2993330615 | (Southern Upland Way); not on maps; deduced from description in W. S. Crockett, *The Scott Country* (1905), p. 372 |
| 55.70955, -3.03786 | NT3488446723 | NCR 1; not on OS; on A. Armstrong, 'Map of the Three Lothians' (1773), and J. Ainslie, 'Map of the Southern Part of Scotland' (1821); near Piper of Peebles Grave; *see* pp. 65–7 |
| 55.58557, -3.21573 | NT2346633107 | |
| 55.56268, -3.34106 | NT1551830706 | |
| 55.63368, -2.99199 | NT3764538237 | 'Early Knowe' is the name of the neighbouring hill |
| 55.58447, -2.71410 | NT5508332545 | St Cuthbert's Way; a track to the col is marked 'Foot Path' on W. Crawford, 'Map Embracing Extensive Portions [...]' (1843); below the hill fort of Trimontium |
| 55.27803, -2.98909 | NY3726598656 | Dumfries & Galloway boundary; 'Ewes' is the name of the hamlet and church; 'a narrow pass called Ewes' Doors, which was the only passage for horsemen to enter into Teviot-dale, before the turnpike road was made': William Scott, *The Beauties of the Border* (1821); 'Ewse Doores' (1514) |
| 55.32536, -2.67305 | NT5739203684 | 'Fanna Sware' on OS 1st edn; from 'Fanna Hill' and 'Fanna Bog' |
| 55.53372, -3.30565 | NT1769027440 | Deduced from Fifescar Knowe; *see* 'scar' in Glossary |
| 55.29583, -2.87371 | NT4461900539 | 'Hass' on J. Thomson, 'Roxburghshire' (1822); referring to an infantryman? |
| 55.58486, -2.94894 | NT4028132766 | (Southern Upland Way); 'Fourlordslands' on J. Ainslie, 'Map of Selkirkshire or Ettrick Forest' (1773); 'Four Lords Lands Meet' on T. Mitchell, 'Map of the County of Selkirk and District of Melrose' (1851); the intersection of four estates |
| 55.68697, -2.95442 | NT4009244134 | Not on OS; only on A. Armstrong, 'Map of the Three Lothians' (1773) |
| 55.59385, -3.43068 | NT0993734287 | *See* 'glack' in Glossary |
| 55.60449, -3.09595 | NT3104935087 | Below Grieston Hill; from 'grevestone'? |
| 55.26188, -2.89302 | NY4334596776 | Dumfries & Galloway boundary; 'guile' may be 'gyle' (*see* 'goul' in Glossary) |
| 55.41544, -3.41883 | NT1027814418 | Dumfries & Galloway boundary; name shifted south-west?; *see* note to Windy Gyle (Borders) and 'goul' in Glossary |
| 55.62330, -3.15531 | NT2734437241 | Cross Borders Drove Road; sometimes 'Gipsie Glen' |
| 55.77393, -3.44211 | NT0963454342 | Only on J. Blaeu, 'Lothian and Linlitquo' (1654); probable location; 'hare' name survives in Craigengar ('Creag na Gearra') |
| 55.34369, -2.62960 | NT6016805698 | Deduced from Hass Sike (and Hass Plantation on OS 1st edn) |

| Name | Elevation (m) | Surface | Nearest place | Region |
|---|---|---|---|---|
| **Hass** | 247 | **A road** | Huntford | Cheviot Hills |
| Hass / Bowerhope Hass | 399 | (track) | Tibbie Shiels Inn | Ettrick Forest |
| Hass of Macrule | 420 | | Talla Linnfoots | Tweedsmuir Hills |
| Hawk Hass / Hawkhass | 374 | (track) | Shankend | Teviotdale |
| *Headshaw Hope – Windy Law* | 299 | path | Hownam | Cheviot Hills |
| Henshaw Mouth | 448 | | Carlops | Pentland Hills |
| Holm Nick | 480 | (track) | Tweedsmuir | Culter Hills |
| Howgate Nick | 480 | path | Eddleston | Moorfoot Hills |
| Humbleton Swyre | 315 | | Yetholm Mains | Cheviot Hills |
| Jeffries Corse | 459 | | Westloch | Moorfoot Hills |
| Katie's Hass | 355 | (track) | Glentress | Moorfoot Hills |
| Kings Road Nick | 547 | (track) | Dewar | Moorfoot Hills |
| **Kirkhope Swire** | 362 | **road** | Kirkhope | Ettrick Forest |
| Leithen Door | 440 | track | Colquhar | Moorfoot Hills |
| Little Nick | 596 | | Bodesbeck | Ettrick Hills |
| Ludsgill Sware | 375 | | Arkleton | Liddesdale |
| *Macfumart Head* | 409 | | Stanhope | Tweeddale |
| Maiden Cross | 536 | path | Sourhope | Cheviot Hills |
| **Manor Sware / The Sware** | 241 | **road** | Peebles | Manor Hills |
| Moss Patrick Swire | 450 | | Hermitage | Liddesdale |
| Newark Swire | 438 | | Yarrowford | Ettrick Forest |
| *Newby Kipps – Preston Law* | 428 | (track) | Kings Muir | Manor Hills |
| Nick of Frudds Head  *see* Talla Nick | | | | |
| **Note o' the Gate** | 371 | **B road** | Singdean | Wauchope Forest |
| **Paddock Slack** | 357 | **B road** | Mountbenger | Ettrick Forest |
| Pete Swire | 484 | (track) | Sourhope | Cheviot Hills |
| Pipers Hass | 420 | | Traquair | Traquair Forest |
| Priesthaugh Swire | 385 | track | Shankend | Teviotdale |
| Priesthope Sware (or Swair) | 455 | | Colquhar | Moorfoot Hills |
| Pyatshaw Hole | 254 | | Mowhaugh | Cheviot Hills |
| Randy's Gap | 506 | path | Sourhope | Cheviot Hills |
| Red Scar | 352 | (path) | Stobo | Tweeddale |
| Red Scar Nick / Red Score Nick | 357 | path | Broadmeadows | Ettrick Forest |

| Latitude, Longitude | National Grid | Notes |
|---|---|---|
| 55.38324, -2.49683 | NT6862010031 | |
| 55.47806, -3.18354 | NT2529121108 | Deduced from Hass Sike; second name presumed |
| 55.44014, -3.43576 | NT0926417189 | Below Macrule Hill |
| 55.31564, -2.80942 | NT4872702694 | 'Hankhass' on J. Thomson, 'Roxburghshire' (1822); mentioned in accounts of Mary, Queen of Scots' journey to Hermitage Castle |
| 55.45941, -2.31917 | NT7991418442 | A crossroads on the drove road named 'The Street' on OS maps ('Clattering Path' on Roy's Military Survey of Scotland) |
| 55.81148, -3.38305 | NT1342258445 | Not on OS 1st edn |
| 55.52382, -3.49424 | NT0576426578 | Lanarkshire boundary |
| 55.70976, -3.15465 | NT2754646862 | 'Howgale Nick' on OS 1st and 2nd edn |
| 55.54483, -2.23225 | NT8544327927 | English border (Northumberland) |
| 55.73630, -3.16184 | NT2714349823 | Name attributed to hill? (the caption is much closer to the col on OS 1st and 2nd edn); 'Jeffry's Cross' on A. Armstrong, 'Map of the Three Lothians' (1773); 'Jeffries Carse' on W. Forrester, 'Map of the County of Edinburgh Shewing the Turnpike and Statute Labour Roads' (1850) |
| 55.66227, -3.12521 | NT2931041547 | Name obscure; 'Katie's Well' is nearby |
| 55.71651, -3.11079 | NT3031447568 | Midlothian boundary; 'Kingroadnick' on A. Armstrong, 'Map of the Three Lothians' (1773); 'Kingroad Nick' on J. Thomson, 'Peebles-Shire' (1821); 'King's Road Nick' on OS 1st edn |
| 55.52200, -3.00007 | NT3695825816 | Not on maps; known locally as 'Bottom Swire'; mentioned in the ballad, 'Whaup o' the Rede' (see p. 65); sometimes 'Kershope Swire' |
| 55.67008, -3.11138 | NT3019442402 | A cycle track now leads from the col to the top of Leithen Door Hill |
| 55.34541, -3.28563 | NT1856606461 | Dumfries & Galloway boundary |
| 55.23470, -2.91162 | NY4212393767 | Dumfries & Galloway boundary; name obscure |
| 55.56333, -3.41964 | NT1056330876 | |
| 55.43537, -2.21331 | NT8660115741 | English border (Northumberland); Pennine Way; not on modern maps; location uncertain, deduced from surveys (e.g. 'ingates and passages forth of Scotland', 1543) and maps (from 1633); 'Mayden Crosse', 1543 (probably 'meadhon', 'middle') |
| 55.64596, -3.21720 | NT2349239829 | CR; above Kirkton Manor |
| 55.29471, -2.82952 | NT4742400380 | Not on OS 25 or 50; 'Mosspatrick Sware' on OS 1st edn; 'Moss patrick hoopswyne' (sic) on J. Blaeu, 'Lidalia' (1654); 'Moopatrickhope Swire' on M. Stobie, 'A Map of Roxburghshire or Tiviotdale' (1770); probably the 'Braidlie-swire' mentioned in accounts of Mary, Queen of Scots' journey to Hermitage Castle |
| 55.53557, -2.96525 | NT3917727295 | Not on maps; mentioned by James Hogg in Wat Pringle o' the Yair (1835), from which its location by Newark Burn can be deduced |
| 55.61138, -3.18094 | NT2570835941 | |
| 55.31904, -2.64951 | NT5887902966 | 'Knot o' the Gate' in Walter Scott, Guy Mannering (1815); 'Note oth Gate' on J. Ainslie, 'Map of the Southern Part of Scotland' (1821); 'Knot i' the Gait' in Ordnance Gazetteer of Scotland (1901); at head of Swire Sike, near Rushy Rig, and thus probably Rugheswyre or Ruchswyre on J. Blaeu, 'Lidalia' (1654) |
| 55.54581, -3.09061 | NT3128328552 | CR; known locally, since at least 1964, as 'the Paddy('s) Slacks'; 'paddock' = 'small farm' or (as variant of 'puddock'), 'frog'; see p. 65 |
| 55.50533, -2.22929 | NT8561523530 | (Pennine Way); formerly on the border; not on maps; mentioned in border survey of 1543 |
| 55.59790, -3.03128 | NT3511334291 | Name obscure; see p. 66 on the Piper of Peebles |
| 55.34784, -2.81024 | NT4871706278 | Not on maps; various texts, e.g. Mary, Queen of Scots, 'proceeded up Priesthaugh-swire, between Pencryst-pen and Skelf-hill': R. Chambers, The Picture of Scotland (1828), I, p. 100 |
| 55.65243, -3.03357 | NT3505940362 | |
| 55.50632, -2.28487 | NT8210523653 | OS 1st edn shows a track ending near the col |
| 55.44551, -2.19414 | NT8781716866 | English border (Northumberland); Pennine Way; probably from Scots 'randy' or 'randie' ('rough', 'aggressive', used especially of beggars) |
| 55.64950, -3.34474 | NT1547340372 | Name attached to the burn on OS 10 |
| 55.57111, -2.89348 | NT4375831190 | Southern Upland Way; first name on OS 1st edn; misread as 'Red Lear Nick' on ScotlandsPlaces.gov.uk |

| Name | Elevation (m) | Surface | Nearest place | Region |
|---|---|---|---|---|
| **Redeswire / Carter Bar** | 418 | **A road** | Huntford | Cheviot Hills |
| Riskinhopeswire | 422 | (path) | Muchra | Ettrick Forest |
| Robb's Cross | 477 | | Singdean | Wauchope Forest |
| Roughley Hass | 389 | | Larriston | Liddesdale |
| Roughsware | 398 | | Heriot | Moorfoot Hills |
| Ruchswyre / Rugheswyre *see* Note o' the Gate | | | | |
| Rut Head | 352 | | Howpasley | Teviotdale |
| Saddle Nick | 485 | | Culter Allers Farm | Culter Hills |
| The Scar | 462 | | Gilmanscleuch | Ettrick Forest |
| *Siller Road* | 364 | path | Colquhar | Moorfoot Hills |
| *Smidhope Hill – Capel Fell* | 610 | | Bodesbeck | Ettrick Hills |
| Southerly Nick | 390 | path | Thornylee | Moorfoot Hills |
| Spithope Nick (or Neuk) | 427 | (track) | Catcleugh | Cheviot Hills |
| *Stockcleuch Edge* | 404 | | Linhope | Liddesdale |
| Sunhope Hass | 374 | path | Linhope | Eskdale |
| Swinlaw Gap | 430 | (path) | Blindburn | Cheviot Hills |
| The Swire *see* Kirkhope Swire | | | | |
| Swirehouse / Swarehouse | 320 | path | Falahill | Moorfoot Hills |
| Talla Nick / Nick of Frudds Head | 693 | | Birkhill | Tweedsmuir Hills |
| *Teviot Stone* | 376 | | Jamestown | Eskdale |
| Turf Hass | 313 | | Deanburnhaugh | Teviotdale |
| Tweed's Cross | 437 | (track) | Ericstane | Tweedsmuir Hills |
| *Unthank Hope* | 391 | | Linhope | Liddesdale |
| White Swire *see* Whitelaw Nick | | | | |
| Whitelaw Nick / White Swire | 385 | path | Kirk Yetholm | Cheviot Hills |
| **Whitrope Hass** | 363 | **B road** | Shankend | Wauchope Forest |
| Wigg Hass | 328 | track | Hyndlee | Wauchope Forest |
| Windy Gowl | 325 | | Carlops | Pentland Hills |

| Latitude, Longitude | National Grid | Notes |
|---|---|---|
| 55.35434, -2.47764 | NT6981306806 | English border (Northumberland); 'Rid Square' (or 'Squire'), 'The Read Squire', 'Reidswire', 'Reed Swire', 'Red Swire' or 'Redswire'; 'Carter Barr' on N. Tennant, 'Map of the County of Roxburgh' (1840); 'Carter Bar' on Bartholomew, 'Cheviots' (1912) and OS 1 (1926); 'bar' indicates the turnpike; battle site, 1400 and 7 July 1575 |
| 55.45285, -3.19659 | NT2441818317 | (Southern Upland Way); not on maps; deduced from journey described in James Hogg, *The Brownie of Bodsbeck* (1818) |
| 55.31761, -2.55794 | NT6468902757 | English border (Northumberland); not on modern maps; location uncertain, deduced from surveys (e.g. 'ingates and passages forth of Scotland', 1543) and maps (from 1633); Robbes Crosse 1543; 'Robb' is unknown and there is no cross (and perhaps never was); *see* 'cross' in Glossary |
| 55.25122, -2.74294 | NY5287095478 | Not on OS; on J. Thomson, 'Peebles-shire' (1821) |
| 55.76697, -2.99603 | NT3760453075 | Name attached to a ruin just below the col on OS 1st edn; 'rough' (Scots) perhaps in the botanical sense of 'rush' or 'reed' |
| 55.34571, -3.01458 | NT3575506210 | The source of Rut Sike |
| 55.56640, -3.49551 | NT0578631318 | Lanarkshire boundary; 'Saddle Nick' is also the name of the sike which rises at the col |
| 55.49810, -3.05722 | NT3330923209 | Deduced from Scar Hill and The Scar (*see* Glossary) |
| 55.67190, -3.04647 | NT3427942540 | 'Silver Road' on OS 10; between Dod Hill and Bareback Knowe |
| 55.35221, -3.31590 | NT1666107254 | Dumfries & Galloway boundary |
| 55.63342, -2.95327 | NT4008338174 | Name perhaps refers to the wind |
| 55.35698, -2.36665 | NT7685207057 | English border (Northumberland); 'Spitthope Nick' on Roy's Military Survey of Scotland (1752–5), and on no other map; 'Spitupunk' in 'The passages of the Scottes all along Rydsdayle' (1597); 'Spiddop Nuke' in 'Survey of the Debatable and Border Lands' (1604); the col summit lies 18 m south of the present border |
| 55.25207, -2.90896 | NY4231895698 | Dumfries & Galloway boundary |
| 55.28314, -2.91310 | NY4210099159 | Dumfries & Galloway boundary; name, perhaps, like 'Sunwick', from Old English 'swīn' ('pig'), or, like 'Sunlaws', from Scots 'sind' ('to rinse'); a 'hope' is a small, closed valley |
| 55.40819, -2.32069 | NT7979212742 | English border (Northumberland); (Pennine Way); not on OS; the col and its name are recorded only on Roy's Military Survey of Scotland (1752–5) |
| 55.79364, -2.99344 | NT3780956040 | Midlothian boundary; not on modern OS; 'Swirehouse' on Taylor and Skinner, 'The Road from Edinburgh to Carlisle' (1775); 'Swarehouse (ruins of)', just below the col, on J. Ainslie, 'Map of the Southern Part of Scotland' (1821); 'Sware House' on J. Thomson, 'Edinburgh Shire' (1821); 'Swareuse' on T. Sharp, C. Greenwood and W. Fowler, 'Map of the County of Edinburgh' (1828) |
| 55.44200, -3.32631 | NT1619217258 | Dumfries & Galloway boundary (now shifted a few metres south); second name on J. Blaeu, 'Tuedia' (1654); the source of Talla Water; 'Frudd' is an older river name, common in various forms |
| 55.27548, -3.04629 | NY3362798425 | Dumfries & Galloway boundary; the stone is a boundary marker at the source of the River Teviot |
| 55.36523, -2.96753 | NT3876908341 | Name refers to the peat bog |
| 55.40906, -3.49509 | NT0543513809 | Dumfries & Galloway boundary; OS 1st edn; on modern OS only in Cross Burn, Corse Burn and Corse Dod; 'A name which is considered by the people in the neighbourhood to apply to the small pass where the road from Dumfries to Edinburgh leaves the County of Lanark and enters the valley of the Tweed'; the 'corse' preceded the cross, 'erected as a road mark in so wild and hazardous a mountain pass' (OS name book 1858–61) |
| 55.24472, -2.91520 | NY4191094885 | Dumfries & Galloway boundary; the caption is extended to the col on J. Thomson, 'Roxburghshire' (1822) |
| 55.52961, -2.23323 | NT8537626233 | English border (Northumberland); Pennine Way; 'White Swire' not on maps but in various surveys of the border, e.g. 'White Swyer' in 1543 |
| 55.30667, -2.73469 | NT5345901643 | 'Whitterhope Hass' on OS 1st edn; 'Faddon Nick' on J. Ainslie, 'Map of the Southern Part of Scotland' (1821) |
| 55.33778, -2.67239 | NT5744805066 | 'Wigg' is the name of a nearby hamlet or house |
| 55.77512, -3.36565 | NT1443254377 | 'Windy Goul' on J. Thomson, 'Peebles-shire' (1821) |

| Name | Elevation (m) | Surface | Nearest place | Region |
|---|---|---|---|---|
| Windy Gyle | 540 | path | Blindburn | Cheviot Hills |
| **Windy House** | 376 | **B road** | Crosslee | Ettrick Forest |
| Windy Path | 414 | path | Sourhope | Cheviot Hills |
| Windy Swire | 436 | | Hermitage | Liddesdale |
| Windydoors Hawse | 341 | path | Blackhaugh | Moorfoot Hills |
| **Birkhill Pass / Pass of Moffatdale** | 339 | **A road** | Birkhill | Tweedsmuir Hills |
| Pass of Pease / Coldbrand's Path / Cockburn's Path | 100 | track | Cockburnspath | Pease Bay |

## Caithness · 6 cols

| Name | Elevation (m) | Surface | Nearest place | Region |
|---|---|---|---|---|
| Am Bealach | 295 | | Wag | Langwell Forest |
| An Caol | 427 | | Gobernuisgeach | Langwell Forest |
| Cadha an t-Sagairt | 514 | | Braemore | Langwell Forest |
| Gille Garbh | 395 | | Gobernuisgeach | Langwell Forest |
| Glac Dubh | 338 | | Braemore | Langwell Forest |
| Glac na Goibhre | 529 | | Aultibea | Langwell Forest |

## Dumfries and Galloway · 104 cols 6 passes

| Name | Elevation (m) | Surface | Nearest place | Region |
|---|---|---|---|---|
| Alhang – Alwhat | 565 | | Craigdarroch | Carsphairn Hills |
| Balloch | 97 | (track) | Kirkmaiden | Rhinns of Galloway |
| Balloch o'Lusk | 25 | track | Chapel Rossan | Rhinns of Galloway |
| **Ballochagunnon** | 31 | **B road** | Logan | Rhinns of Galloway |
| Ballyan Hass | 382 | | Gateslack | Lowther Hills |
| Barholm Hill – Ben John | 270 | | Cardoness | Cairnharrow |
| Ben John – Mill Knock | 225 | | Cardoness | Cairnharrow |
| **Billhope Hass** | 314 | **road** | Linhope | Liddesdale |
| Bught Hass | 392 | path | Wanlockhead | Lowther Hills |
| Bught Hass | 316 | track | Durisdeer | Lowther Hills |
| Buittle Slot | 113 | | Dalbeattie | Buittle Hill |
| **Charlie's Moss** | 271 | **road** | Langholm | Eskdale |
| Clashywarrant | 552 | | Craigdarroch | Carsphairn Hills |
| Comb Hill – Laght Hill | 411 | path | Wanlockhead | Lowther Hills |
| Conrick Hass | 424 | | Benbuie | Scaur Hills |
| **Corse Gate** | 156 | **road** | Square Point | Bardarroch Hill |
| **Corse of Slakes** | 274 | **road** | Glen | Glenquicken Moor |
| Corsencon Hill – Ellergoffe Knowe | 390 | (track) | Lagrae | Lowther Hills |
| Craiglour Hawse | 390 | | Carroch | Scaur Hills |
| Craik Cross / Craykcorse | 387 | (track) | Langshawburn | Craik Forest |

| Latitude, Longitude | National Grid | Notes |
|---|---|---|
| 55.43153, -2.23909 | NT8496815319 | English border (Northumberland); Pennine Way; the name, shown as 'Windygyle' in W. Crawford, 'Map Embracing Extensive Portions […]' (1843), is misattached to the hill – correctly 'Windgate Fell' (N. Tennant, 'Map of the County of Roxburgh', 1840) or 'Windygate Hill' (OS, 'Roxburghshire', 1863); the col is near the head of Gyle Burn and Windy Rig; 'Windy Gyle Swire', 1604; sometimes confused with Cocklawgate or Hexpethgate |
| 55.46962, -3.14763 | NT2754620131 | CR; not on maps; known locally as 'Top Swire'; original col nearby at 55.47274, -3.13845 on the drove road (named Hart Leap on OS 1st edn); older name perhaps in 'Windy House', first recorded on OS in 1900 |
| 55.49576, -2.24474 | NT8463622468 | At the col on OS 1st edn; displaced to south-east on modern OS; 'path' occasionally used for 'pass' |
| 55.29425, -2.83511 | NT4706800333 | 'Swair' on W. Crawford, 'Map of Dumfries-shire' (1804); 'Windy Sware' on OS 1st edn |
| 55.65206, -2.90210 | NT4333140205 | 'Windydurrs' on J. Blaeu, 'Tuedia' (1654); slightly misplaced on modern OS |
| 55.43150, -3.26237 | NT2021516014 | Dumfries & Galloway boundary; not on OS; 'Birkhill Path' on W. Crawford, 'Map of Dumfries-shire' (1804) and J. Thomson, 'Dumfriesshire' (1828); there is another Birkhill Pass in Aberdeenshire |
| 55.91588, -2.33386 | NT7923169249 | Southern Upland Way; 'Pease Dean' (i.e. 'dene') on OS; 'Pass of Pease' in Walter Scott, *The Minstrelsy of the Scottish Border* (1803) |

| | | |
|---|---|---|
| 58.23353, -3.67683 | ND0163328425 | 'The Pass'; deduced from Allt Preas Bhealaich |
| 58.23714, -3.70884 | NC9976428874 | 'Caol' = 'strait' or 'narrow'; deduced from Allt Caol |
| 58.22301, -3.57979 | ND0730327116 | 'Pass of the Priest' |
| 58.22582, -3.75749 | NC9687427687 | 'Rough Gully' (from Coire Gille Ghairbh); 'gille' here is probably a corruption of Gaelic 'gil' ('rift', 'gully', 'mountain stream'), from Old Norse 'gil' ('cleft', 'gully') or 'gill', 'gheall' ('notch') |
| 58.22594, -3.54295 | ND0947427392 | 'Black Hollow' |
| 58.21992, -3.60496 | ND0581726807 | 'Goat Hollow' |

| | | |
|---|---|---|
| 55.28892, -4.13645 | NS6442301502 | Ayrshire boundary; the source of the Afton |
| 54.68452, -4.95184 | NX0981736165 | From *bealach* |
| 54.76121, -4.95943 | NX0968844716 | Only on modern OS 10; from *bealach*, and from Gaelic 'loisg' ('burn')? |
| 54.73489, -4.95298 | NX0997941771 | Deduced from Ballochagunnon Plantation (not on OS 25 or 50); from *bealach* |
| 55.30005, -3.72643 | NS9048902019 | Below Ballyan Scars |
| 54.86669, -4.27633 | NX5401054809 | |
| 54.86835, -4.25980 | NX5507754959 | |
| 55.27089, -2.88588 | NY4381197773 | Borders boundary; Billhope is the valley to the east; *see* p. 105 |
| 55.36287, -3.80802 | NS8549109140 | A 'boucht', 'bought', 'bucht' or 'bught' is a sheepfold |
| 55.34681, -3.76599 | NS8811007285 | A 'boucht', 'bought', 'bucht' or 'bught' is a sheepfold |
| 54.93784, -3.85538 | NX8123261928 | Below Buittle hill; 'slot' = 'hollow', 'dip' or 'gully' |
| 55.16151, -2.96721 | NY3847585670 | |
| 55.29815, -4.11982 | NS6551102497 | Ayrshire boundary; 'Clashywarrant' is the name of the burn which rises at the col between Alwhat and Meikledodd Hill; from Gaelic 'clais' (*see* Glossary) |
| 55.36470, -3.71598 | NS9132909196 | Lanarkshire boundary; Southern Upland Way |
| 55.25743, -4.03189 | NX7096097800 | Below Conrick Hill |
| 55.03599, -3.91061 | NX7799372944 | Name attributed to Corsegate Farm, beyond which the road ends |
| 54.89871, -4.29917 | NX5266258419 | 'Cross of Slakes' on J. Thomson, 'Kirkcudbright-Shire' (1828); *see* pp. 62–3 |
| 55.41194, -4.08961 | NS6780815099 | Ayrshire boundary |
| 55.21044, -4.06903 | NX6844592641 | Below Craiglour Craig |
| 55.32983, -3.09255 | NT3078304519 | Borders boundary; the col, not specifically named, lies at the foot of Craik Cross Hill, which is crossed by a Roman road; an earlier name perhaps in Gowl Sike, which rises at the col; 'Craykcorse' marked one of the boundaries of the Middle March in 1550 |

| Name | Elevation (m) | Surface | Nearest place | Region |
|---|---|---|---|---|
| *Criffel—Boreland Hill* | 424 | | Kirkbean | Criffel |
| Daer Hass | 502 | | Kinnelhead | Lowther Hills |
| Deep Nick of Dromore | 243 | | Castramont | Cairnsmore of Fleet |
| Deil's Barn Door | 420 | | Corsebank | Lowther Hills |
| Deil's Barn Door | 526 | path | Wanlockhead | Lowther Hills |
| Dempster's Hass | 408 | | Auchenbrack | Scaur Hills |
| Door of Cairnsmore | 277 | | Cairnsmore | Cairnsmore of Fleet |
| Drove Hass | 420 | | Corsebank | Lowther Hills |
| Duddiestone Hass | 304 | path | Auchenhessnane | Scaur Hills |
| Ewes Doors | 338 | | Linhope | Eskdale |
| **Fenton Yet** | 249 | **B road** | Boreland | Castle O'er Forest |
| Ford of Munsack | 562 | track | Craigdarroch | Carsphairn Hills |
| Glenbo Hass | 442 | | Durisdeer | Lowther Hills |
| Glendyne Pass | 430 | (path) | Wanlockhead | Lowther Hills |
| Glenwhargen Hass | 400 | | Glenmanna | Scaur Hills |
| Gowdie Slack | 278 | track | Kinnelhead | Lowther Hills |
| Guile Hass | 374 | | Linhope | Liddesdale |
| The Gyle | 527 | | Ericstane | Tweedsmuir Hills |
| *Hags of Poljargen* | 457 | | Craigdarroch | Carsphairn Hills |
| **Hass** | 303 | **road** | Carroch | Scaur Hills |
| The Hass | 277 | (path) | Gateslack | Lowther Hills |
| Hass / Swire | 390 | | Kirkstile | Eskdale |
| Hass o' the Red Roads | 695 | | Capplegill | Tweedsmuir Hills |
| Howcon | 364 | | Corsebank | Lowther Hills |
| Kiddam Hass | 329 | (track) | Garwald | Eskdalemuir Forest |
| Kirkgrain Hass | 555 | (track) | Durisdeer | Lowther Hills |
| Kirtle Nick | 270 | | Debate | Kirtle Water |
| Linn Slack | 294 | | Langshawburn | Eskdalemuir Forest |
| Little Nick | 596 | | Bodesbeck | Ettrick Hills |
| Loup of Laggan | 407 | path | Craigencallie | Galloway Forest |
| Ludsgill Sware | 375 | | Arkleton | Liddesdale |
| *Luke's Stone* | 537 | | Craigdarroch | Carsphairn Hills |
| **Mennock Hass** | 424 | **B road** | Wanlockhead | Lowther Hills |
| Milking Hass | 362 | track | Fingland | Eskdalemuir Forest |
| Moat Hass | 212 | | Airieland | Bengairn Range |
| Mote Hass | 315 | track | Breconside | Scaur Hills |
| Neive of the Spit | 660 | (path) | Palgowan | Galloway Forest |
| Nick of Benniguinea | 283 | | Clatteringshaws | Galloway Forest |
| Nick of Clashneach | 619 | | Cairnsmore | Cairnsmore of Fleet |

| Latitude, Longitude | National Grid | Notes |
| --- | --- | --- |
| 54.93421, -3.64272 | NX9484661184 | |
| 55.29441, -3.62514 | NS9690501237 | Lanarkshire boundary; 'Dairhass' on C. Ross, 'A Map of the Shire of Lanark' (1773); 'Dear Hass' on J. Thomson, 'Northern Part of Lanarkshire: Southern Part' (1822); Daer Water has one of its sources at the col |
| 54.95153, -4.27406 | NX5446364243 | 'Deep Nick of Drumore' on OS 1st edn; 'Drumore' = 'great ridge' |
| 55.43554, -3.91140 | NS7916117401 | One half of a double col (see Drove Hass) or perhaps a remnant of its original name (see 'beàrn' in Glossary); 'deil' = 'devil' |
| 55.36585, -3.78271 | NS8710409430 | See 'beàrn' in Glossary; 'deil' = 'devil' |
| 55.24490, -3.98773 | NX7372796325 | A 'dempster' was a judge or a public executioner |
| 54.95071, -4.31689 | NX5171864242 | On OS, attached to the cliffs above the col, which lay on a well-used smugglers' route; see 'door' in Glossary |
| 55.43483, -3.91189 | NS7912817323 | See Deil's Barn Door (420 m) above |
| 55.24336, -3.90179 | NX7918596001 | 'Duddiston Hass' on W. Crawford, 'Map of Dumfries-shire' (1804) and J. Thomson, 'Dumfriesshire' (1828); 'doddie' or 'duddie' = 'bald' |
| 55.27803, -2.98909 | NY3726598656 | Borders boundary; 'Ewes' is the name of the hamlet and church; 'a narrow pass called Ewes' Doors, which was the only passage for horsemen to enter into Teviot-dale, before the turnpike road was made': William Scott, The Beauties of the Border (1821); 'Ewse Doores' (1514) |
| 55.22719, -3.26871 | NY1940093287 | Below Fenton Heights; 'yet' = 'pass' or 'defile' |
| 55.28716, -4.19345 | NS6079801419 | 'Ford' has the sense of 'col'; particular name obscure |
| 55.33405, -3.73097 | NS9029505809 | Glenbo is a nearby stream or cleuch |
| 55.38894, -3.81750 | NS8496612057 | Not on maps; in F. Groome, Ordnance Gazetteer of Scotland (1884-5) |
| 55.32058, -3.93102 | NS7756504644 | 'Glenquhargen Hass' on J. Thomson, 'Dumfriesshire' (1828); the name of the farm at the foot of Glenwhargen Burn |
| 55.33674, -3.52632 | NT0328205805 | (Southern Upland Way); also 'Goudie' and 'Goudy'; 'gowd' (Scots) = 'gold', but the word is also 'a pet-name for a light yellow-coloured [i.e. 'golden'] cow' (Dictionary of the Scots Language) |
| 55.26188, -2.89302 | NY4334596776 | Borders boundary; 'guile' may be 'gyle' (see 'goul' in Glossary) |
| 55.41544, -3.41883 | NT1027814418 | Borders boundary; name shifted south-west?; see note to Windy Gyle (Borders) and 'goul' in Glossary |
| 55.27185, -4.15654 | NX6308999642 | |
| 55.19612, -4.05834 | NX6907891027 | Not on OS; only on W. Crawford, 'Map of Dumfries-shire' (1804) |
| 55.28984, -3.74487 | NS8929000912 | |
| 55.21115, -3.04036 | NY3389791261 | Deduced from Hassgair Heads and Swire Sike |
| 55.40302, -3.38870 | NT1215812998 | The 'red roads' were probably tracks made by sheep exposing the red sandstone; Red Gill is nearby |
| 55.42359, -3.90776 | NS7935416065 | Name obscure; 'how' is probably 'hollow' |
| 55.31664, -3.25990 | NT2014003230 | Below Kiddam Hill |
| 55.32488, -3.71095 | NS9154004757 | Lanarkshire boundary; the source of Kirk Grain |
| 55.14870, -3.15020 | NY2679384422 | North-east of Kirtlehead Hill |
| 55.30882, -3.14946 | NT2713402239 | The 'linn' is Bogle Linn waterfall |
| 55.34541, -3.28563 | NT1856606461 | Borders boundary |
| 55.05448, -4.41618 | NX4575976000 | 'Loup = 'leap'; source of White Laggan Burn |
| 55.23470, -2.91162 | NY4212393767 | Borders boundary; name obscure |
| 55.26782, -4.18267 | NX6141599245 | The boulder named 'Luke's Stone' lies 300 m east of the col |
| 55.39131, -3.78111 | NS8727812261 | 'Menock Hass' on Roy's Military Survey of Scotland (1752-5), OS 1st edn and Bartholomew; distinct from Mennock Pass |
| 55.32376, -3.24530 | NT2108104006 | Perhaps referring to sheep |
| 54.86337, -3.93687 | NX7578353784 | Not on maps; in R. Cunningham, 'Geognostical Description of the Stewartry of Kirkcudbright', Prize-Essays and Transactions of the Highland and Agricultural Society of Scotland (1843), p. 726; source of Hass Burn, below Dungarry Fort (or 'moat'); distinct from Mote Hass |
| 55.28754, -3.88407 | NS8044400886 | 'Moat Hass' on OS 1st edn; 'mote' or 'moat' refers to the nearby earthwork on Druidhill Burn |
| 55.12943, -4.48366 | NX4174684490 | Name obscure (Scots 'neive' = 'fist') |
| 55.06142, -4.23486 | NX5736476388 | 'Nick of Kenneth's Hill'? |
| 54.96545, -4.33208 | NX5080065914 | Perhaps 'Cleft of the Horses' |

| Name | Elevation (m) | Surface | Nearest place | Region |
|---|---|---|---|---|
| Nick of Corners Gale | 572 | | Glen Trool Lodge | Galloway Forest |
| Nick of Curleywee | 555 | | Craigencallie | Galloway Forest |
| Nick of Disgee | 395 | | Knockgray | Carsphairn Hills |
| Nick of Frudds Head  *see Talla Nick* | | | | |
| Nick of Knock | 258 | | Darngarroch | Galloway Forest |
| Nick of Milldown | 246 | | Bennan Cottage | Galloway Forest |
| Nick of Mochrum | 235 | track | Merkland | Mochrum Fell |
| Nick of Orchars | 237 | track | Clatteringshaws | Galloway Forest |
| Nick of Rushes | 474 | | Craigencallie | Galloway Forest |
| Nick of Sheuchan | 375 | | Garlies Castle | Galloway Forest |
| Nick of Slannyvenach | 292 | | Dallash | Galloway Forest |
| Nick of the Brushy | 604 | | Glen Trool Lodge | Galloway Forest |
| Nick of the Dead Man's Banes | 317 | track | Clatteringshaws | Galloway Forest |
| Nick of the Dungeon / Wolf Slock / The Wolf's Slock / Hass of the Wolf's Slock | 494 | | Glen Trool Lodge | Galloway Forest |
| Nick of the Lochans | 643 | | Knockgray | Carsphairn Hills |
| Nick of the Lochans | 510 | | Glen Trool Lodge | Galloway Forest |
| Nick of the Saddle | 559 | | Dallash | Cairnsmore of Fleet |
| Nick of the Saddle | 349 | (track) | Glen Trool Lodge | Galloway Forest |
| Nick of the Sware | 453 | (track) | Craigdarroch | Carsphairn Hills |
| Nick of Trestran | 256 | | Glen | Pibble Hill |
| Nick of Whirstone | 98 | (track) | Ringford | Whirstone Hill |
| Peat Hass / Peat Hause | 347 | (track) | Carsphairn | Galloway Forest |
| Reedies Hass | 428 | | Foulbog | Eskdalemuir Forest |
| *Roughbank Height – Broad Head* | 386 | | Kirkstile | Eskdale |
| Smart's Hass | 432 | (path) | Polgown | Scaur Hills |
| *Smidhope Hill – Capel Fell* | 610 | | Bodesbeck | Ettrick Hills |
| Snappers Slack | 593 | (track) | Gateslack | Lowther Hills |
| **Sorbie Hass** | 175 | **road** | Kirkstile | Eskdale |
| Square Nick | 428 | | Wanlockhead | Lowther Hills |
| Stockcleuch Edge | 404 | | Linhope | Liddesdale |
| Sunhope Hass | 374 | path | Linhope | Eskdale |
| Sware | 62 | path | Palnackie | Bengairn Range |
| The Sware | 301 | | Gateslack | Lowther Hills |
| **Swyre / Swair** | 129 | **road** / track | Dunscore | Nithsdale |
| Talla Nick / Nick of Frudds Head | 693 | | Birkhill | Tweedsmuir Hills |
| *Teviot Stone* | 376 | | Jamestown | Eskdale |
| Thickside Hass | 336 | | Davington | Eskdalemuir Forest |
| Thief's Slack | 370 | | Garwald | Eskdalemuir Forest |
| Tweed's Cross | 437 | (track) | Ericstane | Tweedsmuir Hills |

| Latitude, Longitude | National Grid | Notes |
|---|---|---|
| 55.06281, -4.43388 | NX4466176967 | Name obscure ('white hill'?) |
| 55.06179, -4.42754 | NX4506276839 | Below Curleywee (perhaps meaning 'hill of the winds') |
| 55.23712, -4.23826 | NX5777495942 | Misplaced to west on modern OS; the source of Disgee Strand; 'gee' perhaps reflecting pronunciation of 'gaoth' ('wind') |
| 54.95062, -4.17262 | NX6095563935 | 'Knock' from 'cnoc' ('hill') |
| 55.04166, -4.14869 | NX6279974016 | First part of name probably from 'meall' ('hill') |
| 55.05031, -4.00238 | NX7217474701 | Below Mochrum Fell |
| 55.01564, -4.21908 | NX5821071262 | 'Orchar' is a Scots variant of 'orchard' |
| 55.06587, -4.37141 | NX4866177170 | Probably 'rushes' in the English, botanical sense |
| 55.03591, -4.46339 | NX4267174040 | Below Sheuchan Craig; perhaps 'small seat' (diminutive of 'suidhe') or Scots 'sheuch' ('drainage trench') |
| 55.03011, -4.38448 | NX4769173220 | 'Moorland of the Crows'? |
| 55.05577, -4.45991 | NX4297276242 | Name obscure (brushwood?); close to Nick of the Brush (which is not a col) |
| 54.99278, -4.24697 | NX5634568776 | See p. 61 |
| 55.12930, -4.42602 | NX4542084346 | 'Nick of the Dungeon' attached to watercourse on OS 25; 'Wolf' names not on OS; perhaps from diminutive of 'dùn' ('hill' or 'fort') |
| 55.25048, -4.20251 | NX6009497356 | Given the absence of small lochs, the name probably derives from 'knockans' ('small hills') |
| 55.07357, -4.46449 | NX4274978233 | See above |
| 54.98013, -4.33239 | NX5083467548 | |
| 55.05495, -4.49532 | NX4070776231 | |
| 55.28185, -4.22508 | NS5877100892 | |
| 54.92375, -4.27676 | NX5419061158 | Name perhaps from St Drostan, follower of St Columba |
| 54.92796, -4.04552 | NX6902061169 | Below Whirstone Hill (name obscure) |
| 55.18974, -4.28224 | NX5480590762 | |
| 55.35981, -3.21344 | NT2317207982 | Near the source of Reedie Sike |
| 55.23329, -3.02449 | NY3494393709 | |
| 55.32119, -4.00091 | NS7313304837 | (Southern Upland Way); personal name |
| 55.35221, -3.31590 | NT1666107254 | Borders boundary |
| 55.28919, -3.67092 | NS9398400725 | 'Snapper's Slack' on OS 1st edn; a 'snapper' (Scots) was a 'snapmaker' or gunsmith |
| 55.19558, -3.00598 | NY3606089496 | Slightly misplaced on OS 25; sometimes 'Sorby' or 'Sowerby'; Sorbie is the small settlement at the col's eastern foot; occasionally 'the Gates of Eden' (late 19th c.) |
| 55.36031, -3.75020 | NS8914908762 | Name locally used and attributed to a fancied resemblance to a carpenter's square; however 'square' is an occasional synonym of 'sware' or 'swire', and a nearby burn is called The Sware |
| 55.25207, -2.90896 | NY4231895698 | Borders boundary |
| 55.28314, -2.91310 | NY4210099159 | Borders boundary; name, perhaps, like 'Sunwick', from Old English 'swin' ('pig'), or, like 'Sunlaws', from Scots 'sind' ('to rinse'); a 'hope' is a small, closed valley |
| 54.89570, -3.85328 | NX8124357236 | Not on OS; deduced from Sware Plantation on OS 10 |
| 55.29565, -3.73206 | NS9012001538 | |
| 55.15008, -3.75828 | NX8804785383 | Second name on J. Thomson, 'Dumfriesshire' (1828) |
| 55.44200, -3.32631 | NT1619217258 | Borders boundary (now shifted a few metres south); second name on J. Blaeu, 'Tuedia' (1654); the source of Talla Water; 'Frudd' is an older river name, common in various forms |
| 55.27548, -3.04629 | NY3362798425 | Borders boundary; the stone is a boundary marker at the source of the River Teviot |
| 55.31248, -3.23950 | NT2142602744 | Name from the former settlement of Thickside ('brushy thicket') |
| 55.30818, -3.27257 | NT1931902303 | (Romans and Reivers Route) |
| 55.40906, -3.49509 | NT0543513809 | Borders boundary; OS 1st edn; on modern OS only in Cross Burn, Corse Burn and Corse Dod; 'A name which is considered by the people in the neighbourhood to apply to the small pass where the road from Dumfries to Edinburgh leaves the County of Lanark and enters the valley of the Tweed'; the 'corse' preceded the cross, 'erected as a road mark in so wild and hazardous a mountain pass' (OS name book 1858–61) |

| Name | Elevation (m) | Surface | Nearest place | Region |
|------|------|------|------|------|
| Unthank Hope | 391 | | Linhope | Liddesdale |
| Well Head / Well Path | 406 | track | Durisdeer | Lowther Hills |
| Wet Slack | 361 | (track) | Garwald | Eskdalemuir Forest |
| White Hass | 274 | (track) | Kirkstile | Eskdale |
| Windfell Nick / Windy Hass | 564 | | Bodesbeck | Ettrick Hills |
| Windy Hass *see* Windfell Nick | | | | |
| *Windy Standard – Millaneoch Hill* | 583 | | Craigdarroch | Carsphairn Hills |
| Wolf Slock *see* Nick of the Dungeon | | | | |
| Wrae Hass | 212 | (path) | Kirkstile | Eskdale |
| **Birkhill Pass / Pass of Moffatdale** | 339 | **A** road | Birkhill | Tweedsmuir Hills |
| **Crawick Pass** | 216 | **B** road | Corsebank | Lowther Hills |
| **Dalveen Pass** | 273 | **A** road | Durisdeer | Lowther Hills |
| Enterkin Pass | 340 | path | Wanlockhead | Lowther Hills |
| **Hass** | 118 | **road** | Poldean | Lowther Hills |
| **Mennock Pass** | 208 | **B** road | Wanlockhead | Lowther Hills |

## Dunbartonshire · 1 col

| | | | | |
|------|------|------|------|------|
| *Owsen Hill – Dumbreck* | 471 | | Strathblane | Campsie Fells |

## Fife · 3 cols

| | | | | |
|------|------|------|------|------|
| Glen Vale | 282 | (track) | Nether Urquhart | Lomond Hills |
| **Macduff's Cross** | 134 | **road** | Newburgh | Ochil Hills |
| The Seven Gates | 235 | track | Abernethy | Ochil Hills |

## Inverness – Islands · 65 cols

| | | | | |
|------|------|------|------|------|
| *Acairseid Mhòr* | 40 | | Dry Harbour | South Rona |
| Am Bealach | 331 | | Bualintur | Skye (Minginish) |
| Am Bealach | 109 | | Lorgill | Skye (Duirinish) |
| Am Bràigh | 52 | | Dry Harbour | South Rona |
| Am Màm | 189 | (track) | Camasunary | Skye (Strathaird) |
| An Slugan | 188 | (path) | Torrin | Skye (Red Hills) |
| Bealach a' Bhàsteir (or Bhasadair) | 838 | | Sligachan | Skye (Cuillin Hills) |
| Bealach a' Bhràig Bhig | 369 | path | Kilmory | Rùm |
| Bealach a' Chaòl-reidh | 349 | | Borve | Skye (Trotternish) |
| Bealach a' Chruidh | 147 | (path) | Torran | Raasay |
| Bealach a' Chùirn | 489 | | Rigg | Skye (Trotternish) |
| Bealach a' Garbh-choire | 796 | | Culnamean | Skye (Cuillin Hills) |
| Bealach a' Ghlas-choire | 639 | | Sligachan | Skye (Cuillin Hills) |

| Latitude, Longitude | National Grid | Notes |
|---|---|---|
| 55.24472, -2.91520 | NY4191094885 | Borders boundary; the caption is extended to the col on J. Thomson, 'Roxburghshire' (1822) |
| 55.33569, -3.71030 | NS9161105959 | Dumfries & Galloway boundary; Roman road; not on OS; 'Wellpath' on C. Ross, 'A Map of the Shire of Lanark' (1773); 'Well Head' on W. Forrest, 'The County of Lanark' (1816); 'Well Path' on J. Ainslie, 'Map of the Southern Part of Scotland' (1821); 'path' is occasionally used for 'pass' in this region |
| 55.29382, -3.29201 | NT1805500728 | |
| 55.20778, -3.01266 | NY3565490860 | Name perhaps from the seedheads of bog cotton |
| 55.34013, -3.30463 | NT1735005896 | Second name from W. Crawford, 'Map of Dumfries-shire' (1804) and *Antiquities Ecclesiastical and Territorial of the Parishes of Scotland* (1850), p. 244 |
| 55.29136, -4.16434 | NS6266101828 | Ayrshire boundary |
| 55.18578, -3.00482 | NY3611888405 | Above Wrae and below Wrae Hill |
| 55.43150, -3.26237 | NT2021516014 | Borders boundary; not on OS; 'Birkhill Path' on W. Crawford, 'Map of Dumfries-shire' (1804) and J. Thomson, 'Dumfriesshire' (1828); there is another Birkhill Pass in Aberdeenshire |
| 55.42909, -3.88784 | NS8063216643 | Not on maps; name in common use |
| 55.34998, -3.73241 | NS9024807584 | OS 1st and 2nd edn attach the name to the river, Bartholomew (1912) and OS 25 to the road |
| 55.36402, -3.76242 | NS8838509194 | 'Entrakin Path' on G. Taylor and A. Skinner, 'The Road from Edinburgh to Wigtoun and Whitehorn' (1775); 'Enterkin, the frightfullest pass, and most dangerous that I met with': Daniel Defoe, *A Tour Thro' the Whole Island of Great Britain*, III (1726), p. 12 |
| 55.28320, -3.43099 | NY0920699719 | NCR 74; not on maps; deduced from Hass Cottage, 55.28791, -3.43668 |
| 55.37439, -3.81817 | NS8488110439 | Distinct from Mennock Hass; Mennock is the village at the western end of the pass; nearby, an earth-and-stone cross marks the presumed site of an ancient church; 500 m south-east, by Glenclach Burn, a horizontal stone cross marks the site where, during a snowstorm in 1925, a district nurse fell off her bicycle and died |
| 56.00936, -4.29419 | NS5706081978 | Stirling boundary |
| 56.23597, -3.29858 | NO1960305584 | Perth & Kinross boundary; probably from 'Gleann a' bhealaich' ('Valley of the Pass') |
| 56.33626, -3.24815 | NO2293216688 | NCR 776; Walter Scott, *MacDuff's Cross* (1823): 'the summit of a Rocky Pass near to Newburgh' |
| 56.32483, -3.28080 | NO2088915453 | Perth & Kinross boundary; CR; a meeting of seven ways, of which six remain |
| 57.53748, -5.97451 | NG6222156671 | |
| 57.21361, -6.33383 | NG3843321976 | Deduced from Allt Mòr a' Bhealaich; 'The Pass' |
| 57.37167, -6.69150 | NG1807140980 | Deduced from Loch a' Bhealaich; 'The Pass' |
| 57.56789, -5.96165 | NG6318860008 | On OS 1st edn; 'Braig' on later editions; 'The Neck' |
| 57.18554, -6.09711 | NG5252817970 | 'The Pass' |
| 57.24549, -6.01307 | NG5799524334 | 'The Gullet' |
| 57.24769, -6.19902 | NG4680125256 | 'Executioner's Pass'; probably referring to the treacherous, jagged ridges of the mountain, Am Bàsteir |
| 57.01388, -6.38358 | NM3400399962 | Little Brae Pass' |
| 57.46393, -6.22657 | NG4663749405 | 'Bealach an Tearnaidh' on OS 1st edn ('Pass of the Descent'); misplaced on OS 50; 'Pass of the Narrow Plain' |
| 57.48001, -5.99621 | NG6054750356 | Not on OS 1st edn; 'Cattle Pass' |
| 57.51100, -6.19837 | NG4865154534 | 'Cairn Pass' |
| 57.20139, -6.21674 | NG4541420174 | 'Pass of the Rough Corrie' |
| 57.23958, -6.18614 | NG4752224307 | 'Pass of the Grey Corrie' |

| Name | Elevation (m) | Surface | Nearest place | Region |
|---|---|---|---|---|
| Bealach a' Mhàim | 347 | (path) | Sligachan | Skye (Cuillin Hills) |
| Bealach a' Leitir  *see* Bealach nan Lice | | | | |
| Bealach a' Mhòramhain  *see* Bealach a' Mhorghain | | | | |
| Bealach a' Mhorghain | 534 | (path) | Balnaknock | Skye (Trotternish) |
| Bealach Amadal | 496 | | Glenuachdarach | Skye (Trotternish) |
| Bealach an Dubh-bhràigh | 272 | | Harris | Rùm |
| Bealach an Fhuarain | 515 | | Harris | Rùm |
| Bealach an Locha | 204 | | Drynoch | Skye (Glen Drynoch) |
| Bealach an Lòin | 68 | | Kyleakin | Skye (Kyle Akin) |
| Bealach an Òir | 455 | | Kinloch | Rùm |
| Bealach an Tearnaidh  *see* Bealach a' Chaòl-reidh | | | | |
| Bealach Bairc-mheall | 466 | | Kinloch | Rùm |
| Bealach Bàn | 251 | | Dunan | Scalpay |
| Bealach Beag | 457 | | Rigg | Skye (Trotternish) |
| Bealach Bharcasaig | 254 | | Orbost | Skye (Duirinish) |
| Bealach Breac | 243 | | Sconser | Skye (Red Hills) |
| Bealach Brittle / Bealach Bhreatal | 214 | track | Glenbrittle | Skye (Minginish) |
| Bealach Chaiplin | 516 | | Glenuachdarach | Skye (Trotternish) |
| Bealach Coire na Banachdich | 850 | path | Glenbrittle | Skye (Cuillin Hills) |
| Bealach Coire na Circe | 358 | | Sligachan | Skye (Cuillin Hills) |
| Bealach Coire Sgreamhach | 475 | | Kilbride | Skye (Red Hills) |
| Bealach Eadar dà Bheinn | 282 | | Grula | Skye (Minginish) |
| Bealach Hartaval | 493 | | Rigg | Skye (Trotternish) |
| Bealach Mhic-Coinnich | 745 | | Camasunary | Skye (Strathaird) |
| Bealach Mòr | 339 | | Borve | Skye (Trotternish) |
| Bealach Mòr | 297 | (path) | Mugeary | Skye (Loch Portree) |
| Bealach Mòr | 255 | (track) | Drynoch | Skye (Loch Harport) |
| Bealach Mosgaraidh | 511 | | Sligachan | Skye (Red Hills) |
| Bealach na Beinne Brice | 334 | | Sligachan | Skye (Cuillin Hills) |
| Bealach na Bèiste | 456 | | Luib | Skye (Red Hills) |
| Bealach na Croiche | 159 | | Eynort | Skye (Minginish) |
| Bealach na Cruinn-leum | 394 | | Kylerhea | Skye (Kylerhea Hills) |
| Bealach na Feadan | 169 | | Coillore | Skye (Loch Harport) |
| Bealach na Glaic Moire | 761 | path | Glenbrittle | Skye (Cuillin Hills) |
| Bealach na h-Airigh Mhùrain | 258 | | Bualintur | Skye (Minginish) |
| Bealach na Leacaich / Bealach na Lice | 541 | | Glenuachdarach | Skye (Trotternish) |
| Bealach na Sgàirde | 415 | | Sconser | Skye (Red Hills) |
| Bealach nam Mulachag | 578 | | Kylerhea | Skye (Kylerhea Hills) |
| **Bealach nan Carn** | 192 | **road** | Achnacloich | Skye (Sleat) |
| Bealach nan Coisichean | 278 | | Balnaknock | Skye (Trotternish) |
| Bealach nan Lice | 860 | | Sligachan | Skye (Cuillin Hills) |
| Bealach Ruadh | 325 | (path) | Balachuirn | Raasay |
| **Bealach Udal** | 283 | **road** | Kylerhea | Skye (Kylerhea Hills) |
| Bealach Uige | 295 | | Balnaknock | Skye (Trotternish) |
| Beinn an Uisge – Beinn na Còinnich | 271 | | Lorgill | Skye (Duirinish) |

| Latitude, Longitude | National Grid | Notes |
|---|---|---|
| 57.26227, -6.23035 | NG4501326995 | 'Gap of the Pass' |
| | | |
| | | |
| 57.57767, -6.25906 | NG4548562174 | 'Pass of Shingle' (W. Watson, *Celtic Place-names* (1926)); OS old and modern show 'Bealach a' Mhòramhain' ('Pass of the Great River') |
| 57.56926, -6.25672 | NG4556661230 | Name obscure |
| 57.00872, -6.42225 | NM3162099540 | 'Black Neck Pass' |
| 56.97023, -6.31486 | NM3786494842 | 'Fountain Pass' |
| 57.28980, -6.25327 | NG4382430142 | 'Loch Pass' |
| 57.26415, -5.74983 | NG7398225505 | 'Marsh Pass' |
| 56.97449, -6.30408 | NM3854895275 | 'Pass of Gold'; 'òir' is the genitive of 'òr' ('gold') but perhaps a mistake for 'oir' ('edge', 'boundary') |
| 56.99087, -6.30417 | NM3865897096 | Name derived from Barkeval ('precipice hill') |
| 57.28151, -5.96481 | NG6113928170 | 'White Pass' |
| 57.49921, -6.19147 | NG4898353197 | 'Little Pass' |
| 57.37704, -6.62076 | NG2236141285 | 'Bealach Varkasaig' on OS 1st edn |
| 57.30393, -6.06591 | NG5519931023 | Deduced from Allt a' Bhealaich Bhric; 'Speckled Pass' |
| 57.22454, -6.31741 | NG3950223129 | 'Pass of confusion'; also spelled 'Bealach Bhraigh Daile' |
| 57.55985, -6.25730 | NG4546560186 | 'Milking Pass' |
| 57.21533, -6.23672 | NG4430421799 | 'Pass of the Pock-Marked Corrie' |
| 57.26970, -6.23649 | NG4469527844 | 'Hen (i.e. grouse?) Corrie Pass' |
| 57.22945, -5.99235 | NG5914022478 | 'Pass of the Loathsome Corrie'; 'Bealach Coire Sionnaich' on OS 1st edn ('Fox Corrie Pass') |
| 57.23777, -6.30971 | NG4005924571 | 'Pass between Two hills' |
| 57.52189, -6.22156 | NG4733855831 | 'Harta Fell Pass' |
| 57.22105, -6.08698 | NG5337721882 | 'Mackenzie's Pass' (named after a famous guide) |
| 57.48271, -6.19696 | NG4854051383 | 'Great Pass' |
| 57.37818, -6.23980 | NG4524839919 | 'Great Pass' |
| 57.33717, -6.30108 | NG4127935590 | 'Great Pass' |
| 57.27523, -6.12159 | NG5165428033 | Variously interpreted; perhaps 'Pass of the Mossy Plot' (land used for a shieling – but unlikely because of the terrain), or from 'sgaradh' ('separation', 'severance') |
| 57.27549, -6.24117 | NG4445328505 | 'Pass of the Speckled Hill' |
| 57.23772, -6.07929 | NG5395223708 | 'Pass of the Monster'; *see* pp. 75–6 |
| 57.24900, -6.36601 | NG3674526036 | 'Gallows Pass' |
| 57.20402, -5.74396 | NG7396718797 | 'Bealach na Greigh-léim' on OS 1st edn; 'Herd's Leap Pass'; 'léim' is applied to a col in Ireland |
| 57.35007, -6.37061 | NG3719137292 | 'Whistle Pass' (*see* Glossary) |
| 57.23394, -6.22235 | NG4530023814 | 'Great Hollow Pass' |
| 57.20378, -6.33445 | NG3832720886 | 'Grass Pasture Pass' |
| 57.55061, -6.24437 | NG4617459110 | 'Pass of the Flat Stones' |
| 57.28711, -6.12045 | NG5180329350 | 'Pass of the Scree' or 'of the Gap' (*see* 'scarth' in Glossary) |
| 57.23848, -5.70113 | NG7676122489 | 'Cheese Pass' |
| 57.09711, -5.93350 | NG6183907552 | Not on maps; identified from A. Forbes, *Place-Names of Skye* (1923): 'On [the] road from Tarskavaig and district to Kilmore burying-ground. Hereabouts funeral parties rested and partook of refreshments (falair); these cairns marked where coffins rested or were laid for the above, and passers-by were expected to throw or place a stone on such cairns'; 'Pass of the Cairns' |
| 57.60290, -6.29387 | NG4358365111 | 'Bealach a' Choisiche' on OS 1st edn; 'Walkers' Pass' |
| 57.24761, -6.20665 | NG4634125276 | 'Pass of the Flat Stones'; 'Bealach a' Leitir' on OS 1st edn ('leitir' = 'hillside') |
| 57.38003, -6.03438 | NG5759939373 | 'Red Pass' |
| 57.22193, -5.72306 | NG7533820720 | NCR 79; 'Gloomy Pass' or 'Pass of Distress'; *see* p. 75 |
| 57.59439, -6.28028 | NG4433464113 | Above Glen Uig and the village of Uig |
| 57.39827, -6.65930 | NG2020843803 | |

| Name | Elevation (m) | Surface | Nearest place | Region |
|---|---|---|---|---|
| Ben Cleat – Ben Meabost | 198 | | Elgol | Skye (Strathaird) |
| **Ben Totaig – Beinn na Crèiche** | 136 | **road** | Totaig | Skye (Duirinish) |
| Bràigh na Cloiche | 217 | | Ramasaig | Skye (Duirinish) |
| Gleann a' Phuill | 248 | | Lorgill | Skye (Duirinish) |
| Gleann Duibhal | 449 | | Harris | Rùm |
| Màm a' Phobuill (or Phopuill) | 289 | | Sligachan | Skye (Red Hills) |
| Meall Acairseid | 50 | path | Dry Harbour | South Rona |
| **Quiraing Pass / Bealach na Cuith-raing** | 260 | **road** | Digg | Skye (Trotternish) |
| Scoval – Beinn Bheag | 135 | path | Feriniquarrie | Skye (Duirinish) |
| Slochd Gille Phàruig | 152 | | Skinidin | Skye (Duirinish) |

## Inverness – Mainland · *236 cols 11 passes*

| | | | | |
|---|---|---|---|---|
| Aisir Mhic a' Ghobhainn  *see* Aisre Ghobhainn | | | | |
| Aisre Cham | 971 | | Ben Alder Cottage | Ben Alder Range |
| Aisre Ghobhainn | 887 | | Ben Alder Cottage | Ben Alder Range |
| Am Bealach | 768 | | Corrour Shooting Lodge | Ben Alder Range |
| Am Bealach | 758 | | Corrour Shooting Lodge | Ben Alder Range |
| Am Bealach | 731 | | Luibeilt | Nevis Range |
| Am Bealach | 615 | (path) | Letterfinlay | Glengarry Forest |
| Am Bealach | 589 | (track) | Lynaberack | Cairngorms |
| Am Bealach | 499 | | Inchnacardoch Hotel | Inverwick Forest |
| Am Bealach | 360 | (path) | Druimindarroch | South Morar |
| Am Bealach | 236 | | Tarbert | Ardnamurchan |
| Am Bealach | 199 | | Arnipol | Ardnish |
| Am Màm | 548 | track | Altnafeadh | Glen Coe |
| An Cadha / An Còs | 330 | | Achnabat | Loch Ness |
| An Crasg | 665 | (track) | Bun Loyne | Beinneun Forest |
| An Diollaid | 699 | | Barrisdale | Knoydart |
| An Eag | 493 | | Bogroy | Strathspey |
| An Lairig | 1134 | (path) | Feshiebridge | Cairngorms |
| An Lairig | 515 | | Comra | Strath Mashie |
| **An Slochd Beag** | 374 | **road** | Slochd | Monadhliath Mountains |
| An Slugan / Sluggan Pass | 337 | track | Auchgourish | Cairngorms |
| An Tarsainn | 485 | | Inverailort | Moidart |
| Bealach a' Bhaca | 511 | | Liatrie | Glencannich Forest |
| Bealach a' Bharnish | 820 | | Moy | Monadhliath Mountains |
| Bealach a' Bhò Chrubaich | 461 | | Barrisdale | Knoydart |
| Bealach a' Bhòta | 500 | | Lettermorar | North Morar |
| Bealach a' Chadha Riabhaich | 857 | path | Kinlochmore | Nevis Range |
| Bealach a' Chàil | 488 | | Levishie | Levishie Forest |
| Bealach a' Chàirn Deirg | 675 | | Camusrory | Knoydart |
| Bealach a' Chait | 663 | | Glenfinnan | Glen Finnan |
| Bealach a' Chaorainn | 471 | (path) | Kinlocharkaig | Glen Finnan |
| Bealach a' Charrain | 510 | | Resourie | Ardgour |

| Latitude, Longitude | National Grid | Notes |
|---|---|---|
| 57.16517, -6.08960 | NG5284515677 | |
| 57.44844, -6.68155 | NG1925749472 | |
| 57.41486, -6.70474 | NG1760945836 | 'Neck of the Rock' |
| 57.40516, -6.67767 | NG1915844645 | 'Bog Valley'; perhaps related to Creag a' Bhealaich-airigh to the south |
| 57.00644, -6.38105 | NM3410399124 | |
| 57.25693, -6.12429 | NG5136826008 | 'The People's Pass' |
| 57.54685, -5.97182 | NG6244357704 | |
| 57.62786, -6.29380 | NG4376367886 | Names in common use; not on maps; Quiraing is the active landslide to the north-east |
| 57.46073, -6.69401 | NG1860550890 | |
| 57.42290, -6.65209 | NG2082846512 | Slochd Ille Phàruig on modern OS ('gille' and 'ille' are equivalent); personal name ('gille' = 'lad' or 'servant'; 'Phàruig' = 'Patrick'); *see* 'sloc' in Glossary |

| | | |
|---|---|---|
| 56.83550, -4.48976 | NN4819974323 | Misplaced to north on modern OS; 'Crooked Pass'; the third-highest col in Scotland and fourth-highest in the British Isles |
| 56.84490, -4.48891 | NN4828975367 | 'Aisir Mhic a' Ghobhainn' on OS 1st edn; 'Blacksmith Pass' |
| 56.79682, -4.53093 | NN4552970111 | Perth & Kinross boundary; deduced from Meall a' Bhealaich; 'The Pass' |
| 56.78504, -4.54228 | NN4478768826 | Perth & Kinross boundary; deduced from Allt, Carn, Coire and Meall a' Bhealaich; 'The Pass' |
| 56.79235, -4.93054 | NN2111070588 | Deduced from Coire Bhealaich; 'The Pass' |
| 56.99985, -4.92682 | NN2232693664 | Deduced from Càm Bhealach and Allt Càm Bhealaich; 'The Pass' |
| 57.00444, -4.01469 | NN7773192170 | Deduced from Coire Bhealaich |
| 57.17571, -4.70705 | NH3644712681 | Deduced from Loch a' Bhealaich; 'The Pass' |
| 56.92217, -5.76506 | NM7096287520 | Deduced from Lochan a' Bhealaich; 'The Pass' |
| 56.70207, -5.81416 | NM6661063207 | Deduced from Druim a' Bhealaich; 'The Pass' |
| 56.87609, -5.71070 | NM7399082214 | Deduced from Lochan a' Bhealaich; 'The Pass' |
| 56.67596, -4.91384 | NN2157957595 | (West Highland Way); deduced from Allt a' Mhain (Mhaim on OS 1st edn); 'The Pass'; above the Devil's Staircase |
| 57.34247, -4.34449 | NH5899930426 | 'The Pass'; 'An Còs' ('The Hollow' or 'Crevice') on OS 1st edn, referring to the summit of the pass |
| 57.12737, -4.87820 | NH2587707727 | Deduced from Màm a' Chroisg ('Hill of the Crossing') |
| 57.07847, -5.61259 | NG8115704404 | 'The Saddle' |
| 57.32618, -3.83712 | NH8948127675 | Deduced from Carn nan Eagan; 'The Nick' |
| 57.08174, -3.71175 | NH9634500272 | Aberdeenshire boundary; deduced from Sròn na Lairige ('Sròn na Leirg' on OS 1st edn); 'The Pass'; the highest col in the British Isles; *see* p. 87 |
| 56.99028, -4.36852 | NN5619191284 | Deduced from Loch and Coire na Lairige; 'The Pass' |
| 57.29051, -3.90888 | NH8504923824 | NCR 7; 'The Little Gully' |
| 57.19371, -3.74855 | NH9443412790 | 'A very narrow, rocky, and precipitous glen, called the Sluggan, said to mean the "swallow" or "swallowing"': Queen Victoria's Journal, 6 September 1850; 'The Gullet' |
| 56.85804, -5.66984 | NM7637080071 | Deduced from Allt Tarsuinn ('Cross Stream') |
| 57.37335, -4.90557 | NH2538935166 | 'Pass of the Notch' |
| 56.94393, -4.63795 | NN3962686727 | 'Pass of the Breach'? |
| 57.08516, -5.49607 | NG8825304780 | 'Pass of the Lame Cow' |
| 56.92981, -5.74044 | NM7250688287 | 'Pass of the Mound' |
| 56.75298, -4.96727 | NN1867866304 | |
| 57.23903, -4.67925 | NH3840519660 | 'Pass of the Kale'; 'Bealach an Aodaich' on OS 1st edn ('Pass of the Cloth') |
| 57.02944, -5.45140 | NM9064598444 | 'Red Cairn Pass' |
| 56.90041, -5.40247 | NM9289783942 | 'Pass of the Cat' |
| 56.92648, -5.38210 | NM9428186780 | 'Rowan Pass' |
| 56.79177, -5.44841 | NM8949171997 | 'Carran' = corn spurrey (a weed) |

| Name | Elevation (m) | Surface | Nearest place | Region |
|---|---|---|---|---|
| Bealach a' Chip | 923 | | Achriabhach | Nevis Range |
| Bealach a' Chòinich | 591 | | Alltbeithe | Kintail |
| Bealach a' Choire Bhàin | 564 | | Be-Ach | Morvern |
| Bealach a' Choire Bheithich | 627 | | Kinbreack | Loch·Arkaig |
| Bealach a' Choire Bhuidhe | 490 | | Glenaladale | Moidart |
| Bealach a' Choire Chreagaich | 741 | | Forest Lodge | Cairngorms |
| Bealach a' Choire Chruaidh | 639 | | Camusrory | Knoydart |
| Bealach a' Choire Dhuibh | 340 | | Glenaladale | Moidart |
| Bealach a' Choire Leacachain | 710 | | Letter Finlay | Loch Lochy |
| Bealach a' Choire Mhòir | 439 | | Glenaladale | Moidart |
| Bealach a' Choire Odhair | 802 | | Black Mount | Black Mount |
| Bealach a' Choire Odhair | 688 | | Barrisdale | Knoydart |
| Bealach a' Choire Odhair | 617 | | Barrisdale | Knoydart |
| Bealach a' Choire Réidhe | 799 | | Kinloch Hourn | Glen Shiel |
| Bealach a' Ghamhna  see Bealach Fèith na Gamhna | | | | |
| Bealach a' Ghlinne | 222 | | Killundine | Morvern |
| Bealach a' Mhàma | 285 | path | Arnipol | South Morar |
| Bealach a' Mhonmhuir | 583 | | Achnalea | Morvern |
| Bealach an Amais | 651 | | Lundie | Glen Affric |
| Bealach an Aodaich  see Bealach a' Chàil | | | | |
| Bealach an Easain | 628 | | Clunes | Glengarry Forest |
| Bealach an Fhalaisg Dhuibh | 753 | | Inverailort | Moidart |
| Bealach an Fhiodha | 398 | | Inverguseran | Knoydart |
| Bealach an Fhìona | 701 | | Inverailort | Moidart |
| Bealach an Fhuarain | 615 | | Kinloch Hourn | Knoydart |
| Bealach an Fhuarain | 601 | | Inchvuilt | Glencannich Forest |
| Bealach an Lagain Duibh | 310 | path | Upper Glendessarry | Glen Dessarry |
| Bealach an Sgrìòdain | 651 | | Resourie | Ardgour |
| Bealach an Sgùrr | 551 | | Luibeilt | Nevis Range |
| Bealach an Toiteil | 699 | | Kinloch Hourn | Glen Shiel |
| Bealach an Torc-choire | 764 | | Camusrory | Knoydart |
| Bealach an Tuill Chéilte  see Bealach Toll Sgàile | | | | |
| Bealach an Tuill Ghaineamhaich | 734 | | Liatrie | Glencannich Forest |
| Bealach Aon Achadh na h-Airidhe  see Bealach Caràch | | | | |
| Bealach Bàn | 598 | | Barrisdale | Knoydart |
| Bealach Bàn | 412 | | Gaskan | Moidart |
| Bealach Beag | 651 | | Tighnacomaire | Ardgour |
| Bealach Breabag | 833 | (path) | Ben Alder Cottage | Ben Alder Range |
| Bealach Buidhe | 696 | | Kylesknoydart | Knoydart |
| Bealach Caol Creran | 449 | | Invercharnan | Bidean nam Bian Range |
| Bealach Caol na Droma Bige | 870 | | Kinloch Hourn | Cluanie Forest |
| Bealach Caol na Droma Mòire | 821 | | Kinloch Hourn | Cluanie Forest |
| **Bealach Caràch** | 139 | **A road** | Kylesbeg | Moidart |
| Bealach Càrn na h-Urchaire | 648 | | Ardechive | Glengarry Forest |
| Bealach Choir' a' Ghuirein | 722 | | Achnasaul | Glengarry Forest |
| Bealach Choire a' Chait | 727 | (path) | Lundie | Ceannacroc Forest |
| Bealach Choire Shalachain | 498 | | Lochuisge | Morvern |
| Bealach Clach nam Meirleach | 627 | | Invercharnan | Bidean nam Bian Range |
| Bealach Coir' an Fheòir | 420 | | Gaskan | Moidart |

| Latitude, Longitude | National Grid | Notes |
|---|---|---|
| 56.75158, -5.00495 | NN1636866249 | 'Hill Top Pass' |
| 57.18368, -5.20916 | NH0614714885 | Ross & Cromarty boundary; 'Bog Pass' |
| 56.61028, -5.59584 | NM7943152274 | 'White Corrie Pass' |
| 57.00509, -5.17445 | NN0731994919 | Not on modern OS; 'Pass of the Corrie of the Beast' |
| 56.84869, -5.55003 | NM8361778646 | 'Yellow Corrie Pass' |
| 56.93036, -3.83904 | NN8817783624 | Perth & Kinross boundary; 'Pass of the Rocky Corrie' |
| 57.02713, -5.44263 | NM9116498160 | 'Hard Corrie Pass' |
| 56.83709, -5.60424 | NM8024577529 | 'Black Corrie Pass' |
| 56.99518, -4.92759 | NN2225793146 | Deduced from Coire Leacachain; 'Coire Leacach' on OS 1st edn; 'Pass of Flat-Stone Corrie' |
| 56.82889, -5.59788 | NM8058576596 | Not on OS 1st edn; 'Big Corrie Pass' |
| 56.57029, -4.83405 | NN2597945633 | Inverness boundary; deduced from Coire Odhar and Stob a' Choire Odhair; 'Dun Corrie Pass' |
| 57.04301, -5.51105 | NG8710400138 | 'Dun Corrie Pass' |
| 57.08717, -5.58718 | NG8274705290 | 'Dun Corrie Pass' |
| 57.14268, -5.30576 | NH0009010604 | Ross & Cromarty boundary; 'Smooth Corrie Pass' |
| | | |
| 56.57554, -5.88418 | NM6152849376 | 'Pass of the Glen'; the glen is Gleann nan Iomairean |
| 56.90672, -5.70709 | NM7439585608 | 'Pass of the Hills' |
| 56.65780, -5.51811 | NM8447157313 | 'Pass of the Murmur(ing Stream?)' |
| 57.21689, -5.05178 | NH1582018143 | 'Pass of the Find' |
| | | |
| 57.00206, -4.98143 | NN1902194053 | 'Pass of the Waterfall' |
| 56.84537, -5.63320 | NM7852878543 | 'Pass of the Black Heath-burning' |
| 57.08062, -5.71957 | NG7469004991 | 'Timber Pass' |
| 56.83938, -5.66728 | NM7641577988 | 'Wine Pass' (on a smugglers' route from the shores of Loch Ailort) |
| 57.04994, -5.40322 | NG9368100577 | 'Fountain Pass' |
| 57.37865, -4.93013 | NH2393935819 | 'Fountain Pass' |
| 56.99711, -5.44510 | NM9084594828 | 'Black Hollow Pass' |
| 56.80004, -5.48745 | NM8715573038 | 'Pass of the Mountain Torrent' |
| 56.82658, -4.80894 | NN2869174085 | 'Bealach an Sgòir' on OS 1st edn; 'Pass of the Cliff' |
| 57.14554, -5.38846 | NG9510411167 | Ross & Cromarty boundary; 'Pass of the Place of Smoke' |
| 57.03116, -5.55842 | NM8416398969 | Misplaced to north-west on modern OS; 'Boar Corrie Pass' |
| | | |
| 57.35149, -5.01543 | NH1867833021 | Ross & Cromarty boundary; 'Sandy (or 'Gravelly') Holes Pass' |
| | | |
| 57.09497, -5.59792 | NG8214206192 | 'White Pass' |
| 56.79958, -5.62202 | NM7894073414 | 'White Pass' |
| 56.78950, -5.43022 | NM9058971689 | 'Little Pass' |
| 56.79956, -4.44654 | NN5069270229 | 'Bealach Breabach' on OS 1st edn; 'breabag' = 'rocky col' or 'cleft' |
| 57.01004, -5.61009 | NM8090596784 | 'Yellow Pass' |
| 56.60947, -5.07998 | NN1107150643 | Argyll & Bute boundary; 'Pass of the Strait of the (River) Creran' |
| 57.13025, -5.25834 | NH0289209083 | Ross & Cromarty boundary; 'Pass of the Defile of the Big Ridge' |
| 57.13197, -5.26847 | NH0228809303 | Ross & Cromarty boundary; 'Pass of the Defile of the Little Ridge' |
| 56.80898, -5.81927 | NM6696175114 | 'The Winding Pass'; 'Bealach Aon Achadh na h-Airidhe' on OS 1st edn ('Pass of the One-field Shieling') |
| 57.00612, -5.02814 | NN1620594630 | 'Shot Cairn Pass' |
| 57.00971, -4.99677 | NN1812794945 | 'Scab Corrie Pass' |
| 57.17977, -5.12911 | NH1096314225 | Ross & Cromarty boundary; 'Bealach Coir' a' Chait' on OS 1st edn; 'Cat Corrie Pass' |
| 56.61783, -5.57511 | NM8074753048 | 'Foul Corrie Pass' (at the foot of Sgùrr Shalachain) |
| 56.61560, -5.06872 | NN1179351294 | 'Thieves' Stone Pass' |
| 56.78934, -5.65347 | NM7696072377 | 'Grass Corrie Pass' |

| Name | Elevation (m) | Surface | Nearest place | Region |
|------|---------------|---------|---------------|--------|
| Bealach Coire a' Chaorainn | 782 | | Kinloch Hourn | Glenquoich Forest |
| Bealach Coire an Dubh-alltan | 714 | | Kilmalieu | Morvern |
| Bealach Coire Dhorrcail | 700 | | Barrisdale | Knoydart |
| Bealach Coire Easain | 935 | | Luibeilt | Nevis Range |
| Bealach Coire Ghàidheil | 717 | path | Alltbeithe | Carn Eige Range |
| Bealach Coire Laoghan | 900 | | Clashgour | Black Mount |
| Bealach Coire Mhàlagain | 699 | | Kinloch Hourn | Glen Shiel |
| Bealach Coire Mhic Gugain | 460 | | Glengalmadale | Morvern |
| Bealach Coire na Ceannain | 924 | | Killiechonate | Nevis Range |
| Bealach Coire na Cìche | 586 | | Caolasnacon | Glen Coe |
| Bealach Coire nan Cearc | 740 | | Glenfinnan | Glen Finnan |
| Bealach Coire nan Clach | 756 | | Glenaladale | Moidart |
| Bealach Coire nan Gall | 733 | | Upper Glendessarry | Glen Dessarry |
| Bealach Coire nan Gall | 611 | | Ranochan | Moidart |
| Bealach Coire Sgoireadail | 540 | (path) | Kinloch Hourn | Kinlochhourn Forest |
| Bealach Coire Thollaidh | 564 | | Kinbreack | Glen Kingie |
| Bealach Cumhann | 655 | (path) | Ben Alder Cottage | Ben Alder Range |
| Bealach Cumhann | 570 | | Achriabhach | Nevis Range |
| Bealach Dearg | 944 | | Dalness | Bidean nam Bian Range |
| Bealach Dearg | 863 | | Inchvuilt | Loch Monar |
| Bealach Dubh | 722 | (path) | Ben Alder Cottage | Ben Alder Range |
| Bealach Dubh | 262 | | Stoul | Morar |
| Bealach Dubh-liath | 975 | | Lundie | Ceannacroc Forest |
| Bealach Duibh Leac | 730 | path | Kinloch Hourn | Glen Shiel |
| Bealach Eala-choire *see* Bealach Ile Coire | | | | |
| Bealach Easain | 548 | | Kilfinnan | Glengarry Forest |
| Bealach Easan | 528 | | Invercharnan | Bidean nam Bian Range |
| Bealach Fèith 'n Amean | 536 | | Achnalea | Ardgour |
| Bealach Fèith na Gamhna | 531 | (path) | Cougie | Guisachan Forest |
| **Bealach Fèith nan Laogh** | 343 | **road** | Glenhurich | Sunart |
| Bealach Fhaolain | 710 | | Dalness | Bidean nam Bian Range |
| Bealach Fhionnghaill | 579 | | Dalness | Bidean nam Bian Range |
| Bealach Fraoch Choire | 729 | (path) | Kinloch Hourn | Glen Shiel |
| Bealach Fraoch-choire | 674 | | Cougie | Glen Affric |
| Bealach Fuar-chathaidh | 697 | | Clashgour | Black Mount |
| Bealach Gaoith | 598 | | Resourie | Ardgour |
| Bealach Ile Coire | 730 | | Camusrory | Knoydart |
| Bealach Leamhain | 739 | (path) | Aberarder | Ardverikie Forest |
| Bealach Leathann | 745 | | Strathan | Glen Finnan |
| Bealach Mam a' Bhearna | 493 | | Resourie | Ardgour |
| Bealach Mhinniceig | 493 | | Kinloch Hourn | Knoydart |
| Bealach Mòr | 80 | | Achnaha | Ardnamurchan |
| Bealach na Breun-leitire | 426 | | Knockfin | Glen Affric |
| Bealach na Brionn Choille | 298 | | Tighnacomaire | Ardgour |
| Bealach na Cloiche Duibhe | 795 | | Inchvuilt | East Benula Forest |
| Bealach na Craoibhe Chaorainn | 284 | | Drumfern | Gleann Dubh Lighe |
| Bealach na Creige Duibhe | 791 | | Inchvuilt | Glencannich Forest |

| Latitude, Longitude | National Grid | Notes |
|---|---|---|
| 57.11229, -5.32979 | NG9847107294 | 'Bealach Coir' a' Chaoruinn' on OS 1st edn; 'Rowan Corrie Pass' |
| 56.66588, -5.46585 | NM8771858048 | 'Black Stream Corrie Pass' |
| 57.06780, -5.57238 | NG8353003089 | OS name book (1876–8) translates as 'Pass of the Corry of the Difficult or Dangerous Tooth' |
| 56.80686, -4.89725 | NN2321172115 | 'Bealach Coire an Easain' on OS 1st edn; 'Waterfall Corrie Pass' |
| 57.26555, -5.15486 | NH0984923840 | Ross & Cromarty boundary; 'Bealaich [sic] Coir'a' Ghaidheil' on OS 1st edn; 'Pass of the Gaels' (or 'Highlanders'') Corrie' |
| 56.56951, -4.90901 | NN2137245739 | Argyll & Bute boundary; 'Pass of Little Calf Corrie' |
| 57.15725, -5.40075 | NG9442612507 | Ross & Cromarty boundary; 'Pass of the Corrie of the Little Sack'; sometimes 'Pass of Corryvarligan' in 19th c. |
| 56.63700, -5.50231 | NM8532054949 | 'McGuigan Corrie Pass' |
| 56.83670, -4.85574 | NN2588375329 | 'Bealach Coire nan Ceann' on OS 1st edn; 'Pass of the Corrie of the Head(land)s' |
| 56.68614, -5.05999 | NN1267859117 | Deduced from Coire na Cìche; 'Pass of the Corrie of the Pap' (i.e. the Pap of Glencoe); the 'Corrynakiegh' of Stevenson's *Kidnapped* (ch. 21)? |
| 56.90858, -5.39270 | NM9353784821 | 'Hen (i.e. grouse?) Corrie Pass' |
| 56.84554, -5.52879 | NM8489378228 | Deduced from Coire nan Clach ('Coire na Làrach' on OS 1st edn); 'Rock Corrie Pass' |
| 57.00493, -5.41414 | NM9276895604 | 'Strangers Corrie Pass' |
| 56.86021, -5.59542 | NM8091880072 | 'Strangers Corrie Pass' |
| 57.13411, -5.34573 | NG9762609768 | 'Bealach Coire Sgoir'adail' on OS 1st edn; 'Pass of Mare's Cleft Corrie' |
| 57.04443, -5.23940 | NN0358499481 | 'Dug Corrie Pass' |
| 56.81156, -4.51532 | NN4654271716 | 'Narrow Pass' |
| 56.78605, -4.98428 | NN1779970029 | 'Narrow Pass' |
| 56.63824, -5.01702 | NN1507553672 | 'Red Pass' |
| 57.44340, -4.95891 | NH2252343098 | Ross & Cromarty boundary; 'Red Pass' |
| 56.82542, -4.49078 | NN4809673204 | 'Black Pass' |
| 57.00036, -5.73427 | NM7331196113 | Deduced from Allt a' Bhealaich Dhuibh; 'Black Pass' |
| 57.17377, -5.10580 | NH1234113493 | Ross & Cromarty boundary; not on modern OS; 'Dark-grey Pass'; the second-highest col in Scotland and third-highest in the British Isles |
| 57.14691, -5.36049 | NG9680311236 | Ross & Cromarty boundary; 'Black Stone Pass' |
| | | |
| 57.02716, -4.91320 | NN2328396667 | 'Waterfall Pass' |
| 56.62498, -5.09218 | NN1040152402 | 'Waterfall Pass' |
| 56.71206, -5.43091 | NM9011563077 | 'Pass of the Mountain Bog' (if as Culnamean/Cul nam Beann) |
| 57.22952, -4.90433 | NH2478119159 | 'Bealach a' Ghamhna' on OS 1st edn; 'Bullock Bog Pass' |
| 56.73965, -5.53707 | NM8377966476 | 'Calves Bog Pass' |
| 56.63656, -5.04339 | NN1345053557 | 'Fillan's Pass' (saint's name) |
| 56.62637, -5.04937 | NN1303352439 | 'Fingal's Pass' |
| 57.14448, -5.32331 | NG9903810855 | Ross & Cromarty boundary; 'Heather Corrie Pass' |
| 57.23035, -5.00037 | NH1898919503 | 'Heather Corrie Pass' |
| 56.59513, -4.88483 | NN2297748527 | 'Cold (Snow-)drift Pass' |
| 56.79313, -5.49178 | NM8685272283 | 'Wind Pass' |
| 57.03372, -5.52668 | NM8610399154 | 'Bealach Eala-choire' on OS 1st edn; 'Swan Corrie Pass' |
| 56.88727, -4.48072 | NN4896080064 | 'Bealach Sleamhuinn' on OS 1st edn; 'Elm Pass' |
| 56.93396, -5.40642 | NM9284387686 | 'Broad Pass' |
| 56.74216, -5.45767 | NM8864766508 | 'Gap Hill Pass' |
| 57.08942, -5.44422 | NG9141705094 | 'Kid-skin Pass' |
| 56.75190, -6.14248 | NM4686069915 | Misplaced on OS 25; 'Great Pass' |
| 57.29828, -4.86522 | NH2746326710 | 'Pass of the Foul Hillside' |
| 56.74936, -5.35096 | NM9520966984 | 'Fair Forest Pass' |
| 57.36598, -5.04239 | NH1712934705 | Ross & Cromarty boundary; 'Black Stone Pass' |
| 56.88260, -5.36168 | NM9528381838 | 'Rowan Tree Pass' |
| 57.36658, -4.98486 | NH2059034619 | 'Black Rock Pass' |

| Name | Elevation (m) | Surface | Nearest place | Region |
|------|---------------|---------|---------------|--------|
| Bealach na Cruaiche | 605 | | Roybridge | Nevis Range |
| Bealach na Faire | 207 | path | Coille Mhorgil | Glen Kingie |
| Bealach na Fèithe | 177 | | Gearradh | Ardgour |
| Bealach na Gaoithe | 268 | | Glenuig | Moidart |
| Bealach na Géire | 355 | | Glenfinnan | Ardgour |
| Bealach na h-Aon-luirg | 596 | | Lundie | Ceannacroc Forest |
| Bealach na h-Eangair | 845 | | Camusrory | Glen Dessarry |
| Bealach na h-Imrich | 596 | | Cougie | Glen Affric |
| Bealach na h-Imrich | 249 | track | Inchlaggan | Loch Loyne |
| Bealach na Sgàirn | 412 | | Durinemast | Morvern |
| Bealach na Sguabaich | 337 | | Kilfinnan | Glengarry Forest |
| Bealach na Staoineig | 490 | | Luibeilt | Nevis Range |
| Bealach nam Biodag | 38 | | Acharacle | Ardnamurchan |
| Bealach nam Botàichean | 769 | | Ardchuilk | Glen Strathfarrar |
| Bealach nam Fiadh | 829 | | Corrour Shooting Lodge | Rannoch Forest |
| Bealach nan Aingidh | 488 | | Inversanda | Ardgour |
| Bealach nan Carn | 382 | (track) | Scotstown | Sunart |
| Bealach nan Creagan Dubha | 497 | | Arnisdale | Knoydart |
| Bealach nan Each | 313 | | Branault | Ardnamurchan |
| Bealach nan Sac | 235 | (path) | Stoul | North Morar |
| Bealach nan Sgòr | 804 | | Corrour Shooting Lodge | Ben Alder Range |
| Bealach Odhar | 839 | | Clashgour | Black Mount |
| Bealach Odhar | 649 | | Bun Loyne | Beinneun Forest |
| **Bealach Ràtagain / Mam Ratagan** | 339 | **road** | Ratagan | Kintail |
| Bealach Ruadh | 103 | | Achnaha | Ardnamurchan |
| Bealach Scamodale | 511 | | Scamodale | Ardgour |
| Bealach Sgairt Dea-uisge | 128 | path | Shielfoot | Moidart |
| Bealach Sgùrr an Lochain | 890 | | Kinloch Hourn | Glen Shiel |
| Bealach Sleamhuinn  *see Bealach Leamhain* | | | | |
| Bealach Sloc an Eich | 340 | path | Glencripesdale | Morvern |
| Bealach Sneachda | 865 | | Ardchuilk | Glen Strathfarrar |
| Bealach Toll an Lochain | 827 | | Inchvuilt | East Benula Forest |
| Bealach Toll Easa | 872 | path | Liatrie | Carn Eige Range |
| Bealach Toll Sgàile | 911 | | Inchvuilt | Glen Strathfarrar |
| Bealachan Lochain Ghaineamhaich | 766 | path | Kinlochetive | Lorn |
| *Beinn a' Chaorainn − Beinn Odhar Bheag* | 700 | | Glenaladale | Moidart |
| **Beinn Chlaonleud − Meall a' Choire Bheithich** | 202 | **A road** | Achagavel | Morvern |
| Beul a' Chasain | 662 | | Easter Drummond | Monadhliath Mountains |
| Beul a' Mhàim | 267 | | Trislaig | Ardgour |
| **Beum a' Chlaidheimh** | 384 | **B road** | Tullochgribban High | Strathspey |
| Black Mile Pass  *see Mile Dorcha* | | | | |
| Cadha an Onfhaidh | 662 | (path) | Upper Glendessarry | Glen Dessarry |
| Cadha Giorraid | 388 | path | Killiehuntly | Cairngorms |
| Cadha Mòr | 256 | (path) | Kinloch Hourn | Kinlochhourn Forest |
| Cadha na Coin Duibh | 754 | (track) | Baileguish | Cairngorms |
| Cadha na Gaoithe | 355 | | Bun Loyne | Ceannacroc Forest |
| Cadha nam Bò Ruadha | 764 | | Kinloch Hourn | Kinlochhourn Forest |

| Latitude, Longitude | National Grid | Notes |
|---|---|---|
| 56.83751, -4.81401 | NN2843275314 | 'Pass of the Hill' |
| 57.04583, -5.18894 | NN0665199492 | 'Pass of the Watchman' |
| 56.71447, -5.35942 | NM9450263128 | 'Pass of the Bog' |
| 56.81726, -5.79182 | NM6868775942 | 'Pass of the Wind' |
| 56.84512, -5.44262 | NM9014477914 | 'Pass of Bitterness' |
| 57.16197, -5.03542 | NH1653511989 | 'One Track Pass' |
| 57.01174, -5.45031 | NM9061196472 | Deduced from Allt Bealach na h-Eangair; 'Pass of the Orator' |
| 57.23688, -4.99643 | NH1925920219 | 'Pass of the Flitting' (transhumance) |
| 57.08497, -5.03962 | NH1589903433 | 'Pass of the Flitting' (transhumance) |
| 56.59177, -5.83095 | NM6489650997 | 'Howling Pass' |
| 57.04532, -4.89389 | NN2454098638 | 'Pass of the Besom' |
| 56.75690, -4.79601 | NN2916366300 | 'Juniper Notch Pass' |
| 56.73952, -5.80636 | NM6731967345 | 'Pass of the Daggers' |
| 57.44601, -4.86626 | NH2809343150 | Ross & Cromarty boundary; 'Bealach nam Bogan' on OS 1st edn; 'Pass of the Bog' |
| 56.75477, -4.58541 | NN4202665557 | Perth & Kinross boundary; 'Deer Pass' |
| 56.71454, -5.39691 | NM9220963249 | 'Pass of the Wicked' |
| 56.72823, -5.59877 | NM7994165403 | 'Pass of the Cairns' |
| 57.10334, -5.62629 | NG8047407214 | 'Black Rocks Pass' |
| 56.73849, -6.06378 | NM5157968136 | 'Pass of the Horses' |
| 56.98071, -5.70418 | NM7501893828 | 'Pass of the Burdens' |
| 56.77645, -4.55072 | NN4423667889 | Perth & Kinross boundary; 'Pass of the Cliffs' |
| 56.57431, -4.92737 | NN2026746321 | Argyll & Bute boundary; 'Dun(-coloured) Pass' |
| 57.11950, -4.91314 | NH2372506941 | 'Dun(-coloured) Pass' |
| 57.22045, -5.47645 | NG9020919768 | Ross & Cromarty boundary; 'Pass of the Small Fortress' (Ratagan is the village at the eastern foot of the col); 'We rode on well, till we came to the high mountain called the Rattakin': James Boswell, *The Journal of a Tour to the Hebrides* (1785); *see* p. 75 |
| 56.73144, -6.16344 | NM4544167718 | 'Red Pass' |
| 56.80777, -5.49981 | NM8644573936 | Scamodale is the place below the col on Loch Shiel |
| 56.77371, -5.81679 | NM6689371183 | 'Pass of the Roaring of Good Waters' (Springs?) |
| 57.13784, -5.29084 | NH0096610021 | Ross & Cromarty boundary; 'Lochan Hill Pass' |
| 56.65169, -5.82666 | NM6553257647 | 'Pass of Horse Hollow' |
| 57.44614, -4.89175 | NH2656543229 | Ross & Cromarty boundary; 'Snow Pass' |
| 57.36300, -5.07333 | NH1525434458 | Ross & Cromarty boundary; 'Lochan Hollow Pass' |
| 57.30166, -5.03583 | NH1720427532 | Ross & Cromarty boundary; 'Waterfall Hollow Pass' |
| 57.44678, -4.91765 | NH2501443367 | Ross & Cromarty boundary; 'Bealach an Tuill Chéilte' on OS 1st edn; 'Hidden Hollow Pass' |
| 56.53640, -5.02741 | NN1393842370 | Argyll & Bute boundary; 'Gravelly (or 'Sandy') Lochan Pass' |
| 56.83727, -5.53899 | NM8422477341 | |
| 56.63267, -5.64951 | NM7626954938 | |
| 57.15435, -4.48600 | NH4972009795 | 'Mouth of the Path' |
| 56.82063, -5.17523 | NN0631774400 | 'Mouth of the Path' |
| 57.35686, -3.76773 | NH9374730979 | 'Gap (or 'Wound') of the Sword' |
| 57.01355, -5.37550 | NM9516196446 | Name uncertain (deduced from the burn 500 m west); 'Storm (or 'Roaring') Pass' |
| 57.04940, -3.99812 | NN7888597144 | 'Shorter Pass' |
| 57.11645, -5.40029 | NG9422807967 | 'Great Pass' |
| 57.02649, -3.86008 | NN8718894358 | Not on OS 1st edn; 'Pass of the Black Dog' |
| 57.15591, -5.00772 | NH1818011240 | 'Pass of the Wind' |
| 57.13592, -5.36294 | NG9659510021 | 'Red Cow Pass' |

SCOTLAND

| Name | Elevation (m) | Surface | Nearest place | Region |
|---|---|---|---|---|
| Cadha Raineach | 769 | | Inchvuilt | Loch Monar |
| Cadha Riabhach | 747 | path | Upper Glendessarry | Glen Kingie |
| Cadha Riabhach | 670 | | Alltbeithe | Glenaffric Forest |
| Caol Lairig | 299 | (track) | Bohuntine | Glen Roy |
| Chalamain Gap | 700 | path | Glenmore | Cairngorms |
| Col | 359 | | Turret Bridge | Glen Roy |
| Corrieyairack weather station | 768 | track | Melgarve | Monadhliath Mountains |
| Creag Mhigeachaidh – Geal-charn | 670 | (path) | Feshiebridge | Cairngorms |
| Creagan a' Chaise – Carn Tuairneir | 644 | | Lynemore | Hills of Cromdale |
| Cùl Mhàm | 540 | | Achnalea | Morvern |
| Diollaid a' Chàirn | 876 | | Ben Alder Cottage | Ben Alder Range |
| Diollaid Coire Eindart | 958 | (track) | Baileguish | Cairngorms |
| Diollaid na Maoil Uidhre | 508 | | Kilmalieu | Morvern |
| Doire nan Gad | 272 | A road | Achagavel | Morvern |
| Drochaid nam Meall Buidhe | 519 | | Inchvuilt | Loch Monar |
| Dubh Bhealach | 350 | | Larachbeg | Morvern |
| Eag a' Chait | 570 | path | Glenmore | Cairngorms |
| Eag a' Gharbh-choire | 580 | | Glenmore Lodge | Cairngorms |
| Eag a' Mhadaidh Ruaidh | 656 | | Resourie | Ardgour |
| Eag Bheag | 510 | | Lainchoil | Cairngorms |
| Eag Coire a' Choinneachaidh  see Chalamain Gap | | | | |
| Eag Mhòr | 412 | path | Lainchoil | Cairngorms |
| Erchite Hill – Meall na h-Uaighe | 351 | | Achnabat | Loch Ness |
| Fiar Bhealach | 740 | | Coille Mhorgil | Glenquoich Forest |
| Garbh-bhealach | 955 | | Cougie | Carn Eige Range |
| Glac a' Chatha | 474 | | Brinmore | Monadhliath Mountains |
| Glac an Lòin | 415 | | Easter Drummond | Monadhliath Mountains |
| Glac Breabag | 338 | | Easter Drummond | Monadhliath Mountains |
| Glac Falaichte | 78 | track | Tarbet | North Morar |
| Glac Mhòr | 121 | (path) | Ardtornish | Morvern |
| Glac na Mòine | 422 | | Inchvuilt | Loch Monar |
| Glas Bhealach | 965 | | Lundie | Ceannacroc Forest |
| Glas Bhealach | 665 | | Resourie | Ardgour |
| Glas Bhealach | 615 | | Corrlarach | Ardgour |
| Gleann na Cloiche Sgoilte | 404 | | Glenhurich | Ardgour |
| Lag a' Mhàim | 529 | track | Glensanda | Morvern |
| Lagan a' Bhuic | 422 | | Eignaig | Morvern |
| Làirig Dhochard | 632 | | Glenceitlein | Black Mount |
| Lairig Eilde | 489 | (path) | Dalness | Bidean nam Bian Range |
| Lairig Gartain / Làirig Ghartáin | 489 | (path) | Dalness | Bidean nam Bian Range |
| Làirig Ghrù / Learg Ghruamach | 836 | (path) | Glenmore | Cairngorms |
| Lairig Leacach | 511 | track | Inverroy | Nevis Range |
| Learg an Laoigh  see Lairig Pass (pass) | | | | |
| Learg Ghruamach  see Làirig Ghrù | | | | |
| Learg Mheuran | 733 | (path) | Coileitir | Lorn |

| Latitude, Longitude | National Grid | Notes |
|---|---|---|
| 57.43711, -4.95976 | NH2244142400 | Ross & Cromarty boundary; 'Bracken Pass' |
| 57.02307, -5.35871 | NM9623297455 | 'Brindled (or 'Grey') Pass' |
| 57.21198, -5.09761 | NH1302917722 | 'Brindled (or 'Grey') Pass' |
| 56.93765, -4.81438 | NN2886886456 | 'Narrow Pass' |
| 57.12610, -3.71162 | NH9647705209 | 'Eag Coire a' Choinneachaidh' on OS 1st edn; also 'Eag Coire na Còmhdalach' ('Nick of the Corrie of the Meeting') |
| 56.99636, -4.78151 | NN3113492907 | Marked as 'Col' on OS 1st and later edn; *see* Glossary (perhaps meaning a flat area) |
| 57.05142, -4.60600 | NN4202598612 | The unnamed col lies 500 m from the summit of the Corrieyairack Pass (*see* below) |
| 57.09625, -3.85584 | NH8765702115 | |
| 57.29738, -3.49568 | NJ0996723966 | Moray boundary |
| 56.65928, -5.50233 | NM8544657428 | 'Back (or 'Nook') of the Pass' (*see* Glossary) |
| 56.85016, -4.47680 | NN4904975926 | 'Cairn Saddle' |
| 57.01168, -3.81628 | NN8980392638 | 'Saddle of Eindart Corrie' (Eindart is a stream which rises at the col) |
| 56.65218, -5.45248 | NM8846056483 | 'Saddle of the Dappled Headland' |
| 56.65392, -5.63570 | NM7724057255 | 'Withes Copse' is the nearest named feature |
| 57.38845, -5.10285 | NH1360837370 | Ross & Cromarty boundary; 'Ridge Pass of the Yellow Hill' |
| 56.57777, -5.80237 | NM6656449343 | 'Black Pass' |
| 57.13804, -3.71300 | NH9642706540 | Not on OS 1st edn; 'Cat Nick' |
| 57.16867, -3.63564 | NJ0119009834 | 'Rough Corrie Nick' |
| 56.79858, -5.46866 | NM8829472817 | 'Red Wolf (or 'Dog') Pass' |
| 57.21228, -3.54622 | NJ0670714562 | 'Little Nick' |
| 57.21741, -3.55109 | NJ0642615139 | 'Great Nick' |
| 57.33165, -4.36175 | NH5791829258 | |
| 57.09289, -5.21217 | NH0548904794 | 'Crooked Pass' |
| 57.29215, -5.07448 | NH1482826578 | Ross & Cromarty boundary; misplaced to east on modern OS; 'Rough Pass' |
| 57.32705, -4.18537 | NH6851928392 | 'Hollow of the Pass'; also 'glaic' and 'chadha' |
| 57.16514, -4.50062 | NH4888011028 | 'Hollow of the Marshy Meadow' |
| 57.17822, -4.50090 | NH4883312529 | Not on OS 1st edn; deduced from Allt Glaic Breabaig; below Meall an Tarsáid ('hill of the path across'); 'Rocky Hollow' |
| 56.96490, -5.62965 | NM7945191826 | The 'glac' leads to the col, shown on maps on the track through Glen Tarbet; 'Hidden Hollow' |
| 56.57383, -5.72239 | NM7144948634 | 'Great Hollow' |
| 57.39163, -5.08906 | NH1445337685 | 'Peat Hollow' |
| 57.17247, -5.09499 | NH1298713319 | Ross & Cromarty boundary; 'Grey Pass' |
| 56.75616, -5.46019 | NM8857268073 | 'Grey Pass' |
| 56.82032, -5.39173 | NM9310975000 | 'Grey Pass' |
| 56.76687, -5.46783 | NM8816569287 | The name, 'Cloven Rock', describes the col |
| 56.59033, -5.55527 | NM8180549926 | 'Hollow of the Pass' |
| 56.53248, -5.63275 | NM7670943740 | 'Little Hollow of the Goat' |
| 56.57062, -4.95136 | NN1877645974 | Argyll & Bute boundary; name related to 'docha(i)r' ('injury', 'sorrow', 'pain')? |
| 56.63649, -4.98697 | NN1690953397 | 'Roe Deer Pass' |
| 56.63264, -4.96228 | NN1840452903 | 'Garter Pass' or a personal name, Gartan |
| 57.09145, -3.69515 | NH9737801327 | Aberdeenshire boundary; name obscure; second name, perhaps speculative, on OS 1st edn ('Gloomy' or 'Forbidding Pass'); on OS 1st edn; also known locally as An Làirig Shuas, 'The Western Pass', the eastern being Learg an Laoigh; (A. Diack, *Place-Names of the Cairngorms National Park*) |
| 56.83488, -4.82034 | NN2803475037 | 'Learg nan Leacan' on OS 1st edn; 'Flat Stones Pass' |
| 56.54593, -4.98900 | NN1634543327 | Argyll & Bute boundary; 'meuran' = 'thimble', 'little finger' or 'small branch' |

| Name | Elevation (m) | Surface | Nearest place | Region |
|---|---|---|---|---|
| Learg nan Leacan  see Lairig Leacach | | | | |
| Màm a' Chullaich | 400 | | Eignaig | Morvern |
| Màm Bàn | 723 | | Corrour Shooting Lodge | Corrour Forest |
| Màm Barrisdale | 450 | path | Barrisdale | Knoydart |
| Màm Buidhe | 748 | (path) | Altnafeadh | Bidean nam Bian Range |
| Màm Chluainidh | 435 | track | Lundie | Loch Cluanie |
| Màm Coire an Easain | 685 | | Kings House Hotel | Black Mount |
| Màm Coire Easain | 932 | | Kings House Hotel | Black Mount |
| Màm Meadail | 547 | path | Camusrory | Knoydart |
| Màm na Cèire | 490 | | Achagavel | Morvern |
| Màm na Seilg | 490 | path | Coille Mhorgil | East Glenquoich Forest |
| Màm nan Calum | 396 | | Upper Glendessarry | Glen Dessarry |
| Mam Ratagan  see Bealach Ràtagain | | | | |
| Màm Suidheig | 498 | | Inverie | Knoydart |
| Màm Uchd | 574 | | Camusrory | Knoydart |
| Màm Unndalain | 527 | (path) | Barrisdale | Knoydart |
| Meall Beag – Mon | 392 | | Achallader | Black Mount |
| Meall Tarsuinn – Meall nan Eun | 785 | | Glenceitlein | Black Mount |
| **Mile Dorcha / Black Mile Pass** | 60 | **B road** | Achnacarry | Loch Lochy |
| Pass of Corryvarligan  see Bealach Coire Mhàlagain | | | | |
| Mini-gaig | 766 | | Gaick Lodge | Cairngorms |
| The Saddle | 807 | path | Glenmore Lodge | Cairngorms |
| Sgorr Dhonuill – Sgorr Dhearg | 757 | | South Ballachulish | Beinn a' Bheithir |
| **Slochd Mòr (Slochd Summit)** | 400 | **A road** | Slochd | Monadhliath Mountains |
| Sluggan Pass  see An Slugan | | | | |
| Uinneag a' Ghlas Choire | 901 | | Corrour Shooting Lodge | Ben Alder Range |
| Uinneag Coire a' Chaorainn | 917 | path | Aberarder | Monadhliath Mountains |
| Uinneag Coire an Lochain | 839 | | Crathie | Monadhliath Mountains |
| Uinneag Coire Ard Dhoire  see The Window | | | | |
| Uinneag Min Choire | 935 | | Aberarder | Monadhliath Mountains |
| The Window / Uinneag Coire Ardair | 952 | | Aberarder | Monadhliath Mountains |
| **Chisholm's Pass** | 182 | **road** | Tomich | Glen Affric |
| Corrieyairack Pass / Pass of Corrieyairack | 776 | track | Melgarve | Monadhliath Mountains |
| Gaick Pass | 439 | track | Gaick Lodge | Gaick Forest |
| Lairig Pass | 773 | path | Glenmore Lodge | Cairngorms |
| Lairigmòr | 271 | track | Lairigmòr | Nevis Range |
| Minigaig / Minigaig Pass | 833 | path | Gaick Lodge | Gaick Forest |
| **Pass of Glencoe** | 182 | **A road** | Altnafeadh | Glen Coe |
| **Pass of Inverfarigaig** | 69 | **road** | Inverfarigaig | Loch Ness |
| Ryvoan Pass | 369 | track | Glenmore Lodge | Cairngorms |
| Slochd Mhuic / Slochmuicht Pass | 360 | track | Slochd | Monadhliath Mountains |
| Stairsneach nan Gaidheal | 339 | track | Moy | Monadhliath Mountains |

| Latitude, Longitude | National Grid | Notes |
|---|---|---|
| 56.52586, -5.66377 | NM7476343105 | Col name attributed to hill; 'Boar Pass' |
| 56.76783, -4.56607 | NN4326266965 | Perth & Kinross boundary; 'White Pass' |
| 57.05700, -5.53713 | NG8560401776 | One of the sources of the River Barrisdale |
| 56.64692, -4.95780 | NN1874754480 | 'Yellow Pass' |
| 57.12435, -5.14155 | NH0992608094 | 'Pasture Pass' |
| 56.60592, -4.83336 | NN2618649596 | 'Waterfall Corrie Pass' |
| 56.60951, -4.86363 | NN2434550072 | 'Waterfall Corrie Pass' |
| 57.02152, -5.53844 | NM8532097833 | 'The Pass of Gleann Meadail' |
| 56.65121, -5.73188 | NM7133657273 | 'Pass of the Haunch' (or 'Wax') |
| 57.08592, -5.12714 | NH1060303779 | 'Hunting Pass' |
| 56.96851, -5.36499 | NM9555291404 | 'Calum's Pass' |
| 57.05539, -5.60455 | NG8150801811 | 'Strawberry Pass' |
| 57.01112, -5.56724 | NM8351296768 | 'Breast' or 'Hillside' Pass |
| 57.05070, -5.48618 | NG8865600916 | 'The Pass of Gleann Unndalain' |
| 56.58692, -4.77068 | NN2994647325 | Argyll & Bute boundary |
| 56.56194, -4.95729 | NN1837045023 | Aberdeenshire boundary; 'Tarsuinn' contains the notion of 'crossing' |
| 56.95410, -4.99434 | NN1800388752 | |
| 56.95555, -3.93235 | NN8257886584 | Not on OS 1st edn; *see* 'gàg, gàig' in Glossary; 'mini' may be from 'mion' ('small') |
| 57.11051, -3.62185 | NJ0187003341 | Moray boundary |
| 56.65015, -5.18579 | NN0479055465 | |
| 57.30422, -3.93082 | NH8377025387 | NCR 7; 'Great Gully' |
| 56.82212, -4.56214 | NN4372972997 | 'Window of the Grey Corrie' |
| 56.97773, -4.53105 | NN4626790242 | 'Rowan Corrie window' |
| 57.05249, -4.36929 | NN5638598208 | 'Lochan Corrie window' |
| 56.97582, -4.55243 | NN4496090078 | 'Window of the Smooth Corrie' |
| 56.96138, -4.58963 | NN4263888556 | 'The Window / Uinneag Coire Ard Dhoire' on OS 1st edn; 'Window of High Wood Corrie'; 'in the neighbourhood of Kingussie this object is called "The Window of Heaven"' (OS name book, 1876–8) |
| 57.31667, -4.83242 | NH2952328673 | Name attested before 1842 |
| 57.05106, -4.61411 | NN4153398592 | 'Corrierrik' on Roy's *Military Survey of Scotland* (1747–52); Gaelic name unknown (presumed to have been Màm Choire Ghearraig, which would have referred to the corrie 1,300 m to the east); this is the summit of the pass, 500 m from the unnamed col (*see* Corrieyairack weather station, above) |
| 56.95264, -4.03750 | NN7617586446 | From 'gàg' or 'gàig' ('cleft', 'notch') |
| 57.15918, -3.59028 | NJ0390808713 | So named on OS 100; 'Learg an Laoigh' on OS 1st edn; 'Pass of the Calf' or 'Fawn' |
| 56.73007, -5.07131 | NN1220564036 | West Highland Way; 'Great Pass' |
| 56.93839, -3.95399 | NN8120884712 | Perth & Kinross boundary; *see* 'gàg, gàig' in Glossary, and note to Mini-gaig, above |
| 56.66562, -4.98092 | NN1742056621 | |
| 57.27765, -4.44769 | NH5253023432 | *See* 'gàg, gàig' in Glossary; 'Inverfarigaig Pass' attested 1831 (sketch by J. M. W. Turner) |
| 57.17761, -3.65211 | NJ0021810853 | Not on OS 1st edn, where the place name 'Ryvoan' is 'Rebhoan' |
| 57.28686, -3.91360 | NH8475323425 | NCR 7; 'Sluch Muichk' on Roy's *Military Survey of Scotland* (1747–52); 'Scholm Pass' in Leigh's *New Pocket Road-Book of Scotland* (1836); 'Hog's Hollow' (but commonly translated 'Boar's Den') |
| 57.38211, -4.09801 | NH7396734354 | 'Threshold of the Gaels' or 'Highlanders', a pass used by cattle-rustlers and drovers |

| Name | Elevation (m) | Surface | Nearest place | Region |
|---|---|---|---|---|

# Lanarkshire · 23 cols 1 pass

| Name | Elevation (m) | Surface | Nearest place | Region |
|---|---|---|---|---|
| Bidhouse Hass | 403 | track | Watermeetings | Lowther Hills |
| Big Windgate Hass | 572 | | Leadhills | Lowther Hills |
| Buchswyre | 586 | | Wintercleugh | Lowther Hills |
| Clydes Nick | 489 | (track) | Glenbreck | Tweedsmuir Hills |
| *Comb Hill – Laght Hill* | 411 | path | Wanlockhead | Lowther Hills |
| Daer Hass | 502 | | Kinnelhead | Lowther Hills |
| Deil's Barn Door | 524 | track | Wandel | Culter Hills |
| Holm Nick | 480 | (track) | Tweedsmuir | Culter Hills |
| How Nick | 420 | | Kames | Lowther Hills |
| Howgate Mouth | 380 | track | Rigside | Tinto Hills |
| Hurlburn Swire | 373 | (track) | Crawford | Upper Clyde |
| Ironside Hass  *see Lyonside Hass* | | | | |
| Kirkgrain Hass | 555 | (track) | Durisdeer | Lowther Hills |
| Kyegill Slop | 502 | | Culter Allers Farm | Culter Hills |
| Little Gill Nick | 373 | | Cold Chapel | Upper Clyde |
| Little Windgate Hass | 498 | | Glenochar | Lowther Hills |
| **Lyonsidehass** | 343 | **B road** | Rigside | Tinto Hills |
| Manor Slack Hass | 449 | track | Leadhills | Lowther Hills |
| *Meikle Bin – Black Hill* | 451 | | Lennoxtown | Kilsyth Hills |
| Saddle Nick | 485 | | Culter Allers Farm | Culter Hills |
| **Thief Slack Hass** | 410 | **B road** | Leadhills | Lowther Hills |
| Well Head / Well Path | 406 | track | Durisdeer | Lowther Hills |
| Windgaitslop  *see Kyegill Slop* | | | | |
| Windgate | 427 | track | Lettershaws | Upper Clyde |
| Windgillhass  *see Kyegill Slop* | | | | |
| **Windygates** | 257 | **A road** | Newbigging | Pentland Hills |
| **Beattock Pass** | 320 | **B road** | Glenochar | Upper Clyde |

# Lothians and Edinburgh · 13 cols

| Name | Elevation (m) | Surface | Nearest place | Region |
|---|---|---|---|---|
| **Carcant Nick** | 400 | **B road** | Middleton | Moorfoot Hills |
| *Carnethy Hill – Scald Law* | 445 | path | Silverburn | Pentland Hills |

| Latitude, Longitude | National Grid | Notes |
|---|---|---|
| 55.40256, -3.60858 | NS9823413246 | Near the source of Bidhouse Burn, scene of a battle of Border clans in 1593, 'When the Biddes-burn ran three days blood' ('The Lads of Wamphrey', ballad published by Walter Scott in 1802); 'Biddes' reflects the pronunciation of 'Bidhouse' |
| 55.40278, -3.71841 | NS9128113437 | 'Over Windgait Slop' on T. Pont, 34 (c. 1583–96) and J. Blaeu, 'Glottiana Superior' (1654); 'Big Wingate Hass' on OS 25 |
| 55.34246, -3.67616 | NS9379406660 | Not on maps; 'Burn of the Buchswyre' in a cartulary of Newbattle Abbey (1327) |
| 55.43393, -3.53187 | NT0316816628 | Borders boundary; at the foot of Clyde Law, near the source of Clydes Burn |
| 55.36470, -3.71596 | NS9133109196 | Dumfries & Galloway boundary; Southern Upland Way |
| 55.29441, -3.62514 | NS9690501237 | Dumfries & Galloway boundary; 'Dairhass' on C. Ross, 'A Map of the Shire of Lanark' (1773); 'Dear Hass' on J. Thomson, 'Northern Part of Lanarkshire: Southern Part' (1822); Daer Water has one of its sources at the col |
| 55.52007, -3.58213 | NT0020726284 | The Deil is the Devil; 'barn' is derived from 'beàrn'; 'door' is applied to some cols (see Glossary) |
| 55.52382, -3.49424 | NT0576426578 | Borders boundary |
| 55.48453, -4.01402 | NS7282723035 | Ayrshire boundary; not on OS; J. Thomson, 'Berwick-Shire' (1821); a 'how' (Scots) was a prehistoric burial mound or tumulus |
| 55.59017, -3.71533 | NS9199034284 | 'Howgatemouth' on A. Armstrong, C. Ross, 'A Map of the Shire of Lanark' (1773) |
| 55.45651, -3.67420 | NS9422419348 | Probably Hurle Burle (or Brough) Swyre between Clydesdale and Nithsdale: 'Little knows the wife that sits by the fire, / How the wind blows in Hurle-burle-swyre': J. Kelly, A Complete Collection of Scottish Proverbs Explained and Made Intelligible to the English Reader (1818) |
| 55.32488, -3.71095 | NS9154004757 | Dumfries & Galloway boundary; the source of Kirk Grain |
| 55.52357, -3.55607 | NT0186126636 | This must be 'Windgaitslop' on J. Blaeu, 'Glottiana' (1654); Wingate House and Wingate Bank are nearby; 'Windgillhass' on C. Ross, 'A Map of the Shire of Lanark' (1773) |
| 55.50903, -3.66731 | NS9480025181 | From the name of the stream |
| 55.41382, -3.69739 | NS9264114633 | 'Nether Windgait Slop' on T. Pont, 34 (c. 1583–96) and J. Blaeu, 'Glottiana Superior' (1654); 'Windgate Hass' on W. Forrest, 'The County of Lanark from Actual Survey' (1816) and J. Thomson, 'Northern Part of Lanarkshire: Southern Part' (1822) |
| 55.58624, -3.74564 | NS9006933894 | Only on W. Forrest, 'The County of Lanark' (1816), and OS 1st edn; 'Ironside Hass' on J. Ainslie, 'Map of the Southern Part of Scotland' (1821) |
| 55.40882, -3.74985 | NS8930714159 | The source of Manorslack Gutter |
| 56.00665, -4.14269 | NS6649481373 | Stirling boundary |
| 55.56640, -3.49551 | NT0578631318 | Borders boundary; 'Saddle Nick' is also the name of the stream which rises at the col |
| 55.41640, -3.74625 | NS8955614997 | A defile with convenient (for thieves) rocky bluffs and blind corners on the road from Leadhills to Elvanfoot |
| 55.33569, -3.71030 | NS9161105959 | Dumfries & Galloway boundary; Roman road; not on OS; 'Wellpath' on C. Ross, 'A Map of the Shire of Lanark' (1773); 'Well Head' on W. Forrest, 'The County of Lanark' (1816); 'Well Path' on J. Ainslie, 'Map of the Southern Part of Scotland' (1821); 'path' is occasionally used for 'pass' in this region |
| 55.46404, -3.71035 | NS9195820241 | Deduced from Windgate Burn |
| 55.71756, -3.58710 | NT0040448271 | 'Windgate' on W. Forrest, 'The County of Lanark from Actual Survey' (1816); 'Windy Gate' on OS 1st edn |
| 55.42212, -3.59275 | NS9928615400 | NCR 74; the coordinates refer to the separate cycle path |
| 55.77648, -3.03844 | NT3495954172 | Borders boundary; NCR 1; last shown on OS 1st edn; see p. 64; Carcant is the hamlet on the old road south-east of the col |
| 55.84005, -3.28657 | NT1952761508 | |

| Name | Elevation (m) | Surface | Nearest place | Region |
|------|------|------|------|------|
| Cauldstane Slap | 435 | | Carlops | Pentland Hills |
| **Chapman's Slack** | 365 | **road** | Danskine | Lammermuir Hills |
| Clochmaid (or Cleuchmaid) Gate | 349 | path | Malleny Mills | Pentland Hills |
| Cross | 470 | path | Silverburn | Pentland Hills |
| The Hawse | 106 | path | Edinburgh | Arthur's Seat |
| Kings Road Nick | 547 | (track) | Dewar | Moorfoot Hills |
| Red Gate | 400 | track | Nine Mile Burn | Pentland Hills |
| Swirehouse / Swarehouse | 320 | path | Falahill | Moorfoot Hills |
| West Kip – Cap Law | 459 | track | Nine Mile Burn | Pentland Hills |
| White Craig Heads | 427 | path | Silverburn | Pentland Hills |
| Windy Door Nick | 413 | path | Swanston | Pentland Hills |

## Moray · 20 cols 1 pass

| Name | Elevation (m) | Surface | Nearest place | Region |
|------|------|------|------|------|
| An Cadha Mor  *see* Camore | | | | |
| Balloch | 431 | (track) | Ballochford | Glen Fiddich |
| Balloch More | 404 | (path) | Bridgehaugh | Glen Fiddich |
| *Bin of Cullen – Little Bin* | 210 | (track) | Weston | Bin of Cullen |
| Cadha Dubh | 585 | | Tervieside | Blackwater Forest |
| Camore / Ca Mor / An Cadha Mor | 694 | | Blairnamarrow | Ladder Hills |
| Corse of Garbet | 446 | (track) | Elrick | Strathbogie |
| *Creagan a' Chaise – Carn Tuairneir* | 644 | | Lynemore | Hills of Cromdale |
| Cross | 560 | path | Bracklach | Mount Meddin |
| The Eag | 587 | (path) | Dalestie | Cairngorms |
| **Glack Harnes** | 325 | **road** | Favillar | Dullan Water |
| Glack-en-ronack / Glackenronach | 388 | track | Sheandow | Dullan Water |
| **Glacks of Balloch** | 370 | **A road** | Ballochford | Glen Fiddich |
| The Ladder | 732 | path | Chapeltown | Ladder Hills |
| Làirig an Laoigh | 747 | path | Glenmore Lodge | Cairngorms |
| **Lecht Pass / The Lecht** | 645 | **A road** | Milltown | Ladder Hills |
| Red Sneck | 633 | | Badenyon | Ladder Hills |
| The Saddle | 807 | path | Glenmore Lodge | Cairngorms |
| Slochd Chaimbeil | 745 | | Chapeltown | Ladder Hills |
| Slogg of Buchromb | 315 | | Tullich | Strathspey |
| The Sneck | 970 | | Inchrory | Cairngorms |

| Latitude, Longitude | National Grid | Notes |
|---|---|---|
| 55.81297, -3.41189 | NT1161858647 | Borders boundary; (Cross Borders Drove Road); 'Coldstone Slap' on J. Ainslie, 'Map of the Southern Part of Scotland' (1821); 'Cauld Stane Slap' on OS 1st edn; a 'slap' or 'slop' is a gap or a breach |
| 55.85741, -2.60557 | NT6219062856 | The caption is closer to the col on OS 1st edn; the saddle is clearer on the map than on the road |
| 55.87158, -3.27498 | NT2031765003 | Not on maps; recorded in 1900; J. Baldwin and P. Drummond, *Pentland Place-Names* (2011); 'Middle Stone Pass' |
| 55.83453, -3.30252 | NT1851760912 | Deduced from 'Cross Sward' |
| 55.94278, -3.16610 | NT2726472807 | (NCR 1); not on OS 25 or 50; James Hogg, *The Private Memoirs and Confessions of a Justified Sinner* (1824): 'he approached the swire at the head of the dell – that little delightful verge from which in one moment the eastern limits and shores of Lothian arise on the view'; *see* pp. 68–70 |
| 55.71651, -3.11079 | NT3031447568 | Borders boundary; 'Kingroadnick' on A. Armstrong, 'Map of the Three Lothians' (1773); 'Kingroad Nick' on J. Thomson, 'Peebles-Shire' (1821); 'King's Road Nick' on OS 1st edn |
| 55.83782, -3.33005 | NT1679961311 | Only on modern OS |
| 55.79364, -2.99344 | NT3780956040 | Borders boundary; not on modern OS; 'Swirehouse' on Taylor and Skinner, 'The Road from Edinburgh to Carlisle' (1775); 'Swarehouse (ruins of)', just below the col, on J. Ainslie, 'Map of the Southern Part of Scotland' (1821); 'Sware House' on J. Thomson, 'Edinburgh Shire' (1821); 'Swareuse' on T. Sharp, C. Greenwood and W. Fowler, 'Map of the County of Edinburgh' (1828) |
| 55.82954, -3.31880 | NT1748660376 | |
| 55.84727, -3.26662 | NT2079162288 | 'Heads' from 'cuid' (cattle-fold) |
| 55.88381, -3.22897 | NT2322066312 | First shown on OS 1st edn (1855) |

| Latitude, Longitude | National Grid | Notes |
|---|---|---|
| 57.38700, -3.09141 | NJ3448833479 | Deduced from Little Balloch Hill |
| 57.40250, -3.13661 | NJ3179935249 | Name attributed to hill |
| 57.66458, -2.86572 | NJ4844964185 | |
| 57.33011, -3.22660 | NJ2624727285 | 'Black Pass' |
| 57.19639, -3.27785 | NJ2288212457 | Aberdeenshire boundary; 'The Great Pass' |
| 57.33277, -2.97282 | NJ4153027334 | Aberdeenshire boundary; 'Rough Place Crossing' |
| 57.29738, -3.49568 | NJ0996723966 | Inverness boundary |
| 57.27163, -2.99829 | NJ3989720550 | Aberdeenshire boundary; deduced from Burn of Cross and Hillock of Cross |
| 57.17495, -3.35545 | NJ1814610161 | Aberdeenshire boundary; 'The Notch' |
| 57.41145, -3.19522 | NJ2829536306 | 'Harnes' would be Scots 'harness' but the original name may be Gaelic |
| 57.43056, -3.17885 | NJ2931638416 | Misspelt 'Glach-en-ronack' on modern OS; 'Little Bushy Hollow' |
| 57.39336, -3.07600 | NJ3542534172 | 'Glacks of Balloch Pass' on OS 100 |
| 57.25766, -3.19382 | NJ2807919185 | Aberdeenshire boundary |
| 57.08488, -3.59629 | NJ0335100451 | 'Learg an Laoigh' on OS 1st edn; also known locally as 'An Làirig Shìos', 'The Eastern Pass', the western being the Làirig Ghrù (A. Diack, *Place-Names of the Cairngorms National Park*); 'Pass of the Calf' or 'Fawn' |
| 57.20069, -3.24744 | NJ2472812902 | Aberdeenshire boundary; 'The Lecht' on Roy's *Military Survey of Scotland* (1747–52); Leac a' Ghobhainn on OS 1st edn (caption shifted west on modern OS); 'Hill slope of the Smith' (from the legend of a blacksmith banished from Inverness-shire); 'leac' can also be a hill summit or a flat stone; the geographical summit is at 57.20032, -3.24887 (636 m) on the other side of the Lecht Ski Centre building; the original col name (perhaps 'lairig' or 'learg') has not survived; the second-highest road col in the British Isles |
| 57.28593, -3.14612 | NJ3100922282 | Deduced from Red Sneck Burn |
| 57.11051, -3.62185 | NJ0187003341 | Inverness boundary |
| 57.23534, -3.23250 | NJ2570116742 | Aberdeenshire boundary; deduced from 'Grains of Slochd Chaimbeil'; 'Campbell's Hollow' |
| 57.46653, -3.16773 | NJ3005242408 | *See* 'slogg' in Glossary ('bog', but probably confused with 'sloc(hd)') |
| 57.09160, -3.45678 | NJ1182101010 | Aberdeenshire boundary; not on OS 1st edn |

| Name | Elevation (m) | Surface | Nearest place | Region |
|---|---|---|---|---|
| **Pass of Grange** | 115 | **road** | Davoch of Grange | Strath Isla |

## Na h-Eileanan Siar (Outer Hebrides) · *66 cols*

| | | | | |
|---|---|---|---|---|
| Am Bealach | 113 | | Kinlochroag | Lewis |
| Am Bealach | 103 | | Airidh a' Bhruaich | Lewis |
| Am Beàrn | 218 | | New Valley | Lewis |
| **Am Blaid** | 239 | **road** | Hirta | St Kilda |
| **Am Feadan** | 56 | **road** | Liceasto | South Harris |
| **An Lairig** | 140 | **A road** | Greosabhagh | South Harris |
| Bealach a' Bheannain | 180 | | Eadar Dha Fhadhail | Lewis |
| Bealach a' Chaolais | 101 | | Lochboisdale | South Uist |
| Bealach a' Mhaim | 223 | | Caolas | Barra |
| Bealach a' Sgàil | 251 | | Bun Abhainn Eadarra | North Harris |
| Bealach a' Sgail | 90 | | Lochmaddy | North Uist |
| Bealach Airneabhail | 101 | | Arinambane | South Uist |
| Bealach an Easain | 106 | | Lochboisdale | South Uist |
| Bealach an Ionalaidh | 230 | | Na Buirgh | South Harris |
| Bealach an t-Isean | 605 | | Bun Abhainn Eadarra | North Harris |
| Bealach Bolum | 207 | | Arinambane | South Uist |
| Bealach Càrnach | 125 | | Bhatarsaigh | Sandray |
| Bealach Crosgard | 305 | | Arinambane | South Uist |
| Bealach Eadar Dhà Bheinn | 313 | | Giosla | Lewis |
| Bealach Eòrabhat | 97 | path | Àird Mhige | South Harris |
| Bealach Euna Clibh | 138 | | Eadar Dha Fhadhail | Lewis |
| Bealach Gaoithe | 531 | | Loch Sgioport | South Uist |
| Bealach Garbh | 400 | | Tarbert | North Harris |
| Bealach Garbh | 251 | | Liceasto | South Harris |
| Bealach Heabhal | 87 | | Arinambane | South Uist |
| Bealach Heileasdail | 298 | | Arinambane | South Uist |
| Bealach Maari | 98 | | Trumaisgearraidh | North Uist |
| Bealach Meavaig *see* Bealach Mhiabhaig | | | | |
| Bealach Mhiabhaig | 95 | track | Miabhaig | North Harris |
| Bealach na Beinne | 73 | | Baile Mhic Phail | North Uist |
| Bealach na Ciste | 204 | | Beacravik | South Harris |
| **Bealach na Ciste** | 191 | **A road** | Bun Abhainn Eadarra | North Harris |
| Bealach na Diollaid | 162 | | Lochboisdale | South Uist |
| Bealach na h-Imrich | 129 | | Kinlochroag | Lewis |
| Bealach na h-Uamha | 189 | path | Àird a' Mhulaidh | North Harris |
| Bealach nam Beanna Beag | 66 | | Arinambane | South Uist |
| Bealach Ràonasgail | 263 | track | Mealasta | Lewis |
| Bealach Sheaval *see* Bealach Heabhal | | | | |

| Latitude, Longitude | National Grid | Notes |
|---|---|---|
| 57.54295, -2.85782 | NJ4874950638 | Not on maps; 'Grange' is the name of the parish |
| 58.11445, -6.78641 | NB1821923948 | Deduced from Airigh a' Bhealaich; 'The Pass' |
| 58.08713, -6.69229 | NB2354420521 | Deduced from Allt a' Bhealaich (conflated with another stream on OS 25) |
| 58.25434, -6.51509 | NB3522538399 | Deduced from 'Beinn Bearnach' ('the cleft mountain'); from 'beàrn' ('gap' or 'breach') |
| 57.81133, -8.58570 | NF0914099243 | 'The Mouth'; the road over the col to the summit of Mullach Mòr, shown on OS maps as a track, is metalled and maintained all the way; see p. 90 |
| 57.82148, -6.85518 | NG1193291786 | Deduced from Loch an Fheadain; 'The Whistle' (see Glossary) |
| 57.84633, -6.82510 | NG1380994306 | NCR 780; deduced from Loch nan Learg; 'Loch na Learg' on OS 1st edn; 'The Pass' |
| 58.15187, -7.00408 | NB0572329039 | Not on OS 25 or 50; 'Little Hill Pass' |
| 57.18672, -7.27527 | NF8142123001 | 'Pass of the Strait' |
| 56.95663, -7.52500 | NL6427898634 | 'Gap of the Pass' |
| 57.97710, -6.85139 | NB1329608954 | 'Bealach an Scaill' on W. Bald, 'Map of Harris' (1805); 'Bealach a' Scal' on OS 1st edn; 'Pass of the Trough' |
| 57.57515, -7.14536 | NF9253465569 | 'Pass of the Trough' |
| 57.21301, -7.33190 | NF7823326189 | 'Bealach Arnaval' on OS 1st edn |
| 57.16179, -7.27693 | NF8110620239 | Misplaced to south-east on OS 25; 'Waterfall Pass' |
| 57.83052, -6.94442 | NG0660893060 | 'Washing Pass'? |
| 57.96531, -6.82341 | NB1485407524 | Not on OS; 'Bealach an Isian' on W. Bald, 'Map of Harris' (1805); 'isean' = 'chick', 'fledgling', 'cub' |
| 57.23847, -7.27651 | NF8179328758 | Also 'Bhòlum' or 'Boelam'; Bholuim is the bay to which the col leads |
| 56.89331, -7.51317 | NL6442791540 | 'Pass of the Rocky Place' or 'Quarry' |
| 57.24711, -7.28168 | NF8155629742 | Perhaps from 'crò' ('strait', 'narrow') and 'skarð' ('notch', 'cleft') |
| 58.10441, -6.93402 | NB0945323459 | Deduced from Allt Eadar Dhà Bheinn and by analogy with two other cols of this name; 'Pass Between Two Hills' |
| 57.84752, -6.88871 | NG1004894709 | 'Bealach Yeoravat' on OS 1st edn; name obscure |
| 58.15388, -7.01564 | NB0506029313 | Not on OS 25 or 50; misplaced on OS 10; name obscure ('eun' = 'bird'; 'clib' = 'excrescence' or 'stumble'); but possible corruption of 'cliof' ('cliff') |
| 57.29278, -7.26706 | NF8283034749 | 'Wind Pass' |
| 57.92696, -6.79022 | NB1651303122 | 'Rough Pass' |
| 57.83310, -6.90594 | NG0891193181 | 'Rough Pass' |
| 57.22013, -7.34852 | NF7729327059 | 'Bealach Sheaval' on OS 1st edn; 'Heabhal' is the hill to the west |
| 57.27024, -7.28531 | NF8153732329 | 'Bealach Hellisdale' on OS 1st edn; 'Heileasdail' is the glen to the south-east |
| 57.63739, -7.25481 | NF8653772988 | 'Maari' is the hill to the west |
| 57.99291, -6.90253 | NB1040410930 | 'Bealach Meavaig' on OS 1st edn; placed at the northern end of Loch Scourst, perhaps referring to the track leading to the col, which is otherwise unnamed; 'Miabhaig' ('Narrow Bay') is the name of the loch or inlet to the south |
| 57.67241, -7.19795 | NF9022576618 | 'Mountain Pass' |
| 57.83008, -6.92231 | NG0791692916 | 'Pass of the Chest' or 'Coffin' |
| 57.94514, -6.80062 | NB1604205187 | NCR 780; 'Pass of the Chest' or 'Coffin' |
| 57.17812, -7.28678 | NF8065222099 | 'Saddle Pass' |
| 58.11681, -6.76956 | NB1922824140 | Deduced from Airigh Bealach na h-Imrich; 'Pass of the Flitting' (transhumance) |
| 58.00196, -6.81497 | NB1564411563 | 'Cave Pass' |
| 57.24368, -7.33056 | NF7858129591 | 'Pass of the Little Mountains' |
| 58.10943, -7.03581 | NB0350524461 | Not on OS 25 or 50; 'Bealach Raonasgil' on OS 10; 'raon' = 'plain', 'field' or 'way'; 'asgall' = 'bosom', 'armpit' or 'sheltered place', 'covert' |

| Name | Elevation (m) | Surface | Nearest place | Region |
|---|---|---|---|---|
| Bealach Spin | 349 | | Arinambane | South Uist |
| Bealach Stoicleit | 68 | | Àird Mhige | South Harris |
| Bealach Tigh Iarras | 93 | | Arinambane | South Uist |
| Bealach Yeoravat  see Bealach Eòrabhat | | | | |
| Beinn na Teanga – Giolabhal Glas | 354 | | Ath Linne | North Harris |
| Beinn Tharsuinn – Trolamul | 285 | path | Carragrich | North Harris |
| Beul a' Bhealaich | 168 | | Brevig | Barra |
| Beul na Bearnadh | 319 | | Miabhaig | South Harris |
| Bràigh an Fhorsa | 239 | | Airidh a' Bhruaich | Lewis |
| Bràigh an Iàclachain | 328 | (path) | Àird a' Mhulaidh | North Harris |
| Bràigh' an Tàrain | 270 | | Islibhig | Lewis |
| Bràigh Bheagarais | 411 | | Abhainnsuidhe | North Harris |
| Bràigh Buidh' a' Choire | 302 | | Leverburgh | South Harris |
| Braighe Bruacleit | 293 | | Breanais | Lewis |
| Braighe Cràcabhal | 400 | | Breanais | Lewis |
| Bràighe Griomabhal | 320 | | Breanais | Lewis |
| Briseadh Mhuaithabhal | 323 | | Ceann | Loch Shiphoirt |
| Cadha Torasclett | 165 | | Urgha | North Harris |
| Caol Laibheal a Deas | 380 | | Breanais | Lewis |
| Feadan Dìrigil | 162 | | Abhainnsuidhe | North Harris |
| The Gap | 170 | | Hirta | St Kilda |
| Gill Luisga | 424 | | Ath Linne | North Harris |
| Glac nan Cruachan | 85 | | Taobh a' Deas | South Uist |
| Gleann na Carradh | 366 | | Breanais | Lewis |
| Gleann Stuladail | 354 | | Àird a' Mhulaidh | North Harris |
| Gleann Trolamaraig | 230 | | Rhenigidale | North Harris |
| Gleann Uachdrach | 88 | | Northton | South Harris |
| Globhar Glas | 303 | | Giosla | Lewis |
| Lag Glas | 560 | | Bun Abhainn Eadarra | North Harris |
| Lag Glas | 551 | | Abhainnsuidhe | North Harris |
| Mullach Mòr – Conachair | 324 | | Hirta | St Kilda |

## Orkney · 2 cols

| | | | | |
|---|---|---|---|---|
| Arwick | 48 | | Redland | Mainland |
| **Chair of Lyde** | 111 | **road** | Settiscarth | Mainland |

## Perth and Kinross · 88 cols  8 passes

| | | | | |
|---|---|---|---|---|
| Am Bealach | 768 | | Corrour Shooting Lodge | Ben Alder Range |
| Am Bealach | 758 | | Corrour Shooting Lodge | Ben Alder Range |
| Am Bealach | 680 | | Spittal of Glenshee | Gleann Beag |
| Am Bealach | 371 | | Aldclune | Tummel Valley |
| An Lairig | 848 | | Camusvrachan | Glen Lyon |
| An Lairig | 648 | track | Spittal of Glenshee | Glen Shee |
| An Suidhe  see Learg Mheuran / An Suidhe | | | | |
| **Bandirran Hill – Dunsinane Hill** | 188 | **road** | Collace | Sidlaw Hills |
| **Barry Hill / Am Beàrn** | 148 | **B road** | Shanzie | Hill of Alyth |

| Latitude, Longitude | National Grid | Notes |
|---|---|---|
| 57.26127, -7.31203 | NF7985131458 | 'Thorn Pass' |
| 57.85051, -6.87035 | NG1116194963 | 'Bealach Stocklett' on OS 1st edn; pass between two hills called Stoicleit |
| 57.25270, -7.32405 | NF7905230563 | 'Pass of the House of Earish' (the name of a fairy) |
| 57.92219, -6.80306 | NB1571202607 | |
| 57.90930, -6.72552 | NB2020100888 | 'Trollamul' on OS 1st edn; 'tarsuinn' contains the notion of 'crossing' |
| 56.97924, -7.45993 | NF6843000827 | 'Mouth of the Pass' |
| 57.87327, -6.84928 | NG1259197403 | From 'beàrn' ('gap', 'breach') |
| 58.01543, -6.64234 | NB2593612346 | 'Waterfall Pass'; 'bràigh' = 'neck' |
| 58.01311, -6.85214 | NB1354012960 | Second name obscure |
| 58.13301, -7.02115 | NB0456327017 | A 'tàran' is the ghost of an unbaptised child |
| 58.00338, -6.99691 | NB0491912502 | Second name obscure |
| 57.77412, -6.97885 | NG0409786944 | The caption is attached to the col on OS 1st edn; 'Yellow Pass of the Corrie' |
| 58.12226, -7.04516 | NB0306225928 | Not on OS 25 or 50; name obscure |
| 58.11088, -7.04864 | NB0276224678 | 'Braig Cracabhal' on modern OS; Cracabhal is the hill to the north |
| 58.08945, -7.06557 | NB0158722371 | Griomabhal is the hill to the south |
| 58.01094, -6.63318 | NB2644211809 | Muaitheabhal is the hill to the south-west |
| 57.91439, -6.76914 | NB1766101636 | 'Torascleit' is the hill to the south |
| 58.09710, -7.05300 | NB0239123166 | Deduced from Allt Gil Chaol Laibheal a Deas ('Laibhal' on OS 1st edn); 'caol' = 'narrow' |
| 58.02651, -6.96223 | NB0715514922 | Name attributed to hill; Feadan Dirascal on OS 1st edn; 'feadan' = 'whistle' (see Glossary) |
| 57.81790, -8.56086 | NF1068399828 | See p. 104 |
| 58.01447, -6.79214 | NB1709012857 | The Allt Gill Luisga ('gill' or 'geall' = 'notch') rises at the col |
| 57.11795, -7.29096 | NF7987915432 | Cruachan is the hill to the south-east |
| 58.12242, -7.02329 | NB0434925849 | The caption is closer to the col on OS 1st edn; 'Valley of the Rock' |
| 57.99959, -6.85764 | NB1310711480 | |
| 57.91977, -6.73442 | NB1975602089 | 'Gleann Trollamarig' on OS 10 |
| 57.80589, -7.04867 | NG0022290780 | 'Gleann Uacrach' on OS 1st edn; 'Upper Valley' |
| 58.10334, -6.94660 | NB0870423394 | The name of the 'grey gully' which leads to the col |
| 57.97575, -6.86916 | NB1223508879 | 'Grey Hollow' |
| 57.99882, -6.97930 | NB0592111918 | 'Grey Hollow' |
| 57.82036, -8.58002 | NA0957400212 | |
| 59.10765, -3.06713 | HY3898225019 | From Old Norse 'vik'?; B. Sandnes, From Starafjall to Starling Hill (2010); see 'wick' in Glossary |
| 59.04989, -3.12008 | HY3584218638 | NCR 1; 'Chair of Liod' on OS 1st edn; from 'leið' ('way', 'path') |
| 56.79682, -4.53093 | NN4552970111 | Inverness boundary; deduced from Meall a' Bhealaich; 'The Pass' |
| 56.78504, -4.54228 | NN4478768826 | Inverness boundary; deduced from Allt, Carn, Coire and Meall a' Bhealaich; 'The Pass' |
| 56.83365, -3.41332 | NO1386172244 | Deduced from Càrn a' Bhealaich on OS 1st edn (now Carn Aig Mhala); 'The Pass' |
| 56.73591, -3.80513 | NN8966961928 | Deduced from Creag a' Bhealaich; 'The Pass' |
| 56.63462, -4.21646 | NN6414651395 | Deduced from Allt and Coire na Lairige; 'The Pass' |
| 56.79786, -3.48464 | NO0942368353 | Cateran Trail; 'The Pass' |
| 56.46788, -3.28553 | NO2089531379 | |
| 56.63844, -3.20749 | NO2603650276 | Not on OS; A. Watson, Place Names (2013); 'The cleft' or 'gap'; deduced from earlier name of Barry Hill: Dun Bearnaigh ('Fort of the Gap') |

| Name | Elevation (m) | Surface | Nearest place | Region |
|---|---|---|---|---|
| Bealach a' Choire Chreagaich | 741 | | Forest Lodge | Cairngorms |
| Bealach a' Choire Odhair | 870 | path | Carie | Loch Tay |
| Bealach a' Choire Pharlain | 744 | | Moar | Glen Lyon |
| Bealach a' Choire Rùchain | 630 | | Dalchruin | Forest of Glenartney |
| Bealach a' Mhaim | 631 | | Pubil | Glen Lyon |
| Bealach a' Mhaim | 594 | path | Kinloch Rannoch | Loch Rannoch |
| Bealach an Aoghlain | 813 | | Achallader | Beinn Dorain Range |
| Bealach an Dubh Choirein | 723 | (path) | Ardvorlich | Ben Vorlich (Strathyre) |
| Bealach an Fhiodha | 847 | | Forest Lodge | Glen Tilt |
| Bealach an Neid | 779 | | Pubil | Glen Lyon |
| Bealach an t-Sagairt | 100 | | St Fillans | Strath Earn |
| Bealach an t-Seolaidh | 520 | | Auchinner | Ben Vorlich (Strathyre) |
| Bealach an t-Sithe | 517 | | Badyo | Tummel Valley |
| Bealach an Uillt Dhoimhne | 681 | | Duinish | Craiganour Forest |
| Bealach Baile na Cùile | 430 | | Dunira | Glen Lednock |
| Bealach Beag | 349 | track | Aldclune | Tummel Valley |
| Bealach Beag-laraich | 573 | | Auchinner | Ben Vorlich (Strathyre) |
| Bealach Car | 592 | | Auchinner | Ben Vorlich (Strathyre) |
| Bealach Coire na Circe | 772 | | Cashlie | Glen Lyon |
| Bealach Creag a' Bhannaich | 805 | | Balintyre | Glen Lyon |
| Bealach Dubh | 938 | path | Carie | Glen Lyon |
| Bealach Dubh Choire | 509 | | Invergeldie | Glen Lednock |
| Bealach Garbh | 667 | | Auchinner | Ben Vorlich (Strathyre) |
| Bealach Glas | 745 | | Lubreoch | Loch Lyon |
| Bealach Gliogarsnaich | 573 | path | Ardvorlich | Ben Vorlich (Strathyre) |
| Bealach Iosal | 585 | | Auchinner | Ben Vorlich (Strathyre) |
| Bealach Leathann | 675 | | Corrour Shooting Lodge | Rannoch Forest |
| Bealach na Gaoith | 703 | | Dalriech | Glen Almond |
| Bealach na Maoime Bige | 563 | | Kinloch Rannoch | Loch Rannoch |
| Bealach na Maoime *see* Bealach a' Mhaim | | | | |
| Bealach na Moine | 658 | | Auchinner | Forest of Glenartney |
| Bealach na Searmoin / Bealach na Searbhaig | 570 | track | Killiecrankie | Tummel Valley |
| Bealach nam Fiadh | 829 | | Corrour Shooting Lodge | Rannoch Forest |
| Bealach nan Losgann | 426 | | Rannoch Station | Rannoch Forest |
| Bealach nan Sgòr | 804 | | Corrour Shooting Lodge | Ben Alder Range |
| Bealach of Runavey | 438 | | Auchavan | Glen Beanie |
| Bealach Ruadh | 608 | | Ardtrostan | Strath Earn |
| *Buttergask Hill – King's Seat* | 232 | path | Collace | Sidlaw Hills |
| *Buttergask Hill – Lintrose Hill* | 257 | | Collace | Sidlaw Hills |
| **Cairnwell Pass** | 667 | **A road** | Spittal of Glenshee | Cairngorms |

| Latitude, Longitude | National Grid | Notes |
|---|---|---|
| 56.93036, -3.83904 | NN8817783624 | Inverness boundary; 'Pass of the Rocky Corrie' |
| 56.53844, -4.24457 | NN6207240748 | Deduced from Coire Odhar and by analogy with three other cols of the same name; 'Dun Corrie Pass' |
| 56.60949, -4.46639 | NN4871849122 | Deduced from Coire Pharlain; personal name |
| 56.34956, -4.12144 | NN6899319490 | 'Pass of the Corrie of the Small Round Hill' |
| 56.56329, -4.50892 | NN4592144077 | 'Pass of the Gap' |
| 56.72334, -4.19802 | NN6559461232 | 'Pass of the Gap'; 'Bealach na Maoime' on OS 1st edn ('Pass of the Torrent') |
| 56.55429, -4.68081 | NN3532243475 | Argyll & Bute boundary; 'Bealach an Aoghlan' on OS 1st edn; name obscure |
| 56.33719, -4.23139 | NN6215518328 | Stirling boundary; 'Dark Dell Pass' |
| 56.83409, -3.70893 | NN9582772704 | 'Timber Pass' |
| 56.56971, -4.48314 | NN4753144733 | 'Neid' = 'battle' or 'wound received in battle' (perhaps a visual metaphor since no battle is recorded) |
| 56.38266, -4.09242 | NN7089923118 | 'Pass of the Priest' |
| 56.32039, -4.14909 | NN6718416297 | Not on modern OS; 'Guiding Pass' |
| 56.74266, -3.67864 | NN9742562483 | 'Fairy Hill Pass' |
| 56.75569, -4.32811 | NN5775765095 | Not on OS 1st edn; 'Deep Stream Pass' |
| 56.40533, -4.05602 | NN7322125573 | 'Nook Farm Pass' |
| 56.72568, -3.84982 | NN8690560863 | 'Little Pass' |
| 56.31258, -4.19734 | NN6417215522 | Stirling boundary; 'Bealach Beag na Laraiche' on OS 1st edn; 'Little Pass of the Ruin' |
| 56.33382, -4.15796 | NN6668217808 | 'Bealach Cuir' on OS 1st edn; 'Pass of the Bend' |
| 56.52635, -4.43737 | NN5017039807 | Stirling boundary; deduced from Coire na Circe and by analogy with another col of the same name; 'Hen (i.e. grouse?) Corrie Pass' |
| 56.58166, -4.16272 | NN6725645397 | 'Fox Rock Pass' |
| 56.55547, -4.21977 | NN6365842594 | 'Black Pass' |
| 56.41144, -4.06397 | NN7275426268 | Misspelt 'Baelach' on modern OS 25 and 10; 'Black Corrie Pass' |
| 56.34053, -4.16589 | NN6621518570 | Not on modern OS; 'Rough Pass' |
| 56.57127, -4.57584 | NN4184345117 | Argyll & Bute boundary; not on OS 25 or 50; 'Grey Pass' |
| 56.34134, -4.20432 | NN6384318736 | 'Tinkling (or 'Glittering') Pass' (from the sound of the burns on the stones?) |
| 56.31436, -4.20498 | NN6370615735 | Stirling boundary; not on modern OS; 'Low Pass' |
| 56.75475, -4.54441 | NN4453265461 | 'Bealach Leathan' on OS 1st edn; 'Broad Pass'; this is probably the 'Bellach Triadan' shown on 'Straloch's mapp of Scotland' (c. 1636–52) and on J. Blaeu, 'Scotiae provinciae mediterraneae inter Taum flumen et Vararis aestuarium' (1654) |
| 56.46187, -3.98151 | NN7800031730 | Misplaced to south-west on modern OS; 'Pass of the Wind' |
| 56.71823, -4.20338 | NN6524760674 | Not on modern OS; 'Pass of the Little Torrent' |
| 56.34236, -4.12977 | NN6845418704 | 'Peat Pass' |
| 56.73853, -3.73493 | NN9397162109 | 'Pass of the Sermon'; second name on OS 1st edn, sometimes translated 'Pass of Bitterness'; however, a 'searbhag' is either a 'pickle', a 'bitter, sarcastic female' or, in this case, 'toil' or 'struggle' |
| 56.75477, -4.58541 | NN4202665557 | Inverness boundary; 'Deer Pass' |
| 56.70182, -4.54138 | NN4449859564 | 'Frog Pass' |
| 56.77645, -4.55072 | NN4423667889 | Inverness boundary; 'Pass of the Cliffs' |
| 56.79918, -3.36341 | NO1683068345 | Angus boundary; not on OS; 'Ruynavey bhellach' on Pont, 28 (c. 1583–96) |
| 56.36550, -4.14566 | NN6755221310 | 'Red Pass' |
| 56.48891, -3.24921 | NO2317533679 | |
| 56.49335, -3.24955 | NO2316334173 | |
| 56.88082, -3.41072 | NO1412877491 | Aberdeenshire boundary; from 'Càrn Bhalg' ('Hill of Bags'), perhaps referring to the rounded hills; the highest road col in the British Isles; see p. 73 |

| Name | Elevation (m) | Surface | Nearest place | Region |
|------|---------------|---------|---------------|--------|
| Cave Pass | 282 | track | Dalmarnock | Strath Tay |
| Chapel Pass | 371 | | Dunira | Glen Lednock |
| **Corse** | 139 | **road** | Kinfauns | Kinnoull Hill |
| Cùl Lochan | 614 | | Camghouran | Loch Tay |
| Deep Sneck of Creag Leacachd | 919 | | Auchavan | Cairngorms |
| *Dunsinane Hill – Black Hill* | 260 | | Collace | Sidlaw Hills |
| Farquharson's Sneck / Easter Glacanbuidhe | 668 | | Auchavan | Cairngorms |
| Fionn Lairig | 914 | (path) | Morenish | Loch Tay |
| The Gap | 365 | track | Kippen | Ochil Hills |
| Glack of Glengairney / The Glack | 608 | | Auchavan | Cairngorms |
| Glack of the Barnetts | 532 | | Alrick | Glen Shee |
| *Gleann Pollaidh* | 952 | | Balintyre | Glen Lyon |
| Glen Vale | 282 | (track) | Nether Urquhart | Lomond Hills |
| Green Balloch | 464 | | Balnaguard | Grandtully Hill |
| **Lairig an Lochain** | 553 | **road** | Milton Morenish | Glen Lyon |
| Lairig an t-Sluaigh  *see* Lairig Luaidhe | | | | |
| Lairig Bhreislich | 548 | | Moar | Glen Lyon |
| Lairig Calbh Ath  *see* Lairig Ghallabhaich | | | | |
| Lairig Ghallabhaich | 478 | (track) | Innerwick | Glen Lyon |
| Lairig Innein | 834 | | Cragganruar | Glen Lyon |
| Lairig Laoigh | 596 | | Camserney | Farragon Hill |
| Lairig Liaran | 592 | | Kenknock | Glen Lochay |
| Lairig Luaidhe | 638 | | Kenknock | Glen Lyon |
| Lairig Meachdaìnn | 698 | | Moar | Glen Lyon |
| Lairig Mhic Bhaidein | 725 | | Batavaime | Forest of Mamlorn |
| **Làirig Mìle Marcachd** | 530 | **road** | Garrow | Glen Quaich |
| Lairig nan Laogh | 356 | track | Scotston | Glen Cochill |
| Lairig Shalach | 671 | | Garrow | Glen Quaich |
| Learg a' Bhacain  *see* Lairig Meachdaìnn | | | | |
| Learg Macbheattie  *see* Lairig Mhic Bhaidein | | | | |
| Learg Mheuran / An Suidhe | 431 | | Achallader | Loch Lyon |
| **Learg nan Lunn** | 505 | **road** / track | Lubreoch | Glen Lyon |
| Learg Rioran  *see* Lairig Liaran | | | | |
| Little Glack an Buidhe | 735 | | Auchavan | Cairngorms |
| *Lòn na Cailliche* | 638 | | Achallader | Beinn Dorain Range |

| Latitude, Longitude | National Grid | Notes |
|---|---|---|
| 56.57905, -3.60701 | NO0137944169 | Earlier name in the hill traversed by the col, Craig a Barns / Craigie Barns; *see* 'beàrn' in Glossary |
| 56.39559, -4.02191 | NN7529424427 | Gaelic name unknown; English name perhaps related to Crapoch or Crappich Hill |
| 56.39734, -3.38760 | NO1444823651 | NCR 77; deduced from Corsiehill / Hill o' Corse ('Cross(ing) hill') |
| 56.63025, -4.38413 | NN5384651254 | *See* 'cùl' in Glossary |
| 56.85788, -3.38349 | NO1573574903 | Angus boundary; not on OS; A. Watson, *Place Names* (2013); Creag Leacach ('Flat Stone Rock') is the mountain to the south |
| 56.47120, -3.27581 | NO2150031738 | |
| 56.83657, -3.38214 | NO1577072530 | Angus boundary; first name in A. Watson, *Place Names* (2013); second name on OS; Farquharson was Laird of Invercauld |
| 56.51587, -4.31716 | NN5752438386 | Stirling boundary; deduced from Coire Fionn-Làirige; 'Fair (White) Pass' |
| 56.28092, -3.62986 | NN9918911023 | Deduced from Gap Moss |
| 56.82579, -3.35928 | NO1714171302 | Angus boundary; at the head of Gleann Carnach |
| 56.74029, -3.36162 | NO1680961789 | Angus boundary; 'Barnetts' is probably related to 'beàrn' (*see* Glossary) |
| 56.63417, -4.13908 | NN6888951194 | Glen unnamed on OS 1st edn |
| 56.23597, -3.29858 | NO1960305584 | Fife boundary; probably from 'Gleann a' bhealaich' ('valley of the Pass') |
| 56.60806, -3.73290 | NN9372847585 | 'Green Pass' |
| 56.54536, -4.29113 | NN5923541613 | 'Pass of the Lochan'; the fourth-highest road col in Scotland |
| 56.54145, -4.34586 | NN5585641292 | Stirling boundary; 'Pass of Confusion' or 'Delirium', perhaps 'Pass of the Rout' |
| 56.63263, -4.29601 | NN5926051334 | 'Lairig Calbh Ath' on OS 1st edn ('Pass of the Rushing Ford'?); also 'Làirig Chalabha' |
| 56.56912, -4.18676 | NN6573544048 | 'Anvil (or 'Rock') Pass' |
| 56.66441, -3.91689 | NN8261154157 | Deduced from Creag na Lairige and Lochan Lairig; 'Calf (or 'Fawn') Pass' |
| 56.51307, -4.47888 | NN4756538422 | Stirling boundary; 'Learg Rioran' on OS 1st edn; 'Rioran' is the name of the burn which rises at the col |
| 56.53342, -4.38326 | NN5352640478 | Stirling boundary; 'Pass of the Lead' (referring to lead mines); 'Lairig an t-Sluaigh' on OS 1st edn ('Pass of the People' or 'the (Fairy) Host') |
| 56.60522, -4.41202 | NN5203848529 | 'Learg a' Bhacain' on OS 1st edn; 'bacan' = 'stake'; 'meachdann' = 'small rod', 'twig' |
| 56.47508, -4.62795 | NN3823334536 | Stirling boundary; 'Learg Macbheattie' on OS 1st edn; W. Watson, *Celtic Place-names* (1926), has 'Làirig Mhic Bháididh' ('MacWattie's Pass') |
| 56.55438, -3.94110 | NN8078041953 | Rob Roy Way; not on maps; 'Làirig Mile Marcachd' ('Pass of the Mile of Riding'), 'because at the summit there is a long level stretch on which a rider could put his horse to speed'; 'Larkmonemerkyth' (i.e. Làirig Monadh Marcachd) in 1529: W. Watson, *Celtic Place-names* (1926); name on OS maps survives only in 'Lochan Lairig' and the hill name 'A' Chrois' ('The Cross') |
| 56.55076, -3.75965 | NN9192241250 | Not on modern OS; 'Calves Pass' |
| 56.51383, -3.92953 | NN8136537421 | 'Foul Pass' |
| 56.57001, -4.61865 | NN3920845076 | Argyll & Bute boundary; 'meuran' = 'thimble', 'little finger' or 'small branch'; 'suidhe' = 'seat' (*see* Glossary) |
| 56.51889, -4.52476 | NN4476639172 | Stirling boundary; 'Auld Larignaloan' on J. Stobie, 'The Counties of Perth and Clackmannan' (1783); 'Larig-na-loone' in N. Carlisle, 'Rannoch', *A Topographical Dictionary of Scotland*, II (1813); a 'lunn' is a staff or a stave, a 'loan' was a peg; gated road |
| 56.84257, -3.39279 | NO1513473211 | Angus boundary; not on OS but survives in 'Easter Glacanbuidhe' nearby; A. Watson, *Place Names* (2013); 'Little Yellow Hollow' |
| 56.53851, -4.67776 | NN3544141712 | Argyll & Bute boundary; 'Old Woman's (or 'Nun's') Marsh' |

| Name | Elevation (m) | Surface | Nearest place | Region |
|------|---------------|---------|---------------|--------|
| Lurgan Hill – Torlum | 280 | | Craggan | Strath Earn |
| Màm Bàn | 723 | | Corrour Shooting Lodge | Corrour Forest |
| Màm Lorn | 546 | | Auch | Beinn Dorain Range |
| Màm nan Carn | 910 | | Dalmunzie House | Cairngorms |
| Màm nan Carn | 771 | (path) | Dalmunzie House | Cairngorms |
| Meall Liath – Meall nan Eun | 784 | | Woodend | Glen Lyon |
| Meall Reamhar – Meall nan Caorach | 464 | track | Newton | Amulree Hills |
| The Seven Gates | 235 | track | Abernethy | Ochil Hills |
| The Slack | 277 | | Kippen | Ochil Hills |
| The Sloggan | 467 | | Aldville | Amulree Hills |
| Windy Gate | 312 | track | Cleish | Cleish Hills |
| **King's Pass** | 116 | **road** | Inver | Strath Tay |
| Minigaig / Minigaig Pass | 833 | path | Gaick Lodge | Gaick Forest |
| **Pass of Birnam** | 106 | **B road** | Stenton | Strath Tay |
| **Pass of Chesthill** | 158 | **road** | Balintyre | Glen Lyon |
| **Pass of Drumochter** | 462 | **A road** | Ben Alder Lodge | Drumochter Hills |
| **Pass of Keltney** | 150 | **B road** | Coshieville | Glen Lyon |
| **Pass of Killiecrankie** | 155 | **B road** | Killiecrankie | Tummel Valley |
| **Pass of Lyon** | 138 | **road** | Woodend | Glen Lyon |

## Ross and Cromarty · 156 cols 2 passes

| Name | Elevation (m) | Surface | Nearest place | Region |
|------|---------------|---------|---------------|--------|
| Am Bealach | 556 | path | Lochdrum | The Fannichs |
| Am Bealach | 518 | | Lochluichart | Loch Luichart |
| Am Bealach | 487 | | Wester Gruinards | Strathcarron |
| Am Bealach | 460 | | Porin | Strathconon |
| Am Bealach | 381 | | Badrallach | Loch Broom |
| Am Bealach | 301 | | Kirkton | Loch Alsh |
| Am Briseadh | 650 | | Fain | The Fannichs |
| **An Cumhann** | 589 | **road** | Russel | Applecross |
| An Torc (east) | 508 | | Boath | Loch Morie |
| An Torc (west) | 544 | | Kinloch | Loch Glass |
| Applecross Pass  see Bealach na Bà pass | | | | |
| Bealach a' Chùirn | 467 | (path) | Letterewe | Gairloch |
| Bealach a' Bholla | 865 | | Carnach | Pait Forest |
| Bealach a' Chaoruinn | 635 | | Craig | West Monar Forest |
| Bealach a' Chòinich | 591 | | Alltbeithe | Kintail |
| Bealach a' Choire | 199 | track | Allt-nan-Sùgh | Strath Ascaig |
| Bealach a' Choire Bhric | 869 | | Fain | The Fannichs |
| Bealach a' Choire Bhuidhe | 575 | | Arnisdale | Glenelg |
| Bealach a' Choire Ghairbh | 587 | (path) | Coulags | Glen Carron |
| Bealach a' Choire Réidhe | 799 | | Kinloch Hourn | Glen Shiel |
| Bealach a' Chòmhla | 449 | | Fasag | Torridon |

| Latitude, Longitude | National Grid | Notes |
|---|---|---|
| 56.34590, -3.92027 | NN8141218717 | |
| 56.76783, -4.56607 | NN4326266965 | Inverness boundary; 'White Pass' |
| 56.50193, -4.67252 | NN3560537629 | Argyll & Bute boundary; 'Lorn' is the ancient name of the district to which the col is a gateway |
| 56.88757, -3.56493 | NO0474878446 | Aberdeenshire boundary; name attributed to mountain; 'Pass of the Cairns' |
| 56.87609, -3.57955 | NO0382877189 | Name attributed to mountain; 'Cairns Pass' |
| 56.63287, -4.11723 | NN7022551008 | |
| 56.48224, -3.74603 | NN9256633603 | |
| 56.32483, -3.28080 | NO2088915453 | Fife boundary; CR; a meeting of seven ways, of which six remain |
| 56.29212, -3.62049 | NN9979812255 | Below Rossie Law hill fort |
| 56.50568, -3.70536 | NN9513536149 | A 'sloggan' is the neck of a bottle, a gullet or a narrow pass |
| 56.15231, -3.49483 | NT0723796520 | Below Dumglow hill fort |
| 56.56915, -3.61288 | NO0099243075 | NCR 77; earlier name in the hill skirted by the pass, Craig a Barns / Craigie Barns; see 'beàrn' in Glossary |
| 56.93839, -3.95399 | NN8120884712 | Inverness boundary; see 'gàg, gàig' in Glossary; 'mini' is perhaps from 'mion' ('small') |
| 56.53551, -3.54123 | NO0531139230 | NCR 77; misplaced on OS 50; name attested 1784 |
| 56.59961, -4.12209 | NN6962447035 | Continuation of Pass of Lyon |
| 56.85125, -4.24415 | NN6323875557 | NCR 7; summit sign; 450 m from Inverness boundary; from 'Druim Uachdair' ('Ridge of the High Ground') |
| 56.62217, -4.00145 | NN7729249604 | CR; name first attested on OS 1st edn (1867) |
| 56.73765, -3.76992 | NN9182862066 | NCR 7; 'Killicranky Pass' on A. Rutherford, 'An Exact Plan of His Majesty's Great Roads' (1745); 'Pass of Killiecrankie' on Roy's Military Survey of Scotland (1747–52); 'Killchrankie Pass' on J. Stobie, 'The Counties of Perth and Clackmannan' (1783); 'Killiecrankie Pass' on J. Thomson, 'Perthshire with Clackmannan' (1827) |
| 56.60301, -4.07762 | NN7255447611 | Continuation of Pass of Chesthill; 'sometimes called Cumhang Dhubhghlais, "the defile of the black stream"': W. Watson, Celtic Place-names (1926) |
| 57.68804, -5.06564 | NH1735070601 | Deduced from Allt Leac a' Bhealaich; 'The Pass' |
| 57.59720, -4.76810 | NH3466859729 | Deduced from Loch a' Bhealaich (one on either side of the col); 'The Pass' |
| 57.85726, -4.50623 | NH5138588062 | Deduced from Allt, Carn and Coir' a' Bhealaich; 'The Pass' |
| 57.57117, -4.79536 | NH3292056899 | Deduced from Loch a' Bhealaich; 'The Pass' |
| 57.89209, -5.26971 | NH0628893871 | Deduced from Loch a' Bhealaich; 'The Pass' |
| 57.30539, -5.60019 | NG8324229604 | Deduced from Loch a' Bhealaich; 'The Pass' |
| 57.72888, -5.25273 | NH0642175665 | 'The Breach' |
| 57.41207, -5.70176 | NG7777441798 | Deduced from Allt a' Chumhaing, which rises at the col; 'The Strait' or 'Narrow'; see Bealach na Bà (pass), p. 206; the third-highest road col in Scotland |
| 57.72391, -4.44381 | NH5455273085 | Deduced from Meall an Tuirc ('torc' is 'wild boar' but can also be 'notch' or 'cleft') |
| 57.72584, -4.46626 | NH5322373348 | See previous entry |
| 57.71381, -5.40897 | NG9703874446 | 'Cairn Pass' |
| 57.35275, -5.14249 | NH1104333507 | 'Pass of the Bowl' (probably referring to the form of the cirque) |
| 57.45158, -5.23146 | NH0621644753 | Not on modern OS; 'Rowan Pass' |
| 57.18368, -5.20916 | NH0617214957 | Inverness boundary; 'Bog Pass' |
| 57.32707, -5.51292 | NG8862131741 | 'Corrie Pass' |
| 57.69190, -5.10281 | NH1515571131 | 'Speckled Corrie Pass' |
| 57.15474, -5.47344 | NG9001812450 | 'Yellow Corrie Pass' |
| 57.48192, -5.45239 | NG9313948780 | First shown on OS 2nd edn; 'Rough Corrie Pass' |
| 57.14268, -5.30576 | NH0009010604 | Inverness boundary; 'Smooth Corrie Pass' |
| 57.59775, -5.54732 | NG8812561958 | 'Pass of the Comrade / Companion in Arms' |

| Name | Elevation (m) | Surface | Nearest place | Region |
|---|---|---|---|---|
| Bealach a' Chuirn Ghuirme | 746 | path | Wyvis Lodge | Wyvis Forest |
| Bealach a' Ghlas-chnoic | 403 | path | New Kelso | Loch Carron |
| Bealach a' Ghleannain | 220 | path | Camas-luinie | Glen Elchaig |
| Bealach Alltan Ruairidh | 392 | (path) | Attadale | Attadale Forest |
| Bealach an Fheadain | 136 | track | Plockton | Loch Carron |
| **Bealach an Fhuarain** | 141 | **road** | Auchtercairn | Gairloch |
| Bealach an Làpain | 725 | | Morvich | Kintail |
| Bealach an Lochain Uaine | 850 | | Glenbeg | Inverlael Forest |
| Bealach an Rathaid | 370 | path | Culligran | Corriehallie Forest |
| Bealach an Ruadh-Stac | 563 | | Coulags | Glen Carron |
| Bealach an Sgàirne | 511 | path | Dorusduain | Kintail |
| Bealach an Sgoltaidh | 550 | | Craig | West Monar Forest |
| Bealach an Toiteil | 699 | | Kinloch Hourn | Glen Shiel |
| Bealach an t-Sealgaire | 818 | | Morvich | Kintail |
| Bealach an Tuill Chéilte *see* Bealach Toll Sgàile | | | | |
| Bealach an Tuill Ghaineamhaich | 734 | | Liatrie | Glencannich Forest |
| Bealach Aoidhdailean | 474 | path | Arnisdale | Glenelg |
| Bealach Arnasdail | 604 | | Arnisdale | Glenelg |
| Bealach Bàn | 775 | | Lochdrum | The Fannichs |
| Bealach Bàn | 513 | | Annat | Coulin Forest |
| Bealach Beag | 832 | | Carnach | Carn Eige Range |
| Bealach Beag | 438 | (track) | Garbat | Strathgarve Forest |
| Bealach Beinn an Eoin | 441 | | Achvraie | Coigach |
| Bealach Bhearnais | 596 | | Craig | West Monar Forest |
| Bealach Bhrathan | 206 | track | Lochussie | Strath Peffer |
| Bealach Bog | 825 | | Carnach | Killilan Forest |
| Bealach Buidhe | 825 | | Morvich | Kintail |
| Bealach Buidhe | 94 | (track) | North Erradale | Gairloch |
| Bealach Caol na Droma Bige | 870 | | Kinloch Hourn | Cluanie Forest |
| Bealach Caol na Droma Mòire | 821 | | Kinloch Hourn | Cluanie Forest |
| Bealach Casan | 587 | | Corran | Glenelg |
| Bealach Choire a' Chait | 727 | (path) | Lundie | Ceannacroc Forest |
| Bealach Clais a' Chùirn | 264 | (track) | Wester Lealty | Cromarty Firth |
| Bealach Coire Choinnich | 866 | | Craig | West Monar Forest |
| Bealach Coire Ghàidheil | 717 | path | Alltbeithe | Carn Eige Range |
| Bealach Coire Mhàlagain | 699 | | Kinloch Hourn | Glen Shiel |
| Bealach Coire nan Cadhan | 657 | | Coulags | Glen Carron |
| Bealach Con | 447 | (path) | Dorusduain | Inverinate Forest |
| Bealach Cùlaidh | 342 | | Wyvis Lodge | Wyvis Forest |
| Bealach Cùmhlainn *see* Coulin Pass | | | | |
| Bealach Dearg | 889 | | Alltbeithe | Kintail |
| Bealach Dearg | 863 | | Inchvuilt | Loch Monar |
| Bealach Dhruim nam Bò | 586 | | Arnisdale | Glenelg |
| Bealach Dubh-liath | 975 | | Lundie | Ceannacroc Forest |
| Bealach Duibh Leac | 730 | path | Kinloch Hourn | Glen Shiel |
| Bealach Fraoch Choire | 729 | (path) | Kinloch Hourn | Glen Shiel |
| Bealach Gaoithe | 780 | | Knockban | Gleann Mèinich |
| Bealach Gorm | 472 | | Fain | The Fannichs |

| Latitude, Longitude | National Grid | Notes |
|---|---|---|
| 57.69705, -4.59166 | NH4563570424 | 'Bealach na Carra Guirme' on OS 1st edn; 'Blue Rock Pass' |
| 57.44578, -5.50067 | NG9003944908 | 'Pass of the Grey Hill' |
| 57.29634, -5.42593 | NG9368328056 | 'Pass of the Little Glen' |
| 57.39435, -5.35504 | NG9849038746 | An 'alltan' is a little stream; ' Ruairidh' is the name Rory |
| 57.33165, -5.62494 | NG8190932605 | 'Whistle Pass'; *see* 'feadan' in Glossary |
| 57.74031, -5.64793 | NG8297078134 | Deduced from Meall an Fhuarain (not on modern OS); 'Fountain Pass' |
| 57.17809, -5.29353 | NH0102014507 | Name obscure, perhaps from a personal name |
| 57.79433, -4.92473 | NH2625882056 | 'Pass of the Green Lochan' |
| 57.49734, -4.70251 | NH3814448459 | 'Pass of the Road' (an ancient route rather than a road) |
| 57.47787, -5.45606 | NG9289648341 | First shown on OS 2nd edn; 'Red Cliff Pass' |
| 57.24038, -5.29151 | NH0147721431 | 'Howling Pass'; known as 'The Gates of Affric' |
| 57.42927, -5.25558 | NH0465142340 | 'Pass of the Cleft' |
| 57.14554, -5.38846 | NG9510411167 | Inverness boundary; 'Pass of the Place of Smoke' |
| 57.22965, -5.32657 | NG9930420340 | 'Hunter's Pass' |
| 57.35149, -5.01543 | NH1867833021 | Inverness boundary; 'Sandy (or 'Gravelly') Holes Pass' |
| 57.15036, -5.50056 | NG8835412046 | From the name of the neighbouring mountain and glen |
| 57.14962, -5.55554 | NG8502512136 | The col above Arnisdale |
| 57.67273, -4.95708 | NH2374568610 | 'White Pass' |
| 57.51129, -5.43780 | NG9417952003 | Slightly misplaced on OS 25; 'White Pass' |
| 57.29919, -5.12743 | NH1167527507 | 'Little Pass' |
| 57.63402, -4.64235 | NH4234163527 | 'Little Pass' |
| 58.01370, -5.20989 | NC1047607231 | 'Bealach Beinn Eun' on OS 1st edn; 'Pass of Bird Hill' |
| 57.45299, -5.23504 | NH0600944920 | 'Pass of the Gap' |
| 57.58406, -4.51906 | NH4949357686 | 'Pass of the Brow' |
| 57.33426, -5.29488 | NH0178031884 | 'Marsh Pass' |
| 57.20271, -5.35269 | NG9758117420 | 'Yellow Pass' |
| 57.75419, -5.78868 | NG7468580139 | 'Yellow Pass' |
| 57.13025, -5.25834 | NH0289209083 | Inverness boundary; 'Pass of the Defile of the Big Ridge' |
| 57.13197, -5.26847 | NH0228809303 | Inverness boundary; 'Pass of the Defile of the Little Ridge' |
| 57.15321, -5.45537 | NG9110212224 | 'Bealach Cas' on OS 1st edn; 'Pass of the Path' |
| 57.17977, -5.12911 | NH1096314225 | Inverness boundary; 'Bealach Coir' a' Chait' on OS 1st edn; 'Cat Corrie Pass' |
| 57.72334, -4.35937 | NH5957872844 | 'Cairn Hollow Pass' |
| 57.45094, -5.19901 | NH0815944590 | 'Meeting Corrie Pass' |
| 57.26555, -5.15486 | NH0984923840 | Inverness boundary; 'Bealaich [sic] Coir'a' Ghaidheil' on OS 1st edn; 'Pass of the Gaels' (or 'Highlanders'') Corrie' |
| 57.15725, -5.40075 | NG9442612507 | Inverness boundary; 'Pass of the Corrie of the Little Sack'; sometimes 'Pass of Corryvarligan' in 19th c. |
| 57.46788, -5.47701 | NG9158447294 | 'Gap of the Corrie of the Passes' |
| 57.27641, -5.34437 | NG9848625594 | Only on modern OS; 'Hound Pass' |
| 57.71662, -4.59880 | NH4529372618 | 'Bealach nan Cuilean' on OS 1st edn ('cuilean' = 'whelp', 'cub'); 'cùlaidh' = 'costume', 'uniform', 'armour' |
| 57.17929, -5.27381 | NH0221814583 | Deduced from Sgurr a' Bhealaich Dheirg; 'Red Pass' |
| 57.44340, -4.95891 | NH2252343098 | Inverness boundary; 'Red Pass' |
| 57.15742, -5.52908 | NG8667012921 | 'Cattle Ridge Pass' |
| 57.17377, -5.10580 | NH1234113493 | Inverness boundary; not on modern OS; 'Dark-Grey Pass'; the second-highest col in Scotland and third-highest in the British Isles |
| 57.14691, -5.36049 | NG9680311236 | Inverness boundary; 'Black Stone Pass' |
| 57.14448, -5.32331 | NG9903810855 | Inverness boundary; 'Heather Corrie Pass' |
| 57.56619, -4.93469 | NH2456656697 | 'Wind Pass' |
| 57.69179, -5.20190 | NH0925171394 | 'Blue Pass' |

| Name | Elevation (m) | Surface | Nearest place | Region |
|------|---------------|---------|---------------|--------|
| Bealach Loch a' Mhadaidh | 226 | | Peterburn | Gairloch |
| Bealach Loch Gaineamhaich | 289 | | Russel | Applecross |
| Bealach Lùib nam Feadag | 472 | | Carnach | Killilan Forest |
| Bealach Mhèinnidh | 490 | path | Letterewe | Gairloch |
| Bealach Mhic Bheathain | 755 | | Coille-righ | Killilan Forest |
| Bealach Mòr | 677 | | Balnacra | Glen Carron |
| Bealach Mòr | 514 | | Glensgaich | Strathgarve Forest |
| Bealach Mòr | 258 | track | Plockton | Loch Carron |
| Bealach Mòr | 50 | | Inverkirkaig | Assynt |
| Bealach na Caime | 899 | | Fain | The Fannichs |
| Bealach na Càrnach | 860 | | Morvich | Kintail |
| Bealach na Carra Guirme  *see* Bealach a' Chuirn Ghuirme | | | | |
| Bealach na Ceud Eilde | 587 | | Carnach | Pait Forest |
| Bealach na Cloiche Duibhe | 795 | | Inchvuilt | East Benula Forest |
| Bealach na Con Dhu | 885 | | Carnach | West Benula Forest |
| Bealach na Craoibhe | 850 | | Shiel Bridge | Kintail |
| Bealach na Craoibhe | 496 | (path) | Shiel Bridge | Kintail |
| Bealach na Croise | 424 | | Taagan | The Fannichs |
| Bealach na Dheiragain | 920 | | Carnach | West Benula Forest |
| Bealach na Eas Ban | 623 | | Dorusduain | Inverinate Forest |
| **Bealach na Gaoithe** | 250 | **road** | Alligin Shuas | Torridon |
| Bealach na h-Airidh | 538 | path | Taagan | Torridon |
| Bealach na h-Eige | 844 | | Carnach | Carn Eige Range |
| Bealach na h-Imrich | 506 | | Lochdrum | Braemore Forest |
| Bealach na h-Imrich | 440 | | Leckie | The Fannichs |
| Bealach na h-Oidhche | 501 | | Arnisdale | Glenelg |
| Bealach na Lice | 520 | | Annat | Coulin Forest |
| Bealach na Lice | 420 | path | Annat | Glen Torridon |
| Bealach na Sealga | 212 | | Talladale | Gairloch |
| Bealach na Siunnachair | 710 | | Glenmeanie | Gleann Mèinich |
| Bealach na Sròine | 508 | (path) | Dorusduain | Inverinate Forest |
| Bealach nam Botàichean | 769 | | Ardchuilk | Glen Strathfarrar |
| Bealach nam Bùthan | 554 | (path) | Fasagrianach | Braemore Forest |
| Bealach nam Fàradh  *see* Bealach nan Arr | | | | |
| Bealach nan Arr | 599 | | Russel | Applecross |
| Bealach nan Cuilean  *see* Bealach Cùlaidh | | | | |
| Bealach nan Daoine | 839 | | Alltbeithe | West Benula Forest |
| Bealach nan Spàinteach | 925 | | Morvich | Kintail |
| Bealach Odhar | 731 | | Leckie | The Fannichs |
| Bealach Phuill Domhain | 70 | | Toscaig | Applecross |
| Bealach Ràrsaidh | 365 | (path) | Arnisdale | Glenelg |
| **Bealach Ràtagain / Mam Ratagan** | 339 | **road** | Ratagan | Kintail |
| Bealach Sgùrr an Lochain | 890 | | Kinloch Hourn | Glen Shiel |
| Bealach Sneachda | 865 | | Ardchuilk | Glen Strathfarrar |
| Bealach Toll an Lochain | 827 | | Inchvuilt | East Benula Forest |

| Latitude, Longitude | National Grid | Notes |
|---|---|---|
| 57.78633, -5.75343 | NG7697983597 | 'Wolf Loch Pass' |
| 57.45643, -5.63826 | NG8185146527 | 'Sandy (or 'Gravelly') Loch Pass' |
| 57.35652, -5.26668 | NH0359534279 | 'Pass of the Plover's Glen'? ('lùib' = 'corner' or 'small glen'); 'feadag' ('plover') may also be 'flute' or 'whistle' |
| 57.70873, -5.42107 | NG9628973917 | 'Mining Pass' |
| 57.32348, -5.34971 | NG9842230846 | 'MacBean's Pass' |
| 57.49126, -5.39485 | NG9663849646 | 'Great Pass' |
| 57.64735, -4.60171 | NH4482364916 | 'Great Pass' |
| 57.32784, -5.61165 | NG8268532138 | 'Great Pass' |
| 58.11740, -5.28845 | NC0640018992 | 'Great Pass' |
| 57.69049, -5.13527 | NH1321471063 | Misspelt 'Caine' on OS 25; 'Pass of the Bend' |
| 57.19251, -5.34847 | NG9778016273 | 'Pass of the Rocky Place' or 'Quarry' |
| 57.36252, -5.20262 | NH0747934763 | 'Ceud' = 'first' or 'hundred'; 'eilde' = '(roe) deer' |
| 57.36598, -5.04239 | NH1712934705 | Inverness boundary; 'Black Stone Pass' |
| 57.27641, -5.19018 | NH0777725148 | 'Black Dog Pass'? |
| 57.18538, -5.34841 | NG9774415480 | 'Pass of the Tree' |
| 57.17161, -5.38971 | NG9517314071 | 'Pass of the Tree' |
| 57.69169, -5.24305 | NH0679971499 | 'Pass of the Cross' |
| 57.28607, -5.18563 | NH0810226210 | 'Pass of the Kestrels' |
| 57.26438, -5.37297 | NG9669624341 | Not on OS 1st or 2nd edn; 'Pass of the White Waterfall' |
| 57.56996, -5.63960 | NG8244859160 | Misplaced to south-east on OS 25; 'Pass of the Wind' |
| 57.61889, -5.37159 | NG9873863775 | Not on modern OS; 'Shieling Pass' |
| 57.30391, -5.09001 | NH1395227929 | 'Pass of the Nick' (see 'eag' in Glossary) |
| 57.75448, -4.94929 | NH2460677686 | 'Pass of the Flitting' (transhumance) |
| 57.68398, -5.17474 | NH1082870449 | 'Pass of the Flitting' (transhumance) |
| 57.16694, -5.58321 | NG8345414150 | 'Pass of the Night' (name variously explained: night fishing or an overnight stop on the way to summer pasture) |
| 57.51186, -5.44273 | NG9388752082 | Not on modern OS; 'Pass of the Flat Stones' |
| 57.50124, -5.45227 | NG9325550929 | First shown on OS 2nd edn; 'Pass of the Flat Stones' |
| 57.66914, -5.51902 | NG9022869812 | Contour heights to north-east are incorrect on OS 25; 'Hunting Pass' |
| 57.56408, -4.92904 | NH2489456448 | 'Fox Hunter's Pass' |
| 57.26794, -5.31018 | NH0050024551 | 'Promontory Pass' |
| 57.44601, -4.86626 | NH2809343150 | Inverness boundary; 'Bealach nam Bogan' on OS 1st edn; 'Pass of the Bog' |
| 57.77020, -4.98831 | NH2236279537 | 'Pass of the Bothies' |
| 57.43799, -5.68858 | NG7872244639 | 'Bealach nam Fàradh' on OS 1st edn ('Pass of the Ladders', referring to artificial steps); also 'Bealach nan Aradh'; 'Bealach nan Àrr' on 2nd edn; 'Stags' Pass' |
| 57.26141, -5.20731 | NH0666623528 | 'Pass of the Men' |
| 57.18085, -5.33101 | NG9877114924 | 'Spaniards' Pass'; crossed by Spanish soldiers arriving at (or, more likely, fleeing from) the battle in Glen Shiel (1719) between the Jacobites and the British army |
| 57.70039, -5.28017 | NH0463472574 | 'Dun(-Coloured) Pass' |
| 57.38310, -5.81013 | NG7108938936 | 'Pass of the Deep Mire' |
| 57.15304, -5.61269 | NG8159012698 | Eilean Ràrsaidh is the island on Loch Hourn below the col |
| 57.22045, -5.47645 | NG9020919768 | Inverness boundary; 'Pass of the Small Fortress' (Ratagan is the village at the eastern foot of the col); 'We rode on well, till we came to the high mountain called the Rattakin': James Boswell, *The Journal of a Tour to the Hebrides* (1785); see p. 75 |
| 57.13784, -5.29084 | NH0096610021 | Inverness boundary; 'Lochan Hill Pass' |
| 57.44637, -4.89179 | NH2656343255 | Inverness boundary; 'Snow Pass' |
| 57.36300, -5.07333 | NH1525434458 | Inverness boundary; 'Lochan Hollow Pass' |

| Name | Elevation (m) | Surface | Nearest place | Region |
|---|---|---|---|---|
| Bealach Toll an Lochain | 815 | | Fain | The Fannichs |
| Bealach Toll Easa | 872 | path | Liatrie | Carn Eige Range |
| Bealach Toll Easach | 669 | | Alltbeithe | Kintail |
| Bealach Toll Sgàile | 911 | | Inchvuilt | Glen Strathfarrar |
| Bealach Tom a' Chòinnich | 869 | path | Wyvis Lodge | Wyvis Forest |
| *Beinn a' Chàisgein Beag – Frith-mheallan* | 509 | path | Little Gruinard | Fisherfield Forest |
| Breabag | 819 | | Lochdrum | The Fannichs |
| Briste na Beinne | 675 | | Attadale | Attadale Forest |
| Cab Coire nan Clach | 824 | | Furnace | The Fannichs |
| Cadh' a' Bhàillidh | 587 | | Lochdrum | The Fannichs |
| **Cadh' a' Bhuic** | 42 | **B road** | Badachro | Gairloch |
| Cadh' a' Mheirlich | 282 | | Croick | Glencalvie Forest |
| Cadh' a' Mhoraire | 469 | | Strathcanaird | Coigach |
| Cadh' an Amadain | 840 | | Fasagrianach | Inverlael Forest |
| Cadh' Iosal | 262 | | Dounie | Dornoch Firth |
| **Cadha Beag** | 105 | **A road** | Little Gruinard | Gairloch |
| Cadha Dearg *see* Gate of Ca'-derg | | | | |
| Cadha Dearg Mòr | 809 | | Lochdrum | The Fannichs |
| Cadha Gobhlach | 834 | | Dundonnell | Dundonnell Forest |
| Cadha Mhic Iall Donaich | 797 | | Fasagrianach | Inverlael Forest |
| Cadha Mòr | 335 | track | Redburn | Cromarty Firth |
| **Cadha Mòr** | 216 | **B road** | Easter Fearn | Dornoch Firth |
| Cadha Mòr | 123 | | Little Gruinard | Gairloch |
| Cadha na Bò | 206 | track | Drumrunie | Coigach |
| Cadha na Guite | 814 | | Lochdrum | The Fannichs |
| Cadha Raineach | 769 | | Inchvuilt | Loch Monar |
| Cadha Ruadh | 700 | | Carnach | Killilan Forest |
| *Carn Dubh – Carn na Gobhlaig-beithe* | 437 | track | The Craigs | Glen Calvie |
| **An Ruadh-Bruach** | 131 | **A road** | Balgy | Applecross |
| Coulin Pass / Bealach Cùmhlainn | 286 | track | Craig | Glen Carron |
| Cùl a' Phollain | 621 | (path) | Culligran | Corriehallie Forest |
| Drochaid a' Choire Dhuibh | 582 | | Aultguish Inn | Kinlochluichart Forest |
| Drochaid a' Ghlas Tuill | 716 | (track) | Lochdrum | Strathvaich Forest |
| Drochaid Allt Toll a' Ghiubhais | 469 | (path) | Taagan | Torridon |
| Drochaid Coire Làir | 388 | path | Achnashellach Station | Glen Carron |
| Drochaid Coire Mhadaidh | 544 | (path) | Scardroy | Strathconon |
| Drochaid Coire Roill | 431 | path | Annat | Glen Torridon |
| Drochaid Mhuilich | 601 | | Craig | West Monar Forest |
| Drochaid nam Meall Buidhe | 519 | | Inchvuilt | Loch Monar |
| Drochaid nan Lochan Uaine | 678 | | Achnashellach Station | Coulin Forest |
| Dubh Chlais | 90 | path | Mial | Gairloch |
| Eag nam Fear-bogha | 892 | | Lochdrum | The Fannichs |
| Eag Odhar | 511 | | Aultguish | Corriemoillie Forest |
| Garbh-bhealach | 955 | | Cougie | Carn Eige Range |
| Gate of Ca'-derg | 698 | | Glenbeg | Gleann Beag |
| Glas Bhealach | 965 | | Lundie | Ceannacroc Forest |
| Màm Coire Doimhneid | 526 | path | Camas-luinie | Loch Duich |
| Màm na Dubharaiche | 582 | | Lienassie | Inverinate Forest |
| Mam Ratagan *see* Bealach Ràtagain | | | | |
| Pass of Corryvarligan *see* Bealach Coire Mhàlagain | | | | |

| Latitude, Longitude | National Grid | Notes |
|---|---|---|
| 57.69265, -5.11520 | NH1442171248 | 'Lochan Hollow Pass' |
| 57.30166, -5.03583 | NH1720427532 | Inverness boundary; 'Waterfall Hollow Pass' |
| 57.24416, -5.24684 | NH0410621723 | Deduced from Allt and Coire Thuill Easaich; 'Waterfall Hollow Pass' |
| 57.44678, -4.91765 | NH2501443367 | Inverness boundary; 'Bealach an Tuill Chéilte' on OS 1st edn; 'Hidden Hollow Pass' |
| 57.68861, -4.57638 | NH4650969450 | 'Mossy Mound Pass' |
| 57.78072, -5.41035 | NG9733081893 | |
| 57.70815, -5.04395 | NH1874372780 | Deduced from Coire Breabaig; 'breabag' = 'rocky col', 'cleft' |
| 57.38805, -5.28798 | NH0248437848 | 'Breach of the Ben' |
| 57.71330, -5.27195 | NH0519373986 | 'Mouth of Rock Corrie' or 'Rock Corrie Gap' |
| 57.66653, -4.98731 | NH2191267998 | 'The Bailiff's Pass' |
| 57.69278, -5.70679 | NG7918073038 | 'Pass of the Roebuck' |
| 57.85716, -4.63142 | NH4395888333 | 'Thief's Pass' |
| 57.99049, -5.19799 | NC1105604616 | 'Lord's Pass' |
| 57.79169, -4.94798 | NH2486481823 | 'Fool's Pass' |
| 57.84596, -4.24069 | NH6709686251 | 'Low Pass' |
| 57.85306, -5.47397 | NG9396490133 | 'Little Pass' |
| | | |
| 57.67713, -5.04953 | NH1825669344 | 'Big Red Pass' |
| 57.79405, -5.25384 | NH0670382918 | 'Forked Pass' |
| 57.79068, -4.96089 | NH2409281744 | Personal name |
| 57.68242, -4.37642 | NH5840368325 | 'Great Pass' |
| 57.83650, -4.27206 | NH6519985260 | 'Great Pass' |
| 57.84313, -5.47426 | NG9389089029 | 'Great Pass' |
| 57.97429, -5.04945 | NC1975102407 | 'Cadh' na Bò' on OS 1st edn; 'Pass of the Cow' |
| 57.68816, -5.04766 | NH1842270566 | 'Pass of the Winnowing Fan' or 'Sieve' |
| 57.43711, -4.95976 | NH2244142400 | Inverness boundary; 'Bracken Pass' |
| 57.34439, -5.30677 | NH0111933046 | 'Red Pass' |
| 57.83617, -4.54318 | NH4910585796 | |
| 57.47082, -5.58652 | NG8503747962 | 'The Red Bank' |
| 57.49813, -5.29981 | NH0236950129 | At the headwaters of the River Coulin |
| 57.46016, -4.75976 | NG8503747962 | 'Cùl' appears to refer to the 'back' of Sgùrr a' Phollain but is applied to some other Highland cols (see Glossary) |
| 57.68789, -4.86075 | NH2955970050 | 'Ridge Pass of the Black Corrie' |
| 57.75049, -4.85191 | NH3037976993 | 'Grey Cave Pass' |
| 57.60613, -5.37198 | NG9864462356 | Caption at the col on OS 1st and 2nd edn; displaced on OS 25; 'Ridge Pass of the Burn of Fir-Tree Hollow' |
| 57.49958, -5.35477 | NG9908550452 | 'Ridge Pass of Mare Corrie' |
| 57.48728, -4.99384 | NH2064248072 | 'Ridge Pass of Wolf Corrie' |
| 57.49976, -5.50153 | NG9029750916 | 'Ridge Pass of Darnel Corrie' |
| 57.45874, -5.15786 | NH1066745342 | 'Ridge Pass' (particular name from Strath Mhuilich) |
| 57.38845, -5.10285 | NH1360837370 | Inverness boundary; 'Ridge Pass of the Yellow Hill' |
| 57.51737, -5.39656 | NG9668152555 | Not on OS 25 or 50; 'Ridge Pass of the Green Lochs' |
| 57.74246, -5.69595 | NG8012778529 | 'Black Hollow' |
| 57.70356, -5.02375 | NH1992472215 | 'Archers' Nick' |
| 57.67167, -4.82632 | NH3153568158 | 'Dun-Coloured Nick' |
| 57.29215, -5.07448 | NH1482826578 | Inverness boundary; misplaced to east on modern OS; 'Rough Pass' |
| 57.83274, -4.88856 | NH2859086238 | The summit of Cadha Dearg ('Red Pass') |
| 57.17247, -5.09499 | NH1298713319 | Inverness boundary; 'Grey Pass' |
| 57.27978, -5.43478 | NG9305726241 | 'Pass of the Deep Corrie' |
| 57.25208, -5.39343 | NG9539523034 | 'Pass of Darkness / Shade / Gloom' |

| Name | Elevation (m) | Surface | Nearest place | Region |
|---|---|---|---|---|
| **Pass of Kerrysdale / Gleann a' Bhaile Dheirg** | 39 | **A road** | Charlestown | Gairloch |
| **Bealach na Bà / Bealach nam Bó** | 626 | **road** | Russel | Applecross |
| **Pass of Glen Shiel** | 275 | **A road** | Alltbeithe | Glen Shiel |

## Shetland · 20 cols

| Name | Elevation (m) | Surface | Nearest place | Region |
|---|---|---|---|---|
| Atla Scord | 215 | | Weisdale | Mainland |
| Hamarigrind Scord | 109 | | Voe | Mainland |
| Inni Scord | 133 | | North Roe | North Roe |
| **Lamba Scord** | 71 | **B road** | Setter | Mainland |
| Muckle Scord | 140 | | Setter | Mainland |
| Scallafield Scord | 198 | | East Burrafirth | Mainland |
| Scord | 160 | | Wester Quarff | Clift Hills |
| **Scord of Brouster** | 35 | **A road** | Bridge of Walls | Mainland |
| Scord of Cuckron | 80 | | Girlsta | Mainland |
| Scord of Hamarsland | 112 | | Haggersta | Mainland |
| **Scord of Scalloway / Scord o 'callowa** | 72 | **A road** | Scalloway | Mainland |
| Scord of Scarfataing | 125 | | Roesound | Muckle Roe |
| **Scord of Sound** | 114 | **A road** | Sound | Mainland |
| Scord of Touby | 60 | | Setter | Mainland |
| **Setter Scord** | 128 | **B road** | Voe | Mainland |
| Shurgie Scord | 351 | | South Collafirth | North Roe |
| Stoura Scord | 121 | | Otterswick | Yell |
| Uyea Scord | 220 | | South Collafirth | North Roe |
| Wester Scord | 186 | | Burravoe | Mainland |
| **Whilmini Scord** | 101 | **B road** | Brettabister | Mainland |

## Stirling · 73 cols  8 passes

| Name | Elevation (m) | Surface | Nearest place | Region |
|---|---|---|---|---|
| Am Bealach | 680 | | Cononish | Ben Lui Range |
| An Cunglach | 517 | | Lendrick Lodge | Trossachs |
| The Balloch | 384 | | Cauldhame | Ochil Hills |
| Bealach a' Bheime  *see Bealach a' Mheim* | | | | |
| Bealach a' Choire Mholaich | 439 | | Braeleny | Loch Lubnaig |
| Bealach a' Mheim | 587 | | Glengyle | Trossachs |
| Bealach an Dubh Choirein | 723 | (path) | Ardvorlich | Ben Vorlich (Strathyre) |
| Bealach an Eoin | 59 | | Balmaha | Loch Lomond |
| Bealach an t-Sneachda | 680 | | Craigruie | Ben More Range |
| Bealach an t-Suidhe | 249 | | Braeval | Trossachs |
| Bealach Ard | 159 | path | Balmaha | Loch Lomond |
| Bealach Beag-laraich | 573 | | Auchinner | Ben Vorlich (Strathyre) |
| Bealach Bràigh | 459 | | Rowchoish | Ben Lomond |
| Bealach Buidhe | 805 | | Glengyle | Ben More Range |
| Bealach Buidhe | 782 | | Cononish | Ben Lui Range |
| Bealach Buidhe | 748 | (path) | Rowchoish | Ben Lomond |
| Bealach Choire nan Saighead | 699 | | Ardchullarie More | Ben Vorlich (Strathyre) |
| Bealach Coire an Laoigh | 797 | | Inverlochlarig | Trossachs |
| Bealach Coire na Circe | 772 | | Cashlie | Glen Lyon |
| Bealach Conasgach | 297 | | Malling | Trossachs |

| Latitude, Longitude | National Grid | Notes |
|---|---|---|
| 57.70542, -5.67194 | NG8133274331 | The Gaelic name ('Red Farm Glen') is attached to the northern section of the pass, which is unnamed on OS maps |
| 57.41798, -5.70706 | NG7749242473 | 'Pass of the Cow' / 'Pass of the Cattle' (a pass rather than a col); sometimes referred to as Applecross Pass or 'The Bealach'; this famous climb, like the Mont Ventoux, has its col about 800 m from the summit (see An Cumhann) |
| 57.16650, -5.31832 | NG9945913290 | Battle, 10 June 1719; 'Glenshells Pass' on H. Moll, 'The Shires of Ross and Cromartie' (1725); 'Pass of Glen Sheel' on Roy's Military Survey of Scotland (1747–52) |

| | | |
|---|---|---|
| 60.25990, -1.30682 | HU3846153053 | Personal name |
| 60.32909, -1.26213 | HU4084860786 | 'Rock Gate Pass' |
| 60.59249, -1.41096 | HU3236790039 | 'Inner Gap' |
| 60.27769, -1.26532 | HU4073655059 | 'Lamb Gap' |
| 60.28417, -1.29464 | HU3910655763 | 'Big Gap' |
| 60.30261, -1.29126 | HU3927157819 | The col below Scalla Field hill |
| 60.06699, -1.28558 | HU3986931581 | Deduced from Skerry and Burn of Scord |
| 60.24677, -1.54070 | HU2552951478 | Brouster is the farm to the east of the col |
| 60.24888, -1.24637 | HU4182151862 | The col below the Hill of Cuckron |
| 60.21184, -1.26884 | HU4062247723 | The col below the Hill of Hamarsland |
| 60.14034, -1.25605 | HU4142139768 | NCR 1; not on OS 25 or 50; Scalloway is the town below the col |
| 60.36165, -1.42006 | HU3209564325 | Scarfataing is the place to the east of the col |
| 60.23687, -1.32276 | HU3760550479 | NCR 1; the gap of the Hill of Sound |
| 60.26956, -1.26816 | HU4058954152 | Touby is the ruined croft to the south of the col |
| 60.34319, -1.29774 | HU3886562335 | NCR 1; Setter is the farm at the eastern foot of the col |
| 60.53783, -1.43511 | HU3109783940 | Name obscure |
| 60.55968, -1.07970 | HU5056386593 | 'Gap of the Knoll' |
| 60.53595, -1.39813 | HU3312883748 | 'Island Gap' |
| 60.38869, -1.28070 | HU3975067412 | Easter Scord, 2.5 kms to the south-east, is a gully rather than a col |
| 60.30463, -1.14708 | HU4723758138 | NCR 1; not on OS 25 or 50; name obscure; second part perhaps 'mòine' ('bog') |

| | | |
|---|---|---|
| 56.38207, -4.79802 | NN2733924602 | Deduced from Creag Dhubh a' Bhealaich; 'The Pass' |
| 56.25679, -4.33795 | NN5526509600 | 'The Defile' |
| 56.18129, -3.87673 | NN8360400325 | From bealach |

| | | |
|---|---|---|
| 56.27820, -4.22955 | NN6205611760 | 'Pass of the Rugged Corrie' |
| 56.27295, -4.65097 | NN3594812101 | 'Bealach a' Bheime' on OS 1st edn; 'Pass of the Cut' or 'Gash' |
| 56.33719, -4.23139 | NN6215518328 | Perth & Kinross boundary; 'Dark Dell Pass' |
| 56.08742, -4.54071 | NS4201391201 | 'Bird Pass' |
| 56.37135, -4.44075 | NN4935022569 | 'Pass of the Snow' |
| 56.18897, -4.36250 | NN5348602106 | 'Pass of the Seat' |
| 56.09265, -4.53427 | NS4243591768 | West Highland Way; 'High Pass' |
| 56.31258, -4.19734 | NN6417215522 | Perth & Kinross boundary; 'Bealach Beag na Laraiche' on OS 1st edn; 'Little Pass of the Ruin' |
| 56.19657, -4.66304 | NN3487203632 | 'Brae Pass' |
| 56.33214, -4.61943 | NN3815118612 | 'Yellow Pass' |
| 56.39481, -4.75964 | NN2976525923 | 'Yellow Pass' |
| 56.19109, -4.64206 | NN3615002972 | 'Yellow Pass' |
| 56.31024, -4.25932 | NN6033015386 | 'Pass of Arrow Corrie' |
| 56.30905, -4.55456 | NN4206515892 | 'Calf (or 'Fawn') Corrie Pass' |
| 56.52635, -4.43737 | NN5017039807 | Perth & Kinross boundary; deduced from Coire na Circe and by analogy with another col of the same name; 'Hen (i.e. Grouse?) Corrie Pass' |
| 56.19199, -4.33768 | NN5503702390 | 'Furze Pass' |

| Name | Elevation (m) | Surface | Nearest place | Region |
|---|---|---|---|---|
| Bealach Cruinn a' Bheinn | 455 | | Rowchoish | Ben Lomond |
| Bealach Cùil a' Choire | 676 | | Ardchullarie More | Ben Vorlich (Strathyre) |
| Bealach Cumhang | 250 | | Invertrossachs | Trossachs |
| Bealach Driseach | 365 | | Craigruie | Trossachs |
| Bealach-eadar-dha Bheinn | 862 | | Benmore | Ben More Range |
| Bealach Gaoithe | 549 | | Rowchoish | Ben Lomond |
| Bealach Gaoithe | 296 | (path) | Anie | Trossachs |
| Bealach Ghlas Leathaid | 575 | | Auchtertyre | Forest of Mamlorn |
| Bealach Glas | 666 | | Ardchullarie More | Ben Vorlich (Strathyre) |
| Bealach Iosal | 585 | | Auchinner | Ben Vorlich (Strathyre) |
| Bealach na Bàn Leacainn | 681 | | Inverarnan | Ben More Range |
| Bealach na Cloiche | 619 | | Glengyle | Trossachs |
| Bealach na Craoibhe | 415 | | Blairuskinmore | Trossachs |
| Bealach na Frithe | 849 | | Monachyle | Ben More Range |
| Bealach na h-Imriche | 570 | path | Kinlochard | Trossachs |
| Bealach na h-Imriche | 449 | | Edra | Trossachs |
| Bealach na h-Imriche | 435 | | Frenich | Trossachs |
| Bealach na Seann Lairige | 606 | (track) | Laggan | Trossachs |
| Bealach nam Biodag | 260 | (path) | Anie | Trossachs |
| Bealach nam Bó | 313 | | Glasahoile | Trossachs |
| Bealach nan Cabar | 658 | | Ardchullarie More | Ben Vorlich (Strathyre) |
| Bealach nan Carn | 180 | track | Invertrossachs | Trossachs |
| Bealach nan Corp | 651 | | Anie | Trossachs |
| Bealach nan Corp | 533 | | Glengyle | Trossachs |
| Bealach nan Searrach | 532 | | Ardchullarie More | Loch Lubnaig |
| Bealach nan Sgliat | 477 | (track) | Ardchullarie More | Loch Lubnaig |
| Bealach Pollach | 598 | track | Ledard | Trossachs |
| Bealach Slaidearan | 819 | (path) | Batavaime | Forest of Mamlorn |
| Benmore Glen | 497 | | Benmore | Ben More Range |
| Cruach Ardrain – Stob Garbh | 856 | | Inverlochlarig | Ben More Range |
| Drochaid an Droma | 536 | | Clifton | Ben Lui Range |
| Fionn Bhealach | 600 | | Craigruie | Ben More Range |
| Fionn Lairig | 914 | (path) | Morenish | Loch Tay |
| Fliuch Learg | 473 | | Cononish | Ben Lui Range |
| Garbh Bhealach | 622 | | Inverarnan | Ben More Range |
| Garbh Bhealach | 515 | | Auchessan | Ben More Range |
| Lairig a' Chaorainn | 395 | | Auchinner | Glen Artney |
| Lairig a' Churain | 609 | | Auchessan | Glen Dochart |
| Lairig an t-Sluaigh  see Lairig Luaidhe | | | | |
| Lairig Arnan / Làirig Àirnein | 382 | | Garabal | Glen Fyne |
| Lairig Bhreislich | 548 | | Moar | Glen Lyon |
| **Lairig Cheile / Pass of Glenogle** | 290 | **A road** | Mid Lix | Glen Ogle |
| Lairig Liaran | 592 | | Kenknock | Glen Lochay |
| Lairig Luaidhe | 638 | | Kenknock | Glen Lyon |

| Latitude, Longitude | National Grid | Notes |
| --- | --- | --- |
| 56.20534, -4.63901 | NN3640004550 | 'Pass of Cruinn a' Bheinn' (mountain name) |
| 56.30159, -4.25456 | NN6059314414 | 'Bealach Cùl a' Choire' on modern OS; 'Corrie Nook Pass' (see 'cùl' in Glossary); (see An Cumhann, p. 198) |
| 56.19811, -4.32714 | NN5571403049 | 'Narrow Pass' |
| 56.33262, -4.43992 | NN4924918257 | 'Thorny Pass' |
| 56.37825, -4.54028 | NN4323323559 | 'Bealach-eadar Bheinn' on OS 1st edn; 'Pass Between Two Hills' |
| 56.18816, -4.65302 | NN3545802672 | 'Wind Pass' |
| 56.25831, -4.26718 | NN5965409623 | 'Wind Pass' |
| 56.46118, -4.63342 | NN3783733002 | 'Grey Slope Pass' |
| 56.32562, -4.25658 | NN6055617092 | 'Grey Pass' |
| 56.31436, -4.20498 | NN6370615735 | Perth & Kinross boundary; not on modern OS; 'Low Pass' |
| 56.34231, -4.64192 | NN3680519797 | 'Pass of the White Slope' |
| 56.30105, -4.58818 | NN3995315080 | 'Pass of the Stone' |
| 56.22400, -4.52513 | NN4353906362 | 'Pass of the Tree' |
| 56.37411, -4.50162 | NN4560323011 | 'Frith' = 'forest', 'heath' or 'moor' |
| 56.21836, -4.48164 | NN4621205636 | 'Pass of the Flitting' (transhumance) |
| 56.26747, -4.45006 | NN4836411031 | 'Pass of the Flitting' (transhumance) |
| 56.23012, -4.62227 | NN3754307268 | 'Pass of the Flitting' (transhumance) |
| 56.28480, -4.34354 | NN5502512729 | 'Gap of the Old Pass' |
| 56.25671, -4.27398 | NN5922709459 | Not on OS 25 or 50; 'Pass of the Daggers' |
| 56.23534, -4.45308 | NN4805007462 | 'Pass of the Cattle'; Walter Scott, 'The Lady of the Lake' (1810): 'Above the Goblin Cave they go, / Through the wild pass of Beal-nam-bo' |
| 56.31918, -4.26237 | NN6017416387 | 'Bealach nan Cabrach' on OS 1st edn 'The Deers' Pass' |
| 56.21115, -4.30996 | NN5682804464 | NCR 7; 'Cairns Pass' |
| 56.26926, -4.33055 | NN5577010973 | 'Pass of the Corpses' |
| 56.30624, -4.64400 | NN3652215788 | 'Pass of the Corpses' |
| 56.28755, -4.26725 | NN5975712877 | 'Pass of the Foals' |
| 56.28085, -4.26457 | NN5989812126 | 'Slate Pass' |
| 56.20478, -4.46856 | NN4696804096 | 'Holey Pass' |
| 56.48608, -4.59936 | NN4004035693 | 'Robbers' Pass' |
| 56.36978, -4.55707 | NN4216122655 | The unnamed col is at the head of the glen |
| 56.35851, -4.57231 | NN4117321436 | |
| 56.43654, -4.75584 | NN3018630557 | Argyll & Bute boundary; 'drochaid' = 'bridge' (see Glossary); 'droma' = 'ridge' |
| 56.36105, -4.44418 | NN4909821430 | 'Fair (White) Pass' |
| 56.51587, -4.31716 | NN5752438386 | Perth & Kinross boundary; deduced from Coire Fionn-Làirige; 'Fair (White) Pass' |
| 56.42927, -4.77535 | NN2895129796 | Argyll & Bute boundary; misplaced to north-west on modern OS; 'Wet Pass' |
| 56.33081, -4.66675 | NN3522118576 | 'Rough Pass' |
| 56.39762, -4.48583 | NN4667225591 | 'Rough Pass' |
| 56.28156, -4.13667 | NN6781711952 | 'Rowan Pass' |
| 56.45937, -4.50923 | NN4547932514 | 'Pass of the Brave Man' |
| 56.32355, -4.78516 | NN2786918059 | Argyll & Bute boundary; 'Àirnein' is the name of the river |
| 56.54145, -4.34586 | NN5585641292 | Perth & Kinross boundary; 'Pass of Confusion' or 'Delirium', perhaps 'Pass of the Rout' |
| 56.42070, -4.33499 | NN5606827833 | Rob Roy Way; NCR 7 (col summit on converted railway cycle path is at 56.42054, -4.33531); 'Larig Ilay' on Roy's Military Survey of Scotland (1747–52); 'Lairig Eala' on OS 1st edn; also 'Làirig Ìle'; 'Pass of the Swan' |
| 56.51307, -4.47888 | NN4756538422 | Perth & Kinross boundary; 'Learg Rioran' on OS 1st edn; 'Rioran' is the name of the burn which rises at the col |
| 56.53342, -4.38326 | NN5352640478 | Perth & Kinross boundary; 'Pass of the Lead' (referring to lead mines); 'Lairig an t-Sluaigh' on OS 1st edn ('Pass of the People' or 'The (Fairy) Host') |

| Name | Elevation (m) | Surface | Nearest place | Region |
|------|------|------|------|------|
| Lairig Mhic Bhaidein | 725 | | Batavaime | Forest of Mamlorn |
| Lairig Mhultaibh | 571 | | Edinchip | Glen Ogle |
| Lairig Riarein | 669 | | Auchessan | Glen Dochart |
| Learg Macbheattie *see* Lairig Mhic Bhaidein | | | | |
| **Learg nan Lunn** | 505 | **road** / track | Lubreoch | Glen Lyon |
| Learg Rioran *see* Lairig Liaran | | | | |
| Màm nan Carn | 317 | | French | Trossachs |
| *Meikle Bin – Black Hill* | 451 | | Lennoxtown | Kilsyth Hills |
| *Owsen Hill – Dumbreck* | 471 | | Strathblane | Campsie Fells |
| *Parlan Hill – Cruach* | 425 | | Ardleish | Trossachs |
| Pass of Glenogle *see* Lairig Cheile | | | | |
| **Slochd an t-Seipine** | 315 | **A road** | Auch | Beinn Dorain Range |
| Windy Nick | 877 | | Inverlochlarig | Ben More Range |
| Windy Yet Glen | 192 | | North Third | Touch Hills |
| **Ballengeich Pass** | 71 | **road** | Stirling | City of Stirling |
| **Duke's Pass / Dukes Pass** | 240 | **A road** | Milton | Trossachs |
| **Pass of Aberfoyle / Pass of Aberfoil** | 33 | **B road** | Milton | Trossachs |
| Pass of Achray | 128 | track | Brig o' Turk | Trossachs |
| **Pass of Balmaha** | 48 | **road** | Balmaha | Loch Lomond |
| **Pass of Leny** | 113 | **A road** | Anie | Trossachs |
| **Pass of (the) Trossachs** | 102 | **A road** | Brig o' Turk | Trossachs |
| Wallace's Pass | 69 | path | Stirling | City of Stirling |

## Sutherland · 67 cols

| Name | Elevation (m) | Surface | Nearest place | Region |
|------|------|------|------|------|
| Am Bealach | 252 | | Forsinard | Strath Halladale |
| Am Bealach | 145 | | Keoldale | The Parph |
| Am Bealach | 59 | track | Achiemore | Strath Halladale |
| **An Cadha** | 46 | **road** | Achlyness | Ardmore |
| Bealach a' Bhaid Lònanaich | 100 | | Laxford Bridge | Loch Laxford |
| Bealach a' Bhùirich | 481 | | Newton | Assynt |
| Bealach a' Choire | 400 | | Corriekinloch | Assynt |
| Bealach a' Chonnaidh | 240 | | Polla | Loch Dionard |
| Bealach a' Chornaidh | 573 | | Newton | Assynt |
| Bealach a' Chùirn *see* Bealach Horn | | | | |
| Bealach a' Mhadaidh | 611 | | Inchnadamph | Assynt |
| Bealach a' Phollaidh | 373 | | Achfary | Reay Forest |
| Bealach an Easain Uaine | 388 | | Achfary | Foinaven Range |
| Bealach an Fhuarain | 299 | | Overscaig Hotel | Loch Merkland |
| Bealach an Tùir | 115 | | Achriesgill | Loch Inchard |

| Latitude, Longitude | National Grid | Notes |
|---|---|---|
| 56.47508, -4.62795 | NN3823334536 | Perth & Kinross boundary; 'Learg Macbheattie' on OS 1st edn; W. Watson, *Celtic Place-names* (1926) has 'Làirig Mhic Bháididh' ('MacWattie's Pass') |
| 56.40265, -4.33766 | NN5583525830 | 'Pass of the Sheep' |
| 56.44594, -4.55602 | NN4254131126 | 'Learg Riarein' on OS 1st edn; 'Lairig Riairein' on OS 25; name obscure |
| 56.51889, -4.52476 | NN4476639172 | Perth & Kinross boundary; 'Auld larignaloan' on J. Stobie, 'The Counties of Perth and Clackmannan' (1783); 'Larig-na-loone' in N. Carlisle, 'Rannoch', *A Topographical Dictionary of Scotland*, II (1813); a 'lunn' is a staff or a stave, a 'loan' was a peg; gated road |
| 56.23361, -4.58420 | NN3991707567 | Deduced from Lochan Mhàim nan Carn; 'Cairns Pass' |
| 56.00665, -4.14269 | NS6649481373 | Lanarkshire boundary |
| 56.00936, -4.29419 | NS5706081978 | Dunbartonshire boundary |
| 56.31322, -4.67537 | NN3461216640 | Argyll & Bute boundary |
| 56.45978, -4.71393 | NN3287133039 | Argyll & Bute boundary; (West Highland Way); deduced from Allt Slochd an t-Seipine; name from 'seipinn' (a liquid measure)? |
| 56.33266, -4.60271 | NN3918718631 | Not on OS 25 or 50 |
| 56.08173, -3.98671 | NS7645989437 | Not on OS 1st edn; 'yet' = 'gate' |
| 56.12453, -3.94702 | NS7906394130 | Name attested 1837 |
| 56.20294, -4.39023 | NN5181903720 | 'Duke's Pass' only on modern OS; name in common use; road built by Duke of Montrose in 1885; opened to the public in 1931; previously shown only as 'Srath Buidhe' |
| 56.18347, -4.41909 | NN4995301616 | Not on OS 25 or 50; battle, 1653 (defeat of Cromwellian troops) |
| 56.22750, -4.43208 | NN4932006544 | Not on OS 1st edn; name attested 1887 |
| 56.08558, -4.54529 | NS4172091007 | (West Highland Way); 'Pass of Ballmaha' on C. Ross, 'A Map of the Shire of Dumbarton' (1777); Walter Scott, 'The Lady of the Lake' (1810): 'Sore did he cumber our retreat, / And keep our stoutest kernes [soldiers] in awe, / Even at the pass of Beal'maha.' |
| 56.25088, -4.27386 | NN5921308810 | NCR 7; 'Pass of Leny' on Roy's *Military Survey of Scotland* (1747–52); 'Pass of Lennie' on J. Stobie, 'The Counties of Perth and Clackmannan' (1783); often 'Pass of Leney', 'Lenny' or 'Lenney' in 19th c.; also 'Cumhang Lànaigh' (W. Watson, *Celtic Place-names* (1926)) |
| 56.23033, -4.42176 | NN4997106836 | Not on OS 1st edn; 'The Trosachs, a wild and beautiful pass' between Loch Achray and Loch Katrine: *Onwhyn's Guide to the Highlands of Scotland* (1839) |
| 56.13619, -3.91462 | NS8111395371 | The pass by which William Wallace descended to attack the English at the Battle of Stirling in 1297 |
| 58.33330, -3.88197 | NC8989939849 | 'The Pass' |
| 58.50216, -4.88281 | NC3211860714 | 'The Pass'; 'Bhellachmaddy or Woolfs Way' next to 'Extreem Wilderness' on Pont, 3 (c. 1583–96); also 'Bhellach Maddy' on Pont, 1; *see* p. 92 |
| 58.50919, -3.89612 | NC8962359451 | 'The Pass' |
| 58.40772, -5.02454 | NC2339050569 | 'The Pass' |
| 58.36323, -5.00729 | NC2417645573 | 'Pass of the Marshy Place' or 'Grove' |
| 58.20257, -4.95684 | NC2634027565 | 'Roaring Pass' (perhaps referring to the rutting of deer) |
| 58.19778, -4.83042 | NC3374426713 | 'Corrie Pass' |
| 58.40086, -4.78795 | NC3717649208 | 'Firewood Pass' |
| 58.20829, -5.06327 | NC2011728481 | 'Bealach a' Chornaich' on OS 1st edn; 'Pass of the Folding' |
| 58.16947, -4.90024 | NC2950623737 | 'Wolf Pass' |
| 58.29063, -4.97110 | NC2593537400 | 'Pass of Pools' or 'Holes' |
| 58.36573, -4.84698 | NC3356245443 | 'Pass of the Green Waterfall' |
| 58.21908, -4.70414 | NC4125928778 | 'Pass of the Fountain' |
| 58.43545, -4.98539 | NC2581353552 | 'Pass of the Pillar' or 'Tower'; 'Bealach-an-Tur' on G. Burnett and W. Scott, 'Map of the County of Sutherland' (1855; survey of 1831–32) |

| Name | Elevation (m) | Surface | Nearest place | Region |
|---|---|---|---|---|
| Bealach Bad na h-Achlaise | 127 | | Laxford Bridge | Loch Laxford |
| Bealach Bàn | 603 | | Allnabad | Foinaven Range |
| Bealach Bàn | 145 | | Rhicarn | Assynt |
| Bealach Beag | 255 | | Kinbrace | Strath Beg |
| Bealach Beag | 250 | path | Sangobeg | Durness Peninsula |
| Bealach Beinn a' Bhùtha | 466 | | Kinloch | Glendhu Forest |
| Bealach Beinn Leòid | 702 | | Kinloch | Assynt |
| Bealach Càrn Phadruig | 197 | | Badcall | Ben Auskaird |
| Bealach Choinnich | 606 | | Ledmore | Assynt |
| Bealach Clais nan Ceap | 324 | | Lettermore | Ben Loyal |
| Bealach Coir' a' Choin | 318 | | Inshore | The Parph |
| Bealach Coire a' Chuidhe | 280 | | Inshore | The Parph |
| Bealach Coire an Uinnseinn | 562 | | Polla | Durness Peninsula |
| Bealach Dubh | 333 | | Lettermore | Ben Loyal |
| Bealach Eadar da Shabhal | 563 | | Aultanrynie | Foinaven Range |
| Bealach Easach | 346 | (path) | Crask Inn | Loch Choire |
| Bealach Fir Àshair | 499 | | Aultanrynie | Foinaven Range |
| Bealach Garbh | 198 | | Nedd | Assynt |
| Bealach Horn | 513 | (path) | Achfary | Foinaven Range |
| Bealach Leireag | 265 | path | Little Assynt | Assynt |
| Bealach Loch na Seilg | 423 | | Laid | Durness Peninsula |
| Bealach Lochan a' Bhealaich | 561 | | Aultanrynie | Foinaven Range |
| Bealach Mòr | 605 | | Rhegreanoch | Assynt |
| Bealach na Beinne | 246 | | Tongue | Kyle of Tongue |
| Bealach na Creige Duibhe | 257 | | Mudale | Loch Fiag |
| Bealach na Creige Riabhaich | 455 | | Lochside | Ben Hope |
| Bealach na Féithe | 452 | path | Aultanrynie | Foinaven Range |
| Bealach na h-Earba | 334 | | Achfary | Reay Forest |
| Bealach na h-Earbaige | 363 | | Badanloch Lodge | Achentoul Forest |
| Bealach na h-Imrich | 341 | | Knockan | Cromalt Hills |
| Bealach na h-Uidhe | 629 | path | Inchnadamph | Assynt |
| Bealach na Muic | 377 | (path) | Dalbreck | Ben Armine Forest |
| Bealach na Teangaidh | 260 | | Kinloch | Loch More |
| Bealach nam Fiann | 409 | path | Achfary | Reay Forest |
| Bealach nam Piob | 149 | | Scourie | Scourie Bay |
| Bealach nan Càrn | 495 | | Rhiconich | Foinaven Range |
| Bealach nan Rath | 538 | | Aultanrynie | Foinaven Range |
| Bealach Odhrsgaraidh | 381 | | Polla | Loch Hope |
| **Bealach Strome** | 111 | **A road** | Kylestrome | Loch a' Chàirn Bhàin |
| **Bealach Tharbait** | 52 | **road** | Tarbet | Port of Tarbet |
| Bealach Trallgil | 508 | | Stronechrubie | Assynt |
| Breabag Tarsainn | 572 | | Stronechrubie | Assynt |

| Latitude, Longitude | National Grid | Notes |
|---|---|---|
| 58.35662, -5.00856 | NC2406944841 | 'Pass of the Grove of the Oxter' or 'Bosom' |
| 58.30664, -4.70131 | NC4181638516 | Deduced from Loch a' Bhealaich Bhàin; 'White Pass' |
| 58.19529, -5.27861 | NC0740127630 | 'White Pass' |
| 58.25385, -3.91589 | NC8766131061 | 'Little Pass' |
| 58.52623, -4.71316 | NC4210962981 | 'Little Pass' |
| 58.26771, -4.88430 | NC3091234628 | 'Pass of Beinn a' Bhùtha' (mountain name) |
| 58.21761, -4.86812 | NC3162329013 | 'Pass of Ben Leoid' |
| 58.31446, -5.07861 | NC1975740335 | 'Pass of Patrick's Mound' |
| 58.08743, -4.89127 | NC2964214585 | 'Meeting Pass'; 'Beallach coinich' on G. Burnett and W. Scott, 'Map of the County of Sutherland' (1855; survey of 1831–32) |
| 58.40857, -4.40667 | NC5948249205 | 'Peat Trench Pass' |
| 58.53267, -4.96233 | NC2763664311 | 'Dogs' Corrie Pass' |
| 58.53908, -4.95843 | NC2789565014 | 'Pass of the Corrie of the Pen'; 'Beallach choir a' chui' on G. Burnett and W. Scott, 'Map of the County of Sutherland' (1855; survey of 1831–32) 'Bealach Coire na Caoidh' ('Pass of Lamentation Corrie') on OS 1st edn (1878) |
| 58.46309, -4.81830 | NC3569356207 | Deduced from name of 'Ash Corrie'; 'Coir' an Nois-neach' on OS 1st edn |
| 58.39993, -4.46562 | NC5600348368 | 'Black Pass' |
| 58.35262, -4.79491 | NC3654643856 | 'Am Bealach' on OS 1st edn refers to the same col; the name refers to the two hills on either side, Sàbhal Mòr and Sàbhal Beag |
| 58.19101, -4.42700 | NC5742125034 | Caption on OS 1st edn attached to the valley leading up to the col; 'Waterfall Pass'; 'Bealach ishin' at the col on G. Burnett and W. Scott, 'Map of the County of Sutherland' (1855; survey of 1831–32) |
| 58.29064, -4.78615 | NC3677336938 | Perhaps for 'fir-astair' ('traveller', 'wayfarer') |
| 58.21366, -5.11587 | NC1705629220 | 'Rough Pass' |
| 58.37229, -4.84327 | NC3381046164 | 'Bealach-horn' on G. Burnett and W. Scott, 'Map of the County of Sutherland' (1855; survey of 1831–32); 'Bealach a' Chùirn' on OS 1st edn; 'Cairn Pass' |
| 58.20235, -5.07634 | NC1932027855 | 'Bealach Leirg' on OS 1st edn; 'Pass of the Hill (Slope)' |
| 58.48343, -4.78041 | NC3799758378 | 'Hunting Loch Pass' |
| 58.31428, -4.75078 | NC3895339483 | 'Pass of Lochan Pass' |
| 58.11355, -5.12844 | NC1580118115 | 'Great Pass' |
| 58.47145, -4.37815 | NC6139556144 | 'Pass of the Mountain' |
| 58.25023, -4.62003 | NC4633332050 | 'Black Rock Pass'; 'Bealach-na-craig-a-dhui' on G. Burnett and W. Scott, 'Map of the County of Sutherland' (1855; survey of 1831–32) |
| 58.43024, -4.57241 | NC4989351975 | 'Brindled (or 'Grey') Rock Pass' |
| 58.33478, -4.78256 | NC3718641841 | 'Pass of the Bog' |
| 58.29749, -4.92214 | NC2883738038 | 'Pass of the (Roe) Deer' |
| 58.31517, -4.03387 | NC8094538089 | 'Pass of the (Small Roe) Deer' |
| 58.02361, -5.02805 | NC2126307838 | 'Pass of the Flitting' (transhumance) |
| 58.19003, -4.95392 | NC2645226192 | 'Pass of the Ford' |
| 58.16262, -4.19711 | NC7082921411 | 'Pig Pass'; perhaps short for 'muc-fhiadhaich' ('wild pig' or 'boar') |
| 58.26316, -4.79000 | NC3642033889 | 'Pass of the Tongue' |
| 58.30098, -4.94873 | NC2729638494 | 'The Warriors' Pass', 'Pass of the Followers of Fingal' |
| 58.36146, -5.13243 | NC1684945710 | 'Pass of the Pipes' |
| 58.42447, -4.87653 | NC3211452053 | 'Cairns Pass' |
| 58.30633, -4.73159 | NC4004138553 | 'Fortress Pass' (probably figurative) |
| 58.41721, -4.70584 | NC4204650831 | Not on OS 1st edn; location deduced from Bealach Odhrsgaraidh (first on OS 2nd edn); the col lies 1.8 kms from the *bealach* caption, which would designate the gully leading to the col; name perhaps contains 'sgaradh' ('separation', 'severance') |
| 58.26808, -5.05262 | NC2104535105 | Name from Norse for 'current' or 'stream' |
| 58.39155, -5.13064 | NC1711049053 | Name from village of Tarbet (from 'tairbeart', 'isthmus'); spot height (98 m) on OS is incorrect |
| 58.12897, -4.88521 | NC3019719192 | 'Bealach Thrallgil' on OS 1st edn; 'Am Bealach' on the other side refers to the same col; the River Traligill rises near the col |
| 58.12749, -4.89163 | NC2981219044 | 'Breabag Tarsuinn' on OS 1st edn; a 'breabag' is a rocky col or cleft; 'tarsainn' = 'transverse, across' |

| Name | Elevation (m) | Surface | Nearest place | Region |
|---|---|---|---|---|
| Bristeadh a' Chnoic | 299 | | Ledbeg | Assynt |
| Cadha Cumhann | 556 | | Achfary | Foinaven Range |
| Cadha na Beucaich | 682 | | Rhiconich | Foinaven Range |
| Càrn nan Conbhairean – Meall an Aonaich | 581 | | Duchally | Assynt |
| Crò Coire Mhic Dhugaill | 692 | | Aultanrynie | Foinaven Range |
| Drochaid Beinn Leòid | 546 | | Corriekinloch | Assynt |
| Drochaid Coire nam Mang | 633 | | Kinloch | Ben Hee |
| Glac na h'Imrich | 129 | track | Rhicarn | Assynt |
| Plovers' Gap | 272 | | Altanduin | Borrobol Forest |
| Reidh a' Bhealaich | 211 | | Klibreck | Loch Naver |
| The Whip / Meall Leathad na Craoibhe – Meall Ailein | 494 | | Loch Choire Lodge | Ben Klibreck |

# Northern Ireland

## Antrim · 8 cols

| Name | Elevation (m) | Surface | Nearest place | Region |
|---|---|---|---|---|
| Cave Hill – Collinward | 320 | path | Belfast | Belfast Hills |
| **Divis Mountain TV transmission station** | 364 | **road** | Belfast | Belfast Hills |
| **Glenaan Road** | 289 | **road** | Cushendall | Glenaan |
| **High Town Road** | 272 | **B road** | Belfast | Belfast Hills |
| **Knock Dhu promontory fort** | 280 | **road** | Glenarm | Antrim Hills |
| **Squires Hill – Divis Mountain** | 292 | **A road** | Belfast | Belfast Hills |
| Trostan – Slievenanee | 445 | (path) | Waterfoot | Glenariff Forest |
| West Torr – East Torr | 265 | (road) | Cushendun | Fair Head |

## Armagh · 2 cols 1 pass

| Name | Elevation (m) | Surface | Nearest place | Region |
|---|---|---|---|---|
| **Carrigans Pass / Bealach an Charraigín** | 150 | **road** | Silverbridge | Slieve Gullion |
| **Sturgan Mountain – Courtney Mountain** | 163 | **road** | Belleeks | Sturgan Range |
| **Bealach an Mhaighre / Moyry Pass / Gap of the North** | 80 | **road** | Ravensdale | Feede Mountain |

## Down · 27 cols 1 pass

| Name | Elevation (m) | Surface | Nearest place | Region |
|---|---|---|---|---|
| Altataggart Mountain – Tornamrock | 348 | | Hilltown | Mourne Mountains |
| Bealach an Aoire / Ballaghanery | 534 | path | Newcastle | Mourne Mountains |
| Bearna an Ghiorria / Hare's Gap / Hares' Gap | 435 | path | Bryansford | Mourne Mountains |
| Carn Mountain – Slieve Muck | 535 | | Cabra | Mourne Mountains |
| Cock Mountain – Slievenamiskan | 405 | | Hilltown | Mourne Mountains |
| Craigdoo – Spaltha | 385 | (track) | Cabra | Mourne Mountains |
| Eagle Rock – Shanlieve | 595 | | Hilltown | Mourne Mountains |
| Hare's Gap see Bearna an Ghiorria | | | | |
| Hen Mountain – Cock Mountain | 270 | | Hilltown | Mourne Mountains |
| **Ott Mountain – Slievenamuck** | 405 | **road** | Hilltown | Mourne Mountains |
| Pigeon Rock – Slievemoughanmore | 390 | | Hilltown | Mourne Mountains |
| Pollaphuca / Poll an Phúca / Bearna? | 518 | path | Bryansford | Mourne Mountains |
| **Rostrevor Road (Crotlieve Mountain – Wee Roosley)** | 236 | **road** | Hilltown | Mourne Mountains |

| Latitude, Longitude | National Grid | Notes |
|---|---|---|
| 58.08612, -5.00642 | NC 2285014736 | 'Rocky Pass of the Hill' |
| 58.35423, -4.82733 | NC 3465744115 | 'Narrow Pass' |
| 58.39598, -4.87071 | NC 3231848868 | 'Roaring Pass' (perhaps referring to the rutting of deer) |
| 58.10961, -4.83318 | NC 3316916907 | |
| 58.31285, -4.79723 | NC 3622639436 | 'Strait of MacDougall's Corrie' |
| 58.21855, -4.83634 | NC 3349429038 | 'Ridge Pass of Ben Leoid' |
| 58.26017, -4.70174 | NC 4158333345 | 'Ridge Pass of Fawns' Corrie' |
| 58.18223, -5.24819 | NC 0911726090 | 'Pass of the Flitting' (transhumance) |
| 58.19400, -4.00006 | NC 8252524543 | Only on modern OS; perhaps a translation of Bealach nam Feadag ('feadag' = 'plover' but also 'flute' or 'whistle') |
| 58.30177, -4.32286 | NC 6396737146 | 'Level Ground of the Pass'; 'Ruigh a' Bhealaich' on modern OS ('ruigh' or 'righe' = 'field') |
| 58.25477, -4.35145 | NC 6210831973 | |

| | | |
|---|---|---|
| 54.65094, -5.95345 | J 32145 80013 | |
| 54.60731, -6.00949 | J 28666 75053 | No public access; Divis was the site of the first trigonometrical station in the Ordnance Survey mapping of Ireland |
| 55.08651, -6.15238 | D 18028 28138 | |
| 54.64615, -5.97150 | J 30096 79446 | So named on OS 1st edn |
| 54.89534, -5.92530 | D 33157 07268 | (The Ulster Way) |
| 54.64011, -6.00262 | J 29006 78716 | |
| 55.03625, -6.16273 | D 17514 22527 | (The Moyle Way) |
| 55.19538, -6.09349 | D 21457 40358 | (The Ulster Way); (NCR 93) |

| | | |
|---|---|---|
| 54.10955, -6.51589 | H 97115 18842 | 'Pass of the Little Rock' |
| 54.16834, -6.45564 | J 00912 25469 | |
| 54.06897, -6.37917 | J 06159 14522 | Republic of Ireland border (Louth); presumed location (the pass guarded by Moyry Castle); Battle of Moyry Pass (1600); 'Pass of the Salmon' |

| | | |
|---|---|---|
| 54.15506, -6.10974 | J 23540 24541 | |
| 54.17230, -5.92777 | J 35370 26793 | Mourne Wall; Brandy Pad (smugglers' route); not on modern OS (labelled only 'Bog of Donard'); 'Shepherd's Pass'; known locally as 'The Ballagh'; 'The Passe' on J. Speed, 'The Province Ulster [sic] Described' (1610) |
| 54.19008, -5.97451 | J 32262 28683 | Mourne Wall; Brandy Pad (smugglers' route); the Gaelic name disproves a supposed connection with an O'Hare family |
| 54.16701, -6.03353 | J 28481 26006 | Mourne Wall |
| 54.17756, -6.07420 | J 25793 27107 | |
| 54.19694, -6.04986 | J 27323 29308 | |
| 54.13968, -6.10005 | J 24219 22846 | Batts Wall; the third-highest col in Northern Ireland |

| | | |
|---|---|---|
| 54.17911, -6.08934 | J 24800 27253 | |
| 54.18082, -6.04253 | J 27851 27527 | The Ulster Way; the second-highest road col in Northern Ireland |
| 54.15218, -6.07974 | J 25508 24273 | |
| 54.18627, -5.99557 | J 30899 28220 | Mourne Wall; name in common use, transferred from the neighbouring gully, though perhaps the true name, since shared by a col in the Wicklow Mountains; 'The Pooka's Hole' (a spirit or fairy); earlier name perhaps in 'Slieve Bearnagh' and 'Bearnagh Slabs' (from 'bearna'), which could refer to the cleft rocks at the summit |
| 54.15120, -6.15463 | J 20554 23899 | |

215

| Name | Elevation (m) | Surface | Nearest place | Region |
|---|---|---|---|---|
| **Sandbank Road (Crotlieve Mountain – Tievedockaragh)** | 208 | **road** | Hilltown | Mourne Mountains |
| Slieve Binnian – North Tor | 623 | path | Annalong | Mourne Mountains |
| Slieve Commedagh – Slieve Beg | 554 | path | Newcastle | Mourne Mountains |
| Slieve Commedagh – Slieve Corragh | 630 | path | Newcastle | Mourne Mountains |
| Slieve Commedagh – Slieve Donard | 580 | path | Newcastle | Mourne Mountains |
| Slieve Croob – Slievenisky | 400 | | Dromara | Dromara Hills |
| Slievelamagan – Cove Mountain | 555 | path | Newcastle | Mourne Mountains |
| Slievelamagan – North Tor | 396 | path | Annalong | Mourne Mountains |
| Slieve Loughshannagh – Carn Mountain | 510 | path | Hilltown | Mourne Mountains |
| Slieve Meelbeg – Slieve Loughshannagh | 509 | path | Bryansford | Mourne Mountains |
| Slieve Meelmore – Slieve Meelbeg | 590 | path | Bryansford | Mourne Mountains |
| Slievenaglogh – Slieve Corragh | 538 | (path) | Bryansford | Mourne Mountains |
| Tornamrock – Rocky Mountain | 325 | | Hilltown | Mourne Mountains |
| Windy Gap | 409 | (path) | Hilltown | Mourne Mountains |
| **Windy Gap** | 273 | **road** | Ballyward | Dromara Hills |
| **Spelga Pass** | 260 | **B road** | Hilltown | Mourne Mountains |

## Londonderry · 8 cols

| Name | Elevation (m) | Surface | Nearest place | Region |
|---|---|---|---|---|
| Carn Hill – Boviel Top | 385 | | Dungiven | Sperrin Mountains |
| **Cullion Gap / The Gap** | 338 | **road** | Draperstown | Sperrin Mountains |
| **Dart Pass** | 440 | **road** | Claudy | Sperrin Mountains |
| **Glenshane Pass / Bearna Ghleann Seáin** | 279 | **A road** | Maghera | Sperrin Mountains |
| Meenard Mountain / Muinard Top – Mullaghaneany | 538 | (path) | Draperstown | Sperrin Mountains |
| Mullaghaneany – Oughtmore | 467 | path | Draperstown | Sperrin Mountains |
| Sawel Mountain – Dart Mountain | 540 | path | Claudy | Sperrin Mountains |
| **Sawel Pass** | 340 | **road** | Dungiven | Sperrin Mountains |

## Tyrone · 10 cols

| Name | Elevation (m) | Surface | Nearest place | Region |
|---|---|---|---|---|
| Ballynatubbrit Mountain – Curraghchosaly Mountain | 305 | (path) | Gortin | Sperrin Mountains |
| **Barnes Gap / An Bearnas** | 220 | **road** | Rousky | Sperrin Mountains |
| **Dart Pass** | 440 | **road** | Claudy | Sperrin Mountains |
| Glengink | 235 | | Newtownstewart | Sperrin Mountains |
| **Gortin Gap** | 255 | **B road** | Gortin | Gortin Glen |
| **Mary Gray – Liscabble** | 230 | **road** | Newtownstewart | Sperrin Mountains |
| Meenard Mountain / Muinard Top – Mullaghaneany | 538 | (path) | Draperstown | Sperrin Mountains |
| Mullaghaneany – Oughtmore | 467 | path | Draperstown | Sperrin Mountains |
| Mullaghclogher / Straw Mountain – Mullaghasturrakeen | 440 | (path) | Dunnamanagh | Sperrin Mountains |
| Sawel Mountain – Dart Mountain | 540 | path | Claudy | Sperrin Mountains |

# Republic of Ireland

## Carlow · 6 cols

| Name | Elevation (m) | Surface | Nearest place | Region |
|---|---|---|---|---|
| Barnadown | 442 | | Killedmond | Blackstairs Mountains |
| **Bearna an Charbaid / Corrabut Gap / Corraby Gap / Corrbut Gap** | 359 | **road** | Myshall | Blackstairs Mountains |

| Latitude, Longitude | National Grid | Notes |
|---|---|---|
| 54.15152, -6.13655 | J 21799 24100 | |
| | | |
| 54.14868, -5.98351 | J 31806 24059 | The second-highest col in Northern Ireland |
| 54.18276, -5.94609 | J 34129 27888 | Brandy Pad (smugglers' route) |
| 54.18865, -5.94828 | J 33978 28573 | Mourne Wall; the highest col in Northern Ireland |
| 54.18266, -5.93317 | J 34984 27935 | Mourne Wall; sometimes 'The Donard Col' |
| 54.33570, -5.96773 | J 32237 44902 | |
| 54.17225, -5.96198 | J 33137 26722 | |
| 54.16237, -5.97803 | J 32120 25592 | |
| 54.17416, -6.02300 | J 29147 26821 | Mourne Wall |
| 54.17962, -6.01417 | J 29706 27445 | Mourne Wall |
| 54.18572, -6.00428 | J 30332 28142 | Mourne Wall |
| 54.19161, -5.96016 | J 33193 28880 | Mourne Wall |
| 54.16406, -6.10973 | J 23514 25542 | |
| 54.14693, -6.09320 | J 24645 23665 | Batts Wall |
| 54.32043, -6.04263 | J 27413 43064 | |
| 54.18554, -6.07031 | J 26023 28002 | 'Pass of the Pointed Rock' |
| | | |
| | | |
| 54.91811, -6.83918 | C 74486 08448 | |
| 54.75104, -6.75611 | H 80143 89942 | Locally known as 'Cullion Gap'; 'The Gap' on modern OS |
| 54.81660, -7.08372 | H 58953 96915 | Tyrone boundary; name in common use (from Dart Mountain); the highest road col in Northern Ireland |
| 54.87583, -6.78875 | C 77801 03796 | 'Glenshane Bride' in *Lewis's Atlas* (1837) |
| 54.83219, -6.94147 | H 68071 98779 | Tyrone boundary |
| | | |
| 54.82403, -6.92490 | H 69150 97887 | Tyrone boundary |
| 54.81459, -7.04924 | H 61173 96721 | Tyrone boundary |
| 54.82247, -7.00685 | H 63885 97636 | Name in common use (from mountain name) |
| | | |
| | | |
| 54.70356, -7.27213 | H 46972 84189 | Marked only 'Rock' on OS 1st edn (a standing stone) |
| | | |
| 54.74964, -7.14467 | H 55126 89412 | |
| 54.81660, -7.08372 | H 58953 96915 | Londonderry boundary; name in common use (from Dart Mountain); the highest road col in Northern Ireland |
| 54.70935, -7.30182 | H 43566 85294 | OS 1st edn places Glengink to the east, on the other side of Ballynatubbrit Mountain |
| 54.69300, -7.23462 | H 49403 83039 | The Ulster Way; NCR 92; placed 500 m to the east on OS 1st edn; Gortin is the townland name; perhaps originally from 'Gort na gCeap' |
| 54.71379, -7.32479 | H 43566 85294 | |
| 54.83219, -6.94147 | H 68071 98779 | Londonderry boundary |
| | | |
| 54.82403, -6.92490 | H 69150 97887 | Londonderry boundary |
| 54.79949, -7.16574 | H 53703 94944 | |
| | | |
| 54.81459, -7.04924 | H 61173 96721 | Londonderry boundary |
| | | |
| | | |
| | | |
| | | |
| 52.59859, -6.78576 | S 82326 50350 | Not on OS; from 'bearna', 'gap' |
| 52.65596, -6.76970 | S 83305 56753 | Signpost ('Corrabut Gap') to viewpoint; some forms from http://www.eastwestmapping.ie/placenames-heritage; 'Boulder Gap'? |

| Name | Elevation (m) | Surface | Nearest place | Region |
|------|---------------|---------|---------------|--------|
| **Bearna an Scalaigh / Scullogue Gap / Scollagh Gap** | 190 | **road** | Kiltealy | Blackstairs Mountains |
| **Camlín Gap / Cam-Líne** | 212 | **road** | Cashel | Blackstairs Mountains |
| Mám a Chuliagh / Cooliagh Gap / The Meeting | 375 | path | Gowlin | Blackstairs Mountains |
| **The Ninestones / The Nine Stones** | 439 | **road** | Drumfea | Mount Leinster |

## Cavan · 1 col

| | | | | |
|------|---------------|---------|---------------|--------|
| **Béal an Bhealaigh / Bellavally Gap / Gap of Beal** | 338 | **R road** | Glangevlin | Cuilcagh Mountains |

## Clare · 6 cols 1 pass

| | | | | |
|------|---------------|---------|---------------|--------|
| An Com Breac / Coumbrack | 405 | | Kilbane | Slieve Bernagh |
| **Bealkelly** | 197 | **road** | Ogonnelloe | Slieve Bernagh |
| **Carcair na gCleireach / Corker Road (or Pass)** | 76 | **L road** | Corcomroe Abbey | The Burren |
| **Glennagalliagh / Gleann na gCailleach** | 275 | **road** | Kilbane | Slieve Bernagh |
| Mám Chatha / Maumcaha | 167 | (path) | Ballyvaghan | The Burren |
| Ucht Máma / Ocht Mama / Oughtmama | 189 | | Corcomroe Abbey | The Burren |
| **Khyber Pass** | 91 | **road** | Murroogh | The Burren |

## Cork · 29 cols 1 pass

| | | | | |
|------|---------------|---------|---------------|--------|
| **Allihies Mines Road** | 240 | **road** | Allihies | Slieve Miskish Mountains |
| **An Bhearna / Barna** | 132 | **road** | Killeenleagh | Mount Kid |
| **An Cuasán / Cousane Gap / Bearna an Chuasáin** | 233 | **R road** | Cousane | Maughanaclea Hills |
| An Easca | 360 | track | Bunane | Caha Mountains |
| An Gabhlán / Gowlane | 458 | | Rossmackowen | Caha Mountains |
| Barnagowlane East / Barr na nGabhlán | 348 | path | Barnagowlane | Shehy Mountains |
| **Barnagowlane West / Barr na nGabhlán** | 289 | **road** | Barnagowlane | Shehy Mountains |
| **Barnancleeve / Barnancleeve Gap** | 150 | **road** | Raheenroe | Mount Gabriel |
| **Bealach Scairte / Ballaghscart / Kerry Pass / Healy Pass** | 285 | **R road** | Adrigole | Caha Mountains |
| **Bealbarnish Glen / Bealbarnish Gap** | 105 | **R road** | Cahermore | Slieve Miskish Mountains |
| **Bearna Ghaoithe / Barnageehy** | 210 | **N road** | Barnageehy | Sheep's Head Range |
| **Caha Pass** | 333 | **N road** | Rossnagrena | Caha Mountains |
| Caol an Ghabhláin / Kealagowlane | 225 | path | Derreenacarrin | Caha Mountains |
| *Cathair na Cáithe / Cahernacaha* | 346 | **road** | Lackabaun | Shehy Mountains |
| **Céim an Fhia / Keamaneigh / Pass of Keimaneigh** | 202 | **R road** | Cappaboy Beg | Shehy Mountains |
| **Céim Chorrbhuaile / Keamcorravooly** | 211 | **road** | Ballingeary | Shehy Mountains |
| **Com an Ghadhair / Coomnagire** | 398 | **road** | Ballyvourney | Derrynasaggart Mountains |
| **Com na nÉag / Coomnaneage / The Coom** | 321 | **road** | Lackabaun | Shehy Mountains |
| Eskinanane | 163 | | Allihies | Slieve Miskish Mountains |
| **Firkeel Gap** | 51 | **R road** | Firkeel | Slieve Miskish Mountains |
| **Goulacullin / Gabhal an Chuilinn** | 336 | **road** | Barrboy | Maughanaclea Hills |
| Healy Pass *see Bealach Scairte* | | | | |
| **Keam-a-gower / The Goat's Path** | 193 | **road** | Kilcrohane | Sheep's Head Peninsula |

| Latitude, Longitude | National Grid | Notes |
| --- | --- | --- |
| 52.57588, -6.78151 | S 82656 47828 | Wexford boundary; 'Farmer's Gap'? |
| 52.62575, -6.84643 | S 78167 53305 | Not on modern OS; 'Crooked Line Gap' |
| 52.53510, -6.82696 | S 79649 43239 | Wexford boundary; not on OS; names from http://www.eastwestmapping.ie/placenames-heritage (quoting Patrick Kennedy, late 19th c.) |
| 52.63685, -6.79387 | S 81705 54599 | South Leinster Way |
| 54.16921, -7.81807 | H 11931 24479 | 'Mouth of the Pass' |
| 52.81959, -8.53901 | R 63710 74388 | 'Speckled Hollow' |
| 52.87425, -8.49121 | R 66974 80447 | From 'béal' ('mouth') and 'coill' ('wood') |
| 53.13654, -9.02975 | M 31132 10020 | Not on OS; T. Robinson, 'The Burren' (1999) and various documents; 'The Clerics' Prison' (or perhaps 'Large Rock'); see 'carcair' in Glossary |
| 52.80283, -8.53744 | R 63802 72522 | 'Glen of the Nuns' |
| 53.10522, -9.10936 | M 25750 06614 | 'Pass of the Battle'; on OS 1st edn and T. Robinson, 'The Burren' (1999); sometimes incorrectly located on the road from Turlough to Corcomroe Abbey |
| 53.12030, -9.02337 | M 31533 08207 | Galway boundary; 'Breast of the Pass'; name attributed to hill |
| 53.12429, -9.26491 | M 15370 08909 | Name in local use; on T. Robinson, 'The Burren' (1999) |
| 51.65283, -10.03200 | V 59421 46375 | Beara Way; the road at the col is unsurfaced |
| 51.63037, -9.34396 | W 06990 42776 | 'The Gap' |
| 51.75750, -9.26460 | W 12730 56822 | 'The Nook' |
| 51.78820, -9.55680 | V 92627 60628 | Kerry boundary; deduced from Esk Mountain / Cnoc na hEasca ('hill' of the 'channel', 'fissure', or 'hollow') |
| 51.69836, -9.85084 | V 72086 51107 | Presumed location; 'The Fork' (see 'gabhal' in Glossary) |
| 51.71417, -9.27324 | W 12049 52011 | 'The Fork' |
| 51.71035, -9.29670 | W 10420 51615 | 'Top of the Fork' |
| 51.55813, -9.52649 | V 94184 34987 | Known locally as 'Windy Gap' |
| 51.72187, -9.75683 | V 78648 53562 | Kerry boundary; 'Pass of the Shelter'; road built in 1847 and renamed 'The Tim Healy Pass' in 1931 on the death of the first Governor-General of the Irish Free State; statue (crucifixion) |
| 51.61582, -10.06746 | V 56851 42327 | 'Mouth of the Gap' |
| 51.61934, -9.44845 | V 99731 41687 | Sheep's Head Way; not on OS 1st edn; 'Wind Gap' |
| 51.78497, -9.58694 | W 90540 60313 | Kerry boundary; Beara Way Cycle Route; col summit in tunnel (175 m long, unlit); named after the Caha Mountains ('An Cheacha') |
| 51.71539, -9.61781 | W 88238 52619 | 'Narrow of the Fork' |
| 51.89153, -9.24686 | W 14210 71713 | |
| 51.81419, -9.30185 | W 10270 63175 | Memorial to Battle of Keimaneigh (1822); 'Pass of the Deer' |
| 51.85709, -9.25375 | W 13669 67890 | 'Pass of the Round Hill of the Booley' (temporary hut erected on summer pastures) |
| 51.97089, -9.13030 | W 22371 80412 | Presumed location; OS caption placed 1 km to west; 'Hound Hollow' |
| 51.90470, -9.28765 | W 11428 73227 | 150 m east of Kerry boundary; 'Hollow of Death' (but perhaps 'eag' rather than 'éag', in which case, 'Hollow Gap') |
| 51.66691, -10.07336 | V 56603 48022 | From 'eisc' (see Glossary) |
| 51.60813, -10.12265 | V 53004 41581 | Marked only 'Glen' on OS 1st edn; the lowest col in Ireland |
| 51.73792, -9.24606 | W 13973 54621 | 'Holly Fork' |
| 51.59561, -9.71083 | V 81498 39439 | Gaelic name in W. R. Wilde, 'On the Unmanufactured Animal Remains Belonging to the Academy' (1859), Proceedings of the Royal Irish Academy, VII (1857–1861); statue (pietà) |

| Name | Elevation (m) | Surface | Nearest place | Region |
|---|---|---|---|---|
| Kerry Pass  *see* Bealach Scairte | | | | |
| *Knocknagallaun (east)* | 256 | | Allihies | Slieve Miskish Mountains |
| **Knocknagallaun (west)** | 99 | **R road** | Allihies | Slieve Miskish Mountains |
| Léim an tSagairt  *see* Priest's Leap Pass | | | | |
| **Muisire / Mushera East** | 429 | **road** | Carrigagulla | Boggeragh Mountains |
| **Mushera Gap / Muisire** | 380 | **road** | Carriganimmy | Boggeragh Mountains |
| **Pass of Boffickil** | 89 | **R road** | Allihies | Slieve Miskish Mountains |
| Pass of Keimaneigh  *see* Céim an Fhia | | | | |
| **Priest's Leap Pass / Léim an tSagairt** | 461 | **road** | Bunane | Caha Mountains |
| **Redchair / Redsheard / Bearnadarg / An Bhearna Dhearg** | 191 | **R road** | Ballyvisteen | Ballyhoura Mountains |
| Windy Gap  *see* Barnancleeve | | | | |
| **Vaughan's Pass** | 189 | **road** | Bantry | Bantry Bay |

## Donegal · 21 cols  4 passes

| Name | Elevation (m) | Surface | Nearest place | Region |
|---|---|---|---|---|
| **An Bearnas / Barnes Gap** | 110 | **N road** | Termon | Stragraddy Mountain |
| **An Carbad Mór / Carbat Gap** | 184 | **R road** | Fintown | Bluestack Mountains |
| **An Mám / Maam / Maum** | 105 | **road** | Gortahork | Cloughaneely |
| **An Mám Mór / Gap of Mamore / Mamore Gap** | 250 | **road** | Dunaff | Urris Hills |
| Barnes Gap  *see* An Bearnas | | | | |
| Bealach Gaoithe / Ballaghgeeha Gap | 412 | | Dunlewy | Derryveagh Mountains |
| Béal an Bhearnais  *see* Rocky Gap | | | | |
| Bearna na Gaoithe / Barnanageeha  *see* Mám na Mucaise | | | | |
| **Bearna na Muice Báine / Barnamuckybane** | 190 | **road** / track | Leabgarrow | Aran Island |
| Bearna na Sruthal / Sruell Gap | 476 | | Ardbane | Bluestack Mountains |
| **Bráid an Bhealaigh / Neck of the Ballagh** | 122 | **N road** | Ardara | Mulmosog Mountain |
| Carbat Gap  *see* An Carbad Mór | | | | |
| Casán an Aon Fhir / One Man's Path | 555 | | Teelin | Slieve League |
| Cró an Chaorthainn / Croankeeran | 355 | | Ardbane | Bluestack Mountains |
| *Crockglass – Leamacrossan Hill* | 299 | **road** | Quigley's Point | Inishowen |
| *Crockmain – Mamore Hill* | 302 | path | Dunaff | Urris Hills |
| *Crockmain – Slievekeeragh* | 285 | | Dunaff | Urris Hills |
| *Drumnalifferny Mountain – Slieve Snaght* | 376 | | Muine Beag | Derryveagh Mountains |
| Glengesh Pass  *see* Malaidh Ghleann Gheis | | | | |
| **Grania's Gap / Bearna Ghráinne** | 276 | **road** | Muff | Inishowen |
| **Malaidh Ghleann Gheis / Glengesh Pass / Glen Gesh Pass** | 271 | **R road** | Ardara | Glengesh Hill |
| Mám an Leaca / Maumlack | 412 | | Dunlewy | Derryveagh Mountains |
| **Mám na Mucaise / Gap of Muckish / Muckish Gap** | 246 | **R road** | Falcarragh | Muckish Mountain |
| Mamore Gap  *see* An Mám Mór | | | | |
| Muckish Gap  *see* Mám na Mucaise | | | | |
| Neck of the Ballagh  *see* Bráid an Bhealaigh | | | | |
| One Man's Path  *see* Casán an Aon Fhir | | | | |
| Rocky Gap / Béal an Bhearnais | 498 | | Muine Beag | Derryveagh Mountains |
| *Slieve Main – Split Rock* | 323 | | Drumfree | Inishowen |
| *Slieve Snaght – Slieve Main* | 414 | | Drumfree | Inishowen |
| Sruell Gap  *see* Bearna na Sruthal | | | | |
| **An Bearnas Mór / Barnesmore Gap** | 107 | **N road** | Barnesmore | Bluestack Mountains |
| **An Bhearnach Mhór / Barnaghmore** | 140 | **R road** | Fintown | Bluestack Mountains |

| Latitude, Longitude | National Grid | Notes |
|---|---|---|
| 51.65775, -10.04424 | V 58589 46946 | |
| 51.66406, -10.06365 | V 57272 47703 | |
| | | |
| 52.02398, -8.94824 | W 34960 86141 | |
| 52.01157, -8.99500 | W 31731 84803 | Named 'Mushera Gap' in J. C. Coleman, *Journeys into Muskerry* (1950) |
| 51.70440, -9.94119 | V 65858 51941 | Sometimes 'Boffickle' |
| | | |
| 51.79343, -9.47116 | V 98548 61087 | Kerry boundary; 'Priest's Leap' at the col on OS 1st edn |
| 52.28756, -8.45353 | R 69101 15143 | Limerick boundary; also 'Redchard', or 'Red Chard', 'Red Guard' and 'Richchair'; the name means 'Red Gap' |
| | | |
| 51.66628, -9.44234 | W 00257 46901 | Sheep's Head Way; not on maps; name locally used (Vaughan was a county councillor) |
| | | |
| 55.07199, -7.86089 | C 08934 24970 | 'The Gap' |
| 54.87621, -8.13995 | B 91064 03174 | 'Boulder Gap' |
| 55.11027, -8.12822 | B 91865 29230 | 'Maum Hill' on modern OS; 'The Pass' |
| 55.23216, -7.49774 | C 32004 42908 | 'The Great Pass' |
| | | |
| 54.99512, -8.06639 | B 95799 16405 | 'Wind Gap' |
| | | |
| 54.99074, -8.53265 | B 65953 16045 | Not on OS; 'White Pig Pass' |
| | | |
| 54.76227, -8.09433 | G 93976 90485 | OS caption placed 2.3 kms to south-west (the col is at the head of the gap); 'Gap of the Streams' |
| 54.72690, -8.42019 | G 72975 86625 | 'Neck of the Pass' |
| | | |
| 54.64969, -8.70242 | G 54706 78175 | Not to be confused with One Man's Pass |
| 54.75602, -8.17621 | B 88703 89800 | 'Rowan Hollow' |
| 55.13784, -7.25837 | C 47346 32544 | |
| 55.24502, -7.47783 | C 33260 44349 | |
| 55.24473, -7.46434 | C 34119 44323 | |
| 54.99478, -8.08647 | B 94513 16369 | |
| | | |
| 55.09470, -7.32645 | C 43051 27697 | 'Grania' is a woman's name |
| 54.72029, -8.48800 | G 68601 85917 | Donegal Way; 'Brow of Glen Gesh' |
| | | |
| 55.02252, -8.05134 | B 96764 19455 | Name attributed to hill; 'Hillside Pass' |
| 55.08865, -8.00237 | B 99896 26816 | 'Pig Pass'; from the west, the col is called 'Bearna na Gaoithe', or 'Barnanageeha' ('Wind Gap'); 'Gap of Muckish' only on OS 1st edn; roadside shrine |
| | | |
| 54.98454, -8.10858 | B 93097 15231 | English name on OS 1st edn; earlier name may survive in Lough Maam just below the col |
| 55.17579, -7.36320 | C 40622 36703 | |
| 55.18645, -7.34146 | C 41996 37902 | |
| | | |
| 54.72359, -7.94843 | H 03371 86177 | 'The Great Gap' |
| 54.85414, -8.16384 | B 89525 00721 | 'The Great Gap' |

221

| Name | Elevation (m) | Surface | Nearest place | Region |
|------|--------------|---------|---------------|--------|
| **The Black Gap** | 170 | **R road** | Pettigoe | The Pullans |
| One Man's Pass | 751 | path | Money More | Errigal Mountain |

## Dublin · 4 cols 2 passes

| Name | Elevation (m) | Surface | Nearest place | Region |
|------|--------------|---------|---------------|--------|
| **Barr na Slinneán / Barnaslingan** | 200 | **road** | Kiltiernan | Dublin Mountains |
| *Kippure – Seefingan* | 620 | | Glencree | Dublin Mountains |
| *Piperstown Glen* | 312 | path | Tallaght | Dublin Mountains |
| **Scalp Pass / Pass of the Scalp / An Scailp** | 164 | **R road** | Glencullen | Dublin Mountains |
| **Ballinascorney Gap** | 258 | **R road** | Tallaght | Dublin Mountains |
| **Glencullen / Gleann Cuilinn** | 365 | **R road** | Glencree | Dublin Mountains |

## Galway · 19 cols 2 passes

| Name | Elevation (m) | Surface | Nearest place | Region |
|------|--------------|---------|---------------|--------|
| An Mám / Maum | 348 | | Maum | Maumturk Mountains |
| Béal an Mháma | 275 | | Derryrush | Connemara |
| Bearna na nEang / Barnanang | 467 | | Kylemore Abbey | The Twelve Pins / Benna Beola |
| Col of Despondency | 259 | | Leenaun | Maumturk Mountains |
| *Devilsmother – Knocklaur* | 360 | | Leenaun | Partry Mountains |
| Gabhlán na Lí / Gowlaunlee | 524 | | An Uillin | Maumturk Mountains |
| Mám Chloch an Leamhain / Maumcloghaloon | 220 | path | Maum | Maumturk Mountains |
| Mám Éan / Maumean | 495 | | Derryvoreada | Maumturk Mountains |
| Mám Éan / Maumean / Maumean Pass | 258 | (path) | Derryvoreada | Maumturk Mountains |
| Mám Eidhneach / Maumina / Maam Ina | 419 | | Kylemore Abbey | The Twelve Pins / Benna Beola |
| Mám Gaoithe / Maumgeeha | 477 | | Kylemore Abbey | The Twelve Pins / Benna Beola |
| Mám na bhFonsaí | 494 | | Recess | The Twelve Pins / Benna Beola |
| Mám Ochóige / Maumahoge | 340 | | Derryvoreada | Maumturk Mountains |
| Mám Toirc / Maumturkmore / Maam Turk | 357 | | Leenaun | Maumturk Mountains |
| Mám Uchta / Maumonght | 549 | | Letterfrack | The Twelve Pins / Benna Beola |
| Maumnageeragh / Mám na g-Caorach | 478 | | Kylemore Abbey | The Twelve Pins / Benna Beola |
| Maumnascalpa | 317 | | Kylemore Abbey | The Twelve Pins / Benna Beola |
| *Mullach Glas – Binn Mhór East Top* | 532 | | Maum | Maumturk Mountains |
| Ucht Máma / Ocht Mama / Oughtmama | 189 | | Corcomroe Abbey | The Burren |
| **Kylemore Pass / Pass of Kylemore** | 36 | **N road** | Letterfrack | The Twelve Pins / Benna Beola |
| Salrock Pass (or Gap) | 138 | | Glassillaun | Killary Harbour |

## Kerry · 57 cols 1 pass

| Name | Elevation (m) | Surface | Nearest place | Region |
|------|--------------|---------|---------------|--------|
| An Com / Coom | 581 | | Glencar | Dunkerron Mountains |
| An Comar Caol | 558 | | Tullakeel | Dunkerron Mountains |
| An Com Riabhach / Coumreagh | 449 | | Kenmare | Dunkerron Mountains |
| An Easca | 360 | track | Bunane | Caha Mountains |
| **An Mám / Maum** | 170 | **road** | Anascaul | Dingle Peninsula |
| Ballagh Pass *see* Bearna an Bhealaigh | | | | |
| Ballaghbeama Gap *see* Bealach Béime | | | | |

| Latitude, Longitude | National Grid | Notes |
| --- | --- | --- |
| 54.57524, -7.95250 | H 03120 69662 | Not on OS |
| 55.03421, -8.11300 | B 92822 20761 | Not on OS; not to be confused with One Man's Path |
| | | |
| 53.22039, -6.17013 | O 22274 20421 | Sign at roadside, 'Barnaslingan Forest Recreation Area'; 'Summit of the Shoulder Blades' (but 'barr na' may have been 'bearna') |
| 53.18495, -6.35509 | O 10011 16177 | Wicklow boundary |
| 53.24757, -6.33126 | O 11442 23182 | EastWest Mapping; Piperstown is the townland to the west |
| 53.21957, -6.18108 | O 21545 20311 | Wicklow boundary; road at the col named 'The Scalp' on OS 1st edn; 'scailp' = 'gap', 'cleft' or 'chasm' |
| 53.24631, -6.38747 | O 07693 22956 | Not on modern OS; name attested 1819 |
| 53.23621, -6.28239 | O 14734 21995 | 'Valley of the Holly' |
| | | |
| 53.52868, -9.55817 | L 96720 54298 | OS caption placed 1 km to south-west; 'The Pass' |
| 53.37281, -9.71745 | L 85741 37195 | Not on OS; from T. Robinson, *Connemara: A Little Gaelic Kingdom* (2011); 'Mouth of the Pass' |
| 53.52130, -9.86698 | L 76222 53969 | Misplaced on OS; 'Pass of the Gap' |
| 53.56328, -9.72466 | L 85700 58220 | Not on maps; named by hill walkers |
| 53.60537, -9.62041 | L 92787 62925 | Mayo boundary |
| 53.53165, -9.71583 | L 86274 54869 | 'Fork of the Stone (or Grave)' (OS written record) |
| 53.51315, -9.50992 | L 99883 52501 | 'Elm Rock Pass' |
| 53.52602, -9.70302 | L 87108 54222 | 'Pass of the Birds' |
| 53.49150, -9.65156 | L 90432 50300 | Western Way; 'Pass of the Birds' |
| 53.51400, -9.82725 | L 78836 53088 | Name attributed to mountain; 'Ivy Pass' |
| 53.52354, -9.85043 | L 77326 54190 | Only on OS 1st edn; 'Windy Pass' |
| 53.50885, -9.80061 | L 80589 52470 | 'Pass of the Rims' |
| 53.52130, -9.69291 | L 87766 53681 | Name obscure |
| 53.54548, -9.72440 | L 85743 56421 | 'Boar Pass' (to which the mountains owe their name) |
| 53.51986, -9.88206 | L 75218 53835 | Name attributed to mountain; 'Pass of the Breast', or 'Ridge'; correct spelling is probably 'Maumought': P. Tempan, 'Irish Hill and Mountain Names', www.mountaineering.ie (2010) |
| 53.49595, -9.83544 | L 78241 51094 | On OS 1st edn only; 'Pass of the Sheep' |
| 53.52845, -9.85833 | L 76817 54750 | 'Pass of the Cleft' |
| 53.48183, -9.60986 | L 93175 49160 | |
| 53.12030, -9.02337 | M 31533 08207 | Clare boundary; 'Breast of the Pass'; name attributed to hill |
| 53.55973, -9.87591 | L 75743 58261 | First attested 1853 |
| 53.61155, -9.83962 | L 78296 63965 | On OS 1st edn, 'Salrock', the name of the village, is attached to the summit of the pass |
| | | |
| 51.92210, -9.85951 | V 72122 76014 | Deduced from Coom Lough |
| 51.90830, -9.92753 | V 67402 74601 | Not on OS; 'The Narrow Ravine' |
| 51.96584, -9.74506 | V 80111 80686 | 'Speckled (or 'Grey') Hollow' |
| 51.78820, -9.55680 | V 92627 60628 | Cork boundary; deduced from Esk Mountain / Cnoc na hEasca ('hill' of the 'channel', 'fissure' or 'hollow') |
| 52.15177, -10.01805 | Q 61925 01857 | The Dingle Way; 'The Pass' |

| Name | Elevation (m) | Surface | Nearest place | Region |
|---|---|---|---|---|
| Ballaghisheen Pass  *see Bealach Oisín* | | | | |
| **Béal Dearg / Bealdarrig** | 256 | **road** | Kenmare | Dunkerron Mountains |
| **Bealach Béime / Ballaghbeama Gap** | 265 | **road** | Boheeshil | Dunkerron Mountains |
| Bealach Chom an Chiste / Coomakesta (or Coomakista) Pass | 210 | **N road** | Caherdaniel | Dunkerron Mountains |
| **Bealach Oisín / Ballaghisheen Pass** | 310 | **road** | Knockroe | Dunkerron Mountains |
| **Bealach Scairte / Ballaghscart / Kerry Pass / Healy Pass** | 285 | **R road** | Adrigole | Caha Mountains |
| Bealach Troisc / Ballytrusk | 295 | | Glencar | Dunkerron Mountains |
| Bearna an Bhealaigh / Ballagh Pass | 598 | | Kate Kearney's Cottage | MacGillycuddy's Reeks |
| **Bearna an Choimín / Gap of Dunloe / The Gap** | 241 | **road** | Kate Kearney's Cottage | MacGillycuddy's Reeks |
| Bearna Ghaoithe / Barnageehy | 730 | | Cloghane | Dingle Peninsula |
| Bearna na Gaoithe / Barnanageehy | 505 | | Tonavane | Slieve Mish Mountains |
| Bearna na Gaoithe / Windy Gap / Barnanageeha | 464 | path | Anascaul | Dingle Peninsula |
| Bearna na Gaoithe  *see Windy Gap* | | | | |
| *Beenreagh – Macklaun* | 388 | | Glenbeigh | Horseshoe Range |
| **Caha Pass** | 333 | **N road** | Rossnagrena | Caha Mountains |
| **Caherconree Pass** | 280 | **road** | Fybagh | Slieve Mish Mountains |
| Céim an Daimh  *see Moll's Gap* | | | | |
| *Cnoc Bréanainn – Barr an Ghéaráin / Brandon Peak* | 668 | | Cloghane | Dingle Peninsula |
| Coimín Piast / Cummeenapeasta | 880 | | Kilgobnet | MacGillycuddy's Reeks |
| Coiscéim an Mhadra Alla / Wolfstep | 526 | | Ballyduff | Dingle Peninsula |
| **Com an Liaigh / Coumaleague** | 119 | **road** | Kildurrihy | Dingle Peninsula |
| **Com Ga / Coumgagh** | 116 | **R road** | Ballynana | Dingle Peninsula |
| **Commaun** | 114 | **road** | Glenbeigh | Horseshoe Range |
| Com Uí Dhuibh / Cummeenduff | 541 | | Kenmare | Dunkerron Mountains |
| **Connor (or Conor) Pass / An Chonair** | 411 | **R road** | Lisdargan | Dingle Peninsula |
| Coomakesta Pass  *see Bealach Chom an Chiste* | | | | |
| **Coomanaspig Pass** | 247 | **road** | Portmagee | Skellig Ring |
| **Croaghane / Mount Eagle** | 369 | **road** | Lyre | Glanaruddery Mountains |
| *Cruach Mhór – Cnoc an Bhráca* | 640 | | Kilgobnet | MacGillycuddy's Reeks |
| *Cummeen – Redtrench* | 411 | path | Kilgarvan | Shehy Mountains |
| Cummeenalassa | 760 | | Kilgobnet | MacGillycuddy's Reeks |
| Cummeengrin | 930 | | Kilgobnet | MacGillycuddy's Reeks |
| Eisc na Gige | 730 | (path) | Kilgobnet | MacGillycuddy's Reeks |
| Eskafaun | 591 | | Glencar | Dunkerron Mountains |
| Gap of Dunloe  *see Bearna an Choimín* | | | | |
| **Garranes** | 190 | **road** | Tuosist | Caha Mountains |
| **Gowlaun / An Gabhlán** | 152 | **road** | Lauragh | Caha Mountains |
| Healy Pass  *see Bealach Scairte* | | | | |

| Latitude, Longitude | National Grid | Notes |
|---|---|---|
| 51.94106, -9.74000 | V 80393 77920 | 'The Red Mouth' |
| 51.94150, -9.81175 | V 75461 78090 | Road sign; 'béim' = 'notch' |
| 51.77642, -10.16669 | V 50509 60392 | Not on OS; Ring of Kerry Cycle Route; 'Treasure Coomb Pass'?; Madonna statue |
| 51.94901, -9.93456 | V 67038 79143 | Road sign; 'Pass of the Fawn' |
| 51.72187, -9.75683 | V 78648 53562 | Cork boundary; 'Pass of the Shelter'; road built in 1847 and renamed 'The Tim Healy Pass' in 1931 on the death of the first Governor General of the Irish Free State; statue (crucifixion) |
| 51.92854, -9.91785 | V 68127 76835 | English name on OS 1st edn; 'Cod Pass' |
| 52.00700, -9.65941 | V 86102 85127 | OS caption placed 1 km to north-west |
| 51.99423, -9.64439 | V 87101 83683 | Labelled 'Head of Gap' on OS; 'Common (land) Gap' or 'Hollow Gap'; 'Dunloe' is the name of the electoral division |
| 52.23863, -10.24688 | Q 46564 11981 | Not on OS; presumed location; 'Wind Gap' |
| 52.21812, -9.76520 | Q 79410 08788 | OS caption placed 2.3 kms to south-east; 'Windy Gap' |
| 52.17679, -10.13975 | Q 53678 04879 | Last form from Lough Barnanageeha |
| 51.99843, -9.95225 | V 65970 84673 | |
| 51.78497, -9.58694 | V 90540 60313 | Cork boundary; Beara Way Cycle Route; col summit in tunnel (175 m long, unlit); named after the Caha Mountains ('An Cheacha') |
| 52.18310, -9.87777 | Q 71616 05085 | Name in common use; Caherconree is a mountain named after a ring fort |
| 52.22091, -10.24002 | Q 46972 09995 | |
| 51.99975, -9.69041 | V 83955 84370 | Deduced from Lough Cummeenapeasta and Glasheencummeenna-peasta (a stream), but probably referring to the cirque rather than the col; the second-highest col in Ireland; 'Hollow of the Monster' |
| 52.21378, -10.10258 | Q 56340 08920 | On OS 1st edn, which places it at the foot of the climb by Macha na Bó; in view of the usual meaning of 'céim', the col at An Com Bán (identified here) is just as likely |
| 52.13905, -10.41484 | Q 34723 01271 | The Pilgrims' Route; 'Hollow of the Standing Stone' |
| 52.16889, -10.33701 | Q 40158 04417 | 'Narrow Coomb'? |
| 52.05689, -9.89074 | V 70363 91066 | Kerry Way; probably from 'coimín' ('Little Hollow') |
| 51.95108, -9.74326 | V 80196 79040 | Name on OS 1st edn; 'Black Hollow', applied to the valley, but perhaps originally to the col (see 'coimín' and 'com' in Glossary) |
| 52.18164, -10.20765 | Q 49051 05558 | 'The Narrow Passage'; the Irish Tourist Board and others call this the highest road pass in Ireland (it is the eleventh-highest road col) |
| 51.85625, -10.36734 | V 36950 69703 | Name in common use; the place name, 'Bishop's Hollow', may contain the original name of the col |
| 52.24451, -9.32613 | R 09469 11084 | |
| 52.00654, -9.67349 | V 85134 85098 | |
| 51.88115, -9.38072 | W 04972 70724 | Either name may reflect the col's original name ('cummeen' from 'coimín', 'little hollow', 'glen') |
| 51.99098, -9.72122 | V 81816 83444 | Not on modern OS; name close to col on OS 1st edn; from 'coimín' ('little hollow'), perhaps the cirque rather than the col; the third-highest col in Ireland |
| 51.99534, -9.69786 | V 83432 83891 | The 'coimín' (see Glossary) and its stream are shown on OS 1st edn to the north-west, perhaps referring to the cirque rather than the col; the highest col in Ireland |
| 51.99274, -9.73794 | V 80672 83667 | 'Esknagigeagh' on OS 1st edn; 'eisc' = 'channel', 'fissure' or 'hollow'; the name is now used only in 'Bóthar na Gige' ('The Zigzags'), the old route up to Carrauntoohil |
| 51.93170, -9.84046 | V 73459 77049 | Probably from 'eisc' (see above) and 'fán' ('slope'); on OS 1st edn |
| 51.78471, -9.73221 | V 80515 60512 | 'Groves' |
| 51.78037, -9.76708 | V 78098 60087 | Deduced from Gowlaun Lough; 'The Fork' |

| Name | Elevation (m) | Surface | Nearest place | Region |
|------|-----|------|------|------|
| Hook Gap  *see* Barnancurrane | | | | |
| Kerry Pass  *see* Bealach Scairte | | | | |
| **Knockmoyle – Knockawaddra** | 324 | **road** | Castlemaine | Slieve Mish Mountains |
| *Knocknabreeda – Bunbinnia* | 490 | | Kenmare | Dunkerron Mountains |
| *Knocknakilton – Dromavally Mountain* | 319 | | Anascaul | Dingle Peninsula |
| Lacknacroneen | 366 | (path) | Glencar | MacGillycuddy's Reeks |
| Léim an tSagairt  *see* Priest's Leap Pass | | | | |
| **Leitir Móiníl / Lettermoneel** | 176 | **R road** | Blackwater Bridge | Dunkerron Mountains |
| Mám an Gharráin / Maumagarrane | 294 | | Anascaul | Dingle Peninsula |
| Mám an Óraigh / Maumanorig | 130 | track | Ventry | Dingle Peninsula |
| **Mám Clasach / Maumclasac** | 189 | **road** | Dunquin | Dingle Peninsula |
| **Mám na Gaoithe / Maumnageehy** | 68 | **road** | Ventry | Dingle Peninsula |
| **Mám na gCapall / The Stage** | 148 | **N road** | Flemingstown | Dingle Peninsula |
| Mamanordill / Mám an Fhordaill / Mameordile | 375 | | Kenmare | Mangerton Range |
| Más an Tiompáin / Masatiompan | 665 | path | Cloghane | Dingle Peninsula |
| **Maumnahaltora / Mám na hAltóra / Mameacoolea** | 209 | **N road** | Camp | Dingle Peninsula |
| **Moll's Gap / Céim an Daimh** | 338 | **N road** | Kenmare | Mangerton Range |
| Mullach Bhéal / Mullaghveal | 397 | path | Ballinloghig | Dingle Peninsula |
| **The Paps East – Knocknabro** | 320 | **road** | Headfort | Derrynasaggart Mountain |
| **Priest's Leap Pass / Léim an tSagairt** | 461 | **road** | Bunane | Caha Mountains |
| The Stage  *see* Mám na gCapall | | | | |
| Stumpa Dúloigh | 600 | | Glencar | Dunkerron Mountains |
| Windy Gap / Bearna na Gaoithe | 332 | track | Kenmare | Mangerton Range |
| Windy Gap | 330 | track | Glenbeigh | Horseshoe Range |
| Windy Gap  *see* Bearna na Gaoithe | | | | |
| Wolfstep  *see* Coiscéim an Mhadra Alla | | | | |
| **Barnancurrane / Hook Gap / Bearna (or Béal) an Chorráin** | 210 | **road** | Muckross | Mangerton Range |

# Kilkenny · 2 cols

| Name | Elevation (m) | Surface | Nearest place | Region |
|------|-----|------|------|------|
| **Bearna Copana / Coppanagh Gap** | 240 | **R road** | Graiguenamanagh | Brandon Hill |
| **Bearna na Gaoithe / Windgap** | 158 | **R road** | Windgap | Slievenamon Range |

# Laois · 3 cols 1 pass

| Name | Elevation (m) | Surface | Nearest place | Region |
|------|-----|------|------|------|
| **Bearnagleamdoyne / Glendine Gap** | 450 | **road** | Srahanboy | Slieve Bloom Mountains |
| **The Cut / An Gearradh** | 434 | **road** | Derrycon | Slieve Bloom Mountains |
| **Windy Gap** | 193 | **N road** | Stradbally | South Midlands |
| **Pass of the Plumes / Bearna na gCleití / Pass of Cashel** | 118 | **R road** | Cashel | Cullenagh Mountain |

# Limerick · 10 cols

| Name | Elevation (m) | Surface | Nearest place | Region |
|------|-----|------|------|------|
| **An Caol / Keale** | 240 | **R road** | Thomastown | Ballyhoura Mountains |
| **Barnagh / An Bhearna** | 189 | **N road** | Ballymurragh | Mullaghareirk Mountains |
| **Cúil Fhraoigh / Coolfree** | 309 | **road** | Ballyorgan | Ballyhoura Mountains |
| Galtee Pass | 723 | (path) | Ballygeana | Galty Mountains |
| Lyracappul / Ladhar an Chapaill | 643 | | Ballygeana | Galty Mountains |
| Pigeon Rock Glen | 595 | | Anglesborough | Galty Mountains |

| Latitude, Longitude | National Grid | Notes |
|---|---|---|
| 52.21199, -9.70544 | Q 83477 08008 | |
| 51.95434, -9.73005 | V 81113 79381 | |
| 52.19192, -10.02328 | Q 61692 06334 | |
| 51.97771, -9.79190 | V 76925 82084 | On OS 1st edn; 'lack' is from 'leaca' ('hillside') |
| 51.87364, -9.81760 | V 74870 70550 | 'Hillside of the Neck' (referring to the ridge of land, perhaps with the same sense as 'swire') |
| 52.16455, -10.10315 | Q 56142 03444 | 'Grove Pass' |
| 52.14507, -10.34964 | Q 39208 01795 | 'Hill-Top of the Yellow Stones' (OS Parish Namebooks, 1841) |
| 52.14173, -10.42530 | Q 34017 01593 | 'Furrowed Pass' |
| 52.14602, -10.38295 | Q 36932 01975 | 'Windy Pass' |
| 52.17031, -10.00167 | Q 63103 03888 | Not on maps; 'Horse Pass' |
| 51.94364, -9.62664 | Q 88195 78027 | Not on OS; from Civil Survey of 1654–6; meaning obscure |
| 52.25788, -10.24879 | Q 46500 14126 | (The Dingle Way); marked 'Brandon Monument' on OS 25-inch (1897–1913); 'Cloch Oghaim' (ogham stone) on modern OS; 'Más' ('hip', 'thigh' or 'buttock') is the name of the mountain; 'tiompán' = 'drum', but also a variant of 'treampán' ('trouble', 'difficulty') |
| 52.19742, -9.93207 | Q 67945 06775 | Marked 'Altar' and 'Penitential Stations' on OS 1st edn; 'Pass of the Altar' |
| 51.93803, -9.65714 | V 86083 77450 | 'Keamadav' on OS 1st edn; named after Moll Kissane, pub owner in the 1820s during the building of the road; Irish name means 'Pass of the Ox'; col name on café sign |
| 52.19059, -10.25554 | Q 45806 06654 | Name attributed to mountain; 'summit' and 'mouth' |
| 52.01268, -9.24866 | W 14317 85195 | |
| 51.79343, -9.47116 | V 98548 61087 | Cork boundary; 'Priest's Leap' at the col on OS 1st edn; *see* 'léim' in Glossary |
| 51.94961, -9.77213 | V 78207 78925 | The col lies between two of the peaks of the mountain so named |
| 51.93377, -9.58599 | V 90966 76867 | The Kerry Way; misplaced on modern OS? |
| 52.03233, -9.93168 | V 67483 88407 | The Kerry Way |
| 51.99213, -9.51331 | V 96100 83254 | The Kerry Way; misplaced on old and modern OS, though correctly described in OS written record |
| 52.54710, -7.02630 | S 66105 44373 | 'Copenach: a place abounding in dock leaves' (OS typed record) |
| 52.46184, -7.39407 | S 41235 34613 | |
| 53.04700, -7.65700 | S 23053 99615 | Offaly boundary; Slieve Bloom Way; 'Pass of the Deep Glen'; Irish name in Inquisitionum in *officio rotulorum cancellariae Hiberniae asservatarum*, I (1826); memorial stone at county boundary |
| 53.09075, -7.55771 | N 29682 04520 | Earlier name in Barna ('bearna') Hill to the east? |
| 52.99571, -7.12352 | S 58901 94222 | On OS 1st edn |
| 52.98412, -7.27344 | S 48848 92809 | Modern OS has 'Pass of the Planes' (*sic*); battle, 17 May 1599; the plumes are those of English helmets left on the battlefield |
| 52.33133, -8.43633 | R 70304 20006 | Not on OS; 'The Narrow', or 'Strait' |
| 52.42071, -9.13370 | R 22920 30467 | 'The Pass' or 'Gap' |
| 52.29901, -8.49378 | R 66363 16435 | Name attributed to mountain; 'Heath Nook' |
| 52.36783, -8.16797 | R 88608 23992 | Tipperary boundary; name used by cyclists |
| 52.35405, -8.23012 | R 84370 22470 | 'Fork of the Horse'; name attributed to mountain |
| 52.34958, -8.23553 | R 84000 21974 | |

| Name | Elevation (m) | Surface | Nearest place | Region |
|---|---|---|---|---|
| Poulastanna | 350 | (track) | Rear Cross | Slieve Felim Mountains |
| **Redchair / Redsheard / Bearnadarg / An Bhearna Dhearg** | 191 | **R road** | Ballyvisteen | Ballyhoura Mountains |
| *Slievecushnabinnia — Carrignabinnia* | 750 | | Ballygeana | Galty Mountains |
| *Slievecushnabinnia — Lough Curra* | 725 | | Ballygeana | Galty Mountains |

## Louth · 4 cols 1 pass

| | | | | |
|---|---|---|---|---|
| Bearna Mhéabha / Barnavave / Maeve's Gap | 301 | track | Carlingford | Carlingford Mountain |
| **Bearna na Gaoithe / The Windy Gap** | 210 | **road** | Omeath | Carlingford Mountain |
| Cadgers Pass | 403 | path | Ravensdale | Black Mountain |
| **Clermont Pass** | 425 | **road** | Ravensdale | Black Mountain |
| **Bealach an Mhaighre / Moyry Pass / Gap of the North** | 80 | **road** | Ravensdale | Feede Mountain |

## Mayo · 14 cols 1 pass

| | | | | |
|---|---|---|---|---|
| **Barnaderg / Bearna Dhearg / Sheeffry (or Sheffry) Pass** | 200 | **L road** | Drummin | Sheefry Hills |
| Barr na Coilleadh / Barnacuillew | 212 | (track) | Pollatomish | Broad Haven |
| Béal an Mháma / Bellavaum | 100 | track | Inishturk | Inishturk |
| Bearna Ghaoithe / Barnageehy / Windy Gap / Pass of Barnageeragh | 199 | **road** | Bofeenaun | Glen Nephin |
| *Birreencorragh — Glenlara* | 510 | | Srahmore | Nephin Beg Range |
| *Coire na Binne / Corranabinnia (north-east)* | 467 | | Carrowbeg | Nephin Beg Range |
| *Coire na Binne / Corranabinnia (south-west)* | 584 | | Carrowbeg | Nephin Beg Range |
| *Devilsmother — Knocklaur* | 360 | | Leenaun | Partry Mountains |
| *Glendahurk — Glennamong* | 352 | | Srahmore | Nephin Beg Range |
| *Glenlara — Glendorragha* | 510 | | Cloondaff | Nephin Beg Range |
| Leamadartaun / Léim a' dartáin | 246 | | Srahmore | Nephin Beg Range |
| Mám a' Scardain / Mame-a-Scardane | 265 | | Srahduggaun | Nephin Beg Range |
| Mám an Rata / Mamearatta / Maumaratta | 348 | | Srahduggaun | Nephin Beg Range |
| Maumthomas / Mame Thomaas | 360 | | Rosturk | Nephin Beg Range |
| Sheefry (or Sheffry) Pass  *see Barnaderg* | | | | |
| **Delphi Pass / Dhulough (or Doo Lough) Pass** | 43 | **R road** | Cregganbaun | Sheefry Hills |

## Offaly · 2 cols

| | | | | |
|---|---|---|---|---|
| **An Tulach agus Cromghlinn / Tulla and Crumlin** | 200 | **road** | Longford | Slieve Bloom Mountains |
| **Bearnagleamdoyne / Glendine Gap** | 450 | **road** | Srahanboy | Slieve Bloom Mountains |

## Sligo · 1 col

| | | | | |
|---|---|---|---|---|
| **The Windy Gap / The Gap** | 189 | **R road** | Largan | Slieve Gamph Range |

## Tipperary · 21 cols

| | | | | |
|---|---|---|---|---|
| **An Caolas** | 255 | **L road** | Killea | Devilsbit Range |
| Béal Beag / Gleann an Bhéil | 549 | | Clogheen | Knockmealdown Mountains |
| **Bearna an Bhainbh / County Cross** | 268 | **road** | Middlequarter | Knockmealdown Mountains |

| Latitude, Longitude | National Grid | Notes |
|---|---|---|
| 52.67228, -8.27076 | R 81733 57892 | On OS 1st edn; probably 'Poll an Stanna'; *see* 'poll' in Glossary |
| 52.28756, -8.45353 | R 69101 15143 | Cork boundary; also 'Redchard' or 'Red Chard', 'Red Guard' and 'Richchair'; the name means 'Red Gap' |
| 52.36590, -8.21198 | R 85610 23785 | Tipperary boundary |
| 52.36734, -8.19960 | R 86453 23943 | Tipperary boundary |
| 54.03174, -6.20809 | J 17463 10648 | The Táin Way; associated with Méabh (Maeve), legendary queen of Connacht; 'Golyin Pass' (e.g. on EastWest Mapping) appears to refer to the ridge route |
| 54.06114, -6.27468 | J 13021 13812 | |
| 54.07338, -6.31281 | J 10492 15114 | Not on OS; a 'cadger' is a beggar |
| 54.08437, -6.31743 | J 10160 16330 | The Táin Way; not on OS |
| 54.06897, -6.37917 | J 06159 14522 | Northern Ireland border (Armagh); presumed location (the pass guarded by Moyry Castle); Battle of Moyry Pass (1600); 'Pass of the Salmon' |
| 53.65650, -9.63241 | L 92124 68633 | Western Way; 'Red Gap'; 'Mám Shíofra' ('Pass of the Sprites') name on road sign at junction with Delphi Pass road |
| 54.27321, -9.82178 | F 81370 37571 | Name attributed to hill; 'Top of the Wood' |
| 53.70468, -10.10893 | L 60782 74823 | 'Mouth of the Pass'; placed 1 km to east on OS |
| 53.95239, -9.31439 | G 13758 01129 | Taken by the French expeditionary force of General Humbert in 1798 ('the Year of the French') |
| 53.98317, -9.49919 | G 01699 04796 | |
| 53.97644, -9.66392 | F 90875 04288 | |
| 53.96320, -9.67813 | F 89908 02836 | |
| 53.60537, -9.62041 | L 92787 62925 | Galway boundary |
| 53.95695, -9.64168 | F 92284 02085 | |
| 53.97609, -9.49054 | G 02250 03996 | |
| 53.99570, -9.52290 | G 00173 06223 | 'Heifer's Leap'? (OS Parish Namebooks, 1838), but perhaps from 'léana' ('water meadow') |
| 54.04125, -9.63982 | F 92624 11464 | Not on OS; 'Mame Thomaas' on W. Bald, 'Map of the Maritime County of Mayo' (1830); 'Pass of the Waterfall' |
| 54.01626, -9.62641 | F 93438 08662 | 'Mamearatta' on W. Bald, 'Map of the Maritime County of Mayo' (1830); 'Pass of the Young Hares'; 'Maumaratta' (peak) placed by OS 3 kms to west |
| 53.94802, -9.71371 | F 87532 01203 | Not on OS; 'Mame Thomaas' on W. Bald, 'Map of the Maritime County of Mayo' (1830) |
| 53.65717, -9.76560 | L 83321 68918 | Late 19th c.; from 'Delphi', a fishing lodge |
| 53.05881, -7.70223 | N 20014 00916 | Slieve Bloom Way |
| 53.04700, -7.65700 | S 23053 99615 | Laois boundary; Slieve Bloom Way; 'Pass of the Deep Glen'; Irish name in *Inquisitionum in officio rotulorum cancellariae Hiberniae asservatarum*, I (1826); memorial stone at county boundary |
| 54.09166, -8.95017 | G 37876 16248 | Western Way; 250 m from Mayo boundary |
| 52.80901, -7.93656 | S 04328 73076 | Probable name, deduced from Ballykealy ('baile' and 'caolas'); 'The Strait', or 'Narrow' |
| 52.24295, -7.99089 | S 00672 10082 | Waterford boundary; 'Little Mouth'; presumed location; P. Power, *The Place-Names of Decies* |
| 52.22492, -7.83628 | S 11237 08088 | Waterford boundary; 'Gap of the Suckling Pig'; P. Power, *The Place-Names of Decies* |

229

| Name | Elevation (m) | Surface | Nearest place | Region |
|---|---|---|---|---|
| **Bearna Chille Cais / Kilcash Gap** | 100 | **N road** | Ballinurra | Slievenamon Range |
| Bearna Chloch an Bhuidéil | 517 | | Monard | Knockmealdown Mountains |
| **Bearna na Gaoithe** | 298 | **road** | Doon | Knockmealdown Mountains |
| **Bearna na gCorr / Barnagore** | 299 | **R road** | Curreeny | Silvermine Mountains |
| **Bearna Ráth Cláiris / Rathclarish Gap** | 176 | **road** | Ballinurra | Slievenamon Range |
| Bearnán Éile / Barnane-Ely | 397 | (path) | Ballinveny | Devilsbit Range |
| Brisleach Dearg | 505 | | Middlequarter | Knockmealdown Mountains |
| **Céim Urumhan / Ormond Stile** | 211 | **road** | Templederry | Silvermine Mountains |
| Galtee Pass | 723 | (path) | Ballygeana | Galty Mountains |
| *Galtybeg – Greenane West* | 640 | | Rossadrehid | Galty Mountains |
| The Gap  *see* Vee Gap | | | | |
| **Garryduff Wood** | 249 | **R road** | Rathkea | Galty Mountains |
| Gleann Coise Binne / Glencoshabinnia | 465 | | Ballygeana | Galty Mountains |
| **Keamnacreeva / Céim na Craoibhe** | 260 | **road** | Templederry | Silvermine Mountains |
| Kilcash Gap  *see* Bearna Chille Cais | | | | |
| O'Loughnan's Castle | 744 | | Rossadrehid | Galty Mountains |
| Ormond Stile  *see* Céim Urumhan | | | | |
| Rathclarish Gap  *see* Bearna Ráth Cláiris | | | | |
| *Slievecushnabinnia – Carrignabinnia* | 750 | | Ballygeana | Galty Mountains |
| *Slievecushnabinnia – Lough Curra* | 725 | | Ballygeana | Galty Mountains |
| **Step / The Step** | 389 | **road** | Silvermines | Silvermine Mountains |
| **Vee Gap / The Gap** | 340 | **R road** | Clogheen | Knockmealdown Mountains |

## Waterford · 11 cols

| Name | Elevation (m) | Surface | Nearest place | Region |
|---|---|---|---|---|
| Béal Beag / Gleann an Bhéil | 549 | | Clogheen | Knockmealdown Mountains |
| **Bearna an Bhainbh / County Cross** | 268 | **road** | Middlequarter | Knockmealdown Mountains |
| Bearna an Mhadra / Barnamaddra Gap / Dog's Gap | 511 | path | Kilbrien | Monavullagh Mountains |
| **Bearna an Mháma** | 338 | **road** | Kilbrien | Monavullagh Mountains |
| Bearna Bhéal an Bhealaigh / Gap / The Gap | 466 | path | Kilbrack | Comeragh Mountains |
| **Bearna Chill Chiana** | 271 | **road** | Ballymacarbry | Monavullagh Mountains |
| Bearna Chloch an Bhuidéil | 517 | | Monard | Knockmealdown Mountains |
| Brisleach Dearg | 505 | | Middlequarter | Knockmealdown Mountains |
| Dog's Gap  *see* Bearna an Mhadra | | | | |
| **Harney's Cross** | 299 | **R road** | Clonmel | Comeragh Mountains |
| Ladhar an Iarla / Lyranearla | 367 | path | Clonmel | Comeragh Mountains |
| **Vee Gap / The Gap** | 340 | **R road** | Clogheen | Knockmealdown Mountains |

## Wexford · 4 cols

| Name | Elevation (m) | Surface | Nearest place | Region |
|---|---|---|---|---|
| **An Easca** | 290 | **road** | Askamore | Wicklow Mountains |

| Latitude, Longitude | National Grid | Notes |
|---|---|---|
| 52.41163, -7.48270 | S 35251 28978 | Not on OS; P. Power, *The Place-Names of Decies*; 'Kilcash' is the name of the townland |
| 52.22609, -7.89802 | S 07018 08211 | Waterford boundary; 'Bottle Rock Gap'; P. Power, *The Place-Names of Decies* |
| 52.22898, -8.08071 | R 94535 08531 | (Avondhu Way); 'Wind Gap'; presumed location (from P. Power, *The Place-Names of Decies*) |
| 52.75701, -8.16246 | R 89081 67300 | 'Round Hill (or Hollow) Gap' |
| 52.40867, -7.43378 | S 38583 28674 | Not on OS; 'Gap of the Rath (Ring Fort) of Clarus'?; P. Power, *The Place-Names of Decies* |
| 52.82829, -7.91509 | S 05773 75223 | Name attributed to Devilsbit Mountain; 'Gap of (the Kingdom of) Ely'; the 'bearna' was bitten out by the Devil |
| 52.22400, -7.85719 | S 09809 07983 | Waterford boundary; 'Red Breach'; presumed location; P. Power, *The Place-Names of Decies* |
| 52.77448, -8.11883 | R 92030 69238 | Not on modern OS; 'Ormond Stile' on OS 1st edn |
| 52.36783, -8.16797 | R 88608 23992 | Limerick boundary; name used by cyclists |
| 52.36907, -8.15163 | R 89721 24127 | |
| 52.43302, -8.17873 | R 87893 31248 | |
| 52.37797, -8.15657 | R 89387 25118 | 'Glen beside the Cliff' |
| 52.78539, -8.10217 | R 93156 70450 | Not on modern OS; 'Pass of the Tree'; 'Keamnacreeva' on OS 1st edn |
| 52.36661, -8.11829 | R 91955 23847 | The 'castle' is a rocky outcrop, named after an outlaw (P. Power, *The Place-Names of Decies*) |
| 52.36590, -8.21198 | R 85610 23785 | Limerick boundary |
| 52.36734, -8.19960 | R 86453 23943 | Limerick boundary |
| 52.77591, -8.23102 | R 84459 69415 | Not on OS; name on information panel |
| 52.24197, -7.95590 | S 03062 09974 | Waterford boundary; Avondhu Way; road sign ('The Vee'); the 'Vee' itself is the 'V'-shaped hairpin bend 2.5 kms to the north-east on the Bóthar na gCorr ('Road of the Round Hill' or 'Hollow') |
| 52.24295, -7.99083 | S 00672 10082 | Tipperary boundary; 'Little Mouth'; presumed location; P. Power, *The Place-Names of Decies* |
| 52.22492, -7.83628 | S 11237 08088 | Tipperary boundary; 'Gap of the Suckling Pig'; P. Power, *The Place-Names of Decies* |
| 52.19894, -7.59156 | S 27977 05264 | A dog dressed as mutton was served to St Declan by a pagan; miraculously restored to life, the dog fled through the Bearna an Mhadra, or Dog's Gap |
| 52.16600, -7.60530 | S 27057 01593 | Not on OS; 'Gap of the Pass'; P. Power, *The Place-Names of Decies* |
| 52.27179, -7.55898 | S 30155 13383 | 'Gap of the Mouth of the Pass' |
| 52.24640, -7.67171 | S 22473 10517 | 'Gap of Cian's Church'; presumed location; P. Power, *The Place-Names of Decies* |
| 52.22609, -7.89802 | S 07018 08211 | Tipperary boundary; 'Bottle Rock Gap'; P. Power, *The Place-Names of Decies* |
| 52.22400, -7.85719 | S 09809 07983 | Tipperary boundary; 'Red Breach'; presumed location; P. Power, *The Place-Names of Decies* |
| 52.33379, -7.61682 | S 26170 20260 | (East Munster Way); 'Harney's Cross Roads' on modern OS |
| 52.32420, -7.65908 | S 23295 19178 | 'Earl's Fork'; presumed location; P. Power, *The Place-Names of Decies* |
| 52.24197, -7.95590 | S 03062 09974 | Tipperary boundary; Avondhu Way; road sign ('The Vee'); the 'Vee' itself is the 'V'-shaped hairpin bend 2.5 kms to the north-east on the Bóthar na gCorr ('Road of the Round Hill' or 'Hollow') |
| 52.65841, -6.48225 | T 02750 57396 | Deduced from Askabeg and Askamore ('easca' = 'depression', or 'hollow'); the true name may be lost |

| Name | Elevation (m) | Surface | Nearest place | Region |
|---|---|---|---|---|
| **Bearna an Scalaigh / Scullogue Gap / Scollagh Gap** | 190 | road | Kiltealy | Blackstairs Mountains |
| **Bearna na hEanaí / Annaghgap / Wicklow Gap** | 220 | road | Clonroe Cross Roads | Croghan Mountain |
| Mám a Chuliagh / Cooliagh Gap / The Meeting | 375 | path | Gowlin | Blackstairs Mountains |

## Wicklow · 35 cols  6 passes

| Name | Elevation (m) | Surface | Nearest place | Region |
|---|---|---|---|---|
| **An Bhearn Dearg / Bearna Dhearg / Bearnadearg / Barndarrig** | 245 | road | Greenan | Wicklow Mountains |
| **Ballinabarny Gap** | 320 | road | Rathdangan | Wicklow Mountains |
| **Ballynultagh Gap** | 449 | road | Lackan | Wicklow Mountains |
| Barnacorane | 335 | | Ballinaclash | Wicklow Mountains |
| Barnalugalish | 545 | | Aghavannagh | Wicklow Mountains |
| **Barnameelia** | 312 | road | Aghavannagh | Wicklow Mountains |
| **Barnamire** | 250 | L road | Kilmallin | Wicklow Mountains |
| **Barnaveg / Barnaveag / Bearnaveag** | 491 | R road | Sraghmore | Wicklow Mountains |
| Barnaveguievy? | 475 | (path) | Greenan | Wicklow Mountains |
| Barnaweenyeen / Barnaweelyeen | 614 | | Brockagh | Wicklow Mountains |
| **Barranisky Cross Roads / Barr an Uisce?** | 205 | road | Ballymoyle | Vale of Avoca |
| Billy Byrne's Gap | 598 | | Ballyknockan | Wicklow Mountains |
| Black Gap | 598 | path | Brockagh | Wicklow Mountains |
| Cavanagh's Gap / Red Scar / Wexford Gap | 525 | path | Granabeg | Wicklow Mountains |
| Céim a' Doire / Camaderry | 625 | path | Brockagh | Wicklow Mountains |
| **Céim an Ghiúistís / Deputy's Pass / Devilspass** | 72 | road | Glenealy | Glenealy Woods |
| Cook's Gap | 555 | path | Brockagh | Wicklow Mountains |
| Deputy's Pass / Devilspass  see Céim an Ghiúistís | | | | |
| Djouce Mountain – War Hill | 615 | | Sraghmore | Wicklow Mountains |
| **Drumgoff Gap / Barnaskanabow / Flags Pass** | 455 | road | Aghavannagh | Wicklow Mountains |
| Flags Pass  see Drumgoff Gap | | | | |
| Gap of Imaal / Imaal Gap  see Ballinabarny Gap | | | | |
| Gravale – Carrigvore | 610 | | Glencree | Wicklow Mountains |
| **Kilcavan Gap** | 185 | R road | Coolattin | Wicklow Mountains |
| **Kilmacrea Crossroads** | 165 | road | Rockstown | Vale of Avoca |
| Kippure – Seefingan | 620 | | Glencree | Dublin Mountains |
| Lavarna Gap / Lavarnia Gap / Lavarney Gap | 596 | | Sraghmore | Wicklow Mountains |
| Lough Gap | 758 | path | Aghavannagh | Wicklow Mountains |
| Lugduff Gap / Barnelogduffe / Prezen Gap | 567 | path | Laragh | Wicklow Mountains |
| Maulin – Tonduff | 501 | | Kilmallin | Wicklow Mountains |
| Ónichabhán Gap | 625 | | Granabeg | Wicklow Mountains |
| Pass of Borenacrow  see Lugduff Gap | | | | |
| **Pollaphuca / Poll an Phúca** | 148 | road | Avoca | Vale of Avoca |

| Latitude, Longitude | National Grid | Notes |
|---|---|---|
| 52.57588, -6.78151 | S 82656 47828 | Carlow boundary; 'Farmer's Gap'? |
| 52.76411, -6.35993 | T 10759 69339 | Not to be confused with Wicklow Gap (Wicklow); 'Marsh Path Gap'; pub sign 'The Gap' |
| 52.53510, -6.82696 | S 79649 43239 | Carlow boundary; not on OS; names from http://www.eastwestmapping.ie/placenames-heritage (quoting Patrick Kennedy, late 19th c.) |
| | | |
| 52.90604, -6.33207 | T 12273 85176 | 'The Red Gap' |
| 52.95357, -6.53056 | S 98810 90173 | Road sign; misplaced to south on OS; probably same as Gap of Imaal (or Imail) / Imaal Gap (L. Price, *The Place-Names of Co. Wicklow*); cf. EastWest Mapping: between Benleagh and Camenabologue at 52.99140, -6.46692; probably from 'Baile na Bearna' |
| 53.13815, -6.43953 | O 04481 10842 | 'Ballynultagh' is the name of the townland |
| 52.89754, -6.32210 | T 12965 84246 | EastWest Mapping only |
| 52.92315, -6.37225 | T 09526 87018 | EastWest Mapping only |
| 52.91164, -6.45910 | T 03713 85608 | 'Pass of the Bare Hill'? |
| 53.18729, -6.23011 | O 18359 16637 | Wicklow Way |
| 53.11834, -6.30090 | O 13810 08849 | The second-highest col in Ireland |
| 52.92184, -6.34449 | T 11396 86915 | EastWest Mapping only |
| 53.07450, -6.38696 | O 08158 03837 | EastWest Mapping only; name attested by L. Price, *The Place-Names of Co. Wicklow* |
| 52.85722, -6.15030 | T 24641 80043 | 'Barr' = 'top'; 'uisce' = 'water' |
| 53.10115, -6.44272 | O 04357 06720 | Billy Byrne was a leader of the Irish Rebellion of 1798, but the name may come from *bealach* and/or 'bearna'; cf. Kilmacrea Crossroads and Pass below ('Baile na Bearna') |
| 53.00200, -6.41093 | T 06731 95734 | EastWest Mapping only (also marked 'Barnavog?') |
| 53.02109, -6.52530 | S 99009 97694 | First two names on OS; Liam Price's informant knew it under the last two names (*The Place-Names of Co. Wicklow*); OS places 'Wexford Gap' separately, west of Table Mountain, where no gap exists |
| 53.02360, -6.39828 | T 07526 98156 | Name attributed to mountain; Gaelic attested 1838; 'Pass (or 'Step') of the Oak Wood' |
| 52.94827, -6.16573 | T 23343 90148 | Name supposedly refers to William FitzWilliam, Lord Deputy of Ireland, 1588–94; 'Devilspass' attested *c.* 1805 (A. R. Nevill's map of Wicklow) |
| 53.00952, -6.42375 | T 05852 96552 | EastWest Mapping only |
| | | |
| 53.13541, -6.25058 | O 17132 10830 | |
| 52.92862, -6.38341 | T 08762 87609 | (The Wicklow Way); first two names on EastWest Mapping |
| | | |
| 53.12533, -6.33347 | O 11611 09576 | |
| 52.73811, -6.47424 | T 03104 66276 | Only on 25-inch (1897–1913) and modern OS |
| 52.91146, -6.16690 | T 23369 86050 | Earlier name in 'Ballinabarny' ('Baile na Bearna')?; see Kilmacrea Pass |
| 53.18495, -6.35509 | O 10011 16177 | Dublin boundary |
| 53.11589, -6.35791 | O 09999 08488 | Not on OS; 'Leath-bhearna' ('One Side of the Gap')?: L. Price, *The Place-Names of Co. Wicklow* |
| 52.96448, -6.44247 | T 04704 91512 | The highest col in Ireland beyond MacGillycuddy's Reeks; EastWest Mapping only (marked 'Barnaharskad?') |
| 52.98895, -6.38275 | T 08655 94324 | (Wicklow Way); EastWest Mapping only; 'Pass of Borenacrow' refers to the old Glendalough–Glenmalure road which crosses the saddle |
| 53.15452, -6.23939 | O 17829 12975 | |
| 52.99919, -6.46243 | T 03280 95346 | EastWest Mapping only |
| | | |
| 52.85282, -6.17391 | T 23064 79513 | 'The Pooka's Hole' (a spirit or fairy) |

233

| Name | Elevation (m) | Surface | Nearest place | Region |
|---|---|---|---|---|
| Prezen Gap *see* Lugduff Gap | | | | |
| Red Scar *see* Cavanagh's Gap | | | | |
| **Sally Gap / Sallygap / Bearna Bhealach Sailearnáin** | 496 | **R road** | Sraghmore | Wicklow Mountains |
| The Saddle | 384 | path | Greenan | Wicklow Mountains |
| **Scalp Pass / Pass of the Scalp / An Scailp** | 164 | **R road** | Glencullen | Dublin Mountains |
| **Three Crosses Pass** | 376 | **road** | Laragh | Wicklow Mountains |
| Wexford Gap *see* Cavanagh's Gap | | | | |
| **Wicklow Gap / Bearna Chill Mhantáin** | 472 | **R road** | Brockagh | Wicklow Mountains |
| **Windgate / Windgates / Bearna Gaoithe** | 125 | **R road** | Bray | Bray Head |
| **Ballygobban Pass** | 318 | **road** | Aghavannagh | Wicklow Mountains |
| Camenabologue / Céim na mBulóg / Bullock Pass | 410 | path | Granabeg | Wicklow Mountains |
| **Kilmacrea Pass** | 150 | **road** | Rockstown | Vale of Avoca |
| **The Murdering Pass** | 400 | **R road** | Sraghmore | Wicklow Mountains |
| **Robber's Pass** | 485 | **road** | Sraghmore | Wicklow Mountains |
| **Stoney Pass** | 295 | **road** | Sraghmore | Wicklow Mountains |

| Latitude, Longitude | National Grid | Notes |
| --- | --- | --- |
| 53.13780, -6.31215 | O 13006 10997 | The highest road col in Ireland; 'Gap of Willows Pass'; 'Barneballaghsilurnan' in Civil Survey of 1654–6 |
| 52.93889, -6.35218 | T 10836 88800 | EastWest Mapping only |
| 53.21957, -6.18108 | O 21545 20311 | Dublin boundary; road at the col named 'The Scalp' on OS 1st edn; 'scailp' = 'gap', 'cleft' or 'chasm' |
| 52.96942, -6.31776 | T 13070 92251 | Only on EastWest Mapping; 60 m from memorial to Shay Elliott, the first Irish rider to wear the Tour de France yellow jersey |
| 53.04179, -6.39776 | O 07516 00181 | St Kevin's Way; 'Pass of the Church (or Cell) of (Saint) Mantáin'; road sign; the third-highest road col in Ireland; not to be confused with Wicklow Gap (Wexford) |
| 53.17083, -6.09187 | O 27648 15043 | 'The Wind Gates' in 1636: *Inquisitionum in officio rotulorum cancellariae Hiberniae asservatarum*, I (1826) |
| 52.89976, -6.44266 | T 04847 84310 | EastWest Mapping only |
| 53.00218, -6.44909 | T 04156 95709 | 'Bullock Pass' on EastWest Mapping |
| 52.90651, -6.17231 | T 23019 85490 | Earlier name in 'Ballinabarny' ('Baile na Bearna')?; see Kilmacrea Crossroads |
| 53.12766, -6.29187 | O 14390 09901 | Not on maps; *A Pictorial and Descriptive Guide to Dublin and the Wicklow Tours* (1914–15), p. 132 |
| 53.10757, -6.25313 | O 17037 07728 | (Wicklow Way); not on OS; EastWest Mapping (but conflated with Stoney Pass) |
| 53.09728, -6.22438 | O 18991 06630 | 'Stoney Pass Br.' on OS |

# Index

In lieu of a complete index, this is a list of some of the better known cols and passes, indicating the section of the catalogue (country and county) in which they occur. For example, 'Bealach na Bà **S** R' shows that the pass is in Ross and Cromarty, Scotland.

## Abbreviations

**E England**
Ch Cheshire
Cu Cumbria
Db Derbyshire
Do Dorset
Du Durham
G Gloucestershire
Ha Hampshire
He Herefordshire
IOM Isle of Man
La Lancashire
GM Greater Manchester
N Northumberland
St Staffordshire
Wo Worcestershire
YN North Yorkshire
YS South Yorkshire

**W Wales**
B Bridgend
Cae Caerphilly
Cer Ceredigion
Con Conwy
D Denbighshire
F Flintshire
G Gwynedd
Po Powys

**S Scotland**
Ab Aberdeenshire
An Angus
AB (m) Argyll and Bute (mainland)
Ay Ayrshire
B Borders
DG Dumfries and Galloway
I (i) Inverness (islands)
I (m) Inverness (mainland)
La Lanarkshire
M Moray
NES Na h-Eileanan Siar
O Orkney
P Perth and Kinross
R Ross and Cromarty
Sh Shetland
St Stirling
Su Sutherland

**NI Northern Ireland**
A Armagh
D Down
L Londonderry
T Tyrone

**RI Republic of Ireland**
Car Carlow
Cl Clare
Co Cork
Do Donegal
Du Dublin
G Galway
Ke Kerry
Li Limerick
Lo Louth
M Mayo
T Tipperary
We Wexford
Wi Wicklow

# Acknowledgements

Above all, thanks to Gill Coleridge and Cara Jones, and to Cecilia Stein, my editor, who not only cared for and fashioned this book but also accompanied its author on an expedition to lost cols in northern England and southern Scotland.

At Particular Books and Penguin, I am grateful to Alice Burkle, Annabel Huxley, Rebecca Lee, Imogen Scott and Jim Stoddart, to Neil Gower for the hand-drawn maps and illustrations and to Richard Marston for design, and, farther afield, for logistical and other support, to Alison Robb, Jamie and Callum, and to Stephen Roberts and María Jose Martínez Jurico.

Thanks also to Dr Henry Chapman and Dr Tom Johnson, to Bikeseven (Longtown), Chas Roberts and the CTC, and to Cairneyhill Airbnb (Pitlochry).

Ordnance Survey spot heights are used with permission of the Ordnance Survey (© Crown copyright 2015). Some of the topo-nymic information in the Irish section of the catalogue is derived from the Placenames Database of Ireland created in collaboration with The Placenames Branch (Department of Arts, Heritage and the Gaeltacht). Of all the cartographic sources cited in the catalogue, by far the richest is the vast collection of maps made available by the National Library of Scotland.

This book was informed, inspired and practically co-written (and ridden) with Margaret.